The British steam sloop HMS Lyra disembarking liberated African slaves at Port Victoria in 1866. - Illustrated London News, 5 January 1867.

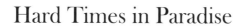

Hard Times in Paradise

For
IAN, JEAN &
BRIGITTE

THE HISTORY OF SEYCHELLES
from Discovery to Independence

Hard Times in Paradise

BEING THE SECOND PART OF
THE HISTORY OF SEYCHELLES
1827-1919

William McAteer

PRISTINE BOOKS
Mahé : Seychelles

First published in 2000 and
reprinted in 2008 by
PRISTINE BOOKS
PO Box 158, Mahé,
Seychelles
e-mail: heureduberger@yahoo.co.uk

Printed in Great Britain by
The Cromwell Press,
Trowbridge, Wiltshire.

ISBN 978-99931-809-1-3

The History of Seychelles collection
ISBN 978-99931-809-3-7

'Travellers ... consider these islands as
a veritable paradise.'
Colonial Office Blue Book, 1901

'Seychelles! Its very name seems
to whisper of Paradise.'
Spectrum Guide to Seychelles, 1990

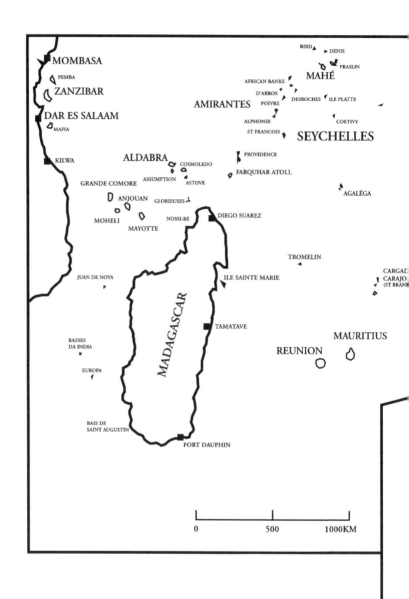

Right: The granitic islands of Seychelles. The island of Aride lies off the map, to the north-west of Curieuse.

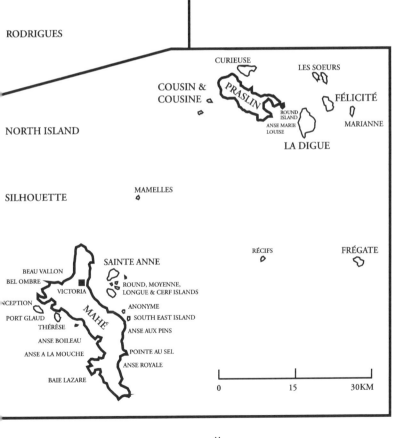

PEROS BANHOS

CHAGOS
ARCHIPELAGO

DIEGO GARCIA

*SEYCHELLES
AND THE
SOUTH-WEST
INDIAN OCEAN*

RODRIGUES

CURIEUSE

LES SOEURS

COUSIN &
COUSINE

PRASLIN

FÉLICITÉ

ROUND
ISLAND

ANSE MARIE
LOUISE

MARIANNE

NORTH ISLAND

LA DIGUE

MAMELLES

SILHOUETTE

RÉCIFS

FRÉGATE

SAINTE ANNE

BEAU VALLON

BEL OMBRE

ROUND, MOYENNE,
LONGUE & CERF ISLANDS

VICTORIA

NCEPTION

ANONYME

PORT GLAUD

SOUTH EAST ISLAND

THÉRÈSE

MAHÉ

ANSE AUX PINS

ANSE BOILEAU

ANSE A LA MOUCHE

POINTE AU SEL

ANSE ROYALE

BAIE LAZARE

| 0 | 15 | 30KM |

ACKNOWLEDGEMENTS

The author would like to thank Assistant Director Alain Lucas and staff of the Seychelles National Archives for making available the material on which much of this book is based. Deserving of special mention is former senior archivist Julien Durup, who was particularly helpful in locating relevant documents.

Ready assistance was also forthcoming at the national archives of Britain, France, the United States, and Mauritius, as well as at the archives of the French Ministry of Foreign Affairs in Paris and Nantes, at the respective libraries of the Foreign and Commonwealth Office and the Church Mission Society in London; at the University of Birmingham; and at the Kendal Whaling Museum, Sharon, Massachusetts, and the whaling museums of Mystic Seaport, Connecticut, and New Bedford, Massachusetts.

In England, Sue Hopson generously gave access to her extensive material on Seychelles, both documentary and photographic. Equally important was her constant encouragement and unfailing assistance. In Seychelles, advice was offered by André Sauzier and Peter Thomson, both of whom read through a large part of the text; their individual contributions to the final shape of the book are gratefully acknowledged, as is that of Keith Fitton, who also undertook with skill and dispatch the unenviable task of editor. Whatever faults and errors remain are wholly of the author's own making.

I should also mention Maureen Kirkpatrick for her medical opinions; Guy Lionnet, for permission to quote from *The Romance of a Palm*; Micheline Georges, who offered papers relating to the Rev. George Ferdinand Delafontaine; Father Morel, for providing photographs from the archives of the Bishop's House, and to Keith Parker and Andrew Carpin for their technical expertise.

Lastly, thanks go to my son, Ian, and daughter Brigitte Gladstone for their invaluable assistance in the production process.

Glacis, Mahé island   William McAteer

CONTENTS

ILLUSTRATIONS

INTRODUCTION

France first laid claim to the uninhabited islands of Seychelles in 1756, forming a settlement fourteen years later to exploit the islands' timber and tortoises. The French settlers and their African slaves grew crops, including spice plants and cotton, and ships on their way from the Île de France (Mauritius) to French establishments in India watered and provisioned there. Otherwise, there was little incentive to develop the islands, for the French feared that sooner or later they would be taken by Britain.

These fears were well-founded. Britain did seize the Seychelles towards the end of the Napoleonic wars, as well as the other French islands in the western Indian Ocean, only the island of La Réunion being returned to France under the terms of the Treaty of Paris, 1815. This book, which is a sequel to *Rivals in Eden* (first published in 1991), covers the period of about one hundred years during which Seychelles was governed by Britain as a dependency of Mauritius before becoming, in 1903, a separate Crown colony.

Compared with the days of French administration, when the islands were touched by war and revolution, the British period of colonisation is usually thought of as being uneventful. It was certainly a time of peace (though the threat of war was always present), but more importantly it was a period of transition. First, there was the abolition of slavery, which overturned completely the social and economic life of the inhabitants; secondly, the coming of the steamship to the islands in the mid-19th century ended what had been their virtual isolation. With an increasing number of visitors — most of them travellers on their way to and from Europe and the Far East — Seychelles became better known to the outside world. For the first time writers, artists, scientists, and soldiers described in detail the beauty of the islands and the exotic flora and fauna to be found there. From these observations there emerged today's image of Seychelles as a tourist's paradise.

Slavery was abolished in Seychelles in 1835, but its legacy was not easily erased, and it continued for many years to emphasize the racial and social divide between Black and White. It also lay at the root of the inhabitants' easy-going lifestyle, where freedom was often equated with idleness, and where morality was perceived in a simple and uninhibited way.

It would have been surprising if strangers had found nothing to criticise or deplore in Seychelles, for the inhabitants were shamefully neglected. There were few schools, for a long time no church nor hospital, and hardly any roads. Officials sent by Mauritius to administer the islands were on the whole efficient and dedicated men, though they were frequently hampered by the incompetence and indolence of their subordinates. They also had to contend with the deadening hand of Mauritius bureaucracy, whose constant complaint was that the Dependency never generated enough revenue to meet its supposed costs. "There has certainly been uncommonly little done for them [the Seychelles]," was the comment of one of the more enlightened Mauritius governors after a visit to the islands.

If the British took scant interest in Seychelles it was because the islands were considered of little commercial value, and retained simply to thwart France's ambitions in the region. With their French language, French Church, and French ways, the inhabitants, like those of Mauritius, were considered of doubtful loyalty, and were treated accordingly. Regrettable as this was, Britain's lack of concern for a subject people has to be viewed in the context of early Victorian England, where a social conscience was only slowly awakening. Education there was still a matter for the Churches and charitable concerns; women and children laboured in mines and factories; the punishment for trivial offences was harsh, with flogging and the death penalty commonplace. Religious differences still evoked hatred and suspicion, and a Roman Catholic's allegiance to the Crown was not always above suspicion.

This history begins at 1827. Although the islands by then had been under British rule for more than a decade, the year marks, in a sense, the closing of one chapter and the opening of another. Quéau de Quinssy, the last and most prominent of the French governors, died in 1827, and the first British troops to be stationed in Seychelles arrived that year from Mauritius. The story concludes at 1919, with the end of World War I, which was a traumatic experience for many Seychellois. Hundreds volunteered to serve as a Carrier Corps with the Allied forces in East Africa, and a great number were to die of disease and neglect. The war also caused widespread suffering and poverty among the people of the islands; it was, in truth, a rude introduction to the harsh realities of the modern world.

Finally, a word about some of the terms used in the following pages. Before the abolition of slavery most of the 'inhabitants' of Seychelles were white, or near-white. The word black, or *noir,* was synonymous with slave, and although the slaves, mainly from Africa and Madagascar, greatly outnumbered the French settlers they were not considered as inhabitants.

On the abolition of slavery freed slaves were sometimes known as "the new population". British officials referred to non-Whites of all hues, including those of pure African blood, as 'coloured', but after the landing of slaves liberated from Arab dhows the term 'African' was used to distinguish those late arrivals from island-born former slaves and their offspring, the coloured Creoles.

French names in the text appear occasionally in the English style. Thus, Napoleon III, but Napoléon Savy, and the French port city of Marseilles, not Marseille.

1

Soldiers and Slaves
1827-1830

Was the slave trading at the Seychelles as clear
as the sun at noon day ?
Yes I think it was, it could not be clearer.

Captain Fairfax Moresby, RN,
to a Select Committee of the House of Commons, 1826

Sometimes it seemed to Lieutenant John Latham as if he had
been fighting the French all his life. Two years old at the
outbreak of war in 1793, he had joined the militia at 17 and
was a veteran of Wellington's Peninsular campaign by the time
he was 21. He had been wounded several times, although it
was an American marksman, not a French grenadier, who had
shattered his right arm at the siege of Fort Erie during the War
of 1812.[1] As a result of that war his regiment, the 82nd Foot,[2]
missed Waterloo, but it later served in France as part of the
army of occupation. In 1819 the 82nd was in Ireland when
orders came to embark for the Indian Ocean island of
Mauritius.

Known to the French as the Île de France, Mauritius had
been seized by Britain towards the end of the Napoleonic
wars. Although it was now a British Crown colony, its
population of French settlers and African slaves lived under
the Union flag in much the same way as before. The settlers
made no attempt to hide their disaffection, and many
remained confident that one day they would have their
beloved Île de France restored to them. As for Latham, eight
years of garrison duty in that stridently Anglophobe colony
must have convinced him that the French were still the enemy.

In November of 1827 Latham received orders to sail with a

1

sergeant and twenty-six men to a group of islands lying about 1,000 miles north of Mauritius. The Seychelles islands had been discovered and settled during the previous century by the French, who administered them as a dependency of Mauritius, an arrangement that the British had continued. On two occasions France had established military outposts on the islands, but this was the first time for British troops to be stationed there. James Holman,[3] a former naval officer who visited Seychelles in 1829, considered the troops useful for protecting the British flag from insult by freebooters and the like, and although the detachment would have little chance of repulsing a determined aggressor, it could harass an enemy from the mountainous interior until relief came.

There are few sights more impressive than the islands of Seychelles at daybreak. As the schooner *Radama* slowly approached the anchorage between the main island of Mahé and Sainte Anne on the morning of 15 December, Latham and his men would have noted how different were the dark granitic peaks, thickly mantled in green, from the sharp outlines of the volcanic island they had left a month earlier. The tiny houses clustered at the water's edge, with a few perching on the lower slopes of the mountain, hardly constituted a town; more a village, so small that the French had not bothered to give it a name, and knew it simply as l'Établissement, or the Bourg de Mahé.

Of course the islands' population was smaller than that of Mauritius, less than one-tenth the size, but it was of a similar racial mix: about five hundred French settlers, most of whom came from Mauritius or the neighbouring island of Bourbon (Réunion). There were also about 4,500 slaves, mainly of African or Malagasy origin. Authority in Seychelles was represented by the acting Government Agent, George Harrison, who, until the departure in disgrace of his predecessor, had commanded the island police force. With the effective strength of the police now reduced to three, it had been partly to allay the settlers' fears of a slave uprising that the British troops had been sent. The soldiers also had the task of preventing the inhabitants indulging their habit of slave trading.

Harrison had arranged accommodation for the soldiers in the police barracks, which stood some way up the hill from the governor's old house, a rundown building that Harrison used as his office. His only worry was the additional expense, for Mauritius had already asked him to advance money to Latham for pay and provisions. "It would be leading all parties into error were I to hold out the hope that the revenues to be collected at this Dependency will enable me at all times to meet Lieutenant Latham's demands upon me," he warned in a letter to Mauritius.

Seychelles had fallen on bad times since the collapse of cotton[4], and had it not been for the maize grown on the outer islands Mahé would have been unable to feed itself. No cash crop had yet proved itself a profitable substitute for cotton. Attempts to grow sugarcane seemed unlikely to succeed given the export restrictions imposed by Mauritius, while coffee production was barely sufficient for local needs. Cloves had been disappointing, and only a small quantity of tobacco was grown. The only worthwhile exports from the Dependency were small quantities of coconut oil, wood, tortoises and turtles. There were also some shipbuilding orders from Mauritius. In a report written in 1830 Harrison estimated that the Dependency's exports in 1827 had amounted to not much more than 15,000 dollars,[5] a figure that had continued to fall. The only other source of revenue was an annual tax of two shillings and sixpence paid by the inhabitants on each slave aged between six and sixty.[6]

In discussing his problems with Latham, Harrison must have recounted the largely sorry tale of the Seychelles under British administration, from that first day in 1811 when Lieutenant Sullivan of the Royal Marines had been left in charge with only his side-arms and powers of persuasion to sustain him. Sullivan was still remembered on the islands for his swashbuckling raid to free a batch of newly imported slaves at Praslin, although the inhabitants, aided and abetted by the former French commandant, Quéau de Quinssy, contrived to see that the slave trader escaped justice.

In 1813 Sullivan departed, and was succeeded by Bibye Lesage, a lieutenant in the 22nd Foot, one of the regiments that had taken part in the invasion of Mauritius. Lesage, who tended to turn a blind eye to slave trading, was in charge for two years, until the setting up of a permanent civil administration under Edward Madge as Government Agent. Madge ruled Seychelles from 1815 to 1826, for much of that time in intermittent conflict with Quinssy. Accused by Madge of a variety of offences from drunkenness to aiding the escape of a slave trader, Quinssy, or Quincy, as he later spelt his name, was sent under arrest to Mauritius. There he was quickly freed by the British authorities and allowed to return to Seychelles   to resume his duties as *juge de paix*, and to continue his skirmishing with Madge.

Quinssy died in July 1827, and lay buried at the Établissement, near the flagstaff where the tricolour had once bravely flown. It had been in 1793, while serving as a captain in the Pondichéry Regiment at the Île de France that he had been appointed commandant of Seychelles. Because he had no means of resisting an attack by the English, Quinssy adopted a policy of negotiating a capitulation of the islands each time an enemy ship appeared over the horizon. In this way he saved Seychelles from the ravages of war, and at the same time defended the honour of *la patrie.* Although Quinssy's death symbolised the end of the French Seychelles, the settlers continued to resist the conqueror's half-hearted attempts to Anglicize them, thereby retaining enough of their Gallic heritage to ensure that future visitors would remark on the French modes and manners of the people.[7]

Britain had little interest in Seychelles, and would have given up the islands of the western Indian Ocean if France had been willing to surrender its footholds in India. But France refused, and consequently under the Treaty of Paris only the island of Bourbon (Réunion), which was noted for not having a good natural harbour, was given back. Mauritius and the Seychelles, including the smaller islands of the Amirantes, remained in British hands. Only later, when the two Powers looked more closely at their maps, did the question of exactly which islands were included in the Seychelles dependency become a matter of conjecture and mild contention.

In addition to their language, laws, and customs, the former French islands had been allowed to retain the institution on which their economies were based, slavery. Britain had abolished the slave trade in 1807, but slavery itself remained in place in British possessions overseas, notably in the rich, sugar-growing colonies of the West Indies. It was natural, therefore, that Britain should allow slavery to continue in the newly acquired French islands of the Indian Ocean and Caribbean.

4

This hardly satisfied the abolitionists in Britain, whose influence in Parliament and the country was growing stronger. They were not convinced that by prohibiting the trade the system would die of its own accord. They knew that slave owners would always find ways to replenish their stocks.

Nowhere was this more true than in Mauritius, where the British governor, Sir Robert Farquhar, had from the start been cautious in enforcing the anti-slaving regulations for fear of upsetting the colony's political peace and economic stability. As a result Mauritian planters were able to import thousands of slaves each year from Africa, Madagascar, and the Comoro islands, often in ships flying the French flag. Seychelles was particularly useful for this illegal traffic, as slaves could be landed easily on one of the smaller islands and from there be dispersed to their eventual buyers. The Seychelles had always been a convenient transit stop for slave ships, and it continued to be so under the British.

Four months after the arrival of the British troops Harrison received a report that a schooner under French colours had arrived at D'Arros island, demanding water. The captain had not disclosed his cargo, but he had been provided with water and had sailed off two days later. Harrison immediately suspected a slaver and considered sending Latham in pursuit, but concluded that the schooner would already be well on the way to its probable destination, Bourbon. In a letter to Mauritius he felt obliged to absolve the Seychelles inhabitants of involvement in the affair, saying it was not possible to prevent slave ships approaching the outlying islands, but that he was "firmly persuaded in my own mind that they (the inhabitants) will never participate in any transactions they so lately pledged themselves to set their faces against".[8]

Whether his trust was justified is doubtful. The law permitting inhabitants to move slaves from one island to another was a great temptation to purchase illegally imported slaves and subsequently send them on to Mauritius under the pretence that they formed part of an existing stock. The transfer of slaves to Mauritius increased substantially during the 1820s, as the prosperity of the smaller islands began to falter. Many of these transfers were legitimate, the owners having decided to quit Seychelles for good or move slaves to their sugar plantations in Mauritius. Records for the year 1828 show that Quéau de Quinssy's son Charles and his daughters Clémentine and Sophie shipped a total of eighty slaves to Mauritius. Other settlers who did likewise included: Le Beuze (110 slaves), Lavoquer (97), Dugand (87), Chaurel (36), Savy father and son (160), Sauveur Antoine Audibert (102), Jean Planeau (263), and Louis Marie Tirant (33).

However, transfers were often fraudulent. Julien Langlois, who, with his brother Clément, was believed to bring in slaves regularly from Africa in the *Courrier des Seychelles*, was granted a licence in 1827 to transfer eighty-four slaves to Mauritius, although the previous year he was registered as having only forty-eight. It is unlikely that the balance had been purchased legitimately.

Madge, whose name was linked with the Langlois brothers' activities, was one of the biggest slave owners in Seychelles. He connived at the illegal trade, if not actually participating in it. Captain Fairfax Moresby, senior naval officer at Mauritius, gave evidence to a parliamentary committee on Madge's involvement, and subsequent probing of the latter's behaviour led to his replacement by Harrison in 1826. No formal charge was made, and Madge returned to Mauritius with eighty slaves to take up the post of assistant registrar of slaves.

The authorities attempted to cut the worst abuses of the transfer system by introducing stricter registration, especially as regards personal identification. Checks frequently turned up wide discrepancies in a slave's vital statistics. Georges Rougier Leganne was refused permission to transfer an adult slave to Mauritius when, on examination, the man was found to be seven inches shorter than he had been in 1815, and 17 years younger than his proper estimated age. Cases like this sparked a rush by slave owners at Mahé to amend details of the slaves they wanted to transfer.[9] In most cases they were allowed to do so, resulting later in the utter confusion of Seychelles' slave registrations   If Leganne was one slave-owner who was cheating, how many others successfully passed 'new' slaves through the net? In July 1827 one finds the Mauritius controller of customs complaining that the only document for eleven slaves shipped from Seychelles in the *Jeune Laure* was a list of names. There was nothing to show whether or not these corresponded with the registration certificates made out before the slaves' departure. It was not until the following year, when a complete ban was imposed on the transfer of plantation slaves from Seychelles to Mauritius, that this abuse was halted.

The ban had been recommended by the Commission of Eastern Enquiry, a three-man body appointed by Parliament in 1822 to visit and report on three of the territories acquired by Britain in 1815, namely the Cape and Ceylon from the Dutch, and Mauritius. The Commissioners were at work for some nine years, three of those spent in Mauritius, compiling reports that were to serve as policy guides for future governors. Much of their attention was directed at slavery, and their recommendations helped to strengthen the case for its complete abolition. The Commissioners found among officials at Mauritius an ambivalent attitude to slavery, which encouraged settlers to evade the regulations. The government itself owned slaves, inherited from the former French administration, and when slaves were held forfeit on account of some abuse by a settler they became government property. It was only in the last years of slavery that the administration took steps to free immediately slaves that came into its hands in this way.

In his slave dealings Madge was probably more blatant than most, but he was certainly not alone. Harrison owned slaves,[10] as did others, for it was easier to go along with the system even if it meant promoting something that British officials should have been attempting to control and, indeed, discourage. Their attitude was akin to that of the former naval officer Holman, who, while regretting that there were selfish people who would often indulge in cruelty and injustice, thought that this was "not a reason for passing indiscriminate censure on the proprietors of slaves". He argued that people in Europe failed to appreciate "the misery and torment" that slaves could cause too indulgent a master. This, "added to their laziness, and a constant desire to pilfer, forms the worst feature of their character". It seemed that, to Holman, it was the slave who was to blame, not the system.

Although Britain had hesitated to abolish slavery in its colonies, it was ready to heed the voices of the humanitarian lobby calling for conditions of the enslaved to be improved. As a result the so-called Melioration laws were passed, which attempted to restrict the arbitrary power of the slave-owners. Abolishing the flogging of females, limiting the daily hours of work, ensuring that slaves were given a rest day on Sunday, and allowing slave families to stay together[11] were among measures recommended by the Colonial Office in May 1823. Often enough they were implemented half-heartedly by officials on the spot, or completely ignored by the planters. Nonetheless they were an important advance, especially when buttressed some years later by the government's decision to appoint a Protector of Slaves in the four former French colonies of Demerara, Trinidad, St Lucia, and Mauritius.

While it is probably true that slaves of the Indian Ocean islands were treated less harshly than those of the West Indian colonies, Mauritius was now rapidly expanding its sugar industry in response to Britain's decision to equalise the import tariff from each region of its empire. As a result there was an inevitable worsening in the conditions of the plantation slave, whose "labour being very profitable to his owner ... was more rigorously exacted". This contrasted with the situation in Seychelles where a declining economy meant that slaves were only moderately worked, as little revenue could be derived from their labour. Their masters would have liked to have shipped most of them off to Mauritius to work in the cane fields, but this was no longer possible.

Major William Colebrooke, one of the Eastern Enquiry Commissioners, who visited Seychelles on his way to Ceylon in April 1829, found the slaves robust and healthy, in contrast to the general condition of plantation slaves at Mauritius. In Seychelles there was plenty of fish, and slaves could raise plantains and breed stock, whereas in Mauritius they were inadequately fed on imported supplies, mainly Bengal rice. Although the Seychelles slave might be ill provided with clothing — the men wore a waistcloth, the women a chemise and petticoat — "from the mildness of the climate they do not appear to suffer on this account", and their thatched huts were superior to the slave habitations at Mauritius. Holman, too, thought Seychelles slaves were better fed, and that they were worked less harshly than the poorer peasantry in parts of Europe. One afternoon he was guest at the home of Charles Dorothée Savy on Sainte Anne island; he described the idyllic scene of Mrs Savy, surrounded by her daughters, supervising female slaves in the making of hats, baskets, and flowers from the young leaves of the coco de mer palm.

Although the working hours of domestic slaves may have been longer, the work itself was less arduous than that of a field hand, and usually there was greater freedom to move about. When the ban on transferring plantation slaves to Mauritius was imposed some slave-owners got round this by declaring their slaves as domestics. Mauritius customs house records show that the unusually high number of seventy-four 'domestics' was sent from Seychelles between April 1828 (when the ban on plantation slaves came into force) and the following December. The authorities subsequently stipulated that only two domestics were allowed per family, causing a barrage of complaints until the directive was eased in favour of those with large families. When Harrison received word that a settler had been accompanied on frequent voyages to Mauritius by different domestic slaves on each occasion, he said there was nothing he could do about it. Latham himself took with him two domestic slaves when he returned to Mauritius in December 1829.

Holman had commented favourably on prospects for sugar in Seychelles after visiting cane fields in the Beau Vallon area (where he and Harrison lunched with Lieutenant Latham and the captain and officers of HM sloop *Jaseur*). The plantation was a joint venture by four gentlemen who had procured "the wheels and iron-work of an excellent mill from England, for which they paid 3,900 dollars". Holman noted that despite five months' drought, "they have had very fair success". However, sugar was never to make its mark in the Dependency, thus sparing Seychelles slaves the back-breaking labour of the cane field.

Harrison, who visited three sugar estates, forecast correctly that they would not succeed unless Mauritius agreed to allow Seychelles to export direct to India and elsewhere. With the exception of a single token shipment of sugar to India in 1831, it was many years before this particular tourniquet was eased.[12]

According to Harrison slaves in Seychelles did not pose the same threat to settlers as they did in Mauritius. Although there were many *marrons* − slaves who had escaped − Harrison pointed out that "an unarmed man may traverse the island [of Mahé] at night without harm, and doors and windows of homes may be left open in perfect safety". Despite this relaxed atmosphere, and the agreeable impressions of Holman and Colebrook, the underlying brutality of slavery remained. Regulations could be passed to make life more acceptable to the enslaved, but masters were often reluctant to observe such restrictions.

A favourite punishment, known as *Zenga*, involved the victim having to hold a rock or some heavy article above the head, continually raising and lowering it to the ground. "When she failed to touch the floor [on lowering the rock], he beat her with a whip or rattan cane; and when the said *sieur* St Jorre went to sleep he forced the individual Janine to keep watch on the girl Eliza in order to prevent her from sleeping." So read the testimony of the female slave Nancy (aged about 46, from Mozambique), in a case arising from St Jorre's alleged purchase of two Malagasy slaves whom he registered in 1826 as being Seychelles-born Creoles.

Female slaves were defenceless against sadistic behaviour, as well as sexual abuse, something that was probably more common and widespread than existing records indicate. Harrison, in a deposition to the *juge de paix* on 21 April 1828, described the condition of one slave girl named Rosette, who was brought before him after escaping from her owner, a Mr Breton. She wore a collar and chain much heavier than that allowed by law, and her body was so severely marked by blows of a whip or cane that he had no hesitation in determining that her punishment exceeded the number of strokes allowed by the government. The surgeon who examined her described the extensive scars and bruising on both buttocks, some more recent than others, as indicating successive thrashings with a whip.[13] Although it had been recommended that females should not be flogged, it was not until 1830 that an Order in Council formally forbade it.

White masters had no monopoly on whipping. One of the cruellest slave-owners was a coloured woman, Babette Loizeau, herself a former slave, whose punishments were described by one official as proverbial. Harrison received a hint in March 1829 that all might not be well at the Mahé habitation where Babette and her sons lived, when word reached him from Mauritius that a Marie Bassac feared her daughter Henriette was being ill-treated by the Loizeaus. Harrison assured the Mauritius authorities that there was no cause for alarm.

However, some years later Babette was fined £30 for cruel and inhuman treatment of three slave girls, and two of her sons were also fined and given short prison terms for aiding and abetting her. One son, Domzil, incurred further penalties for administering a second flogging to one of the girls. Babette thereupon petitioned the Governor, unwisely making "calumnious attacks upon the local authorities". Instead of having the sentences set aside, she was warned about her language, and jailed. She was later released, with the agreement of both the Governor and the Protector of Slaves, on paying a fine of two male slaves.

Justice in Seychelles was administered by a tribunal consisting of a *juge de paix,* with two assistants and a recorder. Fines of up to 120 dollars and imprisonment of fifteen days could be imposed. In serious criminal cases a copy of the trial and judgement would be sent to Mauritius for confirmation, resulting in lengthy delays between the passing and execution of sentence. Holman observed that the criminal law hardly applied to slaves, the masters preferring to administer their own punishment, or perhaps none at all if the offence related to a third party, as a flogging and imprisonment would mean the temporary loss of the slave's labour. The death penalty, according to Holman, was rarely carried out.[14]

Although slaves were now allowed to give evidence in court, there were many obstacles to overcome before their testimony could be used to convict a settler. In one case, involving a vessel from Seychelles, the principal witnesses, who had been part of its slave cargo, were barred from giving evidence to the Mauritius court because they "were not aware of the nature and obligation of an oath". By such means was justice perverted.

Not surprisingly, attempts by slaves to escape were common. Captain William Owen, who had visited Seychelles in 1824 while surveying the surrounding seas in HM ships *Leven* and *Barracouta,* expressed surprise that despite the difficulty in obtaining slaves owners should treat them as carelessly as they did. He thought slaves attempted to escape not only because of the cruelty they might suffer, but also because they lacked female company. He noted that it was not uncommon to find twenty men on an island with only two female companions.

One of Owen's officers, Lieutenant Boteler, described the

Barracouta's encounter with a large pirogue off the African coast in October 1823. "In her sat four black men, haggard and emaciated in their appearance, while a fifth lay stretched at full length under the seats, apparently in a dying state." The men lowered the tattered cotton sheet that had served as a sail, but seemed to hesitate about coming on board. The *Barracouta*'s crew encouraged them by friendly gestures, and a voice from the boat inquired what nationality the ship was. Told that it was English "they uttered a cry of joy and paddled alongside". Boteler noted that the men had escaped from an island of the Amirantes. They had been at sea for seventeen days, with only a small amount of water and rice, and had covered a distance of 750 miles, "scarcely credible, considering the means they had for its performance".

Holman also referred to the frequency with which slaves tried to escape "in boats of various sizes ... in which they have vainly hoped to reach their own country, all the slaves on the islands having come either from the east coast of Africa or Madagascar". It was for this reason, he noted, that the Blacks in Seychelles were known as Mozambiques. Although desertion was an offence punishable by death it was almost never carried out, and in any case the desire to be free was irresistible.

In November 1829 a detachment of the 99th Regiment[15] arrived from Mauritius to relieve Latham and his men. During his two years in Seychelles Latham had not faced any major threat from either external or internal sources, his principal concern being to maintain discipline on a small island that offered few diversions for his men. Their conduct, presumably, had been considered satisfactory, as on his return to Mauritius in December he was promoted to captain. On 30 September 1831 the 82nd Foot embarked for England, and landed at Cowes, Isle of Wight, the following March. In April 1833 Latham sold his commission for £1,800 (worth today about £145,000) and retired from the army. That summer Parliament approved An Act for the Abolition of Slavery throughout the British colonies.

2

A French Visitor
1830-1837

... pour l'Angleterre, cette possession n'est rien du tout;
mais ne pas la voir entre nos mains leur importe beaucoup.
Capitaine Aimable-Constant Jehenne, 1841

On 30 December 1829 the French warship *Favorite* sailed from Toulon on a mission ordered by the Minister of Marine and Colonies, Vice-Admiral the Comte de Rigny. The voyage which was to take the 26-gun frigate around the world would last for almost three years. In addition to furthering navigational knowledge by charting certain areas of the Indian Ocean and the China Sea, the *Favorite* would show the flag at various ports in India and the Far East, and offer protection wherever needed to French shipping. The Minister's instructions warned the frigate's captain that in the event of war the ship must at all costs evade capture.

De Rigny had commanded the French squadron at the Battle of Navarino[1] two years previously, and no doubt Captain Cyrille Laplace would have welcomed a similar opportunity to achieve glory in battle; not altogether impossible, for France was on the brink of incursions into both Madagascar and Algeria. Of more immediate interest to Laplace, however, was the chance to add to the discoveries of navigators such as Bougainville, La Pérouse, Crozet, and Grenier.

Laplace had joined the navy as a cabin boy in 1802, and had seen service in the Indian Ocean under the Empire. At the Restoration he had been fortunate enough to remain employed, but there were few plum posts available in the much reduced royal navy, and service under the Republic or the Empire was not a strong recommendation for promotion. It was only with the appointment of Baron Portal as Minister that some sense was brought back into the question of naval command and advancement. Laplace, who had recently completed an expedition up-river in Senegal, caught the Minister's attention with the fluency of his written reports. The result was his promotion to full lieutenant. There followed further service in the Mediterranean and Caribbean, and in 1827 he attained the rank of *capitaine de frégate*, the equivalent of commander. His command was to be the newly built *Favorite*.

Laplace's mission was the continuation of a programme of navigational research embarked on by the French navy in the early 1820s. Notably, there had been in 1824 the round-the-world voyage in the *Thétis* by the Baron de Bougainville, son of the famous mariner, and the later explorations of Duperry, Dumont-d'Urville and Freycinet. Although Laplace had some discretion in planning his voyage, his orders were to first make for Bourbon, and from there follow the usual route to Pondicherry, then on to the Philippines, Australia, Tasmania, New Zealand, and back home via Cape Horn.

He was advised to chart with extreme care the islands to the north-east of Madagascar, an area where the early Portuguese had for centuries succeeded in scaring away rival ships by liberally scattering their charts with innumerable islands, reefs and shoals. It was not until the mid-18th century, thanks to the exploratory voyages initiated by Mahé de la Bourdonnais and his successors at the Île de France (Mauritius) and Bourbon, that most of the links in the Seychelles and Amirantes island chain were located, and a more realistic assessment of the hazards of the area became possible.

Even so, "the charts of the archipelago ... still leave much to be desired," Laplace was advised by the navy's Hydrographer. "Many of the islands and reefs are badly placed, and the uncertainties are such that a special reconnaissance of the region should be made."[2] This was the view also of Lislet Geoffroy, who had been in charge of charts and plans at the Île de France and had been kept on by the British. In 1817 he had published a new chart of that part of the Indian Ocean.[3] Not absolutely correct, was his own verdict on it, although many points had been verified by French and British mariners, among them the former Seychellois corsair Jean-François Hodoul.

It was thanks to the likes of Hodoul that the French had always been better informed than the English on the hazards of the western Indian Ocean. Captain Fairfax Moresby pinpointed some of these while engaged in anti-slaving operations in 1821-22.[4] At times he employed Hodoul as his pilot, and he complimented him and his son on their navigational accuracy. They were, he wrote, "both of great intelligence and active zeal", and "I found the plan of the Hodouls so correct that scarce the smallest alteration was necessary". In addition to Moresby's charts, the voyages by Owen in the *Leven* and *Barracouta* in 1822-26 had given Britain an edge in an area where it had the advantage of possessing island bases. Part of Laplace's task was to complement and confirm the findings of those British navigators.

After rounding the Cape the *Favorite* ran into a cyclone. The frigate stood up well to this ordeal, and on 1 April 1830 safely reached Bourbon, which had been devastated by the cyclone. A month later, having carried out repairs to the frigate, Laplace set course for Seychelles. He called on the way at the deserted Île du Sable, or Tromelin island, and reported that some other islands — he listed Providence, Saint Pierre, and Saint Laurent — either did not exist or were badly placed on the charts. This uncertainty over the existence or otherwise of certain islands was to continue for several more years. In 1841 Captain Jehenne, in the *Prévoyante*, reported that in his opinion the mysterious island of the Portuguese charts, Roquepiz, was either Agaléga, Coëtivy, or Île Platte.

On 14 May Laplace sighted Mahé, and a few hours later the *Favorite* came to anchor off Sainte Anne island. Having been to Seychelles during the war, he was not unfamiliar with the scenery. Like Delaunay, who in 1770 formed the first French settlement on Sainte Anne, Laplace decided that this was where he would make his base. "Sainte Anne," he wrote, "has a cheerful look. In the centre are high rocks, deprived it is true of the foliage that used to cover them, but which form a dominating backcloth to the plantations of sugarcane that cover the southern end of the island, as well as the clumps of lemon and orange trees, and other tropical fruit." After he had sent an

15

officer to Mahé to inform Harrison of his arrival, Laplace received an invitation to dine that evening with the proprietor of Sainte Anne, the same Monsieur Savy who had entertained James Holman eight months earlier. Laplace later admitted that the evening with the Savy family had been so pleasant that he almost forgot about the needs of his crew, a situation he corrected the following morning by taking on board fresh meat and vegetables, of which there had been little to purchase at Bourbon.

In the afternoon Laplace paid a courtesy call on the 'governor' at the building used by Harrison as his office. In the evening he had the opportunity of seeing Harrison's grander abode outside the town, "where the order and good taste that was very evident there sparked my curiosity to meet the mistress of the house". He was not disappointed. Mrs Harrison, who was from Geneva, was very different from the reserved, coldly polite Englishwoman Laplace had envisaged.[5] Even Harrison exceeded his expectations, for not only had he good manners but he spoke French well, "which, with an Englishman, always indicates a well polished education". The dinner was excellent, and the conversation warm and animated.

The presence of a French warship was always an occasion for celebration in Seychelles, for even in the days when France ruled the islands such visits were rare. None surely could have enjoyed themselves more than the captain and crew of the *Favorite*. In his account of the voyage, Laplace wrote at length on the charms of the Seychelles women, whom he found to be generally well made, of medium height, dark-haired, and with expressive features. Although their dancing — and it seemed that the French officers danced almost every night — was not as skilled as that found in Europe, "their desire to please and the absence of all pretension, had me close my eyes to those points of comparison that would not have been in their favour". The men, too, won his admiration. "Their character is generally good, affable, and hospitable; almost all are sailors, they have courage and are enterprising in their labour. Although their homes are scattered over the island, the settlers enjoy society and its pleasures." There were three rough tracks across the mountains to the west coast. Some of the settlers had horses and mules, and for shorter distances there were slaves to carry them in litters. There was no danger from wild animals, the last crocodile having been exterminated some fifteen years earlier.[6] Personal transportation, however, was still more often than not by sea, in a pirogue.

On the economy of Seychelles Laplace noted, like Holman, that sugar had overtaken cotton as the main crop. There was also fishing, and cattle raising, but contrary winds and calms made exporting difficult. Tortoises and turtles were also important products, with Bourbon and Mauritius consuming about 12,000 creatures a year, "without apparently causing any diminution in numbers in the archipelago". He also remarked on the busy ship repair and construction yards on Mahé, describing them as "one of the best branches of commerce for this little country". He assessed authority in the island as mild, liberal, with little taxation, while his later writing showed he believed, like many others, that slavery was essential for the continuing prosperity of the colonies.

Laplace would have liked to have stopped longer at Mahé. His officers were going to miss the hectic socialising with the young ladies of Mahé, but of more concern to the captain was the quality of his surveys. He was not at all sure that his charts were accurate for, as he explained to the Minister, he had drawn them up hurriedly. Time had been short and on only a few mornings had the weather been favourable for his observations by theodolite from the summit of Sainte Anne.

During his stay Laplace had sailed around the nearby islands, checking positions and taking soundings. He found that Frégate, Marie-Anne [sic], Denis, and the Île aux Vaches-Marines (Bird island) corresponded to Owen's chart. He also drew up a plan of the anchorage at Sainte Anne, but this last task had again been done hurriedly. Early in the morning of Thursday, 20 May, the *Favorite* sailed for Praslin and the Maldive islands. Needless to say, the French officers had danced till dawn.

The appearance of the *Favorite* in the Indian Ocean coincided with the first major attempt by France to restore its influence in Madagascar by reoccupying some of its old settlements on the eastern seaboard. Two months before Laplace left Toulon a military force from Bourbon, commanded by Captain Gourbeyre in the frigate *Terpsichore*, had bombarded Tamatave after Queen Ranavalona[7] failed to respond to a demand by France for territorial concessions. The fort was taken after fierce fighting. According to a report in *The Times* newspaper of 22 February 1830, the French had "murdered the poor inhabitants without mercy".

A British warship, the *Volcan* (Captain Colpoys), which arrived at Tamatave with twenty-four Malagasy seamen returning to their homes after service in the British navy, was forced to sail twenty miles north to Foulepointe to land the men there. Colpoys reported that he did not think the French intended to settle, but were simply seeking plunder. In fact, Gourbeyre was preparing the way for settlers to come over from Bourbon. However, despite his hard campaigning, Ranavalona refused to surrender, and the French were forced to withdraw. As before, only the Île Sainte Marie, on the north-east coast, remained in French hands.

Laplace had learned of Gourbeyre's unsuccessful expedition on his arrival in April at Bourbon, where two of the ships that had taken part in the operations, the *Nièvre* and the *Indefatigable*, were lying in the roadstead. Echoing the advice given by Grenier and Rochon sixty years earlier, Laplace remarked that gifts and seduction often proved to be the best weapons when dealing with people who were "hardly civilised".

Madagascar had always been important as a source of food and slaves, a fact that the English quickly recognised when the Indian Ocean islands passed into their hands. *The Times* reported that one result of Gourbeyre's aggression was that merchant vessels calling at Tamatave could no longer find bullocks or poultry for sale, "for the French seize upon everything within their reach". Even at Foulepointe, where cattle was available, the people were unwilling to sell them to the Mauritian ships captains, who they refused to believe were British subjects because they spoke French.

If Farquhar had had his way the settlements along the Madagascar coast would have been under his direct rule as dependencies of Mauritius, but they had not been specified as such in the Treaty of Paris and Britain eventually abandoned formal claim to them.[8] It remained British policy, however, to extend its influence in Madagascar, and at the same time make sure France made no appreciable gains there. Thus the *Grande Île* remained a bone of contention between the two Powers until near the end of the century.

Farquhar had seen a chance of reducing Mauritius' dependence on a slave-based plantation economy by exploiting the resources of the East African coast. Despite criticism that he was soft on the planters, he believed that the safest way to end slavery was gradually to cut off the supply. His first target was Madagascar, which was both a major supplier of slaves and an important transit stop for slave ships, and here he was fortunate in finding a willing partner in the Merina chieftain Radama,[9] who, unlike his wife and future successor, Queen Ranavalona, welcomed Europeans. Farquhar concluded a treaty in October 1817 whereby Radama prohibited the export of slaves from his territory in exchange for an annual indemnity worth 2,000 dollars, plus gunpowder, English muskets, one full-dress coat, hat and boots, and the right to call himself King of Madagascar. Farquhar also persuaded the East India Company to pressure Sultan Seyyid of Muscat and Zanzibar to prohibit the sale of slaves to Europeans, and he hastily dispatched Captain Fairfax Moresby to Muscat to obtain the Sultan's signature to a draft treaty under which Arab slave ships would henceforth be confined to the coastal waters of Arabia and East Africa. If found outside what became known as the Moresby Line, they would be liable to seizure by British cruisers.

If Britain was to succeed in suppressing the slave trade, it required an equal commitment from the other maritime Powers. Treaties were eventually negotiated with Holland, Spain, and Portugal. France had formally declared the slave trade illegal and agreed to cooperate in its suppression, but its efforts were at best half-hearted. Ever suspicious of Britain's motives, France saw attempts to halt the slave trade as a convenient cover for Britain to extend its trade and influence. It therefore refused to agree to a reciprocal right of search, thus leaving the way open for slavers flying the French flag to evade detection. It was only in the late 1820s, after France had given up all hope of regaining its rich Caribbean colony of St Domingue (Haiti), that a more cooperative attitude emerged. The fall of the Bourbon dynasty in 1830 continued the process, and two years later France agreed to a restricted right of search by warships. It was a step in the right direction, but a satisfactory conclusion to the problem was still a long way off.

Farquhar's successor, Sir G. Lowry Cole, was equally

concerned not to upset the Mauritian planters, and obstructed as best he could the tougher anti-slavery legislation emanating from England. In the year he assumed office as governor, the Society for the Mitigation and Gradual Abolition of Slavery was being formed in London under Thomas Fowell Buxton,[10] who had succeeded William Wilberforce[11] as leader of the anti-slavery movement. Buxton did not mince words, declaring that the society's aim was "nothing less than the extinction of slavery, in nothing less than the whole of the British dominions".

In Seychelles, where officials had only a vague notion of the size of the slave population, it was easier for slave-owners to ignore government regulations concerning the treatment of slaves. In January 1827 an attempt was made to tighten the taking of the biennial census, when every slave-owner had to record the number and names of the slaves he possessed, whether he could show legal ownership or not, and give a detailed description of each slave, including tattoos and other marks. According to Colebrooke, of the Commission of Eastern Inquiry, the 1829 census recorded 6,520 slaves in Seychelles, of whom 2,231 were island-born Creoles. The numbers of males and females were about equal. Births had been double the number of deaths over the past two years, but Colebrooke suspected that not all deaths were reported so that the introduction of 'new' slaves would be easier.

He suggested that slaves be withdrawn from the Amirante islands, where they were out of reach of a magistrate or of medical care. The following year, the assistant registrar of slaves in Seychelles, James Dowland,[12] reported on a visit to the islands of Desroches, Poivre, and Alphonse. At Desroches he found all forty-seven slaves, owned by Hodoul, to be in good health and apparently content, but it was a different story at Poivre and Alphonse. Many of the forty-eight slaves at Poivre were former domestics who had been taken there to labour in the field under the lash of a *commandeur*, or overseer, noted for his severity. Others had been separated from their children or parents, left behind at Mahé. At Alphonse, where there were nineteen slaves, Dowland noted that only four were female, one a girl of 14, "an evil naturally attended with many bad consequences". It is to the credit of the Mauritius governor, Sir Charles Colville, that he instructed Harrison to see that the slave families were reunited, and not to permit any such divisions in future. The overseer at Poivre was to be removed and the 'evil' at Alphonse remedied or he, the Governor, would resort "to some measure of authority". As for the productivity of the islands, Dowland found that Desroches had a fine crop of maize, Poivre's was indifferent, and Alphonse could produce only 15,000lb of haricot beans.

Dowland, who had been sent from Mauritius on what he thought was to be a temporary posting, had little liking for his job. Writing of his "unhappy sojourn" in Seychelles, he said almost everything was uncongenial, and considering all the illegal transactions of the past he found it impossible to reconcile slave numbers and descriptions with past records. As a result his returns to Mauritius were invariably late, and he was warned several times by his superiors. Dowland was probably correct in concluding that the returns he submitted were often false, and that many of the slaves should have been forfeited to the government. His views received little support.[13]

Fortunately for Dowland, relief was at hand. In September 1830 HM sloop *Jaseur* arrived with his replacement, a clerk at the Registry Office in Mauritius named John Ormsby. On the voyage to Mahé, Ormsby had visited the slaves at the island of Rodrigues and the Diego Garcia archipelago, while Dowland, on the return voyage, was to make similar inspections at Coëtivy, Agaléga, Providence, and St Brandon (Cargados Carajos) islands. Ormsby seems to have fared no better than Dowland in sorting out the confusion over slave registrations. In August 1831, the Mauritius advocate-general described the Seychelles returns as "so very inconvenient" that it was difficult for the Governor to take a decision on any slave transfer application that would not incur "severe reflections from those influential persons in England whose eyes are ever watchfully fixed upon all our proceedings relating to the slave population". He recommended that an official be sent with the sole aim of sorting out all past and present returns.

In October of that year, a clerk named Elliott arrived to carry out this task, but soon he was complaining to Harrison that Ormsby was too busy with his own work to help him.

The first Protector of Slaves to be appointed at Mauritius, R. M. Thomas, arrived in the Colony straight from London. He was well-intentioned, but it was not long before he had upset the Secretary of State, Lord Goderich, with his apparent readiness to side with the slave-owners. To give Thomas his due, he insisted that the slaves should not work on Sundays, and he spoke out strongly against the fettering of women. The problem was that he expected the slaves to have the same attitude to work as free, well-paid employees. He also discouraged complaints by ordering a public whipping of any slave who was found to have made false allegations.

Thomas's advice to Ormsby, who had been appointed assistant protector of slaves in Seychelles, was to discreetly let them know that he was their "zealous friend". At the same time he should not raise unrealistic expectations of what he could do for them. Complaints by slaves about their treatment should be made singly, and in an orderly manner. Any wishing to complain had first to obtain a pass from the estate manager — a restriction unlikely to encourage the expression of genuine grievances — but Thomas told Ormsby that if he heard of any mistreatment he should investigate it without waiting for a complaint to be made.

Thomas's notion that he could create a society of happy, hard-working slaves was clearly not sustainable. It was not what the abolitionists aimed at, nor, in the long run, the government. Like all measures concocted to improve the condition of slaves, the appointment of an official to protect slaves' rights tended to be a step towards that ultimate right, liberty, a prospect that threw the Mauritian planters, with their 65,000 slaves, into turmoil. Every principle of their colour-conscious, slave-based society, it seemed, was being undermined. Discrimination against the free coloured population had already been abolished by an Order in Council in June 1829.[14] The following year saw, in addition to the appointment of a protector of slaves, orders against the whipping of females or the infliction of more than twenty-five lashes on males without judicial order; an insistence on the keeping of punishment books; and, worst of all for the slave-owners, a suggestion that as Mauritius must have imported many slaves after 1813, when it was illegal to do so, all slaves should be set free without compensation.

To reinforce these policies, a known abolitionist, John Jeremie, was sent to Mauritius in 1832 as *procureur-général*. The result was near rebellion. The planters refused to make returns, produce punishment books, or cooperate in any way with the officials. Each district on the island determined "to set the law altogether at defiance". Some unsuccessfully petitioned the French government to intervene on the grounds that the terms under which Mauritius was surrendered to the British in 1810 were being violated.[15] To all this the slaves responded with acts of sabotage and increasing desertions.

There was also unrest in Seychelles, where a detachment of the 29th Regiment,[16] under Lieutenant Christopher Humfrey, arrived in June 1831 on board the *Jaseur* to relieve the men of the 99th. Word had reached Mahé of an outbreak of violence on Desroches island, where Hodoul's slaves were obviously not as contented as Dowland had thought. A party of soldiers were immediately sent there. The regimental diary notes that their services were not needed, but the soldiers remained as a precaution until May 1832, when they returned to rejoin the main detachment on Mahé. The same month Harrison informed Ormsby that land grants on the outer islands could be made only on the strict condition that no slaves were employed there. He suspected that slave ships were still calling at the islands, and insisted that all such visits were reported. Ormsby was now on the point of being recalled. His replacement as sub-agent, assistant registrar and protector of slaves was another official from Mauritius, Arthur Wilson.

Resistance to the abolition of slavery in Mauritius was headed by a prominent planter, Adrien d'Épinay, who went to Britain twice to argue the case for the planters. He was instrumental in winning some concessions, including a free Press[17] and the reform of the non-elected Council of Government, originally created in 1825. He also ensured that the principle of compensating slave-owners was confirmed. However, the tide was flowing too strongly in favour of total emancipation for it to be seriously diverted by any rearguard action. The Reform Bill of 1832[18] had given Britain a parliament which could claim some semblance of democratic representation, and in the summer of 1833 it passed a law abolishing slavery in all British colonies. The Emancipation Act came into force in the West Indies the following year, and in Mauritius and Seychelles in 1835. Even then, the planters were to retain the services of their ex-slaves for a few years longer, time enough for thousands of Indian immigrants —

slaves in all but name — to be brought in to work in the cane fields of Mauritius and keep the sugar industry alive.

In Seychelles, the pattern for the future evolved differently. There was no substantial sugar industry to ensure the islands' prosperity, and there would be no large-scale Indian immigration to replace the lost labour of the slaves. The planters had little to look forward to, and many who in previous years had watched others leave with their slaves, themselves prepared to pack up and go.

"On this island, in only a few years, everything, man and his surroundings, has changed under the influence of the emancipation of the slaves," wrote Laplace, when he revisited Seychelles in June 1837, this time in command of the frigate *Artémise*. He looked in vain for the happy, smiling port of call that he had known seven years previously. Instead there was an air of abandonment everywhere, as if the colony had been struck by the plague. He called on the Savy family, and found them thinking of going to India. Even the climate was more oppressive than Laplace remembered, and his crew, who had been so healthy before, fell sick through eating too much fruit.

The general malaise was reflected by the government medical officer, Dr Bernard, who complained to Mauritius about the lack of a proper hospital in Victoria — *une misérable cabane,* was how he described it — as well as a seaworthy boat for him to visit ships. He feared that there was often fraudulent communication with arriving ships, and as the smallpox vaccine sent by Mauritius had proved ineffective many children were at risk. Fortunately, Laplace had a supply of vaccine, and the *Artémise*'s doctor carried out vaccinations during the ship's stay. To Laplace Seychelles displayed "the utter despair in which all the black colonies quickly fall without exception". He believed that with wise and patient policies, freedom could have been achieved without the sacrifices that had produced "the ingratitude of the Blacks, the condemnation of the Whites and the loss of our colonies". He did not elaborate further. Instead, as soon as he could, he sailed off on his second voyage around the world, ordered by the government of Louis-Philippe[19] to give "distant peoples a just idea of the naval power of our country".

3

Whales and Whalers
1834-1851

Moby Dick had in a former year been seen ...
on what is called the Seychelle ground ...
Herman Melville, *Moby Dick*, 1851

Wednesday, 29 January 1834. In the American whaleship *Georgia* the mate, Edward Harris, made the following entry in the ship's journal before turning in for the night: *At 6 pm came to Anchor in Mahee Roads, several ships there, employed in fiting water casks etc. So ends.* Tomorrow there would be a run ashore for the larboard watch, a prospect that normally would have raised a cheer in the 'poorhouse', but after ten months at sea and few whales to show for it the rejoicing had been muted. Harris thought back to the dog Towser, thrown overboard after it went mad. Perhaps it had been a bad omen. Short-handed they were, too, with the skipper unable to find a single recruit at the Western Isles (Azores). They had sighted whales off and on, but most times when they lowered the creatures had escaped. And in any case, with so few hands, it had been hard work cutting in those they managed to bring alongside.

The *Georgia*'s best day had been in November, off the islands of Providence and St Pierre, where they had taken four sperm. They had later called at Providence, but got little except for some old bedsteads. Earlier, they had managed to take some coconuts from Cosmoledo. They had spoken several ships: the first, only five months out, had nothing, but the barque *Emma* had boasted 2,900 barrels of sperm oil. They had also spoken the *Cicero* (William Hussey) and the barque *Amanda* (Latham Cross, Jun.), both of New Bedford, and the *Julius Caesar* (Captain Hebron), of New London. All had reported oil on board. Later, the skipper had bent course for Mahé. On New Year's Day there had come up strong gales from the south-west, a real "Harry Cane" that had turned over the boats. On 11 January they sighted Coëtivy; landed, but got nothing.

The bad weather had followed them all the way to Mahé, where, even in the roadstead, the wind and a heavy swell had capsized the windlass and broken the sampson. Harris kept the crew busy cleaning the ship, and stowing down the water casks, the watches taking it in turn to go ashore. After two weeks in port, with a new sampson and a few recruits on board, the *Georgia* left Mahé, with the *Cicero* in company. It would remain in the western Indian Ocean for the rest of the year, not returning to its home port of New London, Connecticut, until February 1835. The cruise was to prove moderately successful, with a total catch of thirty-three sperm whales and eighteen humpbacks.[1]

That year more than 200 American vessels like the *Georgia* were hunting whales around the world. Yet this was only the beginning of a golden age that would see the number of voyages rise steadily through the 1830s to the 1860s until more than 700 whaleships were flying the Stars and Stripes world-wide. It was "one of the largest and most important branches of business in which this country has yet embarked," remarked the *Whalemen's Shipping List* weekly of New Bedford, on 8 June 1847.

Although whales had always been hunted for their meat, and for the oil which gave light and warmth, the coming of the industrial age caused an unprecedented and ever-growing demand for whale oil, essential for lubricating machinery and in the manufacture of certain foods, soaps, and cosmetics. At the same time whalebone — not bone at all but the horny sieve in the mouth of the baleen whale through which it feeds on the small shrimp-like creatures called krill — had a variety of uses as the 'plastic' of the 19th century, from corset stays and kitchen utensils to horse whips. As whales became scarcer they had to be hunted from bigger boats and farther out to sea. Some whales, such as the blue or sulphur-bottom (the largest animal in the world) and the finback, were too big or too quick to be tackled with only a hand-held harpoon wielded from an

26

open boat, but most of the other whales were vulnerable. They included the right, the sei, the humpback, and lastly even the formidable sperm whale, or *cachelot*, prized for its superior oil and the fragrant, waxy liquid called spermaceti contained in its huge head.[2]

"The Seychelles have, of late years, attracted considerable attention, on account of the sperm whales which are now known to frequent the extensive banks about these islands," wrote Holman, explaining that the sperm whale was of the type furnished with teeth. "Those of an ordinary size, will produce fourteen barrels of oil, one of which is taken from the head in a liquid state," he wrote.

Today we know that the Seychelles bank, in the vicinity of Bird and Denis islands, is a sperm whale breeding ground to which, every season, adult males return after feeding in the Antarctic. Whaling activity in this area was therefore particularly damaging to the natural increase of stocks. Although few people at the time seriously thought of whales becoming extinct, the *Philadelphia Bulletin* of 1847 felt it necessary to reassure its readers.

"It is a singular fact that, notwithstanding the general impression that the whale becomes scarcer yearly, there would seem to be little rational cause for the belief, for there are but few more vessels engaged in that species of fishery now than there were two hundred years ago." The newspaper added that if the size of the US whaling fleet had increased there were also fewer European vessels, and so numbers had probably stayed the same. "Hence we question the fact, so often asserted that whales are becoming scarcer. It is very probable that they are changing their location in order to avoid their pursuers, for the instinct of all animals lends them to do this."

Thomas Smith, a boatsteerer on the London whaler *Coquette*, who spent several months on Denis island in 1828 after falling sick, reported that there were at least thirteen other whaleships in the area during the three weeks the *Coquette* had hunted whales near neighbouring Cow (Bird) island. Smith had a certificate from his captain entitling him to a 130th part of the ship's catch, which was then 700 barrels of sperm oil. This share, or lay, indicated the importance of a boatsteerer, a rather misleading title for one who had to harpoon the whale, attaching one or more irons (harpoons) with lines to the animal. Protocol demanded that once the whale had been brought up close, the officer or mate would exchange places with the boatsteerer, and from the bow repeatedly stab the creature with his lance, seeking its heart or lungs.

During this hazardous operation, with the flimsy whaleboat continually in danger of being crushed by the frenzied lunging and lashing of the wounded whale, the boatsteerer would hold the boat steady with the long steering oar. As little or no wages were paid on a whaleship, his earnings would be a share of the proceeds; in Smith's case a 130th part. The master, in contrast, might have from a fourteenth to a nineteenth lay, while a greenhand on his first voyage would be lucky to get a 250th lay. Holman thought that the system contributed to the generally more insubordinate attitude of the crews, who, "being on shares, as it were ... assume a degree of consequence and independence, from an idea that they are part proprietors." Captains were in fact often part-owners, having purchased a share in the ship with money from their lay. An experienced captain could demand a bonus if he filled his ship, or ask for an extra $1 for every cask of sperm oil over an agreed minimum. Always in demand, whalemen might bargain successfully for a better lay, especially after the discovery of gold in California in 1848, when many of their kind joined the rush to the diggings on the West coast.

British whalers had hunted southern right whales off the Cape of Good Hope and sperm whales east of Madagascar as early as 1789, but it was not until 1823 that the first whaler called at Seychelles. "Of 150 tons burden, called the *Swan*, (it) returned to England and gave such favourable accounts to the owners, Messrs Enderby and Co. of London, as induced them to send her back immediately, where she procured a second cargo in eleven months," wrote Holman. "The ship *Asp*,[3] of 345 tons (belonging to the same owners), reached this port (Mahé) in December 1825, and sailed for England, with a full cargo, in April 1827. Thus did forty men and boys gain from the sea, in the short space of seventeen months, the value of 80,000 dollars in oil."

The English whalers were mostly from London, although there were a few from Hull, a port which was active in the

Arctic and southern oceans until overtaken by Scottish ports in 1850. Compared with the American whaling industry, however, Britain's share was negligible throughout the century, and whaling in the Indian Ocean was virtually a US monopoly.

Four vessels from Nantucket hunted whales off Zanzibar and to the north of Seychelles in 1828, and by 1830 a few New Bedford whalers were making regular appearances in the Indian Ocean. Harrison recorded a total of 82 whaleships, English and American, putting in at Seychelles between 1823 and 1836, although he knew that many others remained at sea so as not to incur anchorage dues. Instead, they called without paying anything at the outer islands, where there was wood, water, coconuts, birds eggs, or even, as in the case of the *Georgia*, old bedsteads. If the islands were inhabited there was usually something to trade. The *William Lee*, of Newport, Rhode Island, left sixty-five pairs of shoes of various sizes with a Praslin woman to sell.

Harrison believed Mahé's main attraction for the whalers lay in its healthy climate, "for in every other respect whaling vessels would probably do better at many of the ports of Madagascar and Johanna (Anjouan), where supplies are so much cheaper". It was these ports that the whalers mostly frequented. Six months after leaving Mahé, the *Georgia* put in at St Augustine's Bay on Madagascar's south-west coast, where it stayed about fourteen days wooding and watering, as well as trading with the natives. Madagascar, however, had a reputation for hostility to Europeans. At the Comoro islands, Anjouan in particular, the people were generally friendly and the islands had always been a regular stopping place for ships from Europe; cattle and fresh provisions were available, at little cost, and articles such as gunpowder and calico could be used as barter. American ships could find consular assistance at Zanzibar and Mauritius (the consular agency at Mahé dates from the 1850s), but Port Louis, despite its long-standing association with American shipping, had the disadvantage of high prices, exorbitant port dues, and an 8 pm curfew.

It is not surprising, therefore, that whaleship crews preferred "a run ashore" at Mahé. Charles Nordoff, recalling Seychelles and its "very innocent and quiet-living people", noted that the whole crew looked forward to calling there. "In fact ... our entire lives hinged upon that delightful name."

Except when forced to put in for water or provisions, or to rest the crew, a whaleship would remain at sea for months on end, processing and storing its catch without aid from the shore.[4] After a whale was killed and towed to the ship, it would be made fast alongside and the messy and often dangerous task of cutting in would begin. First the head would be cut off, and if it was a sperm whale the spermaceti would be ladled out. Then, with men balanced precariously on the revolving carcase — and with sharks often swirling about in the bloody water beneath them — huge "blanket pieces" of blubber would be cut away and winched down into the ship, to be cut into smaller pieces for rendering into oil.

This 'cooking' process was done at the tryworks on deck, where the blubber boiled furiously in large cauldrons, emitting a thick, oily smoke. It is said that the stench from a whaleship "trying out" could be detected twenty miles away. Care had to be taken to make sure the oil did not burn or discolour. While one man skimmed off the cracklings as they came to the surface, others ladled out the boiling oil into cooler pots. When the oil had cooled sufficiently it was put into barrels and stowed below. Sometimes the cook make doughnuts for the crew as the oil boiled. Trying out had to be completed soon after the whale was killed, otherwise the oil might turn rancid. No-one on the whaleship slept until the job was done.

Reefs and shoals were an ever present danger on the Seychelles bank, and several whaleships came to grief.[5] It may have been partly for this reason that Harrison in 1827 asked Mauritius if slaves could be embarked on whaleships "for the purpose of aiding in the navigation of such vessels". Approval was given. How many slaves were thus employed is not known, but sometimes one or more would slip aboard a whaling ship and achieve their freedom that way. The *Coquette*, after calling at Providence island — where the captain had obtained milk in exchange for a bottle of rum — found that two slaves had remained on board. Their names were Joseph and Sylvestre. Claiming that they were free men, they were treated like other crew members, but some months later, hearing that they were being sought by Harrison, the captain returned them to Mahé, and agreed to pay the owner one dollar compensation for each day's lost labour.

Despite their seafaring tradition and fine boat-building,

including the construction of a 300-tonne barque, the *Thomas Blyth*,[6] mentioned by Harrison in his report for 1837, the early Seychelles settlers showed little interest in whaling. Whales washed up on the beach would be cut up and their flesh and oil consumed, but this was the extent of their on-shore whaling. A suggestion by the Commission of Eastern Enquiry in March 1828 that the settlers should improve their fisheries, "including that of the spermaceti whale", brought no response. The seas remained open to Yankee whalers, who averaged thirty-five vessels clearing New England ports for the Indian Ocean each year between 1835 and 1859.

It was customary for the American ships to recruit on the African coast, at the Azores and the Cape Verde islands and also, in mid-cruise, at the Seychelles, where crew members would occasionally quit ship to seek work ashore. It has been estimated that as a result of this recruiting pattern, by the 1840s coloured men made up one-sixth of the labour force in the American whaling industry. Undoubtedly a number of these men were from Seychelles.

Life aboard a whaleship was invariably hard, and brutality by captain and mates was part of an accepted lifestyle that easily translated into riotous behaviour when the men were ashore. "Sailors belonging to whaling ships are certainly more difficult to manage than the crews of any other vessels," noted Harrison. He was commenting on an incident in July 1834 involving the Savy family. Charles Savy, who had so often entertained naval officers at his Sainte Anne plantation, was unfortunately away in Mauritius when less mannered mariners paid a call. There were about thirty of them, sailors from the English whaling barques *Zephyr* and *Harpooneer.* According to Savy, they forced their way into his house. Responding to the cries of the women and children, who had fled upstairs, Savy's son Hylaric and Louis Adam, with two slaves, confronted the mob and were severely beaten. One of the slaves was knocked unconscious, but a barrier on the stairway prevented the sailors reaching the upper floor. Their intent seems to have been pillage rather than rape, for Savy remarked that when help came the sailors withdrew *"sans avoir pu en lever le trésor".*

Savy demanded compensation and protection from whaleship crews, describing them as *"demi sauvage".* He was critical of the Government Agent, whom he accused of being under the influence of the whalers, as well as the troops and *"les six gendarmes pauvres et souffrants"*, dubbed by him as useless. Harrison, who happened to be at Mauritius on account of his health and in order to give evidence on slave registrations to the Commissioners of Compensation, rejected Savy's criticism, but strongly recommended that the *juge de paix* be given more powers to maintain the public peace. It was, after all, common knowledge that the Seychelles authorities lacked sufficient muscle to enforce any of their regulations.

It seems also to have been common knowledge that liquor was readily available at the Sainte Anne establishment – its consumption was even encouraged by Savy and his family if the captains of the *Zephyr* and *Harpooneer* are to be believed – which prompted Mauritius to remind Harrison that there were laws restricting the sale or barter of alcoholic beverages. No action seems to have been taken, however, and it was only in March 1836, after Captain Howard of the *Harpooneer* had been cut up by a Praslin arrack seller named Gontier that the Government Agent formed a committee to tackle the problem of liquor sales. While approving the measure, the Governor, Sir William Nicolay, wondered why Harrison had not acted earlier.

Four months after the Savy affair there was another incident, involving captains of two whaleships. This time the Seychelles authorities reacted forcibly, probably improperly, and almost certainly with malice, thereby attracting the attention of the US consul at Mauritius.

In May 1834 Captain Latham Cross, jun., of the American whaling barque *Amanda* had put in at Praslin, where he decided to abandon his leaking ship, load his cargo of 600 barrels of oil into a London whaler, the *Thames,* and take passage in it to England. The day before its sailing, in early November, Cross invited to his house on Praslin Captain Dunn of the *Thames,* the chief mate Day, and the surgeon. Other guests included François Mellon, of La Digue. During the meal a quarrel arose between Day and Mellon, whereupon, according to Cross, the latter drew a knife. As Dunn tried to separate them, some seamen of the *Thames* put a rope round Mellon's neck and dragged him to the door.

The intention seems to have been to hang Mellon, and Cross claimed that he had to rescue the Seychellois. Mellon then returned to the table, with the matter apparently forgotten. Five days later, as the *Thames* was putting to sea, it was intercepted by an armed pinnace, carrying a summons for Cross and Dunn to appear in court to answer a charge of assault. The two men were kept in prison without food, and interrogated by Judge Fressanges — who, according to Cross, discussed the case with witnesses as he lunched under a tree. They were then taken to Mahé "in the company of slaves and negroes ... without being allowed to procure ... a change of linen". Eventually, after several days of interrogation by the judge, the two men were released. Cross appears to have laid a complaint against Mellon, which was dismissed by Chief of Police Amedée Savy as not serious; Dunn saved the authorities possible embarrassment by dying, and the mate and the sailors were acquitted of assault. The *Thames* eventually sailed for England, with a new captain and mate sent from Mauritius.

Although the whaleships' presence was often troublesome, it helped to keep the islands in touch with the outside world. The captains maintained a useful information network from 'gamming' (exchanging visits or speaking with) other whaleships. Always of interest was where whales might be found, and a stranger would often bring news from home. Whaleships were sometimes willing to provide passage[7] to and from the outer islands; even to England if passengers were not pressed for time. The ships accepted and delivered mail, and sometimes prominent visitors would arrive at Mahé in a whaleship. In August 1836 Dr Robertson informed Harrison that envoys bearing a message from the Sultan of Anjouan to the Mauritius governor had arrived at Praslin in the New Bedford whaler *Anstey Gibbs*. As one of the sailors had smallpox, Robertson ordered the crew and passengers quarantined on Curieuse island. There they remained for three weeks, after which Harrison arranged for the Sultan's envoys to continue their journey to Mauritius in the schooner *Étoile*.

Anjouan occasionally sought outside help when assailed by internal or external threats. Raids by Sakalava tribesmen from Madagascar were common, and the Comoro islands were occasionally at war with each other. Aware of French interest in the area and anxious to maintain the independence of Anjouan — the island with which it had closest ties — Britain would sometimes send a warship to show the flag, although the naval C-in-C at the Cape, Rear Admiral George Elliott, regretted that Mauritius never briefed him properly on what line to take with these "most insignificant islands". A few years later, another group of Anjouan envoys — dismissed by Elliott as "boys sent as ambassadors" — arrived at Mauritius, having made a stop-over at Seychelles. After hearing their pleas for assistance, Mauritius suggested to London that it would be advisable to appoint a British consul to Anjouan. This was done, but not until 1848.

Whaling captains sailed to wherever they thought they would find whales, which meant every sea in the world. They scoured the Atlantic, criss-crossed the Indian and Pacific Oceans, they penetrated the Arctic and, in later years, braved the icy wastes of Antarctica. However, some skippers had one favourite ground to which they regularly returned. Such was Samuel Braley,[8] who each time he left New Bedford would set a course for the Indian Ocean. Perhaps it was the lure of the sperm whale, the fabled Moby Dick of American fiction, that beckoned him. Or, again, it may have been a romantic attachment to someone at Seychelles. We can only guess.

In March 1850 Braley was already several months into his fourth voyage, his second as master of the 276-tonne barque *Arab*, and he was far from happy. Not only was the crew inexperienced, with several men sick, but there had been no sight of a whale. Braley would console himself by writing up his log, a remarkable document in that it was addressed solely to his wife, Mary Ann.

After recording his position on the western edge of the Great Chagos Bank, he continued: "Night has come again, and I am thinking of thee ... it only makes me miserable ... thou are fixed in my inmost thoughts and I must endure a longing that is consuming by inches and will not be appeased by any antidote but holding thee in my arms."

The next day, 20 March, still no whales, and there was trouble among the crew. "I came near to flogging two men for fighting. I went so far as to seace [sic] them up, but on their promising to do better in future I let them off ... Good night." The following morning they sight sperm whales and manage to

34

get one with the lance; the others escape. Cutting in and boiling the blubber was hard work, his crew "so green ... they don't know what to do." Braley, whose wife was a Quaker, admitted: "I have to swear a little occasionally for I get clear out of patience." By 17 April he has almost given up hope. His back is sore, and, at 32, he finds he is getting old. On Sunday, 21 April, he puts in at Diego Garcia, to shift the fresh water to prevent the casks rotting and "to see old friends". He stays there several days, and accidentally cuts his leg with an axe. On 1 May he is back at sea; his leg still painful. "Maddam Austin gave me some salv that seems to agree with it," he informs his wife, adding by way of an afterthought, "Don't be jellous for she is a married woman and her husband with her so there is no chance of course."

On 17 May, just as he is thinking of sending six of his men home and recruiting others, his luck changes. They kill a large sperm whale, which makes 100 barrels of oil. "It is the largest whale that I have ever taken in the Indian Ocean," he notes. Although cheered by this, he is angered by the crew's presumed ailments. "My list of cripples augments daily ... sore legs, sore feet, sore toes and I know not what besides."

On Wednesday, 10 July, Braley puts in at Mahé, where on entering the harbour he strikes the reef. At first he finds the inhabitants indifferent to his plight, but eventually about forty men pull the ship free. They demand $1,150 for the service; Braley thinks $100 would have been sufficient. "Whaleships rarely carried cash, barter being a more convenient form of exchange, and Braley has to leave all his barrels of oil ashore as surety to get his ship repaired. The estimate for this is $1,500. "I fear that I shall have to lose the $1,500 in spite of all I can do as they have my stores in their possession," he writes. "It is swindling in the worst form to take advantage of one in distress ...These beggars almost drive me mad." he complains to Mary Ann.

A year goes by, and the *Arab* is again nearing Seychelles. On Thursday, 26 June 1851, he writes: "Well tomorrow I suppose that I shall see that beautifull island called Mahe ... how I shall find my affairs I cannot guess for the men are such consumate villins." On Friday he is off Sainte Anne, but decides to wait till morning before entering harbour. "Once I should have gon in tonight, but I dred that port more than any

35

other in the world, and I want daylight to enter." he admits. Happily, he enters safely, and finds that his drafts have been honoured and that he is free to take away his oil. It requires a week before all the barrels are on board.

On 27 July Braley leaves Mahé to cruise off Denis island. On board is the local Anglican priest, the Rev. F. George Delafontaine, taking passage to Praslin.

4

Not yet Freedom
1830-1842

The negro ... is thus ... secured from the evils of poverty
... and from the still greater evils of unrestricted idleness.
The Times, 13 May 1833

On 1 February 1835, eighteen months after the passing of the
Emancipation Act, slavery was formally abolished in Mauritius.
Five days later, Chief Secretary George Dick wrote to Harrison
instructing him to inform the slaves of Seychelles, "in the most
impressive manner possible", that they were slaves no longer.

The apparent lack of urgency in implementing the Act
matched the modest benefits it actually conferred on the
servile population. The manumitted slaves, except for those
under seven and over sixty years of age, were now apprentices
for the next seven years, legally bound to work for their
masters as before. If anything, they were expected to work with
even greater willingness, for the Act declared itself in favour of
"promoting the Industry of the Manumitted Slaves".

Arguing in favour of this "industry of freedom", *The Times*
newspaper pointed out that it was not labour "wrung from the
negro by the outrage of corporal punishment, capriciously
inflicted on him by the master, but ... secured to the master by
the control of the law, in like manner as the industry of the
labourer in this country who thinks fit to bind himself for a
specific period". Such, indeed, was the intention, although it
soon became apparent that apprenticeship in the former slave
colonies was a very different thing from what one understood
by that term in England. By an Order in Council it was
stipulated that praedial apprentices, or those attached to a
plantation, and for the most part field hands, would work for

37

seven and a half hours a day, six days a week, with Sundays and holidays free. Those relatively liberal hours were to allow the apprentice time to earn money by working additional hours, or to grow his own crops.

Masters were not required to pay wages, but they had to provide housing, clothing, and food, or, in the absence of the latter, a plot of ground to grow crops. Apprentices who worked extra hours were entitled to receive payment of a shilling an hour. If their master failed to pay them, his goods could be attached. The authorities hoped that, eventually, apprentices would save enough money to buy their freedom. Although the payments were small, some of the more industrious were able achieve this. According to the slave code of behaviour it was more creditable to buy one's freedom than to have it granted, and women particularly sought liberty this way. They would often show off their shoes as a sign of freedom, for neither slaves nor apprentices wore shoes.

Slave-owners naturally were bitter at the loss of their human property, but the compulsory apprenticeship scheme and Britain's agreement to pay generous compensation softened the blow. Compensation varied from colony to colony, but in general a slave-owner could be expected to receive 40 per cent of the declared value of his or her slaves. Harrison had been directed in June 1834 to start collecting evidence from slave sales and transfers to assist the four appraisers to be sent to Seychelles the following June to determine how much each slave was worth. Because slaves had always fetched higher prices in Mauritius, several of the Seychelles slave-owners petitioned the government to evaluate their slaves according to the Mauritius scale, but the Commissioners of Compensation rejected this notion. Records show that slaves in Seychelles were valued at between £80 and £120, and in the final reckoning an average of £30 per slave was paid in both Mauritius and Seychelles, amounting in all to just under £2mn.[1] Planters in the West Indian colonies, owning several hundred thousand slaves compared to Mauritius's 67,000, received about £18mn, not as much as they had hoped for, but a good deal more than some MPs would have given them.

Most abolitionists were opposed to masters retaining the services of their former slaves for seven years (the original proposal before Parliament had been twelve years), but it is difficult to see how the slaves could have been liberated immediately without causing massive hardship and upheaval in the colonies. It had always been recognised that a master freeing a slave should provide him or her with the means of survival: setting him up in a trade, for example, or with a plot of land or a pension; sometimes even with a slave of his own. Of course, if they could get away with it, many masters would have readily rid themselves of a slave no longer able to work because of age or infirmity, or too troublesome, and thus difficult to sell.

Special magistrates were appointed to regulate the apprenticeship scheme, but they were often intimidated by the planters. In Seychelles Wilson, the Protector of Slaves, was appointed a magistrate in January 1835. While the law he had to enforce prescribed light penalties for erring masters, apprentices who broke the rules could find themselves in prison, or even seized up for a flogging. Indolence or carelessness meant an additional fifteen hours of labour. Absence from work for seven and a half hours in any week amounted to desertion, and resulted in a term of imprisonment. If an apprentice was absent for two whole days he or she was officially declared a vagabond, and liable to be jailed for two weeks, with fifteen strokes of the cane; if away for six days the absentee became a runaway, and faced a possible penalty of a month's jail and thirty lashes.

As in the days of slavery, no apprentices were permitted in town after dark. At Harrison's request, Mauritius agreed to send a small gun to signal nightfall so that the apprentices would not "compromise themselves". Several settlers, among them Huteau (who had the concession of Aldabra), wanted to place apprentices on outlying islands. The Governor agreed, but only if it was clearly in the apprentices' interest. That this was not always the case is evidenced by the Governor's refusal to permit one settler, named Albert, to transfer apprentices to certain outlying islands for fishing.

As the years passed, concern in Britain that apprenticeship was simply prolonging the reality of slavery appeared increasingly well-founded. In Parliament MPs reminded Ministers of their pledge that the working conditions for apprentices would be no worse than those of a British labourer, whereas reports reaching London indicated the contrary. The government was also reminded of its promise that if masters flouted the law apprenticeship would be abolished. Government spokesmen at first claimed that cruelty was the exception, but this had little impact at the public meetings held all over England to discuss the issue.

The fact that slaves were still being shipped illegally from Africa was an additional aggravation. The trade "flourishes to a most fearful extent," noted *The Times* of 11 January 1836. In that year Portugal finally prohibited the export of slaves from any of its dominions (it was the last European power to do so), but according to *The Times* many states, even those that supported anti-slaving legislation, still engaged in it.

France had not yet abolished slavery in its colonies (this did not occur until the Revolution of 1848, which ushered in the Second Republic). The Anglo-French agreement of 1831 had given both countries mutual right of search and seizure of suspect ships, but because of French susceptibilities it was too limited to be effective, and slave captains frequently used the French flag to run slaves into Bourbon, where there was a continuing demand for labour on the sugar plantations. Because of increasing difficulties in shipping slaves from Africa some Bourbon planters cast their eyes towards India, from where they could bring in coolies under contract. These workers, from Pondicherry and Karikal, were slaves in all but name. Mauritius also considered recruiting labour from India as it became clear that the apprenticeship scheme was unlikely to last the full seven years. Increasing desertions and more frequent purchases of freedom, as well as the mounting opposition in Britain to apprenticeship, were warning signs to the planters. Local ordinances were drawn up in 1836 and 1839 to fix the terms for importing Indian labour, but both were disallowed by the Secretary of State, Lord Glenelg, who described them as "in some material respects even less equitable than that of slavery itself".

In the West Indies, Bermuda and Antigua had set an example by declaring all slaves free immediately. Now, with almost two years of the apprenticeship scheme still to run, the other colonies were being pressured to move to complete freedom. In April 1838, with Jamaica on the point of liberating its apprentices, Glenelg sent Mauritius two dispatches urging the Indian Ocean colony to do the same. These were considered by the Mauritius Council of Government and rejected. In October, two months after apprenticeship ended in Jamaica, Glenelg tried again. Again he was rebuffed.

The following month, an Order in Council was issued by London empowering the Governor to proclaim that apprentices living in Mauritius were, as from 1 February 1839, "absolutely free and discharged of and from the then remaining term of their apprenticeship". Domestic apprentices were to be freed first, praedials attaining full liberty on 31 March. This news sent shivers of apprehension through the island. Everyone knew that in the wake of freedom came riots and disorder. As one American in Mauritius observed, "all large bodies of men, when all restraint is suddenly withdrawn ... launch into violent excesses". Some of those fears were to be realised, when the streets of Port Louis swarmed with apprentices celebrating their freedom, "much to the annoyance of the more quietly disposed population".

In Seychelles, the approach of Liberation Day had been viewed with equal concern, especially as there were now no British troops on Mahé, the last detachment having been withdrawn because of indiscipline.[2] Instead, the police had been armed with sabres and light muskets. Nevertheless, a group of inhabitants petitioned the Governor to bring the soldiers back. Reluctantly he agreed, stipulating only that the people would have to meet the cost of repairing the barracks.

The troops arrived in January 1839, the detachment being provided by the 35th (Royal Sussex) Regiment.[3] The barracks were not yet ready, but Wilson (who by then had succeeded Harrison as Government Agent) was able to quarter the troops in buildings known as the Établissement Dugand. As it turned out, there was no need for a military presence, the Seychelles apprentices, to the "sincere gratification" of the Governor, celebrating their liberation in "a joyful but restrained manner". With nothing to detain them, the soldiers of the Royal Sussex returned to Mauritius. It was the last time British troops would be stationed in Seychelles until the outbreak of World War II.

After the festivities it had been hoped that the former apprentices would return voluntarily to work. It was not to be. In Mauritius about 5,000 signed one-year contracts, probably because they did not fully understand that they were free, but by 1841 none was working in the cane fields. The planters had prepared for this, and already 20,000 labourers from India had arrived, with more on the way. It was the start of a migration from the Indian sub-continent that would change totally the demographic face of the island.

In Seychelles the freed apprentices also abandoned their work places. Why should they labour for the pittance that was offered to them, when they could work for themselves, at their own pace? Their preference was a few days' labouring hard, to earn just enough to live in idleness for the rest of the month. Many were allowed to squat on their former master's land, others went off into the mountains, or became fishermen, small traders, or artisans. "They live poorly, and content themselves with little, because they prefer that mode of life which requires the least amount of regular labour." So stated a report by Mauritius to the Secretary of State, but it could equally well have referred to the former apprentices in Seychelles.

Although the ending of forced labour is sometimes perceived as the cause of Seychelles' economic decline, that had begun a decade earlier with the collapse of the cotton market. Sugar's early promise failed to overcome the Mauritian stranglehold on Seychelles exports and, as Harrison had forecast in 1830, "a loss of revenue, non-payment of taxes and general despondency ... will be the result". Many estates were abandoned and the settlers, with their slaves, moved away.[4] During the decade from 1830, the population of the islands fell by half, from 8,500 to 4,360, and not surprisingly Seychelles became a "miserable place" for ships calling for refreshment. A little rice was grown, but there were few sheep, fowls, or pigs. Only fish, and the maize that grew plentifully on Silhouette, Marianne, and some of the Amirante islands, kept Mahé from starving.

Captain Edward Belcher of HMS *Sulphur*, who visited Mahé in February 1842, found that business had completely stagnated. Money was scarce, bills were not negotiable, and "we even experienced difficulty in arranging for the few supplies obtained". He attributed lack of labour to the settlers' inability or reluctance to pay, for they "cannot make their minds up to swallow the bitter pill of paying those whose services they still maintain they are entitled". He saw little likelihood of "this heavy cloud" dispersing. "Unless some speculative characters drop in with their spare thousands, it is very evident that this beautiful and very capable group [of islands] will fall into insignificance".

Like their counterparts in Mauritius, the Seychelles settlers had thought of recruiting labour from India, but all requests to do so were turned down. The Indian government, alarmed at the atrocious conditions experienced by emigrant workers going to Mauritius, had halted the traffic, and it was not until 1842 that it was resumed, under much closer supervision. In contrast to Mauritius, Seychelles began to move towards the cultivation of less labour-intensive crops, and by the early 1840s coconut oil had become the main export. Years later, it was noted that "never since then has Seychelles been able to provide enough food to feed itself".[5]

* *

In October 1829 a leper colony had been set up on Curieuse island, off Praslin's northern coast, after Harrison informed Mauritius that he had found a man with leprosy on Mahé. He thought that possibly there were others, and suggested that if Mauritius wanted to keep lepers all in one place, Curieuse might be acquired for this purpose. It would, he noted, be a "desirable place of residence for the leprous and other diseased Blacks scattered over the various islands of this archipelago, Agaléga, and Diego Garcia". Most of those unfortunates had been cruelly abandoned by their masters, whose only concern was to prevent the disease spreading to other slaves. Harrison's suggestion of forming what would become a refuge for them — however imperfect — can be regarded as a humanitarian gesture.

He had, however, a double purpose. Reports had reached him that the coco de mer palm was being threatened by indiscriminate cutting and neglect on Praslin and Curieuse, the only two islands of Seychelles where the celebrated palm grows naturally. By declaring Curieuse an asylum for lepers Harrison knew that he would scare others away, and thereby preserve more easily the stands of coco de mer on the island. As an additional measure of conservation, he suggested that the Governor should order proprietors on Praslin and the small nearby island of Ronde to plant two hundred coco de mer

43

trees on every hundred acres of land. To all this the Governor agreed.[6]

The inhabitants of Praslin and La Digue had no desire to see lepers settled close by, and Harrison got little help in setting up a camp. He managed, however, to erect sufficient huts from coco de mer leaves to house the lepers. George Forbes, third mate of the whaling barque *Greenwich* of London, ashore since 1826 because of ill-health, was appointed superintendent of the settlement. There was also a resident doctor and a policeman.

Rations of rice, salt, and sugar were arranged for the lepers, who were expected to supplement this by fishing and growing vegetables. It was far from being a paradise. The surgeon of the *Jaseur*, who visited Curieuse in July 1830, reported that the lepers — sixty-four men, twelve women, and two children — had only bandages to cover their feet. He suggested leather should be provided for making sandals. Several lepers had lost toes and fingers, and six of the most helpless were in the small hospital. Coconuts were required for their consumption, as there were few on the island, and maize and cassava needed to be added to the rice-only diet. The following year HM sloop *Curlew* visited the island, and a subsequent report criticised the doctor and Forbes' wife for punishing the lepers for not washing.

As yet little had been done to improve their diet. Without a pirogue the lepers were unable to fish, and were dependent on supplies from Praslin and La Digue. Mauritius gave permission for them to be given coconuts at eight dollars per 1,000, but the supply of this and other foodstuffs was irregular and subject to arbitrary price rises, to the annoyance of the new medical superintendent, Dr Patrick Robertson. Robertson eventually gave up trying to organise a supply of turtles and fish from the inhabitants of La Digue, and obtained permission through Harrison for a pirogue to be provided for the lepers, so that they might catch their own fish. Robertson remained at Curieuse until his death by drowning in June 1846. There were rumours that he himself had caught the disease.

Occasionally Harrison received requests from Mauritius to accommodate unruly slaves, who the police thought would benefit from a spell in Seychelles. One, known as Petit Jean, had served as an overseer with the police in Mauritius.

Although "incorrigibly bad" he was deemed extremely intelligent, and the Police Commissioner thought he should be given a similar position at Seychelles. Petit Jean was duly sent to Mahé on board the *Curlew,* along with another slave, Edward William. On their arrival they were dispatched to Curieuse. No record has been found of the fate of Petit Jean, but in 1833 Edward, whose behaviour at the leper settlement had proved unsatisfactory, was returned to Mahé, where he was made assistant to a new overseer with the police, a slave named Castor. The latter had for years led a band of *marrons,* or runaway slaves, in the mountains, before giving himself up to become a tracker of fugitive slaves, a task which earned him "a sort of celebrity".

Meanwhile, the French had not forgotten the usefulness of Seychelles as a dumping ground for undesirables. In 1837 an application was sent to Mauritius by the Bourbon governor asking that seven persons found guilty of attempted insurrection might, as an alternative to prison, by sent to Seychelles. This request was promptly rejected.

For most British officials, a Seychelles posting was not regarded with much favour, and there were few volunteers when a vacancy arose. As a result it was often the least worthy, those Mauritius wanted to get rid of, who were sent to Seychelles. Harrison always had difficulty in getting policemen transferred from Mauritius, and consequently he looked for recruits wherever he could, frequently off a whaleship. In August 1832 he warned Mauritius that he had only two gendarmes fit for duty, and that he had therefore recruited two Englishmen, one a sailor from a whaling ship and another "who arrived from Praslin". The sailor, Joseph Thomson, had been put ashore by his captain for insolence, but, as Harrison pointed out, he was big and tough, and capable of subduing drunken sailors. As for the second recruit, George Dill, his appearance was in his favour, although Harrison doubted whether he would behave himself with only 14 dollars a month; he had decided, therefore, to pay him 20 dollars, the same as Thomson. Six months later Thomson was dead, and another man of unspecified profession appointed in his place.

Portuguese names appear frequently in Harrison's list of recruits, indicating that they were probably from the Azores or Cape Verde islands, where American whaling ships frequently took on crew. Mauritius also allowed Harrison to use "from time to time" unarmed troops, but off-duty soldiers were one of his problems, frequently involved in drunken brawls. Eventually, at the request of the officer commanding the detachment, the canteen near the barracks was closed.

Harrison left Seychelles at the end of 1837 for Mauritius, where he continued in government service as collector of international revenue. Although he had acted as Government Agent of Seychelles for ten years, and had been highly praised by at least one governor, he had never been confirmed in his post, lacking, perhaps, the necessary seniority. Wilson remained in charge for just over a year, before he was superseded at the beginning of 1839 by Charles Augustus Mylius, Seychelles' first Civil Commissioner. Mylius came to his post full of energy and enthusiasm, with the clear intention of putting Seychelles on a new and sounder footing.

5

Anglicans arrive
1839-1851

It is a great pity that a strong effort was not made
to instruct the African slaves when they were liberated
sixty years ago. As a race they are lost to us.
Rev. Henry Buswell, Church Missionary Society, 1894

In 1841 the small town of Seychelles known as l'Établissement
was officially named Victoria. The Civil Commissioner,
Mylius, considered it appropriate that the Colony — a term he
sometimes used for Seychelles until rebuked by his
superiors[1] — should be associated with Britain's recently
married young Queen.[2] He had suggested the name Port
Victoria, but instead of endorsing his choice Mauritius had
insisted that the inhabitants must first be consulted.

Mylius was aware that many people were opposed to the
name Victoria,[3] but he managed to collect sufficient signatures
for an appropriate petition, and this was subsequently
forwarded to the Queen. He also submitted to Mauritius a list
of proposed street names. In addition to Victoria and Albert
Streets, these included names such as Quincy, Market,
Hangard, Lodge, and Huteau. Except for Victoria Street, all
have survived.

Other street names, few of which were approved, were of
former British administrators and old French families like
d'Offay, Hodoul, St Jorre, Nageon, and Savy. Mylius pointed
out that he had not put his own name down for a street, but
felt that the new wharf, which had been "built with rocks
blasted under my directions", should rightly bear his name.

Eventually London approved the name of Victoria for the
town, a decision that probably displeased Mylius, who

47

henceforth in all his correspondence used the name "Port Victoria". Officially, this designated only the town's port, and Mylius's action was to lead years later to some uncertainty over the exact name of the Seychelles capital.[4]

The Civil Commissioner had arrived in Seychelles on 11 February 1839, accompanied by his Mauritian wife and three daughters. Although he just missed "the day of liberation" for non-praedial, mainly domestic apprentices, he was able to witness during the next few months the freeing of those who worked on the plantations. Informed of "the boon that Her Most Gracious Majesty had been pleased to bestow" on them, the latter generally accepted the delay in according them freedom, although there is evidence of at least one incident of disorder.[5]

Some settlers, like Mamin, the owner of Marie Louise island, had made a deal so that the apprentices were freed early but would stay until the work in hand had been completed. The widow Lefèvre, née Lebeuze, wrote to Mylius assuring him that she would free her apprentices on St Joseph and D'Arros islands in June, and provide passages for those wishing to leave. In the meantime she complained about her vegetable gardens being raided by apprentices who considered that the produce which they had grown belonged to them.

By now Mylius was beginning to realise how little real power he had as Civil Commissioner. He had been disappointed to learn that a major symbol of his authority, the detachment of British troops which had been stationed in Seychelles off and on since 1827, was to be finally withdrawn, further evidence, he thought, of the government's lack of interest in the islands.[6] He had hoped that, with the post of Government Agent renamed Civil Commissioner, he would be able to implement a new policy of economic development for Seychelles, but none – or almost none – of his proposals was accepted. Instead, he received a rebuke for quarrelling with the stipendiary magistrate, Lorenzo Clément, along with a reminder that his powers were no more extensive than those of his predecessors.[7] To Mylius, these powers were already so circumscribed as to reduce the job of Civil Commissioner "almost to a nonentity".[8]

Mylius felt particularly the lack of a church on Mahé. He had complained to Mauritius soon after his arrival that the inhabitants lived out their lives without the benefit of any Christian teaching or tradition. This, coupled with the state of the cemetery, where pigs sometimes dug up bodies for food, "places this colony in the very lowest state of degradation in point of Morals and Religion".

He asked for permission to build two churches and two schools on Mahé, and also schools on Praslin, Silhouette, and La Digue, all under Church of England missionaries. He called for roads and bridges to be built, as well as a market, so that produce could be properly distributed. He also wanted a hospital on Mahé, with dispensaries at Praslin, Silhouette, and La Digue. Anticipating a refusal on account of cost — "for I am not ignorant of the sweeping charge of the Mauritius against this remote and in a great measure abandoned little spot " — Mylius requested that the issue be submitted to London, "convinced as I am that Her Majesty and the people of England will not allow so degrading a state of things to exist in one of Her Colonies for the paltry saving of a few thousand pounds".

This was strong stuff, and in Mauritius' view completely unrealistic. Seychelles was costing Mauritius about £3,000 a year, mainly in pay and allowances to its officials, compared with an annual revenue of about £800 from Seychelles customs duties and taxes. Mylius, it was felt, would have to be fobbed off with vague promises. A careful reply was drafted, assuring Mylius that the Governor was sympathetic to his requests, and would try to send clergymen to Seychelles, although there was presently a shortage of clerics in Mauritius. Money might be forwarded to build a church, but this would have to be repaid. As regards schools, the government had no power to establish any, but would seek advice from London. It was also unable to provide a hospital. The Governor, however, considered that a market was a good idea, and said he would advance funds for that.[9] As regards the shortage of labour in Seychelles, Mauritius could not send any convicts to build roads, and restrictions by the Government of India precluded any recruitment of labour from there (Mylius had asked for 1,200 Indian immigrants).

Although Governor Nicolay thought Mylius wanted far too much, he did raise with London the question of churches and schools and, stung perhaps by Mylius's reference to the degrading state of one of Her Majesty's colonies, recommended that funds should be made available to cover the cost of buildings and salaries of the preachers and teachers. He said he was not sure whether these should be wholly Protestant, and wanted more information from Mylius. He repeated that it was not possible to provide medical services. While praising the energy of the Civil Commissioner, Nicolay added: "The poverty of the inhabitants of the Seychelles is sufficient alone to preclude all hopes of those Islands ever arriving at the flourishing state which he [Mylius] anticipates."

At the Colonial Office, the Governor's letter was referred to the Minister, but as little was known about Seychelles it took time to compile a dossier for Lord John Russell to study. On one page of the dossier someone had noted that Mauritius was not interested in Seychelles, but that the islands were important to Britain's naval empire and "it appears to me that the possession of them involves her in the responsibility of supplying the inhabitants with the means of living as Christians". Either public funds should be used, the writer suggested, or an approach be made to the missionary societies for assistance.

Seychelles had first attracted the attention of the Anglican missions in June 1830, when a preacher named William Morton called there on his way to take up a teaching post at King's College, Calcutta. The slave population, mainly without any Christian belief, must have seemed a rich source of souls to save, and during his short stay Morton baptised over 450 people, and would in time have baptised everyone according to Harrison, who added: "He appeared to me to be a very superior man, and one who would do a great deal of good in a place like this."

Harrison's comment was taken up by the then Mauritius governor, Sir Charles Colville, who offered Morton the post of Protestant preacher at Mahé, adding: "I have no doubt that the inhabitants will pay one-half of the expense of the erection of a suitable place of worship." Two years later, having resigned his post in Calcutta, Morton was back in Seychelles, where he and his family were accommodated in the old government house. The place of worship which Colville hoped the inhabitants would help to build did not materialise, and Morton had to make do with preaching in the pavilion where, during the week, Harrison had his office. Morton quickly

Creole girls in traditional costume.

Photographs depicting 'liberated African slaves,' from an album of Chief Civil Commissioner of Seychelles, Arthur Barkly (1882-88).

Bishop Clark

Father Léon Des Avanchers

Father Ignatius

Church of the Immaculate Conception, Victoria.

St Paul's Anglican Church, consecrated in 1859 by Bishop Ryan (inset).

Government House, 1905. Built in 1851, it was finally demolished in 1959.

An imaginary portrait of the boy king Louis XVII, whose disappearance during the French Revolution led to one of Seychelles' most enduring legends.

Sir Arthur Gordon

Taking a rest while crossing the mountains of Mahé. The lady traveller is in a 'fotey brankar,' or chair fixed to two poles, and carried by four men.

Prempeh, in robes and head-dress, poses with followers and guards.

The house at Le Rocher, outside Victoria, where Prempeh lived during his years of exile in Seychelles.

Boys working in the garden at Venn's Town.

A sketch of Venn's Town by founder Rev. William Chancellor.

became disillusioned, and within eighteen months he had left Seychelles for good. "His feelings towards the inhabitants, and theirs towards him, appear to have most materially changed," commented one observer, who blamed Morton for never having tried to preach in French. It was clear that in future any churchman sent to Seychelles would have to be able to speak fluent French.

Without church or pastor, Mylius himself undertook to preach each Sunday to a congregation of some 300 to 400, mostly former slaves and apprentices, now generally referred to as the new population.[10] He also presided at marriages, christenings, and funerals. Mylius showed concern, too, for the former French settlers, who had never had the benefit of a resident priest, and he repeatedly recommended that a priest be sent to minister to their needs.[11]

In 1840 Mauritius dispatched another Anglican clergyman to Seychelles to report on the state of religion in the Dependency. The Rev. Langrishe Banks was pleased to find that the black population was "more docile and respectful than that of the Mauritius", and he was able to perform 542 baptisms and conduct twenty-six marriages during his stay. He preached each Sunday in an improvised schoolroom – the morning service in French, with English in the afternoon. He expressed satisfaction at the morning's turnout, the worshippers being mainly black but with "a reasonable proportion of white and mulatto people". He found it remarkable that so many of the settlers, who if they acknowledged any creed at all would be Roman Catholic, attended "the preaching and services of a Church of England clergyman". Less well attended were the services in English, unless there happened to be a whaleship in port.

Banks' report was to raise hopes in Mauritius that the people of Seychelles would in time become good Anglicans, an expectation that was seemingly borne out some years later by the welcome given to the visiting Bishop of Colombo. Banks had pointed out that the black majority of the population (which totalled 4,369 on Mahé) regarded slavery as essentially French, while freedom had been "the boon of England". As a result, he considered they were more likely to identify with the English Church. Banks was not being unduly optimistic. The opportunity for the Anglicans was there, yet they failed to grasp it. Instead, personal arrogance, short-sightedness, and lack of government support were eventually to ensure the religious and educational predominance of the Roman Catholic Church.

Mylius's successor as Civil Commissioner, Robert Keate, admitted some years later that the Anglican Church "had not ... made that progress which was anticipated, and with so much reason, at its first introduction into the islands". He blamed the personality of the preacher for the lack of success.

In Mauritius, France had ensured that the Roman Catholic Church was strongly entrenched, and although Protestant bodies such as the Society for the Propagation of the Gospel (SPG) and the London Missionary Society opened schools there in 1835, little headway was made.[12] The Seychelles appeared an easier target, but with the Anglicans slow to commit themselves it was left to a non-sectarian body, the Mico Charity, to open the first school on Mahé.[13] Previously families had had to depend on a tutor for the education of their children (during the French regime, some settlers had employed Jacobin deportees in that capacity). Others enrolled their children at one or other of the small tutorial schools on the island,[14] or tried to send them to Mauritius, where the Royal College had been established since 1791.[15]

The Mico Charity school was run by a Mr and Mrs George Clarke, who arrived from Mauritius in April 1839. No catechism, nor books of "peculiar religious tenets" were taught at their school, and every child was free to attend the place of worship of his parents. Held at first in the open air, the school later rented premises at La Rosière, where on weekdays there were over 100 pupils, including adults, and a similar number on Sundays. One observer noted the cleanliness and neatness of the pupils, and Mylius praised the work of the Clarkes.

In 1843 the Mico Charity decided to withdraw from Mauritius, handing over its ten schools to the government. The school in Seychelles was also closed, but the educational gap there was quickly filled after Banks' report had persuaded the Bishop of London to press the British government to finance the appointment of a chaplain to Seychelles, at an annual stipend of £300 a year. The SPG, which contributed a further £100, selected a Swiss clergyman, the Rev. Ferdinand George Delafontaine, who arrived at Mahé on 5 July 1843.

Although Mylius claimed that the school was ready for him, Delafontaine later referred to the Mico Charity school having been closed for several months "for various reasons not favourable to Mr Clark [sic]". At the beginning of August he opened a boys' school, with fifty-six pupils, and two weeks later a school for girls, which eventually had forty-six on its roll. Two teachers, one a Roman Catholic, were appointed on the advice of Mylius, but the non-sectarian principles of the Mico Charity were abandoned; Delafontaine enrolled only those children whose parents attended his church. As an official at the Colonial Office forecast more or less correctly, "all Christian communities are less shocked with the total blindness of any portion of mankind, than with having it ... directed towards their theological rivals ... the Roman Catholics will tread on the heels of the Mico schoolmaster, and the Methodists on theirs, and the Negroes at Seychelles will learn Christianity and controversy together.[16]

Financial difficulties dogged Delafontaine's school from the start. He pared £1 off the teachers' monthly salaries, although in Mylius's opinion he himself was one of the better off missionaries. In addition to his stipend as Civil Chaplain and the annual grant from the SPG, he had other "little school pickings". The SPG was, in fact, on the point of withdrawing its aid, but agreed to continue paying £50 a year towards the school. In 1846 Delafontaine opened another school, at Anse Royale, but after a year he had to close it due to lack of funds. In 1850 he moved the school at La Rosière to the site where St Paul's Cathedral now stands. This building consisted of three rooms, two for the school and one for worship.

Delafontaine remained ten years in Seychelles. During that time he preached regularly in his makeshift chapel, and supervised the day-to-day running of the school. He also worked hard at perfecting his English, although he found that the few English families in Seychelles knew French "quite well". When word circulated that British troops might return to Seychelles, Delafontaine was delighted at the prospect of holding services for them in English and offering spiritual guidance in their own language.[17] He was to be disappointed; no troops were sent.

One of Delafontaine's major worries was that a Roman Catholic priest would appear before he had succeeded in firmly planting Anglican beliefs among the people. In June 1845 he had heard that Rome was trying to recruit a priest for Seychelles. The fact that no priest materialised that year, or in 1846, or even in 1849, did nothing to alleviate his anxieties. In the end Delafontaine was given eight years to promote the Anglican creed without challenge. Even so, his mission was hardly a success, and when he finally left Seychelles in 1853 there were fewer pupils at the school than when it had opened.[18] Intolerant as any Calvinist from his native Switzerland, Delafontaine put religious principle before education. When asked why he refused to admit to his school any child whose parents were not Anglicans, his answer was that he could not conscientiously omit the Gospel from being taught in the schoolroom.

Delafontaine had no time for Mylius's interest in the religious needs of the Roman Catholics; he foresaw "much evil ... from the presence of the idolatrous practices of a popish clergyman", and complained to the SPG that Mylius had criticised him and his ecclesiastical character "in the most improper manner".[19] Mylius, described by a subordinate as "one of the most honorable, efficient, upright, and zealous public officers",[20] thought Delafontaine was a bad-tempered bigot. Worse, he had been named in a case alleging "criminal conversation" with the wife of one of the inhabitants, while his insulting behaviour towards the head of the police and the government medical officer, whom he "calumniously and grossly" abused in open court "to the great merriment and sarcasm of an anti-English audience, clearly proves that he is not the messenger of peace and charity".

Mylius also protested that Delafontaine had procured the post of civil chaplain under false pretences, and wanted to know if an alien could be a minister of the Anglican Church. He regretted that Seychelles had not been sent "an English minister of the Church of England, to make English Protestants and English subjects of the late slave population".

Like other observers, Delafontaine deplored the misery and poverty of the people. "While the nature of the soil if cultivated could enrich the inhabitants by its astonishing fertility, it is covered with brambles and the fruit which — uncultivated and despite the landowners' laziness — it does produce, stays and rots on the plants on which it grows. The most hopeless misery dominates almost every home and this situation, allied to moral depravity, make these islands the most desolate spot on earth," he noted in a letter to the SPG.[21]

The collapse of cotton, mass emigration to Mauritius, and the consequent depression prior to emancipation had resulted in many estates being abandoned or neglected. According to Keate, the slaves had "already contracted habits of indolence, which they soon began to look upon as identical with freedom, and had made the fatal discovery that in these islands life was sustainable almost without the necessity of exertion". Keate likened Seychelles to a new colony, which needed inputs of energy, capital, and labour, adding: "Planters now have little of first, little of second, and ex-slaves without religion, education or civilisation are as useful as aborigines of New South Wales or Van Dieman's Land at the period of their colonisation".

While the settlers would have agreed with much of this analysis, they regarded British neglect and misrule as the main cause of their misery. In a petition to the Governor in January 1849 a group of twenty leading settlers said that "religion, morality and justice have become empty words in this country, which reverts rapidly to a savage state". They charged that "the Seychelles have been looked upon as a place of refuge for persons without capacity, or as a place of exile for those whose services were not desired elsewhere, and particularly at Mauritius." Although this was unfair to the likes of Harrison and Mylius, the complaint had some truth. The settlers could also have pointed out that the Governor had as yet not found the time to pay a visit to Seychelles.

Several times Mylius had drawn attention to frequent "acts of gross injustice" in the Dependency. He was especially bitter at the appointment as stipendiary magistrate of the *juge de paix,* Guillaume Antoine Anne Fressanges ("totally ignorant of English," Mylius claimed). Fressanges now had the "diabolical power ... to dispose, at will, and free from all responsibility, of the liberty, fortune and very existence of anyone he thinks proper". As a result poor, illiterate men, women and children had been detained for up to eight months, and then simply released without redress, for any appeal by the poorer classes was impossible. Mylius grieved for the former slaves, who, although British subjects, were the victims of an "arbitrary power" that threatened their liberty and well-being. In contrast to the powers of the stipendiary magistrate, he, Mylius, was severely restricted in what he could do and, with no prosecutor to enforce his decrees, was held virtually in contempt by the public.

Having by now spent ten largely frustrating years in the Dependency, Mylius decided that his health required him to leave. The government medical officer, who took over until Mylius's successor arrived, wasted no time in threatening to have Fressanges removed "for the due protection of Her Majesty's subjects in this distant colony". Outrageous was how Dr Ford described Fressanges' behaviour, adding that his court was a mockery of justice. He oppressed innocent and respectable people, both Creoles of the colony and British subjects, while "protecting and supporting dishonest and notoriously ill-conducted individuals, or aliens, who may most probably have left their country for their country's good".

Three months later, Seychelles' new Civil Commissioner, Robert Keate, recommended that Fressanges be replaced on grounds of age and infirmity. He pointed out that although there might be personal animosity working against Fressanges, the *juge de paix* was incapable of carrying out the duties of district magistrate. A more competent person was needed, and if he were an Englishman unconnected with local interests so much the better.

Mauritius was always reluctant to remove an official from Seychelles because of the difficulty in finding a replacement, but it could hardly ignore Keate's criticism of Fressanges, and after some months, although remaining *juge de paix,* he was replaced as district magistrate by a practising barrister from Calcutta, Charles Molloy Campbell. Campbell arrived in June 1852, and soon was vying with his predecessor in setting new, bizarre standards of judicial and social behaviour. We will return to Campbell later.

Although justice, or the lack of it, troubled the settlers, their principal complaint was lack of labour. Since 1842, when India lifted its suspension on emigration, there had been a steady influx of indentured labour into Mauritius to fuel the island's sugar industry, pushing up the population there to over 180,000. When the Seychelles settlers first asked for Indian labour the ban on emigration was in force, making it easy for Mauritius to refuse. In 1842 the Seychelles petition was again rejected on the grounds that Mauritius had made special arrangements to supervise the condition of their immigrants. At their third attempt, seven years later, the Seychelles settlers were told by the Mauritius colonial secretary, George Dick, that he had no power to act in the matter. Nor did he hold out hope for an early visit by the Governor, Sir George Anderson, who "fears that he will scarcely be able to find the time for that purpose". As regards the settlers' dissatisfaction with the administration, Dick promised that if he received any specific case of wrongdoing he would investigate.

The settlers had in their 1849 petition emphasised what the Seychelles economy could offer. Already, there had been moves away from traditional food crops to the less labour-intensive coconut plantations, where the settlers estimated production at 100,000 veltes of oil in seven or eight years. Seychelles could also supply all the fish Mauritius needed, plus provide England with whale oil. Cattle could be reared, and with a harbour capable of sheltering 1,000 ships (a considerable advance on Morphey's estimate of 200 ships in 1756)[22], Mahé could become an excellent maritime base. What was required, however, was "a paternal and intelligent administration" which would give the inhabitants a legitimate share in running the country. While the ex-apprentices needed to be led back to labour and a regular life, the introduction of Indian emigrants would, it was thought, encourage industrious men to settle in Seychelles.

Mylius had recognised the need for immigrant labour, and Keate was of similar opinion, saying that "unless permission is granted to the proprietors of the soil to procure labour for working it by means of immigration, the land of these islands must shortly fall out of cultivation altogether". The difficulty was the expense involved; the islands were too remote; they were off the shipping routes, and communications were bad. Keate identified about twenty planters who he thought could afford migrant workers. Three of those were growing sugar-cane and manufacturing rum, mainly for domestic consumption, and eight were coconut oil producers; some were in timber, and a few were growing coffee, cloves, cocoa, rice, and tobacco. Others were raising cattle for sale in Mauritius. While recognising that none could afford large-scale immigration from India, Keate supported the idea of the settlers bringing in labour from Madagascar and the African coast, using their own vessels. Engagement of the workers would be for three years, and wages would not exceed two dollars a month, with food.

A Seychellois lawyer at the Mauritius Bar, Napoléon Savy, son of Savy of Sainte Anne, had also taken up the settlers' case. He suggested to the Governor that the nearly £4,000 paid by Mauritius on account of Seychelles should be made available for immigration. The Mauritius colonial secretary referred him to the recommendation that workers be brought in from the East Coast of Africa, Madagascar, and the Comoro islands, adding that although eighteen months had elapsed since then, "His Excellency the Governor is not aware that advantage has been taken of this permission, or that any immigrants have been introduced".

Savy, who claimed he spoke "for the unanimous voices of the whole community of Seychelles", then wrote to the Secretary of State, the Duke of Newcastle, repeating the claim that it was unfair not to give a share of migrant labour to Seychelles, which had been "reduced to a state of decay and misery which reflects no credit upon our local government and the several able Commissioners who have ruled over them". He added that it was impossible to get labour from Zanzibar "except by purchase, which constitutes at once slave trade". But London was not convinced; in any case, an application from a self-styled representative of the Seychelles people could hardly be considered.

Unlike the planters in Mauritius, the French in Bourbon did not have access to labour from India. Their earlier experience with workers recruited from the French possessions there had not been a success, for the settlers had difficulty differentiating between freely engaged Indian coolies and African slaves. As an official appointed to supervise immigrants noted: "The mentality of the country, addicted to having a servile population, regards free labour as another form of slavery." As a result of their harsh treatment the workers absconded in droves, turning to begging and crime. Of the 3,102 recruited in 1830, only 1,367 still remained at Bourbon in 1847. Fortunately for the settlers, they still had their slaves, whose numbers they could top up by illicit recruitment in Madagascar and the African coast. Although France had committed itself to abolishing the slave trade, Bourbon's urgent need of labour encouraged the turning of an official blind eye to the exact status of those who were to work in the sugar-cane fields.

The purchase of so-called free African labour was streamlined in 1845, when France made a deal with Sultan Seyyid Said (who had by then moved his capital from Muscat to Zanzibar) to recruit in Zanzibar. According to some observers the French bought so many slaves in Zanzibar that it diminished the numbers being transported in dhows to Arabia more effectively than the interceptions by British cruisers.

France was still resentful at having lost so much of its colonial empire, while Britain, sensitive to any threat to India, viewed with concern French efforts to reassert themselves in the Indian Ocean. In 1841 Nossi-Bé had been ceded to France.[23] Two years later, the French added to this acquisition the island of Mayotte, in the Comoros. In both places the Sultan of Zanzibar had maintained a tenuous claim and, with Anglo-French relations already embittered over French support for Muhammad Ali in Egypt, Britain's Foreign Secretary, Palmerston, contemplated backing the Sultan's claims.[24] For a few days the situation looked serious, but fortunately Palmerston was replaced by the more pacific Lord Aberdeen, and war was averted.

Among other potential flashpoints was Mauritius, an island the French had not altogether given up hope of repossessing. Their warships frequently called there for repairs (Bourbon lacking the necessary facilities), and given the French navy's keen sense of honour and self-esteem, a confrontation was almost inevitable. The first serious *contretemps* had occurred in September 1839, when insults, intentional or otherwise, were offered to the other's national flag by the French armed transport *Isère* and the British merchant ship *Greenlaw*. With neither the French nor the British (in the form of Governor Nicolay) considering that an adequate apology had been made by the other, the Governor issued an ultimatum to the French ship. This it ignored, and sailed from the harbour without giving the usual salute.[25]

Later, a letter to *The Times* criticised Nicolay's "vain warlike display, which can only tend to make him and the British appear absurd in the eyes of the world". The French, despite their moral victory, were not pleased either. *Le Temps* of Paris described as humiliating the fact that French officers explained how the supposed insult to the British flag was accidental, and declared: "Our flag insulted, our navy outraged in the person of the commander of the *Isère* ... these are wrongs which cannot be passed over in silence."

A few years later Mauritius witnessed a further display of Anglo-French enmity when, in August 1846, the C-in-C Cape, Admiral James Dacre, flying his flag in HMS *President*, was visiting the island. The Admiral had arranged to give a ball on board ship. Among those who received an invitation was the French consul, Barbet de Youy, who was subsequently surprised and not a little annoyed when two officers from the ship called the following day to cancel his invitation.

When he complained to the Governor, Sir William Gomm, he was told that the Admiral had withdrawn the invitation because Barbet had not formally visited the flagship to pay his respects. Barbet's response was to write an insulting letter to the Admiral. He subsequently refused all appeals to withdraw the letter. The Governor sought the mediation of the US consul, an Englishman named Hollier Griffiths (he was later to become, albeit briefly, acting Civil Commissioner of Seychelles), but Griffiths supported Barbet's stand, saying that he had not called on the Admiral either, and that he had no intention of going to the ball.

As the affair escalated, Bourbon expressed anxiety about deteriorating relations with Mauritius, and offered to send a warship to bring Barbet away. By November, the British government had called for Barbet to be withdrawn. The following March, *Le Cernéen* of Mauritius reported that the French government, much to the anger of the parliamentary opposition, has agreed to satisfy the demands of Lord Palmerston, and that Barbet de Jouy would be transferred to Honolulu.

Barbet's successor, Fourcaud, arrived in Mauritius in September, and reported that he had been well received by the Governor. Admiral Dacre was also on the island, but the consul succeeded in avoiding him, and soon afterwards Dacre sailed in the *President*, accompanied by the sloop *Brilliant*, for the Seychelles.

In 1848, the year of revolution in Europe, France finally abolished its monarchy. It also abolished slavery throughout its overseas possessions, including the island of Bourbon or, as it was renamed once more, La Réunion. Ironically, France, the first country to outlaw colonial slavery in 1794 (restored in 1802 under Napoleon), had needed another revolution to bring itself into line with most European Powers. Not that the French were lacking in anti-slavery sentiments. Under the Orléans monarchy there had been an active humanitarian lobby, seeking to end not only the slave trade but slavery itself. Two years before slavery's eventual abolition, laws had been passed forbidding corporal punishment of women, outlawing the use of chains, and restricting flogging to a maximum fifteen strokes. Slave rations had been improved, hours of work cut to nine and a half a day, and — a remarkable advance — schooling was made compulsory for children between eight and 14.

As the day of liberation, 28 December 1848, approached, those who were being freed in Réunion had to enter into contracts of one or two years' duration with their former masters. Legally married women were exempt, leading to a spate of marriages, and a campaign by the settlers to make marriage more difficult. In the end, two-thirds of those freed quit their masters' employment. Forced to leave their huts they became vagabonds, liable to three to six months' forced labour if arrested. These developments resulted in the French stepping up the recruitment of labour from Madagascar and the African coast, a campaign which persisted until Britain, in 1859, reluctantly agreed to allow the French to recruit coolies from India. Only then did France prohibit further recruitment of free labour from East Africa, Madagascar, and the Comoro islands.

Although lack of labour was the main cause of the Seychelles settlers' despair, a longer standing grievance was the absence of a resident priest. Except for occasional visits by ships' chaplains during the early days of the French settlement, the inhabitants had remained throughout without moral instruction or guidance in their faith. Now, under British administration, it appeared that they were no better off

Yet the Church had not been totally indifferent to the needs of Seychelles. The Apostolic Vicar in Mauritius, Mgr Collier, had approached the Holy Ghost Fathers and the Jesuits to send a mission to Seychelles. Both turned the idea down; perhaps they considered the islands too small to justify the expense. In time Collier's perseverance would no doubt have been rewarded, had not chance — or, as some would have it, divine intervention — brought to Seychelles an extremely "turbulent priest", Father Léon des Avanchers.

6

Catholics triumph
1851-1861

You thought your last ruler was
a sneezer, but I am a snorter
From anonymous satire on Robert Keate, Governor of Natal
Four Books of the Prophet Ignoramous , 1872

A remarkable man, Father Léon des Avanchers. On his first mission abroad he learns that the people of Seychelles are without the benefit of a priest, and he decides to help. After obtaining permission from his superiors, he takes passage in a schooner to Mahé, where he is given a rapturous welcome.

The British 'governor' refuses to let him stay, but Des Avanchers defies him, and continues preaching, instructing, and baptising. At the end of three weeks he is forced to leave. By then he has accomplished what Church leaders in Mauritius had been attempting half-heartedly for years: the renewal of the Catholic faith in Seychelles.

It was at Aden that Des Avanchers first heard of the plight of the Seychellois. He had left France almost two years earlier to join a mission to the Galla tribe of Ethiopia[1] but because of difficulties in entering the country he had got no further than the Arabian coast. The head of the mission, Bishop Massaïa, who had himself been trying to enter Ethiopia for some years, had gone off with his frustrations to Rome, leaving Des Avanchers in Aden to continue studying English and Arabic.

While thus occupied, Des Avanchers met the skipper of a Seychelles schooner, the *Joséphine Loizeau,* and it was arranged that he would sail to Mahé. There was some delay in arranging his departure, and eventually Des Avanchers had to make his own way across the Gulf of Aden to Berbera, where the schooner was taking on board a number of mules.[2] At the Somali port Des Avanchers began religious instruction for the crew, none of whom had been baptised.

To his friend d'Abbadie in Paris[3] he wrote: "It is so sad that all these inhabitants ... should have been abandoned without a priest. The people of these islands, called the Séchelles, approached their bishop in Mauritius several times, but their prayers have not yet been granted, or rather they were heard, but instead of a Catholic priest a Protestant minister was sent, who so far has succeeded in winning over about one hundred people."

It was true that the Anglicans had little to show for twenty years' unhindered effort in Seychelles. Not only had they made relatively few converts, but the essential symbol of a proper church was still missing – the money for it was there, but no decision had yet been taken on size or site.[4]   The Civil Commissioner, who believed the coloured population needed education to protect them from the blandishments of the Roman Church, was anxious to keep Catholic priests away from the islands for as long as possible, preferably for ever. He therefore counselled Mauritius against hurrying to grant the settlers' request for a priest; better to wait awhile, he advised, citing the importance of maintaining religious harmony in the Dependency.[5]

The settlers were tired of waiting. Disappointed by the Mauritius bishop's apparent indifference, they directed their prayers elsewhere, and miraculously,[6] or so it seemed, there arrived in Seychelles a Capuchin priest.[7] Although only 26, Father Léon des Avanchers, in simple habit and with a long dark beard, must have appeared an imposing, patriarchal figure as, barefoot, he stepped ashore at Mahé on the morning of 1 March 1851. Word of his arrival spread quickly. "The heads of families requested me to say Mass, and arranged for a place where the Whites came to see a priest and take part in a Catholic service," he reported. "That same day I began to baptise a large number of children, and every day afterwards taught them the catechism."[8]

Keate received Des Avanchers coolly, and it seems that the priest in turn acted arrogantly when he formally sought permission to stay in Seychelles. He had drawn up a public notice that hinted he might need protection from government persecution, and although on second thoughts he cancelled this ill-conceived missive, Keate heard of it, and accused him of threatening civil disturbance.[9] Des Avanchers subsequently assured Keate that he respected "the legitimate authority which represents God, and I hope that the best understanding will exist between you and myself".

Nonetheless, the Civil Commissioner was determined that Des Avanchers should leave as soon as possible. He told him that permission for a foreigner to reside in Seychelles could be granted only by the Governor, and that as the *Joséphine Loizeau* was bound for Mauritius it would be convenient if Des Avanchers remained on board the ship and sought the necessary permission to stay in Seychelles when he reached Mauritius.[10]

Des Avanchers then suggested that, as a French national,[11] he might be granted the privilege of remaining in Seychelles until the Governor's decision was known. Keate wrote back: "Sir, in reply to your letter of yesterday's date (7 March 1851), which you placed personally in my hands, I have the honor to inform you, as I did in conversation, that the circumstances of your arrival in this port will be made known to His Excellency the Governor of Mauritius by me without fail by the vessel on board of which you are a passenger, and that as you have come into this Dependency not merely to reside as a stranger, but to perform certain official functions, I cannot, however much I may regret putting you to inconvenience, take upon myself to accede to the demand you now make for temporary leave of residence without previously communicating with His Excellency". When Des Avanchers protested that he was being deported, Keate assured him that "so far from being expelled from an English colony, you are on your way to one, where you will without doubt be treated with the respect that is due to you".

Naturally the settlers were pressuring Keate to allow Des Avanchers to stay, but all they got from the Civil Commissioner was an assurance that he would forward any petition they might have to the Governor. He predicted that such a petition would be favourably received, "especially if accompanied by a statement of the extent to which you propose to furnish means for his [Des Avanchers'] maintenance". Keate still doubted the settlers' willingness to pay for a priest, an expense which would fall wholly on them for, unlike the Anglicans, they would not benefit from a government subvention.

Keate's immediate worry was the growing support among the people for Des Avanchers, who daily went out to talk to the inhabitants, teaching them the catechism and baptising the children, many of whom had previously been considered Anglicans. "This people, who up to then had resisted all the approaches of the Protestant minister, came in large crowds to hear the word of God," wrote Des Avanchers, who had rented as a church the building formerly used by Delafontaine. When the latter objected, Keate informed Des Avanchers that the building could be used only for English services.

Des Avanchers was not surprised, for he was, in his own words, engaged in 'a spiritual revolution', and he realised that Keate, the nephew of an Anglican bishop, would be receptive to the intrigues of Delafontaine and the police chief, Lablache, who, according to Des Avanchers, had a warrant out for his arrest. Nevertheless, he continued preaching and baptising, even though he feared that those he baptised had received insufficient instruction. "What could I do?" he wrote later. "Overwork, anxiety, and continuous uncertainty, all these things determined me to do the best I could. As a result, I think I must have baptised 2,500 persons, if not more." He would never know exactly, being unable to keep a register.

Des Avanchers tried repeatedly to persuade Keate to permit him to stay, at least a while longer. First, he referred to the danger of cyclones; then it was because he no longer had a cabin on the *Joséphine Loizeau*, the captain having loaded with additional freight. Lastly, there was the question of his health, which, he told Keate, made it imperative that he should wait for a passage in the *Trois Frères*, which was to sail for Mauritius in early April.

Much as he wanted to get rid of Des Avanchers, Keate realised that any precipitate action that upset the colony's Roman Catholic population would not be regarded favourably by the Governor. He therefore assured Des Avanchers that he would have been happy for him to sail in the *Trois Frères*, thus giving him more time in Seychelles, but that unfortunately this was not possible as the ship would not sail until May.

At this point, Des Avanchers capitulated. On 20 March,

two days after receiving Keate's letter, he sailed from Mahé, much to the sorrow of the inhabitants. He regretted having given in, and later claimed he had done so because he feared his continued defiance would cause a disturbance.

Although his final attempts to avoid departure hardly enhanced his priestly dignity, Des Avanchers had succeeded in giving spiritual comfort to the former French families of Seychelles; he had made many converts among the African population and, lastly, he had opened a church, dedicated to the Immaculate Conception, at La Rosière. Through zeal, determination, and guile he had forced his way into Seychelles, and few would doubt that he was departing in triumph. Only later would the full extent of his victory become clear.

Des Avanchers' visit had convinced Keate that Seychelles could no longer be regarded as an Anglican preserve. The only hope was that the government would ensure that an English priest was appointed, someone "who can temper his zeal and avoid discord and dissension". He abhorred the idea of "a foreign branch of the Church" being subsidised, but thought that, under the circumstances, the government should pay half the cost of a priest as long as the latter was ministering solely to the French population. Inhabitants of English origin and those with no hereditary faith, in other words the African population, should still be the responsibility of the Anglican clergyman.

Keate forwarded, as promised, a petition from the settlers to Governor Higginson, asking that Des Avanchers be allowed to return to Seychelles, where, they claimed, his short stay had already resulted in an improvement in the morals of the community.[12] Fortunately for the government Bishop Collier was temporarily absent in Europe, so no decision could be taken until his return. Meanwhile — and the Seychelles petitioners were so informed — the Governor felt "great satisfaction" that the Bishop's deputy had nominated a priest, Macdonald by name, to Seychelles. The Governor hoped that this would bolster the interests of religion, morality, and education in the Dependency. Privately, Higginson backed Keate for having turned away "a zealous propagandist" after the attorney-general assured him that he had every right to expel a foreign priest, although it would be improper to do so simply because of possible conflict between the Churches, given that "in England, more than in any other country, the principle of religious as well as civil liberty is so fully admitted". The law officer added that even if Des Avanchers was to urge his flock to obey the civil authorities, "it would not be prudent to allow an alien to exercise such a moral power over the generality of a population such as that of Seychelles". Rather, the Bishop should appoint a priest over whom he could exert "a sort of control" — which "perhaps is not the case with the Reverend Léon des Avranchers [sic]". Higginson accepted this advice, and urged the Secretary of State to select a priest for Seychelles who was a British subject. Meanwhile Des Avanchers, who had already gathered his own enthusiastic following in Mauritius, would be offered a post by Bishop Collier until he could be dispatched elsewhere. Thus, did the government hope to solve the problem of a Roman Catholic resurgence in Seychelles.

The Secretary of State, Earl Grey, agreed with Higginson, expressing satisfaction that a suitable replacement had been found for Des Avanchers (he understood it to be the Reverend Macdonald). He warned, however, against "incurring expense for objects of this kind from the general Revenue of the Colony". Charges to the Dependency were in excess of contributions, "and I shall be very unwilling to add to their amount". As usual, money was the stumbling block when it came to implementing policy. Without funds, Higginson did nothing, and in the end it was left to Rome to fix the form, the style, and the personnel of its Church in Seychelles.

Des Avanchers had no desire to stay on in Mauritius under Collier, who had made it clear that he was against the Capuchin being appointed to Seychelles,[13] despite the approval given by the Sacred Congregation for the Propagation of the Faith.[14] Des Avanchers decided therefore to make one last attempt to breach the Mauritius authorities' ban by appealing to Queen Victoria. In his letter, dated 13 May, he claimed that he had been ill used by being forced to leave Seychelles without reason, an act which was "a violation of all principles of nature of Humanity, and of English public policy". His expulsion was "a most unjustifiable restriction of personal and religious liberty", and he asked that Keate's order, and the Governor's confirmation of it, be rescinded. Des Avanchers received a sympathetic reply but, predictably, nothing was done. Massaïa was by now demanding he return to Aden, and

Des Avanchers had little choice but to obey. He determined, before leaving, to bring the Pope's attention to the plight of the people of Seychelles, warning that if a Catholic mission was not promptly established, "the inhabitants, tired of being badgered by the government and feeling the need of a religion, will fall into the arms of heresy — and should that happen one would have to renounce the idea of introducing the Catholic religion there".

During the return voyage in the *Joséphine Loizeau*, the schooner called at Mahé, reportedly to repair a leak, and Des Avanchers went ashore with a letter of encouragement to the inhabitants. He also offered religious objects for the church he had founded, as well as a clock. At first the inhabitants were overjoyed at seeing their priest, and then were plunged into despair on learning that he was not to stay. Few believed they would see him again. As for Keate, he was convinced the stop-over had been deliberately planned.

Back at Aden, Des Avanchers again tried to enter Abyssinia, only to be imprisoned there for several months until freed by the intervention of his superior. When the Congregation then suggested that it would arrange his return to Seychelles Des Avanchers, surprisingly, demurred, citing Collier's opposition, the unfavourable attitude of the Protestants there, and his own inexperience. Instead, he went to Agra, taking with him to India a personal letter of encouragement from the Pope.

In Seychelles, there was understandably much bitterness against Keate, and in a conciliatory gesture the Civil Commissioner permitted the Roman Catholics to say prayers in the building Des Avanchers had used as a church. This decision resulted in possibly the first signs of religious tension in the Dependency. The Catholics claimed that at their gatherings crowds stood around outside, whistling and jeering. They asked for police protection, but Keate accused the worshippers of going beyond what he had permitted, namely, the reading of prayers. He said he had received reports of unauthorised preaching. There was also an accusation that the body of a child had been brought into the chapel contrary to regulations, and money was being collected from "ignorant blacks" attracted by the religious activity

Unauthorised preaching and unruly crowds were not Keate's only worries. There was the problem of stray dogs —

far too many, in his opinion – and he gave orders that they should be destroyed. There were also "perpetual scenes of drunkenness and disorder, especially on Saturday nights and Sundays, among the scattered population of the country districts". Keate blamed this on the widespread manufacture of fermented drinks from sugarcane, pineapple, and coconut. Keate appreciated his tipple as much as anyone, and felt it would be an unjustified interference with personal liberty to ban this cottage industry, although he suggested the government tax every still, and inflict heavy penalties for manufacturing drink illegally.

Despite the generally depressed state of the Seychelles economy, Keate remarked that some of the new population were improving their lifestyle. They were fishing and growing produce which they sold to buy clothes and other necessaries; they were also saving their money, "which they horde and hide in bamboo knots and tin boxes, and with which they even purchase land". A new class of traders and shopkeepers was emerging, and people were spending on dressing up as well as buying rum. Many had, Keate noted, "a peculiar weakness for Eau de Cologne, so called, and Pomatum".

As he had already pointed out, what was holding Seychelles back was lack of capital and the "pernicious system" of *moitié,* under which landowners allowed families to squat on their land in return for half a week's labour. Keate would have had the landowners pay regular wages. He stressed the need for better communication with the outside world as well as within Seychelles, where the only roads were "tortuous and rocky paths which lead from habitation to habitation". He advocated introducing taxes to pay for services such as roads and education. He also supported Seychelles being granted some legislative powers, suggesting that a form of municipal board be set up to oversee schools and cemeteries (as an alternative to burials on private estates), supervise a rural constabulary, and see to the construction of roads and bridges.

None of these schemes was to materialise in Keate's time, for he left Seychelles for good in December 1852. One of his major disappointments must have been that there was as yet no Anglican church in Victoria. Also leaving was the Civil Chaplain, Delafontaine. He had requested sick leave, but Keate, who never had much liking for the Swiss clergyman (now a naturalised British subject), recommended to Mauritius that he be replaced. Keate stressed that the post should be filled quickly, but more than two years elapsed before a new pastor arrived. In the meantime, the Roman Catholic Church was busy with its own plans for Seychelles.

In November 1852, the month in which Des Avanchers travelled to India, the Pope decreed the separation of Seychelles from the Mauritius diocese, and its elevation to an apostolic prefecture. A year later, on 20 September 1853, two Capuchin fathers, Jeremiah di Paglietta and Théophile Pollar, sailed into Port Victoria. Despite the government's opposition to "alien priests" it was an Italian and a Frenchman who would firmly establish the Roman Catholic Church in Seychelles.

The two priests had made a long, roundabout journey to their island parish. Father Théophile, who was in Turkey when the call came, had travelled to Aden, where he joined Father Jeremiah. As there was no vessel bound for Seychelles, they sailed to Bombay, where they boarded a three-masted ship for Mauritius, arriving there on 3 September. Like Des Avanchers two years earlier, the two priests had excited great interest in Port Louis, Father Théophile noting that everyone was full of admiration for "the poor Capuchin missionaries". They were offered a free passage to Seychelles by the skipper of the schooner *Trois Frères*, Étienne Nageon, and before they sailed Bishop Collier and his clergy presented them with cash and religious ornaments, as well as a 500lb. bell for a new Church of the Immaculate Conception.

In Seychelles the priests were warmly welcomed by "the elite of the population", after which Civil Commissioner Wade held an official reception in their honour at Government House. While they waited for a house to be made available, they found accommodation with the family of a Genoese, François Muratorio. On 21 September 1853, the day after their arrival, the Seychelles mission was formally inaugurated in the small church that Des Avanchers had founded at La Rosière. Present were many of Des Avanchers' new converts, as well as "a crowd of unbelievers and heretics of all conditions and all colours". Three months later the two Capuchins received powerful reinforcements when Des Avanchers arrived from India. "The Protestant minister has taken fright, and fled," boasted the Apostle of Mahé.

71

Influenced by Collier, Father Jeremiah had tried to prevent Des Avanchers' appointment as deputy apostolic prefect, and apparently was greatly surprised when he turned up in Seychelles. Other forces, too, seemed intent on thwarting Des Avanchers' mission, for on the voyage to Mahé his ship had run into a cyclone and was saved from destruction only by *"une grâce spéciale"*. All in all, it was hardly an encouraging start to his mission in Seychelles.

The priests' first task was to enlarge the church to allow it to cater for the 500 parishioners in Victoria. Later, while Des Avanchers began opening churches at Anse aux Pins, Anse Royale, and Anse Boileau, Fathers Jeremiah and Théophile embarked on a tour of the islands, visiting Praslin, Curieuse, Félicité, and La Digue. The people threw themselves in front of the priests, trying to kiss their feet. "We had to tell them that we were only mortal," observed Father Théophile.

During the dozen or so years the two priests spent in Seychelles they established twelve wooden churches, carried out some 7,000 baptisms, and regularised thousands of marriages. Des Avanchers, who stayed for just over a year, carried out 1,300 baptisms during that period; he blessed 200 marriages and celebrated 100 first communions.[15] In Victoria he opened a free school in a building previously used by the Masonic lodge. It had forty pupils, and three teachers, but it only lasted for four months. In a subsequent report Des Avanchers fails to give a reason for the closure, saying only that he did not want to attack anyone. The mission also erected six crosses at different sites, "one of which worked wonders after its benediction in 1854", noted Father Théophile.

Typically, Des Avanchers had not sought government permission to build the church at Anse Royale, but when questions were raised in Mauritius about his action the *procureur-général* upheld his right to do so, given that no official funds were involved. Even so, the Catholic mission made it a point from then on always to seek official approval for any new building. In 1857 the first stone was laid for the new Church of the Immaculate Conception in Victoria.

In contrast to the good relations Wade maintained with the other priests, he was frequently at odds with Des Avanchers, and for a time considered sending him away. Only the possibility of disturbances dissuaded him. He did, however, ask the visiting Bishop of St Denis to request the Pope to have Des Avanchers recalled. According to Wade Bishop Desprez agreed, "and only regreted [sic] it was not in his power to order him [Des Avanchers] away himself".

The trouble seems to have originated over an accusation by Father Jeremiah that Des Avanchers had burned a number of Protestant bibles. Although not specifically denying the charge, Des Avanchers rebuked the Apostolic Prefect for spreading rumours against him. The Capuchin priest was also hauled before the magistrate's court for allegedly having blessed a marriage without the necessary certificate. Des Avanchers was acquitted, but he felt betrayed. In his report to the Sacred Congregation he refers to insults, persecution, and lack of understanding, all of which convinced him to request his transfer.

In August 1855 a new Anglican chaplain arrived. He was Dr Auguste Fallet, an elderly medical missionary who spoke only French. Wade had been maintaining the small Anglican school out of his own pocket, and was relieved to be able to hand it over.[16] He told Fallet that while he had admitted non-Anglicans to the school, it was up to him whether or not he wished to reimpose Delafontaine's restricted entry. The following year the Anglican community received a visit from Bishop Ryan of Mauritius, who preached in Delafontaine's makeshift chapel. He expressed satisfaction at the size of the, mainly African, congregation, "after all that had been said about the scattering of the flock since Mr Delafontaine's departure". He also visited the site where St Paul's Anglican church was to be built, and which he subsequently consecrated on 14 May 1859.[17]

Des Avanchers had left Seychelles early in 1855, having received permission from the Congregation. "I do not really feel I shall go there again," he was to confide in a letter to a friend as the schooner taking him from Mauritius to Aden passed close to Mahé. Before leaving he had seen the Bishop of St Denis and had strongly urged that members of a teaching order be sent to Seychelles. Another of his final acts for the Dependency was to negotiate the purchase of land in Victoria for the construction of a convent and school.[18]

After a stay in Paris and Rome, Des Avanchers was back at Aden in 1857, then on to Zanzibar and the East African coast. He urged the Pope to renew the Church's mission on the

Zambezi, which had been founded by the Portuguese in 1586 and long since abandoned. He pointed out that this would thwart English and Muslim ambitions in the area. The project was eventually approved by the Congregation, although shortly afterwards we find Des Avanchers complaining about delay in its implementation. In 1861 Des Avanchers made his way back to Ethiopia, to rejoin Bishop Massaïa. He was to stay there for the rest of his life, some eighteen years, during which he contributed not only to the spread of the Roman Catholic faith but also to the scientific and cultural knowledge of the country.

If religion was potentially a divisive force in Seychelles, so also was race. Part of the trouble was that the Whites still hankered after the old days; they had no wish to mix socially with those they thought of as inferiors. Unfortunately for them there was no longer a clear-cut division of Whites and Blacks. Miscegenation and immigration from Mauritius had produced a substantial population of mixed race, many of whom resented the affected superiority of impoverished Whites. There were other loyalties, too, that tended to harden these racial animosities. The African population saw the British, who had freed them from slavery, as potential allies against their former French masters, while the latter, aware that the racial purity on which they prided themselves was being gradually diluted, felt all the more threatened.

Before he took up his appointment Wade had been warned that tension was growing between the White families and "the mulatto section" of the population. "Violent feelings" had been openly expressed on the street, and he was instructed to deal with the problem. These fears had seemed justified in December 1852, when Adolphe Loizeau called on fellow Coloureds to "draw the dagger, to do what had been done in Brazil and St Domingo (Haiti), and exterminate the white population of this island". This outburst, coming from one of Mahé's largest proprietors, could not be overlooked, and Loizeau was subsequently convicted and jailed for six months. He was later released by Wade on account of ill-health.[19]

Ironically, Loizeau's hatred of Whites was shared by Seychelles' new District Magistrate, James Molloy Campbell. A nephew of Sir Colin Campbell, Chief Justice of Ceylon, Campbell had been born of an Indian mother, a fact that embittered his feelings towards Whites. Thanks to his uncle's influence, he became acting attorney-general in Hong Kong, and in 1852 was appointed to Seychelles, taking over the duties of district magistrate formerly held by the elderly and discredited *juge de paix* Fressanges.

Within a year Campbell had been suspended from office. The immediate cause was his apparent connivance at the cover-up of a murder, although the acting Civil Commissioner Dashwood Ricketts[20] (who had temporarily succeeded Keate) claimed there was sufficient evidence of other dubious transactions to show Campbell to be incapable of holding "the important duties attached to his high situation". Blackmail, embezzlement, fraud, indecorous behaviour and more could be laid at his door, according to Ricketts, although the District Magistrate's inflammatory remarks on behalf of the coloured community (and his preference for the English language over French in his courtroom)[21] were probably what really put him beyond the pale.

"I have warned him over and over again, but to no effect," Ricketts assured the governor, recalling the occasion when Campbell threatened vengeance on any Whites who refused to attend a ball that he and some others had organised. "Mr Campbell exclaimed that he was proud to belong to the latter [coloured] class, and so long as he had power and authority he would use it for their favor and interest, and that he should like to see those who dared to refuse and join their party; he would mark them in his pocket book with a cross in red ink". Campbell denied the accusations, but his "cool falsehood" made the acting Civil Commissioner "quite ill". Although Governor Higginson doubted the precise legality of Ricketts' suspension of Campbell, he backed his action and Campbell's dismissal was subsequently confirmed by London.

In a comment on the case an official at the Colonial Office expressed surprise that "the administration of justice should have been committed, even in the most remote and isolated of our dependencies, to a person capable of perpetrating the series of frauds, oppressions and iniquities which there can be little doubt that Mr Campbell did commit in the space of one year in the Seychelles". The Secretary of State, the Duke of Newcastle, added that the whole matter was a further example of "the vice which seems inherent in everything connected with Mauritius, irregularity and confusion". The initial inquiry into

Campbell's behaviour had been carried out by Charles Telfair, a Mauritius magistrate who had been sent to Seychelles at the same time as Wade. Telfair, assuming the duties of district magistrate at Mahé until the arrival of a replacement, was himself soon a subject of controversy.

Meanwhile Higginson had been sufficiently concerned about what was happening in Seychelles to go there himself, the first governor ever to visit the Dependency. He told the inhabitants that the impoverishment of the islands was due either to influences beyond control, or to their own "want of foresight and providence". He pointedly suggested that as other British possessions had experienced similar difficulties and got over them, it was up to Seychelles to do the same.

Higginson dismissed any lingering hope that the landowners might get labour from Africa or Madagascar; a scheme approved by London had proved too difficult to implement. The Governor also ruled out immigration from India, saying that everyone agreed it was beyond the means of the Dependency. The only solution he could see was "to stimulate the lower orders to more active and remunerative industry", to which they were "indisposed not only by natural indolence but by strong prejudices engendered by their former social condition".

How this radical change of behaviour was to be achieved Higginson did not say, although he listed a series of measures which he hoped would improve living standards in Seychelles. Most important, perhaps, was the lifting of port dues and better port facilities. He also promised that road works would be started, and after the closure of the leper colony on Curieuse island (suggested by Keate in 1851),[22] a new hospital would be built in Victoria.

To pay for these improvements a land tax would have to be imposed, everyone contributing according to his means. Proper land titles would be issued, as well as fishing licences. Higginson hoped also that proprietors would discontinue the *moitié* system and give workers continuous employment and regular wages. In an oblique reference to the recent racial tensions on Mahé, he called on the inhabitants to show more "good fellowship" towards each other. Higginson concluded by referring, somewhat insensitively, to the experience of Mauritius — then riding high on a sugar boom — urging the

Seychellois to follow their fellow colonials' bright example. With that, he hurried back to Mauritius.

Given the lack of capital and official indifference, it was not surprising that development of the Seychelles economy was slow. What investment there was usually resulted from concessions granted to Mauritian planters, and Wade recommended that this trend should be encouraged, for he considered that "few Seychellois have the capital, and none the energy, to benefit the Dependency in general by holding large tracts of land". He claimed that four of the wealthiest and possibly the most intelligent inhabitants of Mahé, with some 700 acres apiece, employed only three men to cultivate them.

Wade also wanted more use of prison labour. Convicts could be hired out at the rate of threepence a day (the cost of their daily sustenance), and he recommended to the Prisons Committee that this scheme should be extended; for example, in the construction of a new pier.[23] He was optimistic that once it was known Victoria was a free port many vessels would want to call, and it was essential that there should be a jetty, about 1,000 yards long, running out into deep water to accommodate vessels of 900 tons or more. Earlier, Keate had envisaged a steamship service to link Seychelles with Aden and Mauritius, thus ending its isolation and bringing about the desired economic recovery. Aden, occupied by Britain since 1839, was an important coaling station used by armed steamers of the East India Company carrying mails between Suez and Bombay, and by the P & O line,[24] which operated between Suez and Ceylon, Madras, and Calcutta. Seychelles mail for Europe had first to go by schooner to Mauritius, and from there by steamship to Ceylon. The alternative was round the Cape. Keate therefore supported a call by the Seychelles inhabitants for a direct steamship link with Aden, but in March 1852 he had to inform them the project had been definitely abandoned.

One measure mentioned by Higginson during his visit to Seychelles was for the creation, with government assistance, of a joint stock company to arrange for the collection, sale, and export of Seychelles produce by fast clipper ships. Wade, who along with Telfair put £100 into the new Union Company, hoped it would encourage business enterprise among the people, as "the real value of money amongst the lower classes is hardly known", preferring, as they do, to barter their produce for drink.

Unfortunately, the Union Company was to be shunned by many of the Whites, who saw no benefit for them and criticised Wade and Telfair for combining with the coloured community against them. There was also bad feeling over the company's take-over of the derelict marine yard in Victoria. These disaffected elements, determined to put their complaints to the Colonial Office, found an eager ally in the Mauritius lawyer Napoléon Savy, and his efforts eventually resulted in an official inquiry being held into alleged improper behaviour and abuse of power by the Civil Commissioner.

One of the complaints related to Wade's dismissal of members of the Prisons Committee for discrepancies in punishing prisoners:, after they had approved the flogging of a black prisoner but refused the same punishment for a white man guilty of a more serious offence.[25] Other accusations related to Wade's preventing complaints being made against Telfair, appointing as a provisional magistrate a person with a known conviction of dishonesty, putting prisoners to hard labour before conviction, and, along with Telfair, employing prisoners without pay at the Union Company yard.

Several Seychellois spoke in favour of Wade, sending a petition to the government expressing satisfaction with the island administration.[26] After the inquiry cleared Wade of almost all charges,[27] the Mauritius colonial secretary accused the complainants of falsehood and frivolous accusations. Writing in a Mauritius newspaper, the elder François Savy said Wade, like his predecessors Harrison, Wilson, and Mylius, had been victimised by those who wanted to govern. Although some of Telfair's judgements were flawed, Savy considered that he, too, was innocent of the charges against him.

Wade had travelled to Mauritius without permission to defend himself before the inquiry. He may at times have felt his life was in danger, for he suggested that protection should be given to officials at Seychelles. The acting governor at Mauritius was of a similar view.[28] He referred to the present "painful contrast" with the Seychelles he remembered of twenty years earlier, when a military detachment had provided a "salutary restraint" on the inhabitants. He proposed that troops should again be sent there.[29]

To conclude this chapter, we turn to two separate incidents that occurred during Wade's tenure of office, one of which is still topical today. The first occurrence was the loss of the British ship *St Abbs*, which resulted in its captain being charged in a Seychelles court with manslaughter.

The *St Abbs*, which had sailed from Greenwich in March 1855 bound for Bombay, ran aground on 14 June on the reefs of Jean de Nove (the Farquhar atoll).[30] As the ship began to break up, the captain, Alexander Campbell Bell, and one seaman managed to reach the shore, but instead of throwing a line to help the rest of the crew and passengers, all young military cadets of the East India Company, the captain abandoned them to their fate.

Just before the ship went down, Cadet Edward Ross[31] and a friend swam ashore, together with two of the crew. All the others were drowned. Some provisions, including crates of brandy and champagne, were salvaged, but the survivors lacked water, and after seventeen days they constructed a raft and managed to reach a larger island. Here they found muddy water and a hut. Another nineteen days passed before they were found by a Seychelles schooner, the *Marie*, that had been hunting turtles and tortoises. "Rice was the best food the *Marie* had, but how truly delicious boiled rice can be," wrote Ross.

They were warmly welcomed on arriving at Mahé. "As soon as Captain Wade heard of our circumstances he most kindly sent for me, and invited me to be his guest," noted Ross. The other survivors also found friendly hosts. Wade sent the captain's report on the shipwreck to Mauritius, but some days later he was transmitting further information to the governor, including depositions by Ross and the surviving crew members.

Wade's suspicions about Captain Bell's behaviour had been roused by the latter's refusal to return to the wreck to try to salvage the cargo, and later, when it appeared that Bell was trying to get away from Mahé in an Arab dhow, he had the district magistrate, Hollier Griffiths, issue a warrant for his arrest. Wade told Mauritius that he would normally have first sought approval from the governor, but considering the circumstances he had Bell charged with manslaughter. A month later — to Ross they were "some of my happiest days" —

the survivors from the *St Abbs* sailed in the schooner *Julie* to Mauritius. Bell went under police guard. "If I see him in charge of a ferry boat when I have to cross the Styx, I shall wait for another turn" was Ross's final comment on the captain.

* *

The following year, in the early morning of 25 September 1856, Louis Poiret, a 70-year-old planter, died at his modest home on Mahé from a gangrenous abscess. The death certificate, witnessed by Charles Jouanis, auctioneer, and Charles Michaud, planter, gives only barest details of the deceased: that he was of French origin, born at Dunkirk, his religion was Roman Catholic, and he was unmarried. The names of his parents were recorded as "not known". The death attracted little attention outside Seychelles, but a half-century later Poiret was to become, and remain so to this day, a cause of widespread speculation and debate.

During his lifetime — of which some forty-five years were spent in Seychelles — Poiret had claimed that his parents were the ill-fated Louis XVI of France and Queen Marie-Antoinette, both of whom died under the guillotine during the French Revolution. The priest Des Avanchers knew of Poiret. In one of his letters to friends in Paris, written in 1853, he noted: "There is at Séchelles an individual who says he is Louis Capet or Louis XVII; according to him he was embarked on a ship that landed him on these islands". He added that there were important papers in this person's possession indicating his royal lineage. However, Des Avanchers had his doubts about this *individu*, for he remarked that "there are so many who claim to be the unfortunate prince (the Dauphin) that one cannot put faith in any of them".

Father Théophile was also to recall the Frenchman who was considered by the Seychellois to be Louis XVII, and who had, as did his children, the unmistakable traits of the Bourbons. Writing in 1870 to his friend the Apostolic Prefect of Trebizonde, in Turkey, Father Théophile said Poiret had died in 1856 at Port Victoria, and that a priest had administered the last rites. He described the funeral as being that of a prince.[32]

Today, mystery still surrounds the death of Poiret, although the claim that he was the uncrowned King of France suffered a setback in April 2000 when it was announced in Paris that the official version of the Dauphin having died in the Temple prison had been confirmed by recent DNA testing. This had been carried out on fragments of a heart that had supposedly been removed from the body and concealed by a doctor during the autopsy ordered by the Revolutionary authorities. [33]

Given the circumstances of the prince's cruel and solitary confinement, his subsequent demise and hurried burial, it is hardly surprising that soon afterwards rumours surfaced in France, claiming that the boy who died was a substitute child, and that the Dauphin had in fact been smuggled out of prison to safety. Within a few years there were about thirty persons claiming to be the missing Louis XVII. [34]

While these pretenders were asserting their claims to the French throne, a young man named Pierre Louis Poiret had already sailed from France to begin a new life in the Seychelles. In time he, too, would claim to be the rightful King of France. Although there is no official record of his arrival in Seychelles, he most probably reached there in 1804. According to some reports he was accompanied by two persons, named Dangreville and Aimé, who subsequently disappeared from view.

Poiret began his stay on Île Poivre, but later moved to Mahé, where he settled at Cap Ternay. There, with nineteen slaves, he grew cotton; he also took a mulatto mistress, who gave him two daughters, both of whom he later legally acknowledged on their respective marriages to Jean Loizeau and Pierre Auguste Pétrousse. Although Poiret was treated with every consideration by the then French commandant, Quéau de Quinssy, there were some who suspected that he was a deportee, like the Jacobins exiled to Seychelles by Napoleon, who would sometimes refer to him derisively as Le Capet or — a name that would stick — Flamand (after the former jailer at the Temple).

In 1817 Poiret was again sent to Poivre, this time by the British government agent Edward Madge, to administer the island for three years. On his return he was given land at Anse Souillac, on Mahé's north-west coast. There he took another mistress, a young woman of Port Glaud, Marie Edesse, with whom he had seven children. Writers have pointed out that the names given to his sons all began with Louis, while his daughters had, in every case, Marie as their first name. Known descendants of Poiret possess copies of various documents and certain articles that point to their ancestor's royal lineage.

When exactly Poiret began claiming that he was Louis XVII is not clear. Certainly until the restoration of the French monarchy in 1815 it is unlikely that he would have wanted to draw attention to himself. Afterwards, there are indications that he resented the way he had been treated. In a letter he is said to have written to his cousin, Archduke Charles of Austria,[35] in 1838, he complained about being abandoned by his uncles, Louis XVIII and Charles X. He signed the letter Louis Capet, adding that in Seychelles he used the name of Louis Poiret, "the benefactor who saved my life in 1793".[36]

After Poiret's death, there seems to have been little further interest in his identity, until the publication on 25 July 1906 of an article in the French newspaper *Le Gaulois.* In it, the newspaper's editor, Louis de Meurville, told of a Frenchman who, in 1865 while in Seychelles, was witness to a deathbed declaration by a Monsieur Louis, who claimed that he was the rightful heir to the throne of France. Meurville's informant was later identified as a Capuchin priest, Father Joseph Schmoderer (1836-1911). As a novice for some years in Réunion, Schmoderer had been sent to Seychelles to restore his health. While staying with the priest in charge, Father Ignatius, he had accompanied the priest to the house of the dying Monsieur Louis.

According to *Le Gaulois* report, while Father Ignatius was preparing to give the last sacraments, Schmoderer overhead the old man repeat his claim to be Louis XVII. The visiting priest urged him, on the point of death, to withdraw the statement and tell the truth. At this Monsieur Louis became angry, and repeated once more that he was the son of Louis XVI and Marie-Antoinette. The only other person present was an old negro servant, who happened to open a cupboard allowing Schmoderer to see cutlery inscribed with the arms of France, and miniature portraits of members of the French royal family. The next day the priest was told by the negro that Monsieur Louis was dead.[37]

Father Ignatius had apparently never questioned the man about his origins, considering him simply to be suffering from delusions. Schmoderer said he later inquired about the dead man from the English 'governor', who told him he knew nothing, having been in Seychelles for only a short time. Five or six years later, while in Rome, Schmoderer met Father

Ignatius, who informed him that an envoy had come from England some months after Monsieur Louis's death, removed seals on the house, and taken away everything that was there.

Some fifty years after the report in *Le Gaullois*, a law lecturer at Clermont-Ferrand University, Mlle Emérentienne de Lagrange, published a book, *Louis XVII aux Seychelles*, in which she recalled that her grandmother, Madame Vetch, who knew Schmoderer, had acted as intermediary for a group of Breton royalists who wanted to finance a scholarship for a Poiret descendant. When Mme Vetch conveyed this offer to one of Poiret's grandsons whom she managed to trace in Seychelles, the young man turned it down, saying that they had all promised their grandfather never to claim his throne nor accept any offers that might be made to them. Mme Vetch died in Seychelles in 1916.

Schmoderer's testimony is tenuous, as it does not tally with the timing of Poiret's death, which is well documented as having occurred on 25 September 1856, nine years before Schmoderer's visit to Seychelles. Is it conceivable that the priest made a mistake? Or did he deliberately concoct a story to impress others? Father Ignatius appears not to have left any written confirmation of the death of a 'Monsieur Louis' in 1865, and no relevant death certificate has been found for that year in the Seychelles Archives.[38]

So was it a hoax? Perhaps not. In August 1936 a series of letters on the Louis Poiret mystery were published in *The Times* newspaper, mostly from former British officials who had served in Seychelles. In one letter, the daughter of Captain Charles Stirling of HMS *Wasp* wrote that her father recalled during his ship's visit to Seychelles in May or August 1861 being told by the Civil Commissioner of an old, infirm man who said he wanted to declare to the Commissioner that he was Louis XVII of France. The man, who apparently had the Bourbon look, made no other request. Captain Stirling was given to understand that the Commissioner intended informing London.[39] The next time Captain Stirling visited Seychelles he learned that the man was dead.

This account implicitly lends supports to Schmoderer's version of a "Monsieur Louis" dying in 1865. We know that Stirling did indeed visit Seychelles in HMS *Wasp* in April 1861, and although he was writing some 30 years after the event, it seems unlikely that he would confuse the date with that of some other visit to Seychelles. Certainly there is nothing in the available records consulted to suggest that Captain Stirling visited Seychelles either before or soon after the death of Louis Poiret in 1856.

Despite the recent scientific findings that indicate, apparently conclusively, that Louis XVII of France died in prison, the true identity of Louis Poiret still remains a mystery. The contradictory testimony we have so far suggests that perhaps there were in Seychelles not just one, but two claimants to the French throne.

* *

On 25 September 1861, Wade died of dysentery. He had served the Dependency well during a difficult period, defusing with firmness and tact the religious and racial animosities that threatened the islands. He welcomed the Catholic mission to Seychelles, and — Des Avanchers notwithstanding — healed much of the bitterness felt by the Catholics. He supported the construction of the Anglican church, promoted the expansion of schools, and tried to integrate the coloured community into the business life of the Dependency. As Seychelles began to emerge from its post-slavery depression,[40] Wade tried to speed economic recovery. He was to suffer personally the loss of his wife and a child through illness, and towards the end of his career he experienced the painful distinction of being the first Seychelles administrator since Madge to be subject to an official inquiry.

One of his final tasks was to deal with the sudden influx into Seychelles of some hundred or so Africans, freed from Arab slave ships by the Royal Navy. It was the first of a series of landings which, continuing with brief interruptions over the next fourteen years, would determine the predominately African composition of Seychelles' multiracial society.

84

7

Land of the Freed
1861-1870

Thank God, the slaves are rescued now,
Redeemed by love, set free.
Slave's Prayer, by R.J.I.

In the hold and on the foredeck of the British warship lay or squatted groups of African men, women, and children, almost all in pitiful condition.[1] Many were emaciated, too weak to stand; they wore little or no clothing other than what the ship's company had given them.

Some had only recently been rescued from a slave dhow taking them to Arabia, and were still fearful, but most were calm, even cheerful, reassured by the routine of the ship and the friendliness of the crew. None had any idea where they were going, or what was to happen to them. Although freed from captivity, they were still prizes of a sort; their liberators would eventually share in bounty money after their charges had been landed in Seychelles, to where the ship, the 485-ton steam sloop HMS *Lyra*,[2] was bound.

The question of where to settle freed slaves had always been a problem for Britain. Returning them to their home villages was not considered feasible, and it was usually the ship's captain who decided where the liberated Africans should be landed, depending on his position, the weather, the state of the vessel, and condition of the crew. During the early years, the Cape had been favoured, but it meant a long haul for cruisers operating north of the Mozambique Channel. During Owen's protectorate at Mombasa in 1824-26 some freed slaves were landed there, but proper settlements were not established in East Africa until near the end of the century. In the 1830s and '40s liberated slaves were often taken to Bombay, where the Church Missionary Society[3] took responsibility for them, establishing what became known as the African Asylum at Nassick, about a hundred miles north-east of the city. This was to continue until its closure in 1875. Aden was also used for landing freed slaves, and several thousands were put ashore there over a period of twenty years. Although it was convenient for naval vessels operating in the Arabian Sea, it was hardly ideal. The ex-slaves were confined to a small outcrop in the harbour known as Slave Island, where they were housed in sheds and supplied with food. The fortunate ones were those who found employment in the port, before being transferred to Bombay.

Cruisers operating south of the Equator sometimes landed their human cargoes at Mauritius, where they were eagerly recruited for the sugar plantations. However, a cholera epidemic in 1855 and the spread of malaria in 1867 seemed to confirm the mistaken belief that the Mauritius climate did not suit Africans.[4] Other places such as Anjouan in the Comoros, the island of Socotra, Lamu on the East African coast, and even Zanzibar itself were considered at various times. It was Colonel C.P. Rigby, British consul at Zanzibar from 1858 to 1861, who seems to have been the first to suggest Seychelles.[5] Possibly he recommended the islands to the captain of the *Lyra*, Commander Radulphus Oldfield, who had impressed Rigby by the way he had prevented dhows from openly loading slaves in Zanzibar harbour, an action that earned the steam sloop the name *Al-Shaitan*, or the Devil.

In late April 1861 the *Lyra* was lying off Pemba. It had destroyed several dhows and was crowded with freed slaves, making it imperative that it should reach a suitable port as soon as possible. Oldfield decided to make for Mahé. "Ship's company sickley," he wrote on 29 April. "Medicines becoming expended in consequence of the demand upon them. Celerity to reach the Seychelles therefore necessary." In addition to the sick, an officer and four seaman had been wounded while trying to board a heavily armed dhow, and one man had already died of his wounds. Another seaman and five of the

Africans would also succumb before, on 12 May, the *Lyra*, alternatively sailing and steaming, sighted the peak of Silhouette island. Another day passed as they made towards Mahé, where they lay off during the night. The following morning, at 9.30, with a pilot on board, the sloop-of-war steamed into Port Victoria, anchoring in ten fathoms and drifting back on the small bower into deeper water. In the harbour lay two visiting French warships. Five days later, two other units of Britain's anti-slaving patrol, the *Wasp* and the *Ariel*,[6] put into Mahé for rest and refreshment.

News of the *Lyra*'s arrival spread rapidly among the settlers. Here, surely, was an answer to their prayers. Ten years previously salvation had come with the appearance of a French priest. Now it was the surprise arrival of two hundred Africans, all in their teens or early twenties, who could be set to work on the island's neglected plantations. Wade was equally surprised by the arrival of the *Lyra*. He had received no instructions from Mauritius, and he was at first reluctant to let the Africans land. It was only after Oldfield had pointed out that many of the freed slaves would surely die if he were to take them on to Mauritius that Wade finally agreed to find temporary accommodation for them at the prison. The next day the business of disembarking began.

At the urgent request of several of the landowners Wade forwarded a petition to Mauritius asking that the Africans be farmed out as apprentices. Apprehensive, however, that they would be ill-used, he also recommended that the former post of protector of apprentices be restored. Unfortunately his advice was ignored, and it was not until 1873 that an official guardian for apprentices was appointed.

In Mauritius, Governor Stevenson was not surprised to hear of the planters' eagerness to take the Africans, for "they get them for little or nothing". It had been a different story when Indian labourers had been on offer. At that time Stevenson was under pressure to cut official expenditure on Seychelles,[7] and perceiving Indian immigration as a way of resuscitating the smaller islands' economy he had sent the Protector of Immigrants, H. Beyts,[8] to Madras to examine the situation. By January 1861 Stevenson had secured London's agreement for up to 1,000 labourers to be sent, but realising what this would cost them, the planters barely responded, and the scheme fell through.[9] Now they would get virtually free labour, for other than the meagre wage they had to pay, they could feed the Africans, unlike Indians, with maize, manioc, beans, and fish.

Oldfield returned to Seychelles the following year, this time in command of HMS *Ariel.* He disembarked sixty-six freed slaves. In addition, one of the dhows he had captured, and which had been renamed *Humble Bee,* arrived two weeks later with a further 193 Africans. Reporting the arrivals to Mauritius, Major R. C. Dudgeon, who had been temporarily posted to Seychelles after Wade's death, noted that most of the Africans were boys and girls under 15 years, and that they had been allotted to planters as labourers or house servants. According to the arrangements approved by Mauritius, the Seychelles planters employed the African apprentices for a period of five years, after which they were expected to shift for themselves. Wages consisted of 1lb of rice a day, 6lb of fish every month, and one dollar paid monthly.

Lieutenant William Devereux, paymaster of HMS *Gorgon* (another of the steam sloops that called at Seychelles with freed slaves), noted that on landing the Africans were ticketed and numbered, with males separated from females. "A day is named for their distribution; we attend and see our chubby little Topseys separated; they are appointed to different families, who undertake to bring them up in the way they should go, also to pay them certain fixed wages; thus all are divided amongst the inhabitants". While some of the freed slaves retained their proper names, many had names chosen for them by the British sailors, such as Peggy, Susan, Sally, Tom and Jim; others were named by their employers often with outlandish names, like Famous, Ebony, L'Endormie, Sud-Ouest, or Nord-Est.

Stevenson suggested that all slaves freed in East African waters should be landed at Mahé, where "they would remain until ... requisitioned by other colonies", but Beyts counselled against this, claiming that the Seychelles planters treated their apprentices badly. This view was supported by the new Civil Commissioner, Swinburne Ward, who arrived in the Dependency in December 1862. He thought many Creole masters were "cruel, cowardly, very exacting, and expect the maximum labour for the minimum of food and general care".

Some of the freed slaves came from Madagascar, but most

were from East and Central Africa, an area dubbed simply as Mozambique.[10] Although they spoke different tribal languages, many understood Kiswahili, the lingua franca of the Coast, a language they continued to use after arriving in Seychelles. Captain George Sulivan, of HMS *Daphne*, made special mention of the Gallas, a tribe located in Ethiopia and in northern areas of present-day Kenya. They were a handsome race, he wrote, "the men powerfully built, and the women positively graceful in form and movement, whilst their bright, intelligent faces and long curly hair gave them quite a civilized appearance." The sailors were not immune to the beauty of the Galla women. Sulivan noted that "they received more attention than any of the others, in the shape of an occasional basin of soup, or plate of meat and vegetables," adding that as a result "the other ebony ladies eye them ... with envy, hatred, and malice."

When Sulivan arrived at Seychelles there had been an outbreak of smallpox aboard the *Daphne*. "The slaves were ordered to be landed on the quarantine island, and the next day every slave was out of the ship. No-one, however, but those belonging to the ship could land there, and we employed the Africans in building a large hut sufficient to hold all of them. We erected a hospital tent for those of our own crew suffering from the disease on the opposite side of the little island, and there they remained till convalescent." A few days later Sulivan visited the freed slaves and found they had divided the large hut into small huts or rooms, in some of which whole tribes were located, and in others married couples.

Sulivan recommended that the Navy establish a coaling station at Mahé — "one of the prettiest islands of the Indian Seas" — using captured dhows as coal lighters and liberated Africans as the labour force. He was opposed to locating freed slaves permanently at Seychelles or at Mauritius, where he considered working for French masters was "little better than ... penal servitude". He advocated the establishment of a depot or depots on the mainland for all liberated Africans.

Sulivan was concerned by the lack of education and religious instruction in Seychelles. The Anglican chaplain[11] had assured him that he was anxious to extend his labours to the liberated slaves "but, with the exception of the few children who have been received in the schools, he is unable to do anything for them for want of assistance". Sulivan referred to the care given to freed slaves at Sierra Leone; unfortunately there was nothing like that on the East coast. As a result, "at Seychelles they unlearn nothing that was evil in their former lives, while they increase it tenfold by drunkenness and debauchery of every kind".

In Sulivan's view the presence of the Roman Catholics in Seychelles — he mistook the Capuchins for Jesuits — did more harm than good. "They have schools too, but they have not much occasion to work amongst the blacks, for the Creole masters, if of any religion, are Romanists, who are not likely to care much for their negroes, except that they do not go to a Protestant church, for, judging from the morality of Seychelles, that is the only thing they look upon as sin".

Sulivan and Rigby were among those who gave evidence at the parliamentary Select Committee which met in London in 1870-71 under the chairmanship of Russell Gurney, a prominent Quaker. Like earlier committees that inquired into the slave trade, the Gurney committee concluded that only through pressure on the Sultan would it be possible to abolish the trade completely. As for the resettlement of liberated slaves they considered Zanzibar itself as first choice, with Seychelles the alternative (already more than 2,000 freed slaves had been landed there). The committee also advocated a strengthening of the navy's anti-slaving patrol on the East Coast, something that was long overdue.

With sometimes only three cruisers on patrol at any one time, and never more than seven, the navy was expected to cover all the sea approaches from Mozambique to the Gulf of Oman and across to the Makran coast of today's Pakistan, a distance of some 6,000 miles. Under the Hamerton Treaty[12] of 1845 slaves could be legally transported only within the Sultan's African dominions, from Kilwa in the south up to Lamu, and including the islands of Zanzibar, Pemba, and Mafia. Dhows starting off on such 'domestic' voyages would frequently make off northwards after passing Kilwa. The navy's cruisers were both steam and sail driven, but there was a shortage of coaling facilities, and under sail a dhow could always make good its escape. The dhows were also experts at using the many creeks and inlets along the way to hide or escape from the attentions of the anti-slavery patrol.

For the ships' crews the work was arduous, exhilarating and often frustrating,. The chase did not always result in a capture and the release of slaves. Sometimes the dhow would have no slaves on board, although there might be sufficient material evidence to condemn it nonetheless. Sometimes it would make for the shore, the crew escaping inland with the slaves; or else in the heat of the chase the Arabs would throw the slaves overboard. The element of uncertainty and excitement appealed to young officers and men, and the bounties they were paid for successful captures was something that rarely came the way of an officer or rating on normal duty. The dangers could be very real, however, especially when a boat crew, attempting to board a dhow, met with determined resistance. Commander Oldfield of the *Lyra*, like many of the other captains, often led these pistol and cutlass operations.[13]

America's insistence on freedom from right of search had long provided a convenient cover for slave ships, but a dramatic shift in American policy occurred in 1862 when Washington, anxious to win support for the North in its Civil War,[14] signed a treaty granting British warships the right of search to within 200 miles of the American and African coasts, and to within ninety miles of Cuba. This effectively extinguished the transatlantic slave trade as well as the involvement of European-owned clippers on the east coast of Africa. There remained only the Arab dhows, a much more elusive adversary, particularly if sailing under cover of the French flag.

Rigby was an outspoken critic of the misuse of the French flag, and strongly opposed the practice of shipping so-called free labourers, or *engagés*, to work in the sugar plantations of Réunion, a trade that had increased over the years despite Britain's agreement to allow France to recruit labour from India.[15] It was estimated that a slave bought for perhaps $10 on the East African coast could be disposed of in Réunion as an *engagé* for up to $120. When the evils of the trade came to the notice of Napoleon III in 1859 a halt was ordered, but the following year, under pressure from colonial sugar interests, the trade was renewed. The only added stipulation was that labourers had to be carried in ships with French officers, who were meant to ensure that only "free men" were taken on board. Understandably, these restrictions made little impact.

Despite the good personal relations between Napoleon III and Queen Victoria, and the recent experience of their countries having fought side by side in the Crimea,[16] the rivalry between the two Powers was never far from the surface. In the Indian Ocean, where both countries had been almost totally excluded from Madagascar by Queen Ranavalona's anti-foreigner policies, Zanzibar was the obvious prize in the struggle for power.

Since Sultan Seyyid's death in 1856 his dominions had been split (one son, Thwain, ruling in Oman and another, Majid, in Zanzibar). France had not immediately recognised Majid's accession, and when, in 1859, Thwain sent an invasion fleet to capture Zanzibar the French consul had been jubilant,[17] telling Rigby that Thwain's seizure of Zanzibar would meet with French approval. The invasion fleet, however, was turned back by Britain, and subsequent French support for another rebellious son, Barghash, resulted in his being exiled to Bombay. Two years later Ranavalona died — "the most bloodthirsty, and the most obstinate and impolitic sovereign in existence"[18] — and Madagascar was reopened to Europeans. As French and English traders and missionaries flocked back to the island, France's pressing interest in Zanzibar waned, and in March 1862 it signed a declaration agreeing to uphold the independence of the Sultan. Britain alone would henceforth decide Zanzibar's fate.

Although Britain and France had agreed not to take any action in Madagascar without prior consultation, according to the French consul, Godeaux, Mauritius was following its own agenda, and had sent a mission to negotiate with Ranavalona's son, King Radama II. This was confirmed within months by the appointment of a British consul to the court at Tananarive, and the dispatch by Mauritius of a second mission. Six months later Radama was assassinated. His widow Rasoherina became queen, but power henceforth lay with her new husband, the Prime Minister, Rainilaiarivony.

In November 1863 Sir Henry Barkly[19] arrived in Mauritius to take over as governor (Stevenson having died in January of that year). Godeaux's successor, Laplace, reported that Barkly was noted for his efficiency and liberalism, and he considered that France would benefit from the change. Laplace was mistaken, however, in thinking that Britain was prepared to concede Madagascar or any of the other islands to which France might lay claim. The status of some of these islands had remained vague. Visited occasionally by fishermen but rarely occupied, they appeared of rather negative value, hazardous to shipping and best avoided. Most were thought of as dependencies of Mauritius, but as neither Britain nor France had laid formal claim to them the question of ownership was left unanswered. Until, that is, something like disputed fishing rights brought matters to a head.

In August 1867, the French vessel *L'Espoir* of Sainte Marie was fishing around the Jean de Nove atoll. The captain, Elie Curandeau, had set up a straw hut on the main island as a temporary store for his catch. A Mauritius fishing vessel, which put in for water, informed Curandeau that the island belonged to a Monsieur Gébert, of Mahé, and that he had no right to operate a fishery there. However, the skipper obligingly offered to seek Gébert's authorisation, and convey the answer to Curandeau on his return. The reply, when it came, was negative, and the Frenchman was told he would have to leave. According to testimony at a subsequent inquiry, Curandeau had intended to sail as soon as he had embarked his catch and water, but strong winds delayed him for several days.

In Mahé, Civil Commissioner Swinburne Ward wanted to dispatch a warship "to arrange the matter". Wisely, Barkly asked instead for the French to investigate, and at the same time suggested Curandeau pay an indemnity to the island's proprietor. In subsequent correspondence with Barkly, Laplace pointed out that marine charts and geographic dictionaries did not show Jean de Nove as a British possession. Not unusual, retorted the Governor, and referred to documents proving that Farquhar had given the use of the island to a Monsieur Boudet of Mauritius in 1813, and that since then there had been unbroken possession.

In due course a board of inquiry set up by the French naval authorities cleared Curandeau of any wrongdoing, but suggested that Gébert had ulterior motives for fostering a dispute, hoping in this way to induce Britain to back a claim that had in fact not been properly registered by Ward. The Civil Commissioner was also criticised for having exaggerated the affair, but Barkly rejected any suggestion of collusion by

Ward, telling French naval commander Hugueteau de Chaillé that the Civil Commissioner "being a gentleman [was] quite incapable of conduct so unworthy of an officer holding Her Majesty's Commission".

The matter might have ended there, had not Chaillé thought to exploit the apparent uncertainty over ownership of the islands and push France's own claims. He decided to visit Mahé, and there, in friendly conversation with Ward, the latter obligingly admitted that he was not at all sure which islands were Mauritius dependencies. "Given the uncertainty of the representative of the British government at Seychelles ... there would be a real interest in broaching the matter ... and making it the subject of a communication to Her Britannic Majesty," Chaillé advised the Minister of Marine. He added that Ward appeared annoyed at having been fooled by Gébert. "I really believe he regrets what has happened."

Chaillé said that when he told Ward that Curandeau had gone to fish off Cosmoledo, the Civil Commissioner observed that that island also belonged to Britain. "Are you absolutely certain?", responded Chaillé. "I don't think that an island lying so close to Madagascar would have been included in treaties relating to the Mauritius dependencies." Ward then admitted he was not sure, and hinted that he had asked Mauritius for confirmation of the island's status without success. Eventually the two men agreed the matter should be taken up by their governments to avoid embarrassment in future.

Britain, however, showed no desire to open discussions which might encourage France to expand further in a region with which it had strong cultural links. London still doubted the loyalty of Mauritius, with governors at times warning of pro-French sentiments on the island.[20] Mauritians in government service were particularly vulnerable to charges of disloyalty, and if these servants of the Crown happened to be of mixed race — or were even thought to be — they were doubly discriminated against. Racialism was usually only hinted at in official correspondence, but it was present nonetheless.[21]

When Wade died in September 1861 the district magistrate, Eugène Dupuy, took over as acting Civil Commissioner but was quickly replaced by a British-born official. Six years later, as tension with France developed over the Curandeau affair, the Secretary of State, Lord Buckingham, questioned the

94

advisability of having a Mauritian (Louis Gustave Trouchet), who was also the French consul, acting as district magistrate in Seychelles. "English authority should be represented by an English officer", he advised, especially as "the islands are of rather increasing importance and ... French influence is increasing and being fostered there".[22]

Such concerns were heightened by news of French intervention in Madagascar, where France had allied itself with the local tribe to establish a protectorate along the north-west coast as a counter to Britain's gains at the Merina court at Tananarive. In the Comoro islands, where the Queen of Mohéli had abdicated, France forcibly blocked Zanzibar's ambitions by earmarking that island for itself. Meanwhile, at Réunion, the naval and military authorities debated the chances of that island successfully defending itself in the event of war against England.

In May 1870 lingering doubts about the loyalty of Mauritius were dissipated by the welcome given to the Duke of Edinburgh, younger brother of the Prince of Wales and the first member of the British royal family to visit the colony. "Enthusiasm unparalleled in the history of this island," was how one official put it, while Laplace reported to Paris that the event showed "how greatly weakened ... were those feelings of hostility that the old Creole society had harboured against the present order". Laplace said the authorities had felt some apprehension before the visit, but everything had gone well, and the Duke made a good impression at the Masonic lodge by drinking to the health of the Emperor.

The departure of the Duke (he sailed on 3 June, in personal command of HMS *Galatea*) coincided with that of Governor Barkly, who left in the French steamer *Mozambique* after what Laplace described as a long and talented administration. Two months later there was cause for further rejoicing by the Franco-Mauritians when news reached the island that France was at war with Prussia. The celebrations were short-lived, however; the following month came the disaster of Sedan[23] and the surrender of Napoleon III. Laplace passed word of the catastrophe to Réunion, which was as yet unaware of the French defeat. In Mauritius the US consul reported that there was "a complete stagnation of trade", although plenty of military activity, with the authorities strengthening the harbour forts "as if England expects to be joining in the fray". Laplace noted, too, that the acting governor had contacted Ceylon about the possibility of starting a steamship service in case the French ships should cease to call.[24]

The government's concern was understandable, as France enjoyed a virtual monopoly of shipping services between Suez and the main islands of the western Indian Ocean. World-wide France had at first lagged behind Britain in creating shipping companies (Royal Mail, Cunard, and P & O all date from the 1840s), but in 1858, spurred by complaints by Réunion that it had to rely on foreign ships for the conveyance of personnel and dispatches, Napoleon III ordered a new shipping service for the region. The result was the Messageries Impériales (later Messageries Maritimes), which in 1864 inaugurated a service linking Suez with Réunion and Mauritius, including a regular call at Seychelles.[25]

Two years later P & O, which had been operating between Suez and Mauritius on a monthly basis since 1860, withdrew, leaving the French company in unchallenged possession of the route.[26] The introduction of regular steamship services, and in particular that of the Messageries Maritimes (maintained until 1919, with an interruption of only a few years), brought to an end Seychelles' isolation. The islands were now on the direct route to Europe, with the added advantage of quicker and more effective contact with Mauritius. Letters from the Seychelles administration could reach there in days, instead of weeks or even months.

Reflecting these improved lines of communication, a Seychelles post office[27] was opened in December 1861, after which the trickle of letters to and from the Dependency grew steadily. Ironically, the opening of the Suez Canal in 1869 did not necessarily speed the passage from Mauritius and Seychelles to Europe; the journey sometimes took longer as what had been a direct service to Suez was henceforth only a branch line to Aden, where passengers had to board another ship for Europe.

It is difficult to over-emphasize the importance of the steamship to Seychelles. Its advent changed the life of the islands as dramatically as the introduction of regular air services was to do a hundred years later. Few may have appreciated it at the time, but a new page was turning for

Seychelles, with gradual political and social advancement matched by renewed commercial prosperity, based not on cotton as at the beginning of the century but on copra, vanilla, and spices. Before turning that page, we must go back to 1862, the year in which the only recorded natural disaster in Seychelles struck the island of Mahé.

8

The Tempest
1862-1875

Having previously been exempt from storms of this kind
... the inhabitants were totally unprepared for such a visitation.
Dr James Brooks, medical officer, 18 October 1862

It could happen [again]; it is quite a bit far-fetched,
but it is not impossible.
Micky Belle, senior meteoroolgist, 22 May 1997

Rain had started to fall on the Friday, 10 October, heavy and sustained. In Port Victoria carpenters from HMS *Orestes* were helping the crew of the American whaler *Charles Carroll*[1] repair storm damage. Captain Alan Gardner of the *Orestes* was glad of the opportunity to keep the men busy, as he had been in harbour for more than a week, delayed by his passenger, the former consul-general at Zanzibar, Colonel Lewis Pelly, who was awaiting the arrival of the P & O steamer *Nepaul*, expected any day .

Throughout the next forty-eight hours the barometer was to fall sharply. The winds steadily increased to gale force throughout Saturday, and by Sunday morning a full storm was in progress. Gardner ordered fires lit to get steam up. At 11.30 he noted that the American whaler was adrift. Soon it would be driven on to the reef. The *Orestes* also began to drag, and Gardner put down two more anchors. Several small boats, including the police launch, had been sunk or were lying wrecked on the shore.

On board, Pelly could sense impending disaster, although he could see very little, "only a scud of foam blown past the side like lace rapidly unrolled". He had no doubt that he was in the midst of a tropical cyclone. Later, he described the experience. "This circular storm, strengthening out of the south-east trade, veered southward, westward, and gave us its full fury from north-west. It then moderated northwards, hung a while at north-east and finally subsided into the south-east trade again." His most lasting impression was the soughing of the wind. "I do not remember to have heard any sound so mournful as the Titanic sobbings of that hurricane — now hushed an instant, as, spent with passion, the tempest gasped for breath."

In Victoria the damage was considerable. Trees had been uprooted, roofs ripped off houses, and palings torn down. Many people had fled their homes, seeking sanctuary in more substantial buildings. The Protestant and Roman Catholic churches seemed safe and appropriate places to be. Some also went to the convent, which had been opened by the Sisters of Saint Joseph de Cluny[2] the previous year.

Police chief R.P. Brunton, who had gone out early on that fateful Sunday with a party of police and prisoners to clear the streets of fallen trees, was reminded of a storm that had hit Mahé the previous year. He was not to know that worse would follow. At some time between 11 am and 12 noon, with the wind just short of hurricane force, the side of one of the Trois Frères mountains, softened by incessant rain, collapsed. The mass of earth and rock, gathering force and volume in its descent, tore through the Bel Air and St Louis areas of the town. Without warning, people were drowning or suffocating in a sea of mud, their houses crushed or obliterated. Trees were uprooted, palms had their tops 'twisted off at the neck', while whole streets disappeared. The lower part of Bel Air cemetery was obliterated by the mud and water.

"The brook by Government House ... burst its banks, and poured in a torrent down the main street of the town, hurrying houses, provisions, men, women and children along its flood towards the sea," recalled Pelly. Fortunately a tree-covered hillock diverted the flow away from Government House, which had been built only ten years earlier on the site of the original residence of the French commandant De Romainville. It was

99

one of the few buildings to escape. Somewhere in the devastation along Royal Street lay the ruins of the convent, the "most solid and beautiful building in Victoria".[3]

Because of the storm Father Jeremiah had decided to say morning Mass in the convent chapel, thinking that it would be more convenient for the parishioners than the church. After receiving communion, the congregation was waiting patiently for a break in the weather. Soon more people arrived, some carrying a seriously injured woman. "She was still conscious," Father Jeremiah wrote later, "almost completely naked; she had a broken leg, with severe injuries to the head, and she was covered with mud." Two of the nuns, Mother Denise and Sister St Victor, found a sheet to cover her.[4] Realising that she would not survive, Father Jeremiah was administering the last rites when, at that moment or shortly afterwards, the avalanche struck. It smashed and crushed the wooden buildings of the convent, burying most of those inside, including the priest and the two nuns.

The remaining nun, Sister Denise, was one of the few to escape. She had gone to the dormitory to bring the children downstairs, thinking they would be safer there, when she suddenly found herself swept away with some of her charges in a torrent of muddy water. Her habit helped keep her afloat as she was carried along towards the house of the Jouanis family, where she was pulled from the water.

Most of those buried by the avalanche probably died instantly; the less fortunate slowly suffocated or bled to death. "The silence of death surrounded me," recalled Father Jeremiah, who was surprised to find that he was still alive. He could not move, his body being firmly pinioned by the wreckage, with a crushing pressure on his chest that made breathing difficult. There was also the fear of drowning, for the mud came up to his chin, and at times it entered his mouth, causing him to choke and vomit. Hoping that the Sisters were still alive, he called out to them, but there was no answer. He gave them absolution, and then commended his own soul to God.

Three hours went by. The priest's limbs grew numb with cold. Fortunately the mud had receded slightly, and Father Jeremiah's breathing became easier. In the strange silence around him, he kept his spirits up by reciting his favourite psalms. "In that position I remained a further two hours, unable to move either my head or feet." The only sound he heard was his own voice. Eventually help arrived, but the rescuers could not at first move him for fear of causing a further collapse of the wreckage. Gradually, as someone held his head free of the mud, others worked his body free. At the same time the bodies of the two nuns were brought out; both had died of suffocation. Seven others in the convent were also dead, although it was only after several days that all the bodies were found.

Father Jeremiah survived, but many months were to pass before he fully recovered. In September 1864 he left Seychelles on sick leave, before being transferred to Chile. The bodies of the two nuns were laid to rest in the Church of the Immaculate Conception.[5] The church building remained unscathed, and there was only slight damage to the Anglican Church of St Paul,[6] where the congregation had been cared for during the storm by the acting Civil Chaplain, Adolphe Vaudin.

Elsewhere in the town the destruction was virtually complete. "The town of Port Victoria has been nearly destroyed," reported the government medical officer, Dr James Brooks, adding that the higher part of the town had been swept into the sea. Brunton found the devastation almost impossible to describe. "Royal, Bazaar, and Benezet Streets have, in many parts, completely changed appearance from the displacement of houses," he wrote. Bishop Ryan, who travelled to Seychelles in the first available ship, described as "very mournful" the view from Government House. "The whole of the richly cultivated ground was now covered with grey mud and sand, the detritus of granite, as the waters had flowed round the elevated land on which Government House stands."

The Mauritius surveyor-general, W.L. Morrison, sent to report on the damage, estimated that half a million tons of debris had engulfed the town, filling the sea frontage with mud and rocks to a depth of from one to two feet. He measured one of the boulders that had been hurled down the mountain, and found it weighed seventy-five tons. Others were even larger. "One enormous rock which was carried a distance of three hundred feet could not have been less than from five hundred to six hundred tons in weight," he reported.

Altogether eighty persons died during the cyclone, twenty-five men, twenty-seven women, and twenty-eight children.[7] About a third of the victims were killed in Victoria. Some families were nearly wiped out. Arthur Barallon, a member of the Anglican Church, lost his father, two sisters, two nephews and three nieces. In addition to the main avalanche, landslides at Plaisance and Petit Paris claimed several lives. The heavy rain also caused landslides at Pointe Capucin, Anse Boileau, and Bel Ombre, but except for the Jouanis property there was little damage between North-East Point and Beau Vallon. Thousands of coconut trees were flattened on low land at Anse aux Pins, Anse Royale, and Baie Lazare. Plantations were also destroyed on Sainte Anne and Cerf islands, and there was damage on Praslin, Silhouette, and Anonyme, although no lives were lost. During the height of the storm, calm weather prevailed over La Digue and Frégate.

When he realised the extent of the disaster, Captain Gardner immediately sent two officers and a party of seamen ashore. They laboured throughout Monday, searching for bodies in the wreckage and assisting police to cut a channel in Royal Street to allow mud and water from the St Louis river to flow to the sea. The *Orestes* also landed a quantity of beef and biscuit for the inhabitants, some of whom — "those of the respectable class" — were temporarily accommodated in Government House. Because the jail had been completely wrecked, prisoners were lodged in one of the outhouses in the Government House grounds. Dr Brooks set up a temporary hospital for the injured, most of whom suffered from broken limbs.

Early on Tuesday morning the steamer *Nepaul* arrived from Mauritius. It reported experiencing very strong winds and high seas throughout the Friday and Saturday, when two of its lifeboats had been carried away. Only on Sunday morning did the weather moderate. After a few hours in port, the *Nepaul* left for Aden. Pelly was on board, homeward bound on sick leave; also the mail for Europe, minus one bag lost in the avalanche.

The next day the *Orestes* departed for Mauritius. It carried a report on the disaster from the acting Civil Commissioner, Dupuy, who informed the Governor that in view of this "unprecedented emergency" he had on his own initiative offered assistance to the destitute, as well as providing food for those cleaning the town.[8] To obtain the necessary labour, Dupuy ordered that all men without passes from their employers should be compulsorily mustered in work gangs, under a constable or 'inhabitant'. Even so, without sufficient tools, the work proceeded slowly. Each day the Anglican church bell rang to announce a free distribution of rice. By the end of the month over £1,000 in aid to Seychelles had been approved by the Mauritius Council, while the mayor of Port Louis, who had been organising a collection for a Lancashire distress fund, changed it to a Seychelles relief appeal.

Swinburne Ward, who arrived to take up the post of Civil Commissioner two months after the disaster, described Victoria as "a perfect wreak [sic]". He noted that although rations were still being issued to the poorer classes, they were expected to help clear the streets if they wanted to receive food. He said the former African slaves had been very useful, although most were women and children. More labour was needed, and he asked Mauritius to send convict labour.

Although reports of damage to some plantations were undoubtedly exaggerated, Dupuy predicted that production of coconut oil would be affected for some years, it being estimated that nearly 30,000 coconut palms had been destroyed. He did not envisage any further deterioration in the "general misery" of the population. He thought planters would be wise not to rely on the coconut in future, although whatever they did "the enervating influence of the Equatorial climate of this Dependency, will ever be a great barr [sic] to the improvement of the welfare of the people".

Some believed good might come from the *Grand l'Avalasse*, the name given locally to the disaster.[9] Here was an opportunity to rebuild, to give the town wider streets, proper drainage, and a realignment of buildings. Pointing out that the town's houses had generally been carelessly constructed, and were too close together, the Surveyor-General said "the calamity may eventually be the means of bringing to pass great improvement", including the building of a hospital and more school accommodation. The landslides outside Victoria also offered an incentive to build new roads, for transport was still largely by sea, which was "generally expensive, frequently very dangerous, and sometimes impracticable". The avalanche had pushed out the coastline, giving Victoria its first experience of land reclamation.

A question sometimes asked is whether the storm that hit Seychelles on 11/12 October 1862 was a cyclone. Those at the scene, or who arrived soon afterwards, certainly thought so. They included Captain Gardner of the *Orestes*, as well as officials sent from Mauritius, an island well acquainted with cyclones. Pelly had underlined the spiralling nature of the storm, with the wind veering all the way round the compass. Its force was reported to range from 4 to 11 on the Beaufort scale, where the higher number represents a "violent storm", with winds up to 63 knots (approximately 117 km an hour). One knot more, and it would have been a Beaufort 'hurricane'. In the modern system of classification, sustained winds of from 48 to 63 knots indicate a "severe tropical cyclone".

Because of their proximity to the equator, the main granitic islands of Seychelles, lying between four and five degrees south, are outside the cyclonic belt; only the southerly coralline islands such as Farquhar, Coëtivy, and Aldabra stand in the danger zone. Cyclones thrive on vorticity — the whirling motion that is their main characteristic — and as they near the equator this vorticity tends to slacken and die out. It is not impossible, however, given a sufficient twist and under certain atmospheric conditions, for a cyclone to venture nearer the equator than is customary.

According to a senior meteorologist[10] this is probably what happened in 1862. "The conditions were suitable for a storm of this calibre to reach our latitude," he said. adding: "Although I would say it was a moderate tropical storm, it was powerful in terms of its proximity to us ... Also it had been raining for several days, loosening the structure of the mountain, which had a huge, projecting head at that time, and with wind gusts of 75 to 80 knots, which you could easily get in a very simple cyclone, that could have triggered the landslide."

A major contributory factor in the disaster is thought to have been the loss of forest cover on the Trois Frères, caused by extensive cutting of timber since the days of the first French settlement. Also, the construction of the St Louis road and the widening of the pass to Beau Vallon would also have made the landslide more likely.

The *Avalasse* was a particularly hard blow for the Sisters of

St Joseph de Cluny. Since their arrival in Seychelles in 1861 they had established a paying school for better-off families — about one hundred children were enrolled, both day pupils and boarders — and a free school and orphanage for poorer children. Now, with only one surviving nun, and the school buildings destroyed, classes had been brought to a virtual standstill. To make matters worse, malicious rumours had begun to circulate attributing the avalanche to the presence of the Sisters on the island.

Father Jeremiah, who had begun making plans for a new convent, found temporary quarters for the nuns' school, but little could be done until more Sisters arrived. He wrote to the Mother Superior at Réunion, imploring her to send "some more of those angels ... to fill the immense gap that has been left". As a result four Sisters arrived during 1863, to resume the task of providing a basic education to a growing number of children. The language of instruction was French, but English was added to the curriculum the following year after the arrival of an Irish Sister. In 1865 the Sisters moved into their new home, which had been built on a site near the present-day cathedral. The latter building, then the Church of the Immaculate Conception, had been redone in stone and coral block the previous year, at a cost of 80,000 francs. At about this time Father Jeremiah left Seychelles, and the mission was placed under the direction of the Capuchin Province of Savoy, with Father Ignatius Galfione of Villafranca as the resident vice-prefect. One of his first tasks after his arrival in October 1864 was to consecrate the new convent chapel.

The high standard maintained in the convent schools was to be a recurring theme in official reports from Seychelles. Sir Arthur Gordon, who succeeded Barkly as governor of Mauritius in 1871, was fulsome in his praise of the Sisters of St Joseph de Cluny, and he deplored the "Protestant bigotry" that had kept the nuns out of Seychelles for so long. By now there were nearly 350 girl pupils benefiting from "the civilising influences that they might not otherwise have had". The Governor also mentioned the good work among boys by the Brothers of Christian Schools,[11] who had opened a primary school, the St Louis College, in 1867.

Unlike previous governors, Gordon was optimistic about the future of Seychelles, which he described as "one of the loveliest spots I have ever seen". On his way out to Mauritius his ship called at Mahé (the first glimpse newly appointed governors had of their colony now that the Suez Canal was open), and he was immediately captivated by what he saw, and which he was later to compare favourably with the "wind-tossed and stunted" scenery of hurricane-prone Mauritius.

"It is impossible not to be struck by the new plantations which are everywhere being formed [in Seychelles]," he wrote, after a second visit to the Dependency in September 1871, "nor to recognize the rapid increase of population and of revenue which has taken place". Seychelles had, in fact, recovered quickly from the effects of the 1862 disaster. Agricultural exports, mostly copra and coconut oil, had increased significantly, made possible by the new steamship services and the influx throughout the 1860s of a more or less steady stream of liberated African workers. The population now stood at about 12,000, of which 9,600 lived on Mahé. With such "rapid progress and improvement" Gordon saw no reason why "the further development of these dependencies is likely to be arrested".

Similar views were expressed by former US consul Derence Atwater,[12] who left Seychelles in 1870 to take up an appointment at Tahiti. He noted the greatly improved appearance of Victoria. Roads had been made up, a piped-water supply introduced, and a market built. Many new houses had been constructed, some of them in stone and coral, and there were roads leading out of town in two directions, of three and five miles respectively.

Victoria was also developing as a major port, although not as fast as it should, according to Atwater. "A little more enterprise on the part of the inhabitants in raising supplies needed by vessels would make the Seychelles the best port in the Indian Ocean for vessels to recruit and give liberty, they being most centrally situated and with communication in all directions," he commented. Atwater was concerned principally about the provisioning of American whaleships, 16 of which put in at Mahé during 1869. This compared with calls by 17 colonial merchantmen, and 12 French and three British merchant ships. Victoria was also becoming an important coaling station[13] for steamships, including men of war, with 20 French and six British warships calling during the year. There was also the coaling twice a month at Mahé of the French mail steamers on the Mauritius-Europe run.

Particularly important for the development of the port was the construction of a deep-water pier. Envisaged ten years earlier by Wade as an extension of the causeway begun by Mylius, the pier had advanced only 100 feet under Ward, and it was not until March 1870 that work began in earnest under Ward's successor, William Franklyn. A master mariner, Franklyn gave the project his personal supervision, pushing ahead with construction until, by September 1871, the pier extended to 1,750 feet. Made of granite blocks, with coral infill, it was 8½ feet high, 20 feet in width, with a crane and trucks running on rails. While Wade had proposed an overall length of 3,000 feet, it was now planned that the pier should extend by an additional 600 feet.[14]

"Never was anything in Seychelles erected with such celerity," wrote the US consul at Mauritius, Nicholas Pike, who accompanied Governor Gordon on his visit to Seychelles in August 1871. For Pike it was "positive proof that the Seychellois can work well". Describing Gordon's ceremonial arrival at Victoria, Pike noted that many planters had come in from the country with their families to greet the Governor. All were dressed in their Sunday best and "looked eager and happy". As the Governor left HMS *Forte* by launch a 17-gun salute was fired, with similar honours from two field guns as he stepped ashore at the new pier. In the harbour were a small French corvette, the *Surprise*, and an armed dhow belonging to the Sultan of Zanzibar; both unable to salute because of insufficient guns. There was also in the harbour an American whaler, the 300-ton *Herald*, of New Bedford.[15]

Gordon greeted the planters who lined the avenue to Government House, where he would stay during his two-month visit, and invited them to call on him to discuss their grievances. Fortunately the Civil Commissioner's residence was large enough to accommodate Gordon in comfort. Described as a long, roomy bungalow-type building, with a deep veranda, it had at one end a suite of rooms known as the Admiral's Wing, so called because the senior naval officer would normally stay there during a flagship's visit. On this occasion, it is probable that Franklyn and his family moved into the guest wing during Gordon's visit.

Although he complained to London about his health,[16] Gordon maintained an active schedule in Seychelles, visiting the main islands and holding discussions, both collectively and privately, with the principal inhabitants. He climbed to the summit of Sainte Anne to see the site for a lighthouse, he visited Praslin and viewed the coco de mer valley (the first British governor to do so). He went to Frégate island and to Curieuse, to see the leper colony. At La Digue, where he was greeted with the firing of pistols, firecrackers, and the ringing of handbells; he found "the little island ... far more lively and go ahead than its bigger neighbours".

He was not impressed by the roads on Mahé, which, with the exception of the road south from Victoria, he likened to garden gravel paths. "As there are no wheeled vehicles, and barely any beasts of burden ... these walks are ... never cut by wheels nor worn by horse hoofs," he wrote. The road south ran as far as Cascade, where a large boulder had fallen during the avalanche and completely buried a house and all its inhabitants. Travelling north from Victoria Gordon saw the 'château' of the last French governor, of which only the foundations remained.

The Governor remarked on the many wild orange trees (*bigarades*) he saw, as well as some magnificent clove trees which he assumed were surviving plants from the Jardin du Roi of the original French settlement. Noting that many of the trees had been cut down to make room for coffee, he predicted that "the singular flora, as well as singular fauna, of Seychelles, will soon be a thing of the past".

Gordon witnessed on Cousin island a hawksbill turtle being caught. "It is beheaded, and ere long we were watching the operation of taking off the plates of the shell by means of fire made in a hole, and repeated applications of hot water." There were thirteen plates in all. Gordon noted that hawksbill turtles were considered poisonous, so much so that their blood was covered up in case dogs licked it. Strange, thought Gordon, for in the West Indies it was freely eaten.[17] Atwater had reported that green turtle, once so plentiful, was becoming scarce on account of the immense number slaughtered not just for meat but also for their inferior shells.

On Frégate island, where the Savy family made plentiful supplies of rum from cane grown there, Gordon was particularly impressed by the coral reef on the island's granite ridge, noting that "the mountain top which forms the island must have gone down 250 feet lower than at present, and remained under water long enough for the growth of the coral reef, which then formed a true atoll, a ring, or nearly a ring, with water in the middle. Then it rose again, and the centre became dry land. The soil ... is exceedingly rich." Pike, who was nearly hit on the head with a coconut when visiting the island, seems to have been more impressed by tales of scorpions and a spider that had a bite which could be fatal. Men took ammonia with them to treat bites, he was told, but even then one could be laid up for ten days, with vomiting, cramps, and swelling.

Both Gordon and Pike were delighted with the scenery and climate. "It is hot, no doubt, but the air is pure," wrote Gordon. What he did not like was "the howling of wild dogs, that rush around in packs, and leave half-gnawed bones, dug up from the cemetery". In this respect, little had changed since Keate's order twenty years previously that all stray dogs should be destroyed.

The fourth son of a former Prime Minister, the Earl of Aberdeen, Gordon was not the typically aloof aristocrat. He mixed easily at all levels of society, although his liberal ideas — which he implemented with steely determination — quickly earned him the hostility of the Mauritian planters.[18] At Baie Lazare, he stayed with Camille LeMarchand, a Frenchman from Marseilles whose purchases of land in the 1860s had made him one of the island's largest proprietors. It was here that Gordon was entertained one evening by estate workers performing an "elephant dance". More an opera than a dance, thought Gordon, who described in detail this example of African theatre.

"A fire was lighted in the middle of a shed," he wrote. "Three naked little black boys crouched and squatted near the blaze beating biscuit tins for tom-toms, with short sticks; the women stood on one side, the men on the other. They sang incessantly, dancing slightly." One of the boys then went out, coming back to report signs of an elephant. He is frightened, but the others go out, singly or in pairs, armed with a bow and arrow or spear, until they finally kill the elephant. "It was a curious bit of savagery brought into civilisation."

Although not approving of the way LeMarchand treated his African labour, Gordon rather liked the Frenchman. "He is, I should say, a rascal, and one of his eyes has a fearful squint; but he is rather a good sort of scoundrel," he commented. About some of the other inhabitants Gordon was less complimentary. He thought Mr Albert, though "not at all a scoundrel", was stupid, and he did not like Mr Dupuy, the principal shopkeeper in Victoria and, according to Gordon, probably the richest man on the island.[19] Among the "most presentable of the *habitans*" was a former French naval officer called Bonnetard, while the Greek wife of the chief medical officer, Dr Brooks, was "rather pretty, ladylike and decidedly clever and pleasing".

Civil Commissioner Franklyn, "fat, short, positive", was a straightforward, practical man whom Gordon could relate to. He found the former merchant navy captain loyal and zealous in carrying out orders, "even when they were opposed to his own", and he praised his efforts to develop the Dependency. Mrs Franklyn, however, was rather dull. Somewhat snobbishly, Gordon deemed her "too quiet and silent to be vulgar, which she manifestly would be if she talked". He was equally unimpressed by Franklyn's daughter. An Anglican, Gordon had no religious prejudices. He got on well with Father Ignatius and the other Roman Catholic clergy, and he was displeased when during a sermon on the board the *Forte* the Anglican chaplain referred to "cowled and scowling monks".

The island's Freemasons, active in the Dependency after an absence of eighteen years, were among those who welcomed the Governor. Pike, himself a mason, visited the temple of the Lodge Réunion Sincère,[20] where he met several of the leading inhabitants. "I quitted the Temple with favourable impressions as to the progress of Masonry in Mahé," he wrote. Pike had earlier been guest at a masonic dinner given by Jean-François Chauvin, of the Exil estate. The American also visited South Mahé, where he met and stayed overnight with some of the inhabitants, including a Swiss immigrant, Felix Pool.[21] Pike commented that "whatever may be the fault of the Seychellois, I must bear testimony that kind heartedness and hospitality are among their most prominent virtues".

Only once was Gordon visibly upset in Seychelles, and that was during a visit to the leper colony on Curieuse island, still there despite the decision by Higginson to close it. Under the direction of the elderly George Forbes, it had become a camp for fifteen old and inform paupers, who mixed freely with the lepers. There were now only half a dozen of the latter, the rest presumably having died. Although Gordon was aware that latest medical opinion considered leprosy not contagious,[22] he was shocked to find that healthy paupers shared accommodation with the sick and diseased, and that there was indiscriminate mixing of the sexes.

The surgeon of the flagship *Forte*, whom Gordon had asked to report on the camp, found that no medical treatment was given, and that the food was inadequate and likely to aggravate the disease. Except in one hut, called the 'hospital', there were no bedsteads or mattresses of any kind. "Each patient is provided with a blanket, which in several cases I noticed [to be] torn and dirty," reported the doctor. One leprous woman had recently given birth. Pike noted that the inmates kept a coffin in their hut ready for use, "which must I should think have a depressing effect at first, but from habit they don't seem to mind it".

"I shall rout out the whole place," Gordon promised himself at the end of his visit. "There is sometimes some satisfaction in being a despot." Instead of closing the camp, however, he urged the Colonial Office to find a suitable doctor for Curieuse, someone who could double up as magistrate for the island of Praslin. When London were slow in responding, Gordon wrote to friends in Britain and found his own candidate for the post, 26-year-old William MacGregor, a recently qualified medical practitioner from Aberdeenshire.

MacGregor arrived at Mahé with his wife in February 1873, and moved to Praslin the following month. He was later to establish himself on Curieuse as superintendent of the camp, taking a lease on the island and building a large house for himself and family (a daughter, Helen, was born there). MacGregor spent more than two years in Seychelles, with a spell of several months in Mauritius. He was a humane and dedicated doctor, who not only improved the lot of the lepers but, as Inspector of Liberated Africans, did much to correct instances of unfair treatment. Gordon described MacGregor as ideally suited for the job; he was "firm, cautious, and thoroughly impartial". He had learned not only to speak

111

Creole but also Swahili, in order to converse with the Africans — "the only white man here at all able to do so".

MacGregor found that generally the former slaves were well fed and housed, and not overworked — "although a few expressed a wish that they had no work at all". They were also sufficiently clothed, with the exception of the LeMarchand estate, where MacGregor considered the lack of clothing an outrage to public decency.[23] The main charge against the planters, however, was that of cheating the Africans out of their wages and rations. MacGregor secured the detection and punishment of two or three large proprietors. "The result has ... been most beneficial to the labourers generally and has caused a more rigid adherence ... to the law," Gordon noted.

Franklyn promised the Governor he would ensure the punctual payment of wages. "I shall also enforce the law recently passed which compels planters to keep proper books and accounts," he wrote. He regretted that employers did not bother to provide religious instruction, nor education of any kind. When he inquired about teaching the Africans to read, the only response was a derisive giggle, yet they [the Africans] were "not wanting in intelligence".

Franklyn would liked to have introduced a system of public relief to avoid the horrors of the previous administration, when "aged and sick Africans, unable to work, [were] being turned out to perish miserably".[24] He considered the planters fortunate in being able to extend and maintain their plantations as a result of the influx of capital and labour. "These improvements are still going on in every direction and fresh capital is being invested, but should that become scarce a sudden check would inevitably take place," he wrote.

The planters were, in fact, concerned at the possibility of being once again without labour, for the number of liberated Africans arriving at Seychelles had seemingly dried up. After an exceptional influx of nearly 800 in 1869 there had been none since, prompting the planters to petition the Queen for a renewal of this source of labour. The Governor agreed to back their request. Unknown to both, the Admiralty had ordered a halt to landings after receiving unfavourable reports from ships' captains about the conditions for apprentices in Seychelles, but the ban was soon lifted.[25] Two weeks after Gordon's departure from Seychelles, HMS *Columbine* steamed into Victoria

112

harbour. As the only cruiser on patrol off the East African coast, it had made several successful captures.

"One dhow we took had over two hundred slaves in her, and I think I have never seen a more disgusting sight in my life," wrote one of the ship's officers in a letter home. "They were packed just like sheep; in fact they were stowed so close that they could not get at them .. and they were dying by the dozen every day. Ever since we have had them on board over twenty have died. They look just like skeletons. I can't make out how any one will buy them, because I should think it would cost more than they are worth to get them alright again." Within days of the Africans being quarantined on Longue island, more than half had been allocated to proprietors of estates "and other respectable persons".

During the voyage to Seychelles in the *Columbine* the freed slaves had slept most of the time. "In the morning they are turned out at 6 o'clock, and the pumps are rigged and we play the hoses on them for about half an hour. They are then put in the sun to dry and the decks are scrubbed. At 9 they come down for their breakfast, which consist [sic] of boiled rice. They then go to sleep until 5 in the afternoon, when they have their second meal, which consists of boiled beans. They then lay down and are covered up for the night." The writer admitted that he would be "heartily glad" to reach Seychelles, adding: "This will be the last of our cruising north of the line as the SW Monsoon breaks this month and now commences our hot weather again."

The *Columbine* was to stay on anti-slaving patrol for several months more, resulting in the writer complaining to his sister: "The Admiral promised to send us [to] India this year, but I am afraid we shall not be able to go, as there are not any ships on the coast now." Nor were they to be relieved the following year. Admiral Cockburn, together with the Viceroy of India, Lord Mayo, was stabbed to death by an Indian convict on the Andaman islands. "The old Admiral liked this ship ... but now I suppose we shall have our coast cruising to do all over again," was the sorry comment.

In January 1872, having made further dhow captures, Captain Tucker of the *Columbine* chartered the German consular steamer *Afrika* to carry more than 150 Africans to Seychelles. Later, at Zanzibar, the ship's officers met members of an expedition sent out by the Royal Geographical Society to find the Scots explorer and missionary David Livingstone,[26] who had not been heard of for several years. It was headed by two naval officers, Commander Dawson and Lieutenant Henn, and included Livingstone's youngest son, Oswald.[27] Before they could set out for the interior, however, the American adventurer Henry Morton Stanley turned up with the news that he had found Livingstone at Ujiji, on Lake Tanganyika. Stanley was hurrying back to Britain to celebrate, and the expedition had little choice but to return with him.

They chartered the *Afrika* to take them to Seychelles, where they could catch the mail steamer for Europe. "We arrived at Seychelles on the 9th of June [1872], about twelve hours after the French mail had departed for Aden," wrote Stanley. "As there is only monthly communication between Mahé and Aden, we were compelled to remain on the island of Mahé one month. Messrs Livingstone, [the Rev. Charles] New, Morgan, and myself, hired a nice little wooden house, which we called the "Livingstone Cottage", while Mr Henn resorted to an hotel." The intrepid journalist concluded: "My life in Mahé is among the most agreeable things connected with my return from Africa ... when at last the French steamer came from Mauritius, there was not one of our party who did not regret leaving the beautiful island."

During his month in Seychelles Stanley had observed how the liberated Africans lived, and he later added his voice to the growing concern by the Church and others about their treatment, claiming to a London newspaper that the apprentices were being sold to the planters as slaves. Bishop William Tozer, of the Universities Mission to Central Africa, also deplored the moral and social atmosphere he had found at Seychelles. Writing to the Church Missionary Society, he noted that "the government has provided neither schools for the [liberated African] children, nor any sort of instruction for the adults. In consequence Seychelles exhibits the strange anomaly of a servile race, permanently settled among Christians who are doing absolutely nothing to wean them from their heathenies, or to teach them the truths of the Gospel".

Other churchmen were saying the same thing, insisting that the liberated Africans must receive instruction and training;

114

otherwise they would grow up "a thriftless, lazy race, from whom no improvement can be expected". Bishop Huxtable, writing to CMS secretary Edward Hutchinson, stressed the duty Britain owed to the Africans. "They are grateful and faithful ... because of the blessing of freedom which England has bestowed upon them. They certainly therefore have the two-fold claim upon us, necessity and affection."

The Colonial Office was sufficiently aroused by such criticism to insist on increased powers for the Inspector of Liberated Africans. MacGregor, who had only recently been appointed to the post, empathized readily with the Africans, his concern for their welfare eventually pushing him beyond both the letter of his instructions and the limits of his own physical endurance. One day, after "hard walking under a tropical sun" and hard talking with the planters, he collapsed and had to lie up for a week at Government House.

As a result of MacGregor's strenuous efforts, Bishop Peter Royston of Mauritius[28] was able to report in 1874 (the year the doctor finally left Seychelles) that "a good deal has been done to ameliorate the outward circumstances of the older ex-African [apprentice] population. Still lacking, however, was the provision of schooling or moral instruction, especially for the children. Royston called for a French-speaking chaplain, preferably with experience of working with "people of half civilized habits". He considered that the current chaplain, Vaudin, had been too long in Seychelles, and needed a change (Vaudin returned to Mombasa the following year).[29]

What rankled Royston particularly was that a number of African boys, rejected by the Anglican chaplain for want of funds and facilities, had been eagerly accepted as pupils by the Catholic nuns, at trifling cost to the government. These boys were probably among the last liberated Africans landed in Seychelles. The Zanzibar slave trade had been ended two years earlier, when Sultan Bargash (who had succeeded Majid in 1870) bowed to British pressure and closed all slave markets in his territories. From now on any freed slaves would find refuge at mission stations along the Coast, notably Frere Town,[30] near Mombasa, set up by the CMS in 1875. Although officially the slave trade was a thing of the past, it was to continue surreptitiously for many more years.[31]

In March 1874 Franklyn died, and was succeeded

temporarily by a former army officer, Captain Arthur Havelock, who had been sent to Mahé earlier to report on irregularities in the paying of wages to African child apprentices. Havelock's report concluded that there had been no proper accounting for the money retained on behalf of the African minors and, by implication, pointed an accusing finger at Ward, who on leaving Seychelles in 1868 had been appointed auditor-general at Mauritius. Others, too, had been involved in the "gross irregularity and carelessness", including a sergeant-major of police with an extravagant life-style. When he was informed of the matter, the Secretary of State refused to accept Gordon's suggestion that the money had been "simply muddled away", adding: "I fear the only result will be his [Ward's] dismissal or enforced resignation".

Havelock strongly supported the idea of an educational institution for the African child apprentices, and with his encouragement Royston, through the CMS in Mauritius, raised the necessary funds. Subsequently, in April 1875, the Reverend William Chancellor[32] and his wife arrived in Seychelles from Mombasa, with the task of setting up a school and training institution for African children. The school, set high in the mountains above Victoria and known as Venn's Town, was to become over a period of some twenty years the focus of Anglican missionary endeavour in Seychelles.

The previous year had seen the departure from Mauritius of Sir Arthur Gordon, who had been virtually driven out by plantation owners opposed to his reforming zeal. With his removal, Seychelles lost the only governor who had shown a real interest in the Dependency. His visit in August-September 1871 had been unprecedented, no other governor having made such a lengthy stay or concerned himself with the islands so soon after assuming office.

Although Gordon's visit has already been described in some detail, we have so far omitted its main purpose, which was to effect major changes in the Seychelles administration. Gordon believed that the trade restrictions imposed by Mauritius should be lifted, and that the Dependency be given a greater say in financial and administrative matters. "There has certainly been uncommonly little done for them," he observed. "Nor has anything like the revenue which ought to have been credited to them, been spent on the dependency."

During his first brief call at Mahé, in February 1871, Gordon had been impressed by Franklyn's advocacy of self-rule. He knew of the unsuccessful petition the inhabitants had addressed to London the previous year, calling for an inquiry into the administration of the islands. He was aware of blatant instances of Mauritius' mismanagement of Seychelles affairs, citing the decision of the Mauritius Council not to approve the construction of any roads in Seychelles on the ground that it would be unfair if one area were to have a road while another remained without. There was also the tax of £16 an acre imposed by Mauritius on Seychelles tobacco, which had effectively killed it as a cash crop.

In proposing greater autonomy, Gordon was not breaking new ground. This was something the Dependency's Civil Commissioners had long cried out for. Even the Secretary of State Earl Grey had, in 1851, suggested a separate legislature for Seychelles, but nothing came of it. To resuscitate Grey's proposal, Gordon had first to get the inhabitants to submit a new petition. He called a meeting, just before he left Seychelles, at which some 700 inhabitants unanimously approved his draft constitutional proposals. They requested greater independence for Seychelles, both legislative and administrative, and the limited introduction to the islands of more liberated Africans.

"Both these requests appear to me reasonable, and I am proposed to recommend them to your Lordship's favourable consideration," Gordon wrote in a covering letter to the Secretary of State, Lord Kimberley. Just over a year later, in November 1872, Seychelles' new legislative and executive body, the Board of Civil Commissioners, met in its first regular session. Franklyn was now styled Chief Civil Commissioner, and the Board consisted of three official members, the newly created Treasurer, the District Judge (with wider powers than the previous District Magistrate), and the government medical officer, with three nominated unofficial members: LeMarchand, François Hodoul, jun., and Charles Dupuy.

Seychelles was now allowed to import most goods directly, instead of having to go through Mauritius, and it had the benefit of its own customs revenue and other taxes. Among the first measures approved by the Board of Civil Commissioners was a land tax of one shilling an acre. It also arranged for the management of a public hospital, the creation of a new cemetery, and the establishment of a refuge for paupers. An Education Board was set up to see to the allocation of government grants to the Dependency's schools, which were to be given irrespective of denomination.

Under what might be termed Seychelles' first constitution, the newly designated Chief Civil Commissioner had greater powers and responsibility. According to Gordon, the post required certain "exceptional qualities", which he listed as: 1) being fit enough to climb mountain paths and voyage "across the rolling swell of the Indian Ocean in an open boat"; 2) fluency in French; 3) an ability to maintain strict financial control; and 4) firmness, coupled with an equable temper and calm judgement, "for he will have to allay many angry quarrels, and guide the whole of the not generally very efficient public servants under his direction".

Much, it seemed, was required of those who would govern Seychelles.

9

Whaling Wives
1868-1888

James Finn comes off drunk and was very insolent.
I boxed his ears and put him down in the hold.
Captain Cutler, of the barque Dolphin, at Mahé

It was seven years since Harriet Allen had been at Mahé, and she was pleased to see that the island was "much improved". Finding accommodation ashore was still a problem. Hotels in Victoria were hardly suitable — "full of man of war's men generally, and ... neither more nor less than drinking saloons" — but friends had come to the rescue and found rooms for her and the two children.

Harriet did not drink, refusing even a glass of wine at dinner, but she was not strait-laced nor overly religious, as were some of the whaling captains' wives. She was an open and friendly woman, intelligent, but very conscious of the passing years. "I am growing old, and just now feel miserable," she confided to herself on her 39th birthday. But she was never despondent for long. She had a sense of humour, and was not above indulging in gossip with the other wives of the whaling fleet.

Many captains took their wives to sea, for despite the hardship of shipboard life they preferred it to the loneliness and anxieties of staying behind. "I do not wish myself at home," Harriet wrote in her diary on 13 April 1870. "Home is something to look forward to by and by. No one needs me there. I am content to be a wanderer."

She had now been wandering for almost two years in the Indian Ocean where the *Merlin*[1] was one of several American

119

whaling barques hunting the sperm whale. Like many captains, David Allen had his favourite whaling ground, in this case, the Indian Ocean, where he had been coming for almost twenty years. Harriet had sailed with him before, in the *Platina*,[2] but this was the first time she had brought the children, Henry and Nellie. "I cling to this life with them," she wrote. "They are mine now, as they can never quite be again." Harriet's only regret was that David did not have a ship of his own, so that he could go "when and where he pleased".

On this voyage he had delayed calling at Mahé, not that he disliked the place but because he feared the crew would like it too much. Harriet's diary hints at some dissatisfaction in the ship, for she observed that life would be enjoyable "if every body was happy and agreeable". Later, as the *Merlin* put in to Victoria on the afternoon of Monday, 16 May 1870, she wondered whether "it may have been better for us, if we had come here last year". It was Henry's birthday — he was now 12 — and she had given him 25 cents. He had received a fishing line from his father, and a handkerchief from Nellie.

The medical officer, Dr Brooks, was one of the first on board, and he later left the ship with Captain Allen, who was unwell. Mrs Brooks sent fruit and flowers for Harriet. The following day she visited Mrs Brooks, whose house she found "as splendid as ever". Mrs Brooks herself "looked finely in a black silk skirt and white waist", and although she was not handsome "her figure, manners and dress make her exceedingly fascinating". The two women talked of old times, and Harriet received news of the Telfairs. He had "died crazy", she was told, and his wife and daughter were now living in England.

As the *Merlin* was staying in port for almost a month, resting the crew, Harriet was able to enjoy the social round of the island. The US consul, Atwater, accompanied her to Government House, where she found the Civil Commissioner "very social" and Mrs Franklyn "a motherly, pleasant lady". On the Queen's Birthday the Allens were among the two dozen or so invited to dinner at Government House, and Harriet had the satisfaction of hearing from Mrs Brooks — who had not mentioned it previously — "some things in reference to the Worth affair".

Janet Worth, another whaling captain's wife, suffered from

sea-sickness, and whenever she could took up residence ashore. It appears that she had recently committed some indiscretion, for three weeks before Harriet's arrival in Seychelles she heard on the fleet grapevine that "Mrs W. has created a sensation in Mahé". Although predicting that she and Mrs Worth "shall not suit each other too well", Harriet was curious to meet this lady of dubious reputation. What she was not prepared for was to have to share rooms with her, an arrangement she agreed to only after Captain Worth told her he could not find suitable accommodation for his wife in Victoria.

"My first impression is that she is very pretty, seen in the evening with her hat on," conceded Harriet. "She has a good deal of quiet ease and assurance in her manner." Harriet could not resist adding: "She is not highly educated". This is all we hear from Harriet on the subject of Mrs Worth, and one can only guess at the nature of her indiscretion. Others who wrote about her give the impression of a woman on whom men doted, including her husband, and who took advantage of it. "She cannot lift a finger to do the least thing for herself," complained the fourth mate of the *Gazelle*, out of New Bedford in 1862 with Janet Worth making her first voyage. "It takes two all the time to tend to her wants, besides 28 dogs at her command. There is no other command in this ship."

Resentful of his lowly position, the fourth mate vented his spite on the captain's wife. Even he, however, fell under the charm of this attractive, spoiled woman. One day, while off duty, he held a long conversation with her on deck. "Very edifying, so much so that most of my watch below went away before I was aware of it," he wrote. "Conversed about love and murder, society, churches, dances, men, and about the price of nutmegs." If Jane was not highly educated, the fourth mate of the *Gazelle* did not seem to notice. As to Mrs Worth's character, and the reason behind her husband's devoted attention, the fourth mate gives perhaps a clue. "Looking into the after cabin today," he wrote, " I saw in a cradle two dolls and beside them sat a pretended mother singing and talking to them as a little girl would."

American whaleships in the Indian Ocean called every so often at one or other of the islands. During the years 1869-70 the *Merlin* visited Anjouan (twice), Grande Comore, Bird island (twice), Diego Garcia, and Zanzibar. Bird island was much frequented, being near the well-known whaling ground. Water and birds eggs could be obtained there, and mail might be waiting collection, while letters home could sometimes be forwarded by another ship. "We sent twelve letters to Mahé by Captain Watkins ... [and he] will bring our letters if they have not been sent to Johanna," noted Harriet Allen on 23 June 1869. Two months later the *Merlin* was at Anjouan. There were several other whalers there, and on 27 August another arrived from Seychelles. On board was Consul Atwater, called to investigate complaints by some of the whaling captains.

Atwater later informed Washington that Anjouan generally was one of the best islands for whalers, both to replenish provisions and because "neither fermented liquors or bad women are to be had there". Unfortunately the inhabitants had the habit of not honouring contracts, masters were often subjected to arrests and delays, runaway sailors were hidden away, and there was "a propensity to steal and be dishonest". Atwater supported the captains' request that a consular agent be appointed, to help maintain harmony between the people and the whaleships as well as look after destitute seamen. The last foreign consul at Anjouan had been William Sunley, a British plantation owner who had been found keeping slaves and consequently forced to resign. The whaling captains had proposed as consul James Duncan, a former officer in the Union army living in Anjouan, but Atwater pointed out that Duncan was himself a deserter. He had also become a Moslem, taken to eastern dress, and kept concubines, "which are, in my opinion, sufficient reasons why he should not be appointed to represent the interests of the United States".

The need for consular representation in Anjouan was underscored in June 1870, when Pike, the US consul in Mauritius, forwarded to Washington a letter from the Sultan complaining about the captain of the New Bedford bark *Pioneer,* who had sailed without paying port charges, as well as abandoning four seamen on the island. The Sultan looked after the men until they found another ship. "The King of Johanna has been very kind and obliging to the American whalers that frequently call there for provisions and I think it would be advisable to notice his complaints as he evidently feels much aggrieved," wrote Pike. The Sultan enclosed a letter from the seamen in which they described their treatment by Captain James Hazard. They claimed that after being eight months at sea, with many of them suffering from scurvy, they had been given shore leave at Anjouan "without a cent ... to Bye our Diners with". They decided to desert, but were caught and brought to the ship, where the captain refused to take them back. A month after the *Pioneer* sailed, they tried unsuccessfully to get away on a French brig bound for Sea Shell [sic]. Three months later the Sultan managed to transfer them to Mayotte, from where a French ship took them to Seychelles. From there they were sent on to Mauritius.

It was not until November 1871 that the *Pioneer* turned up at Port Louis. Pike reported that Hazard became "terribly exasperated" when denied a certificate of exoneration for having abandoned the four seamen. He also objected to Pike taking testimony from the crew, and adamantly refused to pay the charges and dues levied on his ship. "Captain Hazard is still ... giving me much trouble," wrote Pike some months later. "He is drunk and riotous much of the time, and I have been several times on board his vessel to quell insubordination. I have removed from his ship eleven of his crew, including the second, third and fourth mates. This was done because I considered it requisite for the safety of the ship." When Pike demanded that Hazard pay the men the three months' extra wages prescribed by law, he refused. Instead, he was "most abusive and threatens to knock out my brains, of which I have no fear".

Pike was having similar trouble with Captain John Pierce of the barque *Annie Ann*,[3] which had arrived at Mauritius about the same time. "Something radically wrong," concluded Pike after visiting the ship, where he found the crew confined. He arranged to hear their complaints at his office, but while he was doing so, Pierce and Hazard tried to frighten him and the seamen by creating a rumpus outside. They continued kicking the consul's door, trying to break in, but failed to deter Pike.

"I think Captain Pierce is the most brutal man I ever met with," the cook, Henry Williams, told the consul, recalling that while the *Annie Ann* was at Seychelles the captain had accused him of using too much water and wood. As a result he was put in irons for six days and fed only bread and water. On another occasion Pierce threatened to knock his brains out, and almost achieved it by "thumping my head on the shifting board till my senses almost left me and I felt the effects many months afterwards". Others related similar acts of brutality.[4] The ship, partly owned by Pierce, was making its first voyage as a whaler, and it seemed Pierce intended that it should also be its last. When off Denis island the *Annie Ann* had hit a rock, after which Pierce announced that he was going "to make a clean job of the accident ... and make the underwriters pay". In this he succeeded. The ship was duly condemned at Mauritius, and sold by auction, while Pierce shipped home nearly 500 barrels of sperm oil, estimated by Pike to be worth $20,000. Pierce told the crew he did not want them any more; that he was going to the Sandwich Islands (Hawaii), and not returning to the United States.

The affair of Pierce and Hazard was picked up by the Mauritius Press. One editorial writer suggested that the United States should give its consuls more authority in such cases, "for we like to suppose that there is as much regard for human life in the United States as in England". American consuls in places such as Mauritius and Seychelles were relatively powerless to deal with those masters who evaded their responsibilities. Pierce's case may have been exceptional, but it was not unusual for captains to get their ship condemned so that they could discharge the crew, often without paying the wages laid down by law, and sell the oil locally or ship it back to the United States. This made it difficult for the crew to claim their share in the proceeds of the sale.

Pike was not a man to give in easily. He held on to the *Pioneer* ship's papers and eventually, after ten months' delay, Hazard had to sail back to Boston without them.[5] Pike also succeeded by threat of some kind to have three months' extra wages, amounting to $1,680 in all, paid to twenty-eight seamen of the *Annie Ann*. The crews of both ships were repatriated to the United States, presumably at government expense.[6]

Pike also wrote to Washington, suggesting ways of ending abuses by whaling captains.[7] He pressed particularly for checks on how captains disposed of oil in foreign ports, suggesting that no part of it should be sold without the permission of the mates and boatsteerers. Liberty should be given to crews at least once every six months, and there should be a proper accounting of the quantity and price of clothing supplied to the crew to prevent their being cheated.

Incidents such as those involving Hazard and Pierce focussed attention not only on deteriorating relations between masters and crews, but also on rifts between whaleships and local traders. Ships would sometimes sail without paying for supplies; and seamen who deserted and found themselves destitute in a foreign port might turn to robbery or worse. There were, of course, counter complaints by whaling captains, who pointed to frequent cheating and extortion by port authorities and traders.

Desertion was probably the biggest problem facing whalers.[8] Although local authorities usually cooperated in returning deserters, there was no law to enforce this, and in the absence of a treaty between Britain and the United States a consul was virtually powerless to punish any offence, no matter how serious. George Fairfield (US Consul, Mauritius, 1856-62) complained that it was impossible to discipline a ship's crew unless he had his own prison. He referred to one occasion when men were brought in after burning an American ship at sea, and he had to release them.

Reports of deteriorating relations at Seychelles, which had been without a consul for over a year (Atwater having left in October 1870), prompted Pike to accept an invitation to sail to the Dependency with Governor Gordon, "to test the truth with personal observation". Pike, whose visit to Seychelles has been described in a previous chapter, found that Franklyn had not only banned whaling crews from coming ashore, but had stopped ships from purchasing fresh provisions except for cash (formerly they had been allowed to barter with salt, pork, flour, and tobacco). The Civil Commissioner had also forbidden the landing of whaleships' stores, arguing that as there was no bonded warehouse on the island such action was illegal. Thanks to Gordon's intervention, the restrictions were lifted, while Pike, in turn, gave an undertaking that the United States would honour all expenses incurred as a result of wrecks and distressed seamen. He was later to suggest to Washington that it would be advisable to appoint a vice-consul at Mahé as soon as possible.

In her diary Harriet Allen, who had returned to Mahé in February 1871, only hints at bad feelings among the whalemen. Referring to the New Bedford barque *Hecla*, which had been wrecked on Bird island the previous December, she wrote: "We get the idea they were well fleeced. The crew were charged for use of the island ... [they were] unfortunately wrecked on." The *Hecla* was a total loss. Only twenty-eight of its 530 barrels of sperm oil (worth about $75,000) were saved. Two other whaleships, the *Herald* and the *Orray Taft*, brought the crew to Mahé, and, in the absence of a consul, Franklyn arranged to have them shipped to Mauritius. Pike found most of the men suffering from dysentery and ophthalmia, "the latter a very common complaint of seamen in our Whale ships in this ocean".

Harriet stayed three weeks at Mahé. "We are pleasantly situated in this little cottage between the house formerly occupied by Mr Atwater and the entrance to Government House," she wrote. She was not feeling well, but there were compensations. "I have flowers and fruit sent to me every day by different persons ... I enjoy sitting here in the house, windows and doors all open, the prospect from every side very pretty." She was soon to be up and about again, and she and Nellie spent a day with the Franklyns.

There were other visits. "Nellie and I went shopping," Harriet wrote on 14 February. "Called at Dr Brooks. Mrs Vaudin was there." At the end of their visit Dr Brooks saw the two ladies home "as there are 'sailors' about" and "Mrs B. dares not stir alone".

Nellie, who had made friends with the Civil Chaplain's daughter, Anna Vaudin, attended school with her for two weeks. She also visited, with her brother, Henry, the convent school "to see the nuns and the little girls". When she left Mahé Mrs Franklyn gave her a pair of doves, and another friend, Auguste App, presented her with two pigeons, one of which escaped before she got it on board.

All that year the *Merlin* roamed the Indian Ocean. They sighted and sometimes caught sperm whales. As the huge creatures were brought alongside to be "cut in", 10-year-old Nellie would frequently sit in one of the boats to watch the butchery. In July they were again at Mahé. They also visited Bird island several times ("We found all our letters," announced Nellie triumphantly on one occasion), and called at Assumption and Cosmoledo. At the latter the *Merlin* was nearly wrecked. Some of the islands had only a few fishermen, but they could usually get water, turtles, or birds' eggs. Aldabra was also a favourite place to call. Two years earlier, Harriet had described it thus: "The lagoon is a lovely place, especially in the misty light of early evening ... The still water, the many islands, the little bays, capes and byways, the deep-dark shadows ... the only sounds the plashing of our oars and the voices of the sea-birds disturbed in their quiet settlements."

They gammed several other whalers, including, Nellie tells us, the *Annie Ann.* "Captain and Mrs Pierce and little Willie [their son] came on board early in the afternoon ... Mrs Pierce and mother were school girls together. Willie is three years' old, but he gave me a description of catching a whale. We had a very nice time". Harriet had insisted at the start of the voyage on giving the children several hours' tuition every day, much to Henry's disgust. By now he had graduated from cabin boy to taking his turn at the wheel, and was spending long hours at the masthead on the look out for whales.

The *Merlin* stayed for several days at Anjouan, taking on supplies. Here Harriet had friends, including members of the ruling family. The island had just recovered from a cholera outbreak; many slaves had died, and families which could had fled to the countryside. A week after their arrival, the Allens spent Sunday at the summer house of Prince Muhammed. "It was very pleasant to sit there on the verandah and look at the mountains, trees and the sea," wrote Harriet, who however was upset to see two white women as slaves. "Both look half sick and weary of life, and as soon as we were alone gave me to understand that they were disgusted with Johanna." Nellie observed that Carima and Camilla did not join them for dinner. She found the meal rather amusing. "We had soup in a washbowl, and silver forks with jackknives to eat with." After the meal they returned to town to meet the mother of one of Harriet's friends.

Several Anjouanais visited the ship, including, according to Nellie, the son of one of the richest men of the island. He was accompanied on board by six attendants. Nellie shook his hand, and offered him refreshment, but all he would take was bread, water, and sugar. This was on account of his religion, explained Nellie. Prince Muhammed and the captain of the Comoro troops also paid visits, and gifts were exchanged.

Nellie tried to get a mate for her dove, without success. "I engaged twelve men to get me one, and they all said tomorrow," she complained, as the *Merlin* set sail again.[9]

While the Comoros were the most westerly islands (other than Zanzibar) visited by American whalers in the western Indian Ocean, Diego Garcia,[10] almost 2,000 miles away, marked the eastern extremity of their whaling operations. This distant atoll, part of the Chagos archipelago, was administered by Mauritius as a dependency, but many Seychellois lived and worked there as managers and labourers in the Chagos copra industry.

Arriving there for the first time on 7 February 1870, Harriet Allen was surprised to find so many people. "When we landed at sunset [at Pointe Marianne], there seemed to be a multitude of ladies, gentlemen and children to greet us – all in holiday attire. They welcomed us warmly and escorted us to a very picturesque house, where we were all seated upon the large verandah." This was the home of Mr Bonnier, where the Allens would stay while repairs were carried out on the ship. Bonnier was head of the Pointe Marianne settlement. He was about 50 and twice married, his second wife coming from Bourbon, and much younger.

Also present were the chief and deputy of the East Point settlement, Messrs Spurs[11] and Hodoul. Together with the administrator and his family at Minni Minni – the settlement directly across the lagoon from Pointe Marianne – they formed the white population of the island. Harriet was told that there were also about five hundred Blacks, not including children, some of whom she saw from the veranda, "passing to and fro in their Sunday dress". Conversation was slow, at first, as Spurs had to act as interpreter. But Harriet found that the Bonniers knew many English words, and with the little French she and husband had, "we got on finely". Later the guests were ushered into the house to the accompaniment of music from a large hand organ, "a remarkable looking coloured individual performing the part of musician, and keeping energetic time with his foot".

Always the keen observer, Harriet has left a detailed description of the Bonniers' home. "The room was oblong in shape, large and high," she wrote. "In the centre was a large oblong table, covered with books such as *History of Rome*,

128

History of the Crusades, Molière's *Dramatic Works*, periodicals, illustrated papers, English and French alike. Over this table was a compass, from which hung a large globe lamp. There are six doors. Two open upon the verandah, two opposite into the dining room and one at either end into sleeping apartments. [The Allens were to be accommodated in a separate pavilion near the house.] Between the doors leading to the verandah is a comfortable sofa in chintz, over which is a mirror and a small portrait of the first wife. Opposite is an oval window without glass — in which was a small group of statuary and a few instruments. Over the window is a portrait of Mr Bonnier's father. Chairs are placed under the window." Other pictures in the room included, above a wooden settee, "the Derby race (the end). On the opposite side of the room is a corresponding settee, over which is a picture of the commencement of the race".

After some time the table was moved aside and dancing began. There then followed a break for dinner. "The table was brilliantly lighted," noted Harriet, who appreciated the breeze from the large fan, or punkah. After dinner more dancing, which continued late into the evening. Spurs and Hodoul then took their leave and the Allens were escorted to their room. Apart from the mosquitoes, they spent a comfortable night.

Mr Bonnier was a Breton who was, so Harriet was informed, "a warm friend" of the Emperor. He did not like Victor Hugo or the Radicals; he believed in progress and education, but "not a Republic for France", a country he had not seen for twenty-four years. One afternoon Harriet was permitted to share in some intimate disclosures by Mrs Bonnier and Antoinette, 15-year-old daughter of the first wife. "Madame told me today that 'Mr Hodoul loves Antoinette' and has asked for her hand," wrote Harriet. "Antoinette who was sitting by, looked up from her tatting [which Harriet had taught her], smiled and said 'But I do not love him'. Madame then explained that he was 'very good', 'good family', but 'not education'. 'Mr Bonnier does not like'."

When the conversation turned to Spurs, Antoinette remarked: "He has no fault." With this Harriet agreed. "From all I have seen of him, I have formed a similar opinion." During their stay Mr Maugy, administrator of Minni Minni, came over on a visit. Harriet learned that he had lived for seventeen years on Diego Garcia, while most people seemed to have been there for two to three years only. The Allens later visited Minni Minni,where Nellie was induced to dance and made "a good beginning", but Henry failed to muster enough courage to try. Before they left, the Allens entertained on board all the white inhabitants. The *Merlin* arrived back at New Bedford on 3 April 1872, Harriet had been away for almost four years. The following year David Allen went back to the Indian Ocean, in the *Sea Queen*, of Westport. But for Harriet, the life of a wanderer was over.

During the year of the *Merlin*'s return sixty-seven ships cleared New England ports for whaling grounds around the world (three only for the Indian Ocean), compared with a yearly average of 110 during the 1860s. Although there would be brief bouts of recovery,[12] the American whaling industry was in terminal decline. Petroleum, coal gas, and electricity were gradually replacing whale oil as the main fuel for artificial lighting.

The marketing of a harpoon cannon in 1868[13] gave a fillip to the industry by enabling whalers to go after larger and faster species such as finbacks and blue whales. "The whaling fleet is gradually increasing in this ocean," reported Atwater in 1870. Equally optimistic was his successor, Thomas Prentice, who reported that twelve American whaling ships had called at Mahé during the year 1873-74. He assured Washington that there was still an "abundance of whales". However, four years later he was referring to a falling off in the take, and he warned that "the most experienced among the whaling masters, some of whom have been on these grounds for many years, think that the thing is being slightly overdone". Prentice suggested that the whalers should carry articles to barter, such as ironmongery, soft goods, prints and white shirtings, and boots and shoes.[14]

This proposal came too late. From 1879 onwards the number of American whalers calling at Mahé dropped to single figures. Evelyn Mussey, who succeeded Prentice, reported the arrival of only one whaler in 1880 and the same in 1881, with two the following year. He considered the area had been overfished, and that any whalers coming to the Indian Ocean soon left for the Atlantic.

Although Prentice had been surprised to find that none of

the whaling ships were owned by Seychellois — striking proof, he thought, of their lack of energy and enterprise — Atwater had mentioned one merchant ship, condemned and sold at Mahé, that was operating as a whaler. "Should it prove a success other vessels will be fitted out," he predicted. "There is no doubt but that vessels can be manned and provisioned from this port a great deal cheaper than whaling vessels at the States, as native seamen do not command as high wages, and require only rice and salt fish for their food."

This example of local enterprise seems to have continued, off and on, for some years, ironically, at a time when whaling was in decline. The American barque *Mermaid*, when near Denis island on 20 June 1888, reported having "gammed bark *Diamantina* of and from Mahé". The *Diamantina* had been out for a month, but as yet had taken no oil. Five years earlier, on 2 June 1883, the same vessel is recorded as having put in to Mahé with 140 barrels of oil. It sailed again "for Johanna and whaling" on 1 July.[15] The master of the *Diamantina* was Captain Church, almost certainly the same Captain Church, formerly of the New Bedford whaler *Laetitia*, who settled in Seychelles about 1879. After several years trading and whaling he became harbour pilot in 1890, retiring three years later.[16]

With the disappearance of the American whalers, the post of US consul at Seychelles was abolished on 30 June 1887. Marianne North, who met the American consul in 1883, found him to be "a queer, wooden old bachelor, who was allowed £300 a year by the United States for doing nothing". He had one virtue, however: he was the only man on Mahé who did not drink.

10

Venn's Town
1875-1895

English will eventually be the spoken
language of the people here.
Charles Salmon, Chief Civil Commissioner, 1879

The Reverend William Chancellor of the Church Missionary
Society had reason to be disappointed. Arriving with his wife,
Katie, at Mahé in April 1875 to open an industrial school for
African children, he found that the children he was supposed
to teach had already been farmed out as cheap labour to
various plantation owners.

He thought it was a "disgrace to the British government"
that the children and their elders should be treated in this way
after being rescued by British warships from Arab slave dhows.
"What with curtailed wages, stinted rations, insufficient
clothing, bad houses, an excess of work and maltreatment, the
African has been compelled to lie, to steal, to attempt murder
and to run away from his hard task master," he reported.
Fortunately the Chief Civil Commissioner, Charles Salmon,
who was both Irish and a Roman Catholic, supported the idea
of an industrial school, and had shown the missionary "a
greater willingness to cooperate ... than any of his Protestant
predecessors". He assured Chancellor that he would transfer
African children into his care whenever he could, particularly
if there was obvious maltreatment.

Salmon valued the Africans' potential as workers — he
would have liked 100,000 of them in the Dependency — and
he had drawn up new regulations covering their housing,
rations, wages, and clothes. "Thank God, we have a
Commissioner who will stand by the poor persecuted African,"

132

commented Chancellor, although he was later to conclude that Salmon had been motivated by political considerations.

After four months in Seychelles, Chancellor was able to inform London that he had eighteen pupils, accommodated in a small schoolhouse he had constructed near St Paul's Church in Victoria. He hoped to add to this number when more liberated Africans arrived in Seychelles, and was keen to show that they would be well looked after. "It behoves us to seek to work in good earnest as the Captains will not hand over their cargos [sic] to those who will not guarantee to maintain them," he wrote. Unfortunately the number of slaves being freed by the Navy had dropped dramatically, and Chancellor knew that a cruiser would not sail to Seychelles just to land half a dozen or so.

To the Church of England, with only 1,000 adherents out of a population of 9,000 on Mahé, the liberated Africans represented a further chance to increase its flock. Although Chancellor remained convinced that "Rome is doing her best to draw these poor ignorant creatures into the meshes of her net", the Catholic mission schools do not seem to have actively sought out the young liberated Africans. Chancellor, who had previously served in Mombasa, hoped that by speaking to the Africans in Swahili he would win them over to his Church. "These poor creatures still retain their own language when conversing together and are delighted to hear a white man address them with *Jambo, uhaligani*," he noted. But he acknowledged that Swahili was dying out. "Their children do not understand it, and speak the 'patois' of Seychelles. Even the parents prefer speaking the Creole. In a very short time the African dialect will be both unintelligible and useless to the Africans residing here".

Physically, Chancellor was an impressive figure. He was tall and robust, with a military bearing that his luxuriant whiskers and long black beard enhanced, as did the pith helmet he invariably wore. Here was a militant pastor ready to do battle, a man of the same mould as the priest Des Avanchers. He expected no favours from the Board of Civil Commissioners (BCC) — "men without any principles, all but one are Romanists" was how he described them — and so he kept his "guns well run out, pointed and charged". He was proud of the fact that he had been four years in the tropics without a day's illness. His advice was to eat good food, drink wine (claret was best), have good mosquito nets, go to bed early and rise early. It was also important to pay the greatest attention to the bowels. "Never let a day pass, if possible, without evacuating them. I am no smoker but when ever I suffer from constipation I take a cigar and it has the desired effect nearly always," he informed the CMS Secretary in London.

Although Salmon was rounding up African children for him, Chancellor went out himself to search for them. This usually meant going round the coast in the mission's boat, the *Hope*. It was tedious work, particularly when they were unable to use the sail. "Could hardly pull for the heat," he wrote, after an expedition to Pointe au Sel, where he spent two nights camped on the beach. Particularly difficult had been negotiating the narrow channel between Point Larue and South-East island. "Had to beach at midday, and lunched on hard boiled eggs, salt fish and manioc," after which he and his crew of one man and two boys "had to pull another nine miles after Point Larry [sic]". They arrived at Pointe au Sel at about 3 pm, where he pitched his tent, boiled a kettle, and bought a chicken for dinner. At 7 pm several people came to the beach to join in prayers.

The next morning, a Sunday, he rang a bell to announce a church service, which was attended by about twenty people, including six communicants. He baptised a boy of three, a liberated African whose master promised to give him to Chancellor. He also conversed in Swahili with other Africans, one of whom entrusted her two little girls to Chancellor just before he left the next morning to return to Victoria. As the tide was low the boat kept bumping on the reef. "All hands turned out to shove", and eventually they reached deeper water, but not before the missionary had gone up to his waist in water.

On the way Chancellor had to call at Cerf island to make arrangements for a funeral. There was a heavy swell and a lot of screaming by the children before the boat eventually reached Victoria. After a quick lunch and change of clothes, Chancellor returned to conduct the funeral. On the crossing back to Victoria the boat kept sticking on the reef, and Chancellor had to take a turn at rowing. By then it was quite dark, and it was after 9 before the missionary reached home.

Salmon had earmarked a site in the mountains of Forêt Noire for the industrial school. Called Capucins on account of its many Capuchin trees, it had for Chancellor the advantage of being a good distance "from sailors and the loose characters of Port Victoria". It also appeared a suitable place for growing coffee. In October the Governor, Sir Arthur Phayre, visited the Seychelles (following the example of his predecessor, Gordon). He inspected the site for the CMS school and was briefed by Chancellor on how the children were to be taught useful trades, including agriculture. "The soil here, I believe, is capable of producing almost every plant indigenous to the tropics," he told Phayre, who subsequently authorised the leasing of the site at a nominal rent for a period of ten years, with the possibility of renewal.

By now Chancellor had forty children at the school in town, with a matron and her husband to assist him, in addition to several other adults. "We are very careful not to admit the Creoles, knowing that the mission is for Africans only," he assured the CMS. Among the most vocal critics of the industrial school was the planter and Unofficial member of the Board of Civil Commissioners, LeMarchand. A "perfect brute" was Chancellor's description of his antagonist, after hearing from the American consul how LeMarchand – who sneeringly referred to the school as "the university" – had little boys serve naked at table. "This man cannot get a single free man to work for him," wrote Chancellor. "All his hands are appropriated Africans." Although the planters argued that it was a waste of time and money to attempt to teach Africans, Chancellor considered that the real reason was that they feared the Africans, if educated, would become their masters.

In March 1876, almost a year after the Chancellors' arrival, construction work at the Capucins site had progressed sufficiently for the children to move up the mountain to their new home. They started early in the morning, before the sun was up. "The time fixed for leaving was 5 am," reported Chancellor, "but at half-past four they passed my house, talking at the top of their voices. I immediately got up, and having dressed, quickly followed them, but did not catch them up until they had ascended the worst part of the mountain." There was still a long way to go, however, and the smaller children were tiring. One little boy, losing his balance, "returned the way he came, head over heels". Luckily he was unhurt, and the ascent continued until the summit was reached.

"Unfortunately for the poor children this was not the only hill to be mounted. There were two others to be overcome, and when they saw these steep ascents in the distance they began to despair of ever reaching the other side." So Chancellor called a halt until everyone's spirits had revived. Soon afterwards he again found many of the little ones lagging behind, and he had to carry one exhausted girl on his back. As they pushed on through the forest a party of prisoners on their way to work passed them, and each took a child on his shoulders. In this way the march quickened, so that they arrived at the school half an hour before the matron and her husband. All were delighted with their new home; it was, they said, as if their old school had been transported to the top of the mountain. Chancellor named the settlement Venn's Town, after the former CMS general secretary Henry Venn.[1]

Over the next fifteen months work continued on completing the settlement, an arduous task as much of the material had to be brought up from Victoria. The houses and classrooms were constructed of timber, with stone foundations. Fire was used to break the rocks, and coral was brought from the beach to make mortar. Palm fronds were used for the roofs. One of Chancellor's sketches of Venn's Town, which was published in the *Church Missionary Gleaner*, shows that the mission buildings were grouped round rows of recently planted trees, presumably the first stage in the creation of the avenue of stately *sang-dragons* that today is a prominent feature of the mission site.

The day at Venn's Town started just before dawn, when the children put their blankets out to air and began sweeping their dormitories. They then went to bathe in the river. This was followed by prayers, after which they attended the clinic to get their medicine, usually castor oil or Epsom salts. "Some suffer from ulcers," reported Chancellor, "and I am sorry to say many form the habit the children have here of eating earth, dry rice, etc." Breakfast was at 10.30, after which the children marched off to lessons, each carrying "a plateful of good Bengal rice and a vegetable called zamberique" for their lunch. Then more hymn singing and prayers, before the resumption

136

of lessons and an hour's recreation. There was more bathing in the river at 4 pm, after which the premises were thoroughly cleaned before dinner at 5.30. The day ended with prayers and bed at 7 pm. "The children are happy and contented," wrote Chancellor. "I trust, with God's blessing, [they] will in time be brought to know and love the truth as it is in Jesus".

Chancellor admitted that the curriculum at Venn's Town was confined to teaching the three R's, "and of course God's blessed Word, which I am thankful to say they are not backward in". It was therefore little different from the other primary schools in Seychelles, which followed a curriculum well adapted to the needs of the country, according to Salmon, who considered that the children were "learning only what they were competent to learn: to dress decently, to behave modestly, to perform household duties, to read their family prayers and to bring up their children outside of vice". If this was not education, he asked, then what was.

At first Chancellor and his wife were the only teachers at the mission. Their attempts to recruit from Mauritius had not been successful. Chancellor concluded that the people there were too much under French influence, adding with the self-assurance of a Victorian gentleman: "We require a thorough Englishman ... [imbued] with the superiority of the Anglo-Saxon race." As no Englishman was immediately forthcoming, it was a West Indian, Robert Pickwood, who joined the mission in April 1877 as superintendent of manual labour. Pickwood, formerly a goldsmith, had arrived at Seychelles as a sailor and had then served for a time as a policeman. Although a worthy man (he was later ordained as a minister), he lacked the necessary experience to teach useful trades to the boys, a task which in any case he could have hardly fulfilled as Chancellor, now acting Civil Chaplain, found he had to spend most of his time in the town.

Acknowledging his debt to Pickwood, imperfectly educated and trained though he might be, Chancellor said he deserved support and sympathy, as generally "coloured people and coloured children will not receive orders from coloured masters". Pickwood was certainly active. He spoke Creole as well as English and French, and he preached not only at Venn's Town (where many parents joined their children for the services) but also at Pointe au Sel, walking there across rough terrain, a distance of from eight to ten miles. He also visited the Anglican congregations at Port Glaud and Anse à la Mouche.

In November 1878, an English lay preacher, Henry Morris Warry, and his wife arrived to take charge of the school. Warry had previously been a blacksmith in Somerset, and his ambition was to be ordained as a minister. He seems to have had little interest in teaching manual skills to the Venn's Town boys. Marianne North, who stayed three weeks at the mission, dismissed Warry as one who "fancied he had a 'call', and came out to be cured of the idea". Warry was certainly observant of wrongdoing, seeing much sin all around him. If a serving woman washed her clothes on Sunday it greatly grieved him, as did "the poor Mozambiques ... beating their tom toms ... across the valley nearly all day". Miss North thought that under Warry the children spent too much time singing psalms, and "did not puzzle their brains with too much learning".

A more charitable view was taken by Fanny Barkly, wife of the Chief Civil Commissioner Arthur Cecil Barkly, who arrived in Seychelles in 1882. She stayed two weeks at Venn's Town. She recorded that the liberated Africans, who all seemed very happy, were taught to read, write, work, sing, "and many other accomplishments". Many of the girls went into service when old enough, "but all were obliged to wear a badge round their necks, to show that they had originally been slaves, and to produce them when required, at the instance of a judge". In addition to working in the coffee plantations and gardens, they did needlework, and made manioc cakes and manioc flour. "They also threaded necklaces out of small shells, in a pretty pattern, to sell in town, or to the passengers on board the mail steamers". Fanny Barkly felt sorry for Mrs Warry, who "seemed to feel very isolated, living almost always so far away, up in the skies".

Chancellor had already been criticised in a report by the Inspector of Africans for doing nothing to instruct his boy pupils in manual trades or agriculture. One reason was that Chancellor thought many of the children were too young for such activities, but he was warned that the mission would fail if he did not find the right instructors. There was a dearth of skilled tradesmen in Seychelles, the Inspector pointed out. "There is not a shoe maker in the archipelago. A good cooper

138

is not to be found, nor a good blacksmith, nor a tailor, nor even a good carpenter but very rarely. One of the civilising wants of this country is some real good tradesmen or handi-craftsmen." The religious instruction at Venn's Town was no doubt excellent, although, added the Inspector, "I doubt the expediency of teaching the boys English, a language not in use among any class of the population of these islands".

During Warry's tenure as head of Venn's Town there were recurring complaints by children and parents, and several instances of boys and girls absconding. Warry found the children rather dull, and he wondered how many believed the prayers and responses he taught them, and which they so readily recited. "When we consider how these poor children have been brought up in their own homes with every kind of vice and wickedness before their eyes it is no great wonder that we see it thriving itself in them," he commented after several of the older boys had gone to town, where they stole salt fish from Mrs Chancellor's kitchen. Warry's punishment was severe enough, two weeks on a diet of dry rice. Perhaps he wished he could punish delinquent parents the same way, although he would have been still happier if all the children had been orphans, so that "difficulties with the parents would be at an end".

Chancellor had at the beginning asked London to send French primers for use at the school, but Bishop Royston was able to convince him that everything of a French nature should be excluded. "It is considered that we are endeavouring to Anglicise as well as Christianise our little waifs," Chancellor admitted. The question of which language to use in school was — and still is in Seychelles — a subject of some debate, encouraged by the vacillating attitude adopted by successive governments. From the start the mission schools had been left to adopt whatever language they chose. In the Roman Catholic schools this was naturally French, staffed as they were by French-speaking nuns and, at the St Louis College, by the Brothers of Christian Schools — until these lay teachers decided in 1875 to quit after financial disagreements with the mission.

A report by two school inspectors sent from Mauritius[2] in 1878 had advocated that teaching in English be made compulsory, but this was rejected by the Seychelles authorities on the grounds that "it would cause to be thrown aside almost the only education within reach and of present practical use to the people of these islands". In the Anglican schools there was more incentive to use English, although here too French only gradually gave room to English in church and classroom. Meanwhile, the mass of the people, without learning of any kind, were developing their own, distinctive language, Creole, which would eventually pervade all levels of society.

The influence that France could exert in Seychelles through the Roman Church was not lost on Paris. "Over and above the moral and religious aspects, one can say that the mission [since 1880 an apostolic vicariate] has helped considerably in upholding and developing among the population of these islands feelings of friendship towards France, and visitors who arrive here might think themselves on French soil." So wrote the French consular agent in Seychelles, Félix Cheyron, when he urged Paris to support Bishop Mouard, who had succeeded Father Ignatius Galfione as Apostolic Vicar.[3] Cheyron stressed that the mission was short of funds, and that the orphanage run by the nuns was a constant drain on its resources.[4]

That the state should contribute towards the costs of church and charity schools was a principle that had been accepted in England since 1833, and it was subsequently extended to Britain's colonies. Mauritius, for example, which spent about £10,000 on education in 1860, had thirty-one grant-aided as well as twenty-four government schools. However, there was no corresponding assistance to Seychelles until 1867, when a grant of £93 12s, was made to the four Anglican schools. The Roman Catholic schools had to wait until 1871 to get their grant of £41 16s, shared between the nuns and brothers. The following year – Seychelles by then being more or less financially free from Mauritius – the grant to the Roman Catholic mission was increased to £150. The Anglicans received £130, which was a more than generous allocation if calculated on the respective number of pupils.

These grants were approved and allocated by a Board of Education, composed of all the BCC members. Together with the Inspector of Schools, the Board's duty was to supervise education generally in the Dependency, but for the most part it concerned itself only with the grants. These were given to non-profit-making primary schools which could show they had

140

qualified staff, were open to all irrespective of race or religion, and did not offer religious instruction to any particular pupil without the parents' consent. This last, "conscience clause" was to bring protests from Bishop Royston of the Church of England, but his representations were rejected. The Colonial Office also turned down Bishop Mouard, who had applied for more funding, claiming the Anglicans were always favoured.

The Anglican schools were certainly better off. They received more generous salaries for their clergy, they had closer liaison with Mauritius as the Bishop there exercised authority in Seychelles, and they had mostly trained teachers, resulting in a higher grant per child. Even so, although the overall grant-in-aid rose from R.4,000 (four thousand rupees) in 1873 to R.8,000 in 1891, the sum failed to keep up with an increasing number of schools and pupils. As a result there developed among all schools a feeling of having been betrayed by the government. Chancellor had been anxious to secure a government grant for Venn's Town, but considered that the religious bias of the "Popish planters" on the Board of Education would prove an obstacle. However the delay that occurred before a grant was approved seems to have been less the result of Catholic machinations than the absence of a qualified teacher. "It is necessary ... that I should pass an examination for a teacher's certificate," Warry was to inform London. Eventually a small grant was given to Venn's Town.

The regulations concerning grants-in-aid were redrafted in 1885 by the Inspector of Schools, James Brodie,[5] but there were still loopholes for dispute. In one instance Chancellor's successor as Civil Chaplain, the Rev. John Francis Grandjean,[6] challenged the eligibility of St Louis College and St Joseph Convent School to receive grants-in-aid, arguing that the two schools had a large number of paying pupils. The Roman Catholic mission replied that many parents of white children in the *classe payante* were unable to pay the fees but their children were allowed to remain as otherwise the parents, out of pride, would have withdrawn them rather than let them mix with coloured children in the "free school".

Grandjean's argument consequently prevailed, and the proportion of the grant to the Roman Catholic schools was reduced, to the benefit of the Anglicans. Naturally, there was resentment. In this way disagreements were allowed to sour relations between the government and the Catholic mission.

"You have no idea of the disorder that exists in this Dependency," Chancellor had written in one of his letters to CMS headquarters. Similar sentiments had been expressed by Mauritius, which was viewing with concern the feuding that had been going on between Salmon and members of the Board of Civil Commissioners. Central figures in this skirmishing were the Seychelles Treasurer, George Barrow,[7] accused of neglect of duty, Dr Brooks, the Chief Medical Officer, previously thought of as "one of the most ... respectable inhabitants", District Judge Delapeyre, and Salmon himself, whom the Colonial Office considered not discreet enough in dealing with officials' complaints and who lacked "the gifts requisite to make a governor". In the end Barrow was sacked, Salmon was transferred to the small Caribbean island of Nevis, the Judge was returned to Mauritius, and Brooks was offered a post away from Seychelles, which he refused. He held out for some time, but eventually he retired to concentrate on his business interests.

Salmon's departure was the signal for Havelock, Gordon's original nominee for the post, to return to Seychelles as Chief Civil Commissioner. He arrived at the end of 1879, and stayed for eight months, long enough to support a petition from the Board for greater powers. In his previous post of Administrator of the Caribbean island of St Lucia, Havelock had been subject only to supervision by the Windward Islands governor, an arrangement which he thought would be suitable for the Seychelles.

Further constitutional advance for Seychelles was being considered by the Colonial Office, impressed as it was by the flourishing state of the Seychelles economy, but there was little support for this from the Governor, Sir George Bowen, who complained that "this troublesome little dependency" already sent more official correspondence to Mauritius "than the great colonies of Victoria and New South Wales send to London". He repeated the view of his assistant *procureur-général*, Seychelles-born Virgil Naz, that Seychelles' progress was due not to the constitutional advances introduced in 1872 but to rising coconut production and increased labour provided by the liberated Africans.

Despite Bowen's misgivings, London agreed to give the

Dependency a greater say in ordering its own affairs. although Mauritius would continue to exercise a veto on matters of finance.[8] Later, the Secretary of State had to abandon one of his proposed reforms — obliging Mauritius judges to travel to Seychelles to try the most serious cases — after discovering that judges were "not easily driven to leave their easy chairs and comfortably arranged moderate quantum of daily work".

In October 1880 a former Mauritius police chief, Captain F. T. Blunt, took over as Chief Civil Commissioner. After inspecting the dilapidated government buildings in Victoria, Blunt called for a new prison, new courthouse, and a new police station, as well as improved pathways across the island to make communication easier. He told the Board of Civil Commissioners at a meeting in November that he "would raise all these points with the Governor during his next visit. "Captain Blunt is full of ideas," one Colonial Office scribe noted, adding: "I suppose he will have to be content with his paths for the present." But time had run out for Blunt; he died three months later. District Judge Henri Desmarais would normally have taken charge, but as he was embroiled in a scandal[9] involving another official's wife a disapproving Mauritius hastily sent Assistant Colonial Secretary Henry Cockburn Stewart to Seychelles. It was the fifth change of Chief Civil Commissioner in seven years. Stewart acted for only six months, but it served as a useful introduction to his subsequent service as Administrator of the islands from 1895 to 1899.

A firm believer in education, Stewart was shocked by the "deplorable ignorance" he found in Seychelles. While he praised the standard of teaching at the Convent girls' school, he found the two boys' schools in Victoria well below standard. Part of the trouble lay with the parents. "The great difficulty experienced by both missions is the utter want of any interest in their children's education," he noted. He also criticised the government for having done nothing for education except approve grants-in-aid, and he wondered whether visitors to Seychelles would realise it was a British colony, as English was hardly understood, never mind spoken. He recommended that government schools be established on the main islands, with compulsory primary education at least on Mahé. Stewart voiced his views at a Convent prize-giving, addressing his

143

audience with the easy assurance of one who would not have to put his proposals into practice. He sent copies of his speech to Mauritius and to the Colonial Office, and while the latter supported the idea of at least one government school and thought that the teaching of English should become a condition for receiving a government grant, Mauritius stressed that compulsory education would be acceptable only if Seychelles paid for it.

The price of progress was already concentrating the minds of many of the islands' planters, who found that taxes had increased with no apparent advantage to themselves. Instead there was a steep fall in the price of coconut oil and other staple produce, while widespread blight was affecting the coconut plantations. Ordinances for enlarging the powers of the Board of Civil Commissioners and the jurisdiction of the District Court were still in the drafting stage, but Stewart, on the point of returning to Mauritius, was letting it be known that he favoured Seychelles becoming a separate colony, a view also expressed by a visiting colonel of Royal Engineers, Charles Gordon.

The prospect of Seychelles going it alone was too much for a group of 413 inhabitants, who, on 24 June 1882, sent a petition to the British government asking for "a return to the complete state of dependence upon Mauritius which existed prior to the Constitution granted at the instance of Governor Sir Arthur Gordon in the year 1872". Describing themselves as "landed proprietors, members of the learned professions, merchants, planters, traders, and general inhabitants of the Seychelles", the signatories called for the abolition of the BCC and the appointment of an Unofficial member of Mauritius Legislative Council to represent Seychelles' interests.[10]

"Preposterous," expostulated Chief Civil Commissioner Arthur Barkly, as he forwarded the petition to Mauritius for onward transmission to London. Barkly, who had arrived in Seychelles at the beginning of the year, admitted that the signatories represented an important section of the property owners, but it was impossible that such an extraordinary petition could be granted, amounting as it did "to nothing less than a wholesale revolution of the existing order of things". He congratulated himself on having defused the situation by assuring the petitioners that Seychelles was not cutting loose

144

from Mauritius, and that the new laws being drafted would mean more savings, not extra expenditure. He pointed out that there had been a steady rise in revenue from 1872 to 1881, and that there were more schools than ever before. The Colonial Office concurred in denying both the petition and any idea that Seychelles might become a separate colony, although the Secretary of State, Lord Kimberley, had earlier observed that "if Seychelles becomes as important and prosperous as Mr Stewart anticipates, it may become desirable to cut it adrift from Mauritius".

Barkly's upbeat assessment of education in Seychelles was reinforced three years later after Bishop Mouard, on a visit to France, recruited five Marist brothers[11] to take charge of the ailing St Louis College, a move which quickly transformed the school, the number of pupils rising from seventy to 200. However, a government school had to wait until 1891. Such a school had been first mooted by Mylius, and it was always envisaged that by this means education's French connection would be broken. Barkly reported that a public meeting held in Victoria showed that "the majority of the educated and intelligent inhabitants" would like to be able to send their children to a school not under the direct control of any religious denomination.

Finance, as always, was the stumbling block, and it was not until 1888 that Brodie was asked to draft proposals for a government school. He recommended the appointment of a European headmaster, with a local assistant. In addition to the usual primary school subjects, "the rudiments of Latin and elementary geometry and algebra with trigonometry and mensuration" would be taught. There would be no fees for the first four standards, and a charge of 25 cents a month for other standards. Instruction would be in English, and no teacher in holy orders would be appointed.

Naturally the Roman Catholic mission saw the proposal as a Protestant school in disguise and reacted accordingly. Parents who sent their children there were threatened with excommunication, and Bishop Hudrisier,who had succeeded Mouard, appealed to the Governor to halt a school which would "destroy the salutary moral effects of religious education".

Two of the Unofficial members on the Board, Hodoul and

Jouanis, supported the Bishop, but the proposal was carried by five votes to two, and the Government Undenominational School eventually opened on 2 March 1891, with fifty-nine pupils on the roll.

In 1879 the Chancellors had been forced to return to England, after it was confirmed that Chancellor was suffering from a serious eye disease. "We are very grieved indeed to lose them," wrote Warry. Mrs Chancellor's "unwavering faith ... in God's word will I am sure have a very good effect upon the natives, she was and is very much beloved by them and had gained great influence over them by her gentle, loving manner."

Warry had to admit that numbers at Venn's Town had dropped considerably during the year of the Chancellors' departure, from sixty-six at the beginning of 1879 to thirty-five in 1880. Three girls had been married, but the others had simply absconded or been decoyed away by their parents. "The poor people have yet to learn the great privilege of having a Mission School, where their poor children may be fed, provided for and taught, and above all, brought into contact with that Word which alone is able to make them wise unto salvation." He regretted that he did not have the Chancellors' command of Creole and Swahili which "enabled them, combined with a true love for souls, to acquire and maintain great influence over the minds of the poor Africans". Inadequate as the Warrys seem to have been,[12] they remained at Venn's Town until 1885, when they were replaced by a former CMS lay worker from London, Edwin Luckock, and his wife. Pickwood had by then been ordained, and was in charge of the Anglican mission on Praslin.

In February and March 1888 Bishop Royston visited Seychelles and, with his wife and daughter, officiated at Easter services on Praslin. Pickwood conducted the service at the church at Grand' Anse, and Royston gave an address before a congregation of about 300. The bishop's daughter, Louisa, remarked on the strangeness of a church with a leafed roof; the little green lizards running up the wall also caught her eye. Another day they went by the boat *Hope* to Anse Consolation and Anse Marie Louise, on Praslin's south-east coast. At Consolation they visited the Anglican school, up on the hill, run by a blind catechist. Louisa was impressed by the beauty of the Seychelles islands, and by the way the people maintained their faith under difficult circumstances. She added: "Surely we ought to value more our [own] Christian up-bringing and Christian privileges in England".

Royston visited Venn's Town several times. If he was disappointed by the diminishing number of children, he did not show it. "The general results are encouraging and reward their [the Luckocks'] spiritual concern for their young African charges," he noted. However with fewer children to look after — in 1893 there were only twenty-five — the Luckocks moved to Bel Ombre. There they offered Bible classes, a night school, and a lending library, but the response was discouraging, and the following year they returned to England. The CMS issued a statement saying that over the past years the African Institution had become less needed and that it would be closed.[13] Although Luckock believed "the seed of the word of God had not been sown in vain", there seems little doubt that the school had failed in its original aim of teaching useful trades and skills to the young Africans of Seychelles.[14]

* *

In 1877 Abdullah Jaafar Moratham Shah, ex-Sultan of Perak, and three other Malay leaders were exiled to Seychelles. In choosing Seychelles Britain was following the example set by France, which under Napoleon had used the islands as a place of detention for troublesome political opponents. Britain was to continue this policy over the next eighty or so years. The last deportee was Archbishop Makarios of Cyprus,[15] who was exiled to Seychelles in 1956-57.

Unlike the Archbishop, ex-Sultan Abdullah was not a particularly imposing figure. He was short in stature, and at first he spoke no English. But with his shy, engaging manner he soon won the respect, in some cases the affection, of those among whom he was forced to reside. He and the three other detainees, accompanied by wives, children, and other family members, had arrived on 31 August 1877 in the British barque *Cotherstone*, sailing direct from Singapore. News of their arrival must have caused something of a stir. Seychelles had seen many strange visitors, but this was the first time it had been asked to play host to a deposed oriental prince and his entourage, numbering about thirty-eight persons. No-one

147

could know that the deposed Sultan and his companions were destined to remain in Seychelles for seventeen years.

Singapore had laid down a scale of allowances for the detainees. For Abdullah this was R.300 a month, considered by Salmon to be insufficient. The others were allocated smaller amounts, all to be paid on the first of the month. Singapore advised "that the Chiefs should be discouraged from requesting advances according to the habit of their countrymen". A European interpreter had been sent with the party, and Salmon requested two others from Mauritius. Salmon allowed Abdullah to keep three swords of honour (one was from Queen Victoria), but a two-edged sword and a *kris*, the traditional Malay dagger, were retained by the police.

At first there had been doubts in Mauritius about where the Malays should be confined. Félicité, a small island lying two miles north-east of La Digue, had been suggested, but in the end the decision was left to Salmon, who had been sent duplicate warrants allowing for detention on either Félicité or Mahé. Initially the whole party was put into a large house with separate pavilions at Union Vale, north of Victoria, but once suitable accommodation had been constructed on Félicité, two of the detainees, the former Mantri of Larut, Ibrahim bin Jaafar, and the Laxamanna (or chief judge) Mohamed Amin bin Abdul Wakafl, were sent there, while Abdullah and the Shahbander Kadek bin Mohamed remained on the main island. All the detainees were permitted to move about freely if accompanied by the interpreter or a guard, and the only other restriction was that they should be back in quarters by 8 pm.

Salmon's reason for splitting the group between Mahé and Félicité may have been the knowledge that Abdullah and the Mantri had been bitter enemies during the internal power struggle in Perak, which had sparked Britain's intervention in the Malay state. The Mantri and Laxamanna were not happy on Félicité island, but Salmon refused to let them come to Victoria, insisting that if all the detainees were to be together it would have to be on Félicité. He reported that some followers of the Laxamanna were disorderly and ill-behaved, and he was concerned over security. However Havelock, on taking over in 1879, decided otherwise. He considered the Mantri's complaints about a water shortage and the lack of medical assistance on Félicité justified his transferring the detainees to

Mahé, a move that was subsequently approved by Mauritius.

Traditionally British policy in Malaya had been to avoid involvement in the affairs of the native states but, in 1873, with dynastic rivalries and civil wars in several parts of the peninsula threatening the stability of the British possessions of Penang, Malacca, and Singapore (the Straits Settlements), this policy of non-interference was abandoned, and London agreed to British Residents being appointed to the Malay states.

In Perak there were two contenders for the sultanate, the ageing Raja Ismail, who had been named Sultan in controversial circumstances and was supported by the semi-independent Mantri of Larut, and Abdullah, who had been heir apparent and was regarded by many, including the British, as Sultan. The Resident appointed to Perak, James Birch, managed to upset both Abdullah and the Raja Ismail. He announced various administrative reforms which quickly united all factions in Perak against what was seen as a British take-over, and in November 1875 he was murdered while on an up-country tour.

British reaction was to send a brigade of infantry into the state, including a battalion of Gurkhas and a battery of mountain artillery. In a short, sharp campaign[16] the troops crushed resistance, but failed to catch the leaders of the uprising, notably Ismail and the Maharaja Lela, who had planned Birch's murder. Abdullah immediately professed friendship to the British, and cooperated with them in hunting the insurgents, but after the surrender of Ismail in March 1876 and the arrest of Lela, Abdullah and the Mantri of Larut were accused of complicity. Lela and six others were tried and hanged for murder, Ismail was exiled to Johore and Abdullah, with the Mantri and two other chiefs, the Laxamanna and Shahbander, were sent to Seychelles.

Throughout the long years of his detention in Seychelles Abdullah never wavered in claiming his innocence.[17] He frequently sent petitions to the British authorities, including the Queen, to have his case reconsidered, and he won the support of several Liberal MPs who tabled questions in Parliament over his detention. Reading the letters that he wrote to the Queen and the Secretary of State, one is struck by the apparent honesty of the ex-Sultan, who argued that he had been the victim of a plot by other Perak chiefs who resented

149

his having allowed the British to enter Perak. All Abdullah's approaches were rejected by London, but despite this he remained a model prisoner, living with his two (later three) wives, his mother, and his children. Gradually, as the years passed, he began to wear European clothes, but like the others he regularly performed the ritual ablutions and prayers of a Muslim. He learned to speak simple English and a little French; he received Malay newspapers from Singapore, and he smoked a lot. He was a frequent visitor at Government House. "He, with his three wives and suite, lived close to us, and the Sultan always came to our parties," noted Fanny Barkly. "We treated him with the greatest respect, and always found him very polite and good natured."

Abdullah had his allowance increased by R.100 (he was reported to be in debt to several traders), and he was allowed to pay visits to Mauritius in 1882 and 1885. Two years later, on the fiftieth anniversary of Queen Victoria's accession, Abdullah again sent a petition, asking that he should not be overlooked when pardons were granted to mark her jubilee. At the same time thirteen prominent persons in Mauritius called for his release. Some time later a similar petition was put forward, this time with 475 signatures. The new Administrator, Thomas Risely Griffith, gave it his backing, commenting that the former Sultan was "a universal favourite here, and I should personally be very happy to learn that it had been found practicable to comply in any measure with the prayer of the petitioners". Again the appeal was turned down, as was another by "the Planters, Merchants, Traders ... of the Seychelles islands".

Abdullah had earlier asked to be allowed to visit England, where his cause had been taken up by the MP for Canterbury, J. Henniker Heaton. He argued that Abdullah's guilt had never been proved, and said he had been "impressed by the freedom from anger evinced by the deposed ruler and his expressions of loyalty to the Queen".

The Mantri of Larut had already asked to be transferred to Singapore or Penang "for the consolation of his religion", and in March 1889 the Secretary of State announced that he would allow him to reside in Sarawak. However it was not until 16 May 1890 that the Mantri left Seychelles by mail steamer. Abdullah and the others refused to go. According to Heaton, Abdullah felt that by accepting the conditions of a transfer to

Sarawak he "would stultify the position he has always maintained of complete innocence of the charges upon which he was, as he says, unjustly convicted and banished from Perak". Others thought that Abdullah simply preferred to stay where he was rather than "exchange a place where he is free and happy for another where the only benefit is that people speak Malay".

The following year the Colonial Office repeated its offer, with Singapore as the place of residence, and again Abdullah refused, but in January 1891 the Mauritius colonial secretary reported that the former Sultan was being "worked upon" by his wives to accept. At the same time renewed pressure was being exerted in Parliament by several MPs. One pointed out that the Straits Settlement Chief Justice had expressed the view at the time of Abdullah's deportation that he was innocent.

In 1893 Abdullah finally consented to his transfer to Singapore. It was also agreed that, first, he could visit England, where he intended putting two of his sons, aged 12 and 14, into school. He left Seychelles in May 1894, accompanied by Henniker Heaton, and arrived in London the following month after a stop-over in Paris. There he was cordially received. He lunched with a group of MPs, had a meeting with the Secretary of State Lord Ripon, and went on a sight-seeing tour of London. The Colonial Office consented to his using the title of ex-Sultan Abdullah (a distinction that had earlier been refused) for, as one official commented, there was a general wish "to let bygones be bygones".

After Abdullah's return to Seychelles there was a further delay on account of the illness of the ex-Sultan's mother, but finally, on 16 February 1895, Abdullah and his family left Seychelles for good. The other detainees departed two months later. Abdullah and his family lived in Singapore until 1903, after which he was allowed to settle in Perak. He died there in 1922.

There was to be an unexpected sequel to Sultan Abdullah's stay in Seychelles, when a song, popular among the Seychellois and a favourite with Abdullah, was selected in 1957 as Malaysia's national anthem. The ex-Sultan had often heard the song *Rosalie* being played by a French band in Seychelles. His son, Raja Chulan, took the tune back with him to Perak, where it gained instant popularity. In 1888 it was hastily improvised as a sort of anthem during an official visit to London by the then acting Sultan of Perak. It was likewise popular all over Malaya under the name *Terang Bulan,* or *Bright Moon,* and was eventually chosen, with appropriate words, as the national anthem of the Malaysian Federation.[18]

11

Saving the Nut
1881-1896

Little islands are all large prisons.
Sir Richard Burton, *Wanderings in West Africa*

"I may mention that a well known and very gifted officer of
Her Majesty's Service, who lately visited Seychelles, has
elaborated a theory by which the island of Praslin is very
plausibly shown to have been the Garden of Eden, and the
Coco palm the very tree from which the knowledge of good
and evil was derived."

So wrote Mauritius Lieutenant-Governor Napier Broome[1]
to the Secretary of State for the Colonies, the Earl of
Kimberley, who was considering suggestions that the
government help preserve the coco de mer by buying land on
Praslin. The "gifted officer" was Lieutenant-Colonel Charles
George Gordon, and Napier Broome doubtless hoped that
Gordon's strange theory would prompt some learned society
to put up money to buy a substantial tract of the coco de mer
forest.

Although at first sight the coco de mer had appeared to the
French as no more than an interesting but useless curio, the
Seychelles settlers had soon found uses for the palm and its
double-lobe nut. The huge leaves provided thatch for their
houses and wall partitions, as well as weaving material for hats,
mats, baskets, and other articles. The shells of mature fruits
could be readily turned into water gourds, boat balers, or
measuring scoops, and there was also a steady demand for nuts
from Mauritius, India, Arabia and elsewhere. There were
some who warned against the indiscriminate cutting of the

coco de mer forests, but few thought seriously of the possible extinction of this remarkable palm.

Colonel Gordon's interest in the coco de mer had developed in correspondence with Sir Joseph Hooker, who, as professor of botany at Glasgow University, had been instrumental in having the Linnaean Society[2] adopt a resolution calling on the government to preserve the coco de mer palm. A letter from Swinburne Ward had been read at the society's meeting in March 1864, and like Harrison's warning over thirty years earlier, it pointed out that fire and the ruthless clearing of forest would before long render the coco de mer "as rare as it was supposed to be when picked up at sea by wandering mariners".

It was only during Salmon's administration, however, that a regulation was introduced in Seychelles requiring anyone possessing a nut or other part of the coco de mer palm to show how he had come by it. Later, Cockburn Stewart appointed a Conservator of Forests, Charles Button, who visited Praslin every month to ensure that coco de mer palms on Crown land were properly tended, and that all fallen nuts were carefully replanted.

Although the purpose of Gordon's mission to Seychelles in 1881 was to survey the islands' defences,[3] he had taken the opportunity to acquaint himself thoroughly with the coco de mer. He spent two days on Praslin[4] discussing the palm with Cockburn Stewart and Button, whom he described as "a first rate, clever fellow". Gordon undoubtedly approved the measures being taken to protect the palm, but he regretted that the "constant change of the governors of these isles requires continual reiteration of orders".

Gordon was already something of a hero in Britain, and anything he said was likely to attract attention. As a young engineer officer he had served with distinction in the Crimea War, and after his subsequent military exploits in China had been given the name 'Chinese' Gordon. It was the Sudan, however, with which his destiny was to be irrevocably linked. He had served there for five years, first as Governor of Equatoria and, from 1877 to 1879, as Governor-General in Khartoum, before resigning, disillusioned, and returning to England. More than a year later, as a favour to another officer, he accepted a rather humdrum posting to Mauritius. "Looking after the barracks repairs, and seeing that the drains were in order" is how he described his duties as Commander of Royal Engineers on the island. Happily, for this brilliant eccentric, the visit to Seychelles had provided him with a new and absorbing interest.

On his return to Mauritius, Gordon continued to badger Hooker and Sir W . T. Thiselton-Dyer, assistant director at Kew, about the dangers facing the palm, for he was not convinced that the government was doing everything it could to preserve "from final destruction a tree interesting in so many aspects to the whole civilised world". He sent to Kew and the South Kensington Museum samples of the palm and the nut, which he described as "a fruit which cannot fail to attract attention by anyone seeing it". He made copious notes, expounding his theory that the palm was the Tree of Knowledge and that Praslin was all that remained of the Garden of Eden.

In several manuscripts, written at different times and each with noticeable variations,[5] Gordon identified the four rivers mentioned in the Bible as flowing into the Garden of Eden as the Euphrates, Tigris, Nile, and the Jordan. Their courses were not as they are today; according to Gordon they all converged near the island of Socotra, and from there flowed southward to an area situated some hundred miles west of Seychelles. This was the District of Eden, "and the Garden was a spot selected Eastward in it". When the Flood came, all this land was submerged, only the tips of the mountains of Seychelles remaining.

The shape of the coco de mer nut fascinated Gordon. "I have already alluded to the temptation of Eve and surely if curiosity could be excited by any tree, it would be this," he wrote. He noted that the fruit "externally represents the thighs and belly", adding somewhat gratuitously that this was "the true seat of carnal desires".[6] He dismissed the obvious difficulty for Adam and Eve in partaking of such a fruit by suggesting that the coco de mer might have been different at that time. As for the other famous tree of the Garden of Eden, the Tree of Life, Gordon identified it with the breadfruit tree, although he must have been aware that this tree is not native to the Seychelles.

After Gordon's death his sister, Augusta, wrote to Thiselton-Dyer offering specimens of the coco de mer that he had given her. "The fruits are all real," she noted, "with the exception of one model which is the outer shell or husk. It contains the fruit: my brother had it made here and took the greatest pains to have it exact as to size and colour." Gordon had sketched a coco de mer palm as the centrepiece of a proposed coat of arms for Seychelles,[7] which he considered should be elevated to the status of a Crown colony. In due course the palm — without the snake Gordon had entwined round the trunk — and a giant tortoise appeared in the coat of arms approved for the Colony.

During his stay on Mahé Gordon visited the Chinese community in Victoria and spoke "to them as well as I could ... of God's indwelling. It was satisfactory, and they were pleased". Gordon was always happy when mixing with ordinary people, admitting that he hated society and "how society hates me". As he explained to his sister, "I never tell you the sort of life I lead, it is not worth it. It is simply the life I led at home, being asked out, and refusing when it is possible — when I go, getting humiliated, or being foolish". All this from the soldier who, a few years later, would almost single-handedly organise the defence of Khartoum, holding out for almost a year against the forces of the Mahdi[8] until his death on 26 January 1885.

Gordon's constant pressuring of officials about the coco de mer was to have an effect, not least in irritating those who felt that everything possible was being done to preserve the palm. Barkly, who had taken over from Cockburn Stewart, reported that the question of purchasing the land held by the elderly Scots seaman Campbell at Fond Ferdinand and Anse Marie Louise in south-east Praslin (the property was in fact owned by Campbell's Creole wife) would be considered by the Board of Civil Commissioners. He added that if the Board did not endorse the purchase it was because the palms there were not endangered.

He was later to agree with a statement by François Hodoul that while the palms should be protected there was little danger from people taking leaves to make straw hats. "It is a mistake to believe that the hearts of fully grown trees are cut down for [this] purpose," remarked Hodoul. "What is used ... is the centre leaf of small stunted trees shooting out in considerable numbers, on thickets under the large trees." Experience was to show, however, that it was precisely widespread and indiscriminate leaf cutting that stunted or destroyed the trees.

By March 1883 there was still no agreement to purchase the Campbell land. Campbell's widow did not want to leave a place where she had lived so long, and Barkly admitted that he did not have finance to buy the property. He pointed out that once Mrs Campbell died the land would be divided amongst the heirs, and it was likely their shares could be bought more cheaply.

The following year Barkly visited Praslin and reported that the coco de mer ravines were in good condition. He found Mrs Campbell's trees exceptionally large, and there were no signs of destruction. There were also many fine trees at the head of a ravine belonging to an old man named Lamour, who seemed ready to sell. "There is not the slightest cause for apprehending the extinction of the *Lodoicea Seychellarum*," [9] he assured Mauritius, adding that it was flourishing all over the island, as well as at Curieuse.

In 1889, responding to appeals from Kew, the Colonial Office ordered the new Administrator, Thomas Risely Griffith (Barkly having finally left Seychelles the previous year), to obtain a living, viable coco de mer for the Royal Botanic Garden. Griffith arranged for Button to ship several barrels of palms to London during May and July, but all failed, as did a further consignment sent in August. In June the following year, Seychelles dispatched another coco de mer, one which had successfully passed the first stage of growth and was well established in the second. This plant seems to have flourished, for on 4 April 1892 the London *Standard* reported: "During the afternoon of 1st April a plant was placed in the lily tank of the Victoria House at the Royal Garden Kew such as has never before been exhibited to the public in any part of Europe. This interesting exhibit is a fine young plant of the double coconut palm [which] has previously defied all attempts to cultivate it in Europe ... The double coconut may now be seen at Kew at any time."

By now it was clear that Hodoul's opinion that the cutting of coco de mer leaves posed no serious problem was mistaken. Reporting to Mauritius in December 1893, Griffith referred to the many complaints he had received from Praslin of the hearts and leaves of palms being cut. "Someone has found out that the straw plaiting sells well in England for the manufacture of hats there, and it is needless to say the destruction of trees has multiplied considerably," he wrote. Too frequently it was the tender heart leaves that were cut out, which stunted or destroyed the trees, and he asked for a new ordinance to put a stop to it. Subsequently it became an offence to posses a heart, heart leaf or an undeveloped leaf of the coco de mer without a permit.

The following year, Griffith reported that negotiations were at last under way through the Anglican minister at Praslin, Robert Pickwood, to buy the ravines at Fond Ferdinand and Anse Marie Louise. On her death Mrs Campbell had left two heirs to the property, both children of a previous marriage. They were Mrs Germain, who possessed the larger area of thirty-four acres, and a son, Viltère Etève, with seventeen acres. Mrs Germain had for some time held out for R.8,000, but eventually agreed to sell for R.2,000. Griffith succeeded in having the price approved by Legislative Council (successor to the Board of Civil Commissioners), but the intervention of another bidder forced the government in the end to pay R.2,200, described as a "great bargain" by one Council member. The fate of the rest of the land was a foregone conclusion. As owner of one-half, the government could licitate the other portion, and force Etève to sell his share to the highest bidder. "From all accounts he is not likely to be in a position to purchase it himself," commented Griffith, adding that the price the government had already paid was considered fair. The land secured had more than 2,500 fully grown trees, eight hundred young trees, forty-three coconut trees in full bearing, and acres of vanilla. This news delighted Thiselton-Dyer, who suggested to the Colonial Office that the home government might contribute to the purchase price.

Once the government had possession of the land, the production of nuts at Fond Ferdinand and Anse Marie Louise increased dramatically. In 1894 only 150 nuts had been produced, a figure that rose to about 700 by 1901 (in which year the total number of trees on Crown land was put at 5,300). Restrictions on the cutting of the heart and leaves of palms had had an effect, particularly after 1896, when the steamships of Messageries Maritimes stopped calling at Seychelles, thus making it difficult to send coco de mer straw to Europe. The government made no attempt at that time to buy further tracts of the coco de mer forest, which included among its many ravines what was later described as "the best valley of the whole lot", the Vallée de Mai.[10]

After leaving Mauritius in early 1882, Gordon had applied for a year's leave of absence. He went to Palestine, and there resumed his study of the Scriptures and worked on refining his theory on the Garden of Eden. It was while in Palestine that he learned that the government had rejected his recommendations on Seychelles defence.[11] Like the French before him, Gordon had considered it too costly to fortify Mahé. He estimated that to defend Victoria harbour one would need six 10-inch guns (two each on Sainte Anne, Cerf island, and near the White Tower[12] on Mahé), plus mines to cover the sea approaches, barracks for troops, and additional forts and field guns on St Louis hill and near the Trois Frères river. The total cost would be £66,000, with an annual expenditure of £50,000. "It is therefore impossible to expect that any of the actual or annual expense could be defrayed by the Colony itself," his report noted, adding that it was "highly improbable" the War Office would consent to such a large outlay. As an alternative Gordon suggested a mobile defence, based on four twin-screw gunboats, each mounted with a 10-inch gun, and fitted to lay electro-mechanical mines. In addition there would be two fast torpedo boats, and six 9-pounder field guns on shore. The cost of four gunboats would be £77,000, plus an annual expenditure of £15,000.

Gordon also suggested that the elderly, wooden three-decker HMS *London*, which he thought contributed little as depot ship at Zanzibar to the suppression of the slave trade, should be stationed at Seychelles, where it would give "great impetus ... to the Colony, and at the same time an effective defence would be acquired without any extra annual expense to the imperial government". He envisaged the *London* providing the crews for the four gunboats.

Gordon had carried out a similar survey for the defence of Mauritius, and his overall opinion was that fortifying the islands without strengthening the region's naval forces was a waste of money, particularly where the civil population was largely unreliable. The essential was command of the sea. Gordon advocated coaling stations[13] on islands like Diego Garcia. "By establishing these coaling stations, no diplomatic complications could arise, while by their means we could unite all our colonies with us, for we could give them effective support."

Never averse to straying from his brief, Gordon suggested that Seychelles (which he habitually referred to as a colony) should be separated from Mauritius. "Mauritius is declining, the Seychelles are a rising colony," he boldly proclaimed. But Napier Broome considered the Dependency "a poor place, leading a hand-to-mouth financial existence", and warned that "its government requires to be watched, controlled, and advised by a superior authority".

In 1883 France finally unmasked its ultimate aims in Madagascar by bombarding and seizing Tamatave, forcing the Hova government to accept a virtual French protectorate. The settlers in Réunion and Mauritius welcomed the move,[14] as Madagascar promised cheap labour and was still a clandestine source of slaves. According to Gordon it was the ban imposed by the Government of India on further emigration to Réunion.[15] that had prompted "the French government to attack Madagascar, so that they [the colonists] might get labour".

In Seychelles, news of the French attack worried Barkly. He warned that the islands were completely defenceless, and that if Mahé were seized it could not be retaken without considerable losses. Although Barkly's concern seems to have excited little interest in London, the authorities decided that £89,000 should be spent immediately on fortifying Mauritius.[16] A confidential memorandum from the Colonial Office warned that in any forthcoming war Britain's most likely enemies would be France or Russia, "and the worst combination we have any reason to dread is an alliance of France and Russia".[17] This opinion was shared by the Mauritius newspaper *Le Cernéen*, which recalled Gordon's proposal for mobile defence. It also stressed the importance of telegraphic communication, something that Mauritius lacked.

Since the successful laying of a transatlantic submarine cable in 1866,[18] cable ships had been criss-crossing the world, unwinding giant umbilical cords along the ocean floor that connected one seaport to another. By 1870 Suez, Aden and Bombay had been joined. Nine years later another cable, from Aden to Zanzibar, was extended to Durban, from where there was an overland line to Cape Town. If war came the Cape would be vital to Britain's communications with India (the Suez Canal, it was felt, could be easily blocked), and there was concern that the French were well placed in Madagascar to cut the marine cable in the shallow waters off East Africa.

Although France held a monopoly of steamship services between Europe and the islands of the western Indian Ocean, it had shown less initiative in the deployment of submarine cables. In 1887 the French news agency Havas invited the Mauritius government to participate in a project that would link Zanzibar to Madagascar and Réunion. By paying part of the cost Mauritius could have the cable extended to Port Louis. The plan did not materialise, but three years later the Mauritius surveyor-general returned from France with a proposal that the Eastern and South African Telegraph Company (forerunner of Cable and Wireless) should connect Mauritius with Zanzibar through Réunion, Sainte Marie, and Diego Suarez.

The French consul at Port Louis, Albert Drouin, doubted whether Britain would be interested. In a letter to Paris he said London suspected that its dispatches were opened and copied on the French mail ships (of particular interest to France were the Mauritius fortifications)[19], and he believed this was the reason that Britain was paying a subsidy to the British India shipping line to operate a service between Colombo and Mauritius. "Almost all official dispatches are today sent by this route, even although it is one-third longer than that of the Messageries Maritimes," he noted. It was unlikely therefore that Britain would let the Mauritius cable pass through French territory.

Drouin was right. Britain rejected the French proposal, deciding instead to connect Zanzibar to Mauritius via Seychelles. Mauritius would pay £7,000 towards the project and Seychelles £1,000. The cable from Zanzibar to Seychelles was completed in 1893 by the 3,900-ton cableship *Scotia*.[20] Telegraphing his congratulations to the Eastern Telegraph chairman, Sir John Pender, Griffith described the new link as "an undertaking ... tending to the extension of commerce, the advancement of science and the closer union of that great empire of which we form so small a portion". Shortly afterwards the *Scotia* and another cable ship, the *Britannia*, made the connection between Seychelles and Mauritius.

Unfortunately as one new line of communication opened, another was about to close. In 1895 Seychelles was informed by the Messageries Maritimes that as from February 1896 its ships would no longer call at Port Victoria. Instead Colombo would be the intermediate call on the French line's Marseilles-Australia-Nouméa[21] route. The MM service linking Seychelles with Mauritius, Réunion, and Madagascar would also be discontinued. "Now we do not know when, or how, we are to get our letters," moaned the Seychelles Administrator.[22]

* *

The previous year, a steamship of the Messageries Maritimes had been party to the removal from Seychelles of the Dependency's best-known historical relic, the *Pierre de Possession*.[23] This carved stone, erected on Mahé in 1756 to signify France's possession of the then uninhabited Isle de Séchelles, appears to have been of little interest to the British, and at some unknown date it was removed from its original position near Government House. Latterly, it was being used as a boundary mark in Victoria when, in September 1894, it suddenly disappeared.

To give him his due, Seychelles Administrator Risely Griffith acted swiftly. Having established that the Swiss proprietor of the Equator Hotel, Jean Schultess, had given the stone to a visiting French general, who was by then well on his way to France, Griffith ordered Schultess to cable the general and have the stone returned immediately by the next mail steamer. Failure would result in imprisonment for Schultess.

The stone had first been noticed by General Henri Frey the previous July, when his ship called at Mahé on its way to Nouméa, where the general was to inspect French military establishments. Schultess, who was later to claim that the stone had been abandoned on his land, was so impressed by Frey that he agreed to give the stone to the general when the latter called again on his way home from New Caledonia. This he did, taking it out in his launch to the MM liner *Australien* as it prepared to sail for Marseilles. Schultess admitted that for this service the general had promised to try to obtain for him the ribbon of the *Légion d'Honneur*.

On receiving Schultess's cable, Frey immediately agreed to return the stone by the next ship. In a letter he expressed

162

regret for the trouble he had caused, but said that seeing the neglected state of the stone he felt it would be better off in a Paris museum. In a subsequent report to London, Griffith noted that as the stone was being rowed out to the French liner Frey was paying an official visit to Admiral Kennedy on board HMS *Boadicea.* Before leaving Seychelles, Frey asked Schultess if he had remarked the salute fired by the British flagship as the stone went past. "I mention this incident," wrote Griffith, "merely to show that in carrying off the Commemoration Stone of the taking of Possession of the Sechelles Islands by the English [sic], this French general knew he was committing a direct larceny to the prejudice of the Seychelles Government."

It is difficult to imagine Britain and France going to war over a stone, but given the relations between the two countries in 1894, even this incident might have been enough to light the fuse of mutual antagonism and suspicion.[24] The following year Griffith's successor was sufficiently alarmed at France's seizure of Madagascar to propose raising a volunteer force to defend Seychelles, an idea derided by the Governor of Mauritius, who remarked that the close affinity of the Seychelles people with Mauritius was a result of "their love of France", adding that Cockburn Stewart was "seeing things in that rosy colouring which marks the dawn of a windy day".

12

French leave
1881-1901

The money you desire to spend ... is the
money of the people of Seychelles.
Lieut.-Governor Napier Broome
advising Civil Commissioners to keep within Estimates, 10 July 1885

The withdrawal of the Messageries Maritimes service was a
severe blow to Seychelles.[1] The speed and punctuality of the
French steamships had ensured the early arrival in European
markets of the Dependency's vanilla, now a valuable and
flourishing export, while the ships' regular calls at Mahé had
helped reinforce the cultural links of the islands with Europe,
particularly France.

Passengers coming ashore at Mahé included writers, artists,
scientists, as well as the occasional adventurous tourist. They
admired the beauty and tranquillity of the islands; some
recorded their impressions in books and magazine articles,
others would paint and photograph the scenery.[2] Meanwhile
Seychelles' inhabitants were learning more about the world
beyond their horizons thanks to imported newspapers, books,
and magazines.

The MM liners also offered to the more affluent Seychellois
a standard of comfort lacking in the British India steamships,[3]
which, fortunately, had begun operating a new service between
India and Africa before the decision of the French company to
withdraw was known. The BI ships would call occasionally at
Mahé, but this was hardly appreciated by the Seychellois. Not
only were the ships old and slow, with "wretched passenger
accommodation", but the service was uncertain. If the liners

164

would sail punctually "we would be satisfied", conceded Cockburn Stewart, who had arrived in Seychelles in June 1895 to replace Griffith as Administrator.

Stewart kept pressing the Messageries Maritimes to change its mind about discontinuing its service. In this he was aided by the French agent Cheyron, who reported that the French government would agree to the mail ships returning if an appropriate subsidy was negotiated. Stewart considered the company's asking price of F.48,000 a year too high, but he told London that "the inhabitants are prepared to make any sacrifice to secure the Messageries Maritimes steamers again calling at this port".

He added that the planters and traders had been treated so badly by BI that they would gladly submit to extra taxation to have the MM service restored. He still thought the BI service should be retained, for it brought rice from India in exchange for Seychelles' coconuts and coconut oil, a fact recognised by the authorities' decision to impose extra duties and port charges to pay for the increased subsidy demanded by the British company.[4]

According to Stewart, it was the "perpetual quarantining" of its steamers that had caused the Messageries Maritimes to withdraw.[5] The Dependency was just not important enough either in number of passengers or amount of freight for the company to accept unnecessary delays, particularly after the introduction of its fast service to Australia and New Caledonia. There were other reasons also: lack of a sufficient subsidy, the high price of coal at Mahé, plus difficulties over leasing the coal wharf. At the same time Seychelles could argue that it had done all it could to accommodate the French liners, including constructing especially for them a lighthouse on Denis island.

The need for a lighthouse on either Denis or Bird island had long been recognised. Many whaleships had foundered along the northern edge of the Seychelles bank, and in 1872 Civil Commissioner Franklyn noted that the current in the area was strong enough to cause a British warship to pass Bird island thirty miles off course. MM steamers running regularly between Aden, Seychelles, and Mauritius were obliged to reach the area during daylight, and Franklyn suggested that a light should be placed on Bird island to aid their navigation. He also proposed placing a light on Sainte Anne — which was done the following year — but the lighthouse for Bird, an iron structure that would be manufactured in Britain, was considered too expensive.

It was not until 1881 that the proposal was revived, after the Messageries Maritimes warned that without the lighthouse its steamers would omit Mahé altogether when its new Marseilles-Sydney-Nouméa service began. The then acting Chief Civil Commissioner, Cockburn Stewart, sent the PWD superintendent, the port officer, and a qualified naval officer to survey Bird and Denis islands. They reported that Bird would be the better choice for a lighthouse, but Stewart thought the decision should be left to the shipping company.

Denis island was eventually chosen, and construction of a tower of coral blocks began. The project did not go well, and in December, when at a height of 40 feet, the tower collapsed, seriously injuring several workers.[6] The subsequent inquiry blamed the materials, over-haste, and absence of supervision. Barkly, who had recently arrived at Mahé, wanted to make a fresh start, but on the advice of the Board of Civil Commissioners the matter was referred to Mauritius, which decided that because of the sandy soil it would be advisable to have the light on a wooden tripod. This Mauritius undertook to make. Meanwhile the MM steamers continued to navigate without the "indispensable lighthouse", including the 3,385-ton *Natal*, which called at Mahé in December 1882 on its inaugural voyage to Australia. It was probably the largest liner Seychelles up to then had seen.

Finally, in August 1883, a notice in the *Government Gazette* announced that a 70ft-high lighthouse had been erected on the north-west side of Denis island. Its fixed white light, at an elevation of about 60 feet, was visible in clear weather to a distance of twelve nautical miles. Barkly, who had been afraid that without proper supervision the light might be accidentally extinguished, had requested that Mauritius find him a competent keeper, as there was no-one in Seychelles with the necessary qualifications. This was done, but the lighthouse's problems were not yet over.

Two years after its erection, parts of the wooden tripod needed replacing, and by 1889 Mauritius was being informed that despite repairs the structure was still insecure. Once again an iron tripod from England was suggested, and again rejected.

A request by the shipping company that a second lighthouse be erected, this time on Bird island, was turned down. Seychelles could not afford another light, said the authorities, and they found it "difficult to suppose that a ship travelling at the speed of the French mail steamers could be over twenty-five miles out in her reckoning which she would have to be in order to run on Bird island if steaming a course so as to make the light on Denis island".

Eventually, in 1893, a new frame, made of Seychelles Capucin wood, was erected. It stood 66 feet high, with a fixed light that was slightly higher than before in order to clear the top of the casuarina trees. An important improvement was that the light was visible from all points. This structure lasted until 1907, when again it had to be replaced. This time Anglo-French expertise was called on. The metal tripod was made in France and erected by French workers. The rotating light, 100 feet high, was made in England. It is said that when the lighthouse was completed in 1910 the workers threw their tools into the sea, saying it would never need to be repaired. Shortly afterwards, the old lighthouse was removed and re-erected on the island of Mamelles, near the entrance to Port Victoria.

While the absence of navigational aids might affect the punctuality and even the safety of the MM steamships, it was, as Cockburn Stewart had suggested, the Dependency's quarantine regulations that seemed to bother the shipping line most. Not that Seychelles was alone in giving cause for complaint; indeed the Dependency could congratulate itself on having for so long remained free of the diseases that had been spread with such fatal results in Mauritius and Réunion. "Fever and smallpox are almost unknown in Seychelles," wrote General Gordon in 1881, but two years later this was no longer true. Instead, Mahé was in the grip of a smallpox epidemic, made worse by the Seychelles authorities' attempt to conceal the true nature of the disease.

The immediate cause of the fatal outbreak was the arrival on 5 June 1883 from Zanzibar of HM schooner *Undine*[7]. It had a Seychellois passenger on board named D. Bouquié. Although he showed signs of an "eruptive disease", this was diagnosed by the health officer, an Irishman named Robert Lepper, as *varicella,* or chickenpox, and he was allowed ashore. Lepper was planning to go to Mauritius on leave later that month, a fact that was subsequently to cast doubts on the objectivity of his diagnosis. "Had Dr Lepper reported the true nature of Bouquié's disease ... and enforced some measures of quarantine, he [Lepper] could not have left the Seychelles," remarked the Governor, Pope Hennessy, in his subsequent report to London.

Dr Brooks,[8] who had been brought out of retirement by Barkly during Lepper's absence, reported on 30 June that although the disease "may be allowed under the head 'Varicella' it is not to be presumed that it is merely a simple form of ordinary chickenpox as met with in this island", and that from its "unusual severity and gravity" it appeared similar to a disease that had recently spread in Anjouan "with disastrous consequences". Although Brooks did not say so, the epidemic in question was smallpox.

By this time many people in Seychelles were worried by the apparent nonchalant attitude of the authorities. Bouquié had recovered, but his wife was now sick, and there were several others who had been in contact with the couple. Surprisingly, despite Brooks' recommendation that a quarantine be imposed, he and Lepper (the latter having been ordered by the Governor to return to Seychelles on 14 August) continued to issue clean bills of health to vessels sailing from Mahé. But word had reached Mauritius privately about the outbreak, and when the MM mail steamer *Sydney* arrived at Port Louis from Seychelles it was immediately placed in quarantine. The following month the Seychelles schooner *Brisk* was found at Mauritius to have several sick passengers on board. They were landed at the quarantine station, where smallpox was diagnosed. The doctor in charge and another health officer subsequently contracted the disease and died.

In Seychelles, Barkly continued to insist that the disease was chickenpox, and blamed indiscreet persons with no medical knowledge of trying to discredit the doctors. He asked Mauritius to rescind the order putting vessels from Seychelles under quarantine, and gave an assurance that the chickenpox was subsiding. He dismissed the deaths that had occurred as being among "persons of the lowest class, and of African descent, whose manner of living is often such as little fits them to resist any disease".[9] But the epidemic was to get worse, and as the number of deaths rose panic spread through Victoria.

"The bells tolled perpetually, and nothing was to be seen but coffins passing," recalled Fanny Barkly. "All government work was suspended, as the workmen had to be employed continually to make coffins." Most of the shops in the town closed, their owners fleeing to the mountains, where they were frequently overtaken by "the terrible scourge".

Fanny would have liked to have moved out of town with her children, but acknowledged that her husband was right in insisting they show an example and remain in Government House. With shops shut food became scarce, and Fanny noted that they were forced to eat a tortoise from the pen at Government House.[10] Pope Hennessy, who had earlier called at Mahé on his way to take up his post as governor of Mauritius, sent a relief shipment of rice to Seychelles. He also sent "a medical gentleman of high professional reputation" to report on the epidemic.

On arriving in Seychelles Dr Evenor Chastellier was forced to spend several days in quarantine on Longue island before being allowed over to Mahé. There, after examining a number of patients, he had no hesitation in confirming that the disease was *variola vera*, or smallpox. Despite this Dr Lepper continued to issue vessels leaving Seychelles with clean bills of health, maintaining that Mahé was free from "every degree of smallpox". It was only after receiving a warning from the Governor that he added to the certificate a statement that "a contagious eruptive disease, which has caused considerable mortality, is prevalent". Twenty-three deaths had occurred during December, and these were to continue during January 1884. Only in February did the number of deaths begin to fall, but for seven months no-one was allowed to leave Seychelles by mail steamer unless they had first spent a period of quarantine on Longue island.[11]

The smallpox epidemic remains vividly today in the communal memory. The present generation recalls hearing first-hand accounts from grandparents and others of the terror that gripped the island during *la Grosse Vérette*. According to widespread belief, the victims were sometimes buried alive, such was the fear of infection. The Barklys tried to maintain people's confidence, visiting some of the sick, and sending food to the poor. Barkly had to provide Dr Lepper, his wife, and child with a police guard, for "the poor man was constantly bullied and threatened in every way," noted Fanny. The Mauritius Board of Health had also targeted Lepper as having been seriously negligent. The *procureur-général* considered that he should be charged, but Pope Hennessy ruled against this because of "the difficulty of applying the Colonial Regulations". He recognised, however, that Barkly had relied too readily on Dr Lepper's advice, which had "prevented him from seeing in time the gravity of the case", and he criticised the Chief Civil Commissioner for having directed Dr Brooks to continue issuing clean bills of health to vessels leaving Seychelles.

While Dr Lepper may be excused for first failing to diagnose smallpox,[12] his continued refusal to admit the mistake and take immediate preventive action is inexcusable. This, and the ill-advised backing he received from Barkly, not only resulted in many unnecessary deaths but meant that Seychelles was to be subjected to years of virtual harassment by the Mauritius health authorities. There were other misfortunes. Exports faltered during 1883. The clove crop was largely abandoned because of a labour shortage, and the coffee leaf disease that was eventually to kill the industry appeared for the first time. Barkly thought that with patience and economy things would return to normal, but it was several years before recovery began.

As if to emphasize the dread many felt, the sea around Seychelles seemed intent on its own form of destruction as, for two days, enormous waves crashed on the shore. No-one knew that they were witnessing the effects of the cataclysmic birth of the Krakatoa volcano. Erupting from the seabead between Java and Sumatra, the volcano set off tidal waves throughout south-east Asia, killing thousands of people and sending an ash cloud into the atmosphere that was to cut solar radiation for more than a year.

Describing the scene in Seychelles on 27 August 1883, Henry Estridge, the government's Collector of Taxes, wrote that at about 4 pm a tidal wave rushed in, reaching a height well above the usual spring tides. Within a quarter of an hour it had receded, leaving boats high and dry. This phenomena continued all next day, and at sunset there was a lurid glare in the sky. "On the morning of the 29th, the sun at seven o'clock was more like a full moon ... rather green in colour ... the sea

170

flowed and ebbed as on the day before, only to a much less extent. We were not aware till after the arrival of the Mauritius mail what caused this, but then learnt what it was and the great destruction it had caused. Even now the shores of the various islands are covered with pumice."

In October 1885 a seaman from HMS *Bacchante*, flagship of the C-in-C East Indies, was put ashore on Longue island suffering from smallpox. When the news reached Mauritius it immediately imposed a quarantine on the MM mail steamer *Salazie* (4,008 tons) despite its having a clean bill of health from Seychelles. Barkly and his family had recently left Mahé on six months' leave,[13] and the Dependency was in charge of the police chief, George Hollier Griffiths. He protested to Mauritius, saying that Seychelles trade was suffering as a result of such actions. He had been told by the Messageries Maritimes that in future it would refuse to accept passengers from the Dependency unless it was assured its ships would not be quarantined on arrival at Mauritius.

Hollier Griffiths admitted that Seychelles had erred in 1883, but since then it had gone out of its way to adhere strictly to the regulations. He deplored the fact that Mauritius still refused to treat Longue island as an effective quarantine station. At first Mauritius refused to budge, and it was only after a ruling by naval doctors that Longue island was secure for quarantine purposes that the Mauritius authorities relented.

However, quarantine problems continued to pursue Seychelles for the rest of the century. An outbreak of measles in 1888 resulted in an extra medical officer being sent to the islands, prompting Griffith, newly arrived as Administrator, to wonder what all the fuss was about. "Considering that so much prominence has been given to the supposed introduction of measles here through the slackness of the government of this Dependency, and statements made that hundreds were dying in consequence, I think the figures given (thirty-one deaths from measles during the four months ended 31 March 1889) are extremely interesting, and show how mild has been the disease." In November 1891, an outbreak of influenza resulted in the steamer from Mauritius failing to call. In a note to London the Administrator said it was felt influenza should be omitted from bills of health, but in view of the stand taken by the Mauritius sanitary authorities, he could not direct the medical officer not to mention the disease. Eventually it was agreed cargo trans-shipped at Seychelles could be given a clean bill of health as long as there was no direct communication.

In August 1895, Cockburn Stewart freed the flagship HMS *Bonaventure* from temporary quarantine after its arrival from Rodrigues, where influenza had been present. The Admiral later told Stewart that if the quarantine had been enforced he would have sailed immediately for Trincomalee, to "the great inconvenience" of the squadron. Recognising "the evil" of a too rigid quarantine, Stewart switched some members of the Board of Health, but the following year, after the withdrawal of the MM steamers from Seychelles, he was again concerned when partisans of quarantine claimed that the BI liners were "hot beds of disease". Stewart considered Dr Jules Mounier's views on quarantine old-fashioned, and it was perhaps fortunate that the health officer died a few months later.

In 1897 an outbreak of bubonic plague in Mauritius alerted Seychelles. Passengers landing from the BI liners were kept seven days in quarantine, and their luggage and cargo were fumigated. Stewart reported that the steamers were not delayed. "I venture to think that the measures adopted show considerable advance on the old antiquated system which used to prevail," he informed the Secretary of State.[14]

Four years later, encouraged by a generous mail subsidy, the Messageries Maritimes put Seychelles back on its schedules. Now steamers on the Marseilles-Mauritius service called at Mahé on both the outward and return trips. Other ports of call included Diego Suarez and Tamatave. It was a welcome return, though still a far cry from the direct links with Europe, Australia, and the other islands of the western Indian Ocean that Seychelles had previously enjoyed. Nor was the resumed service to last. In 1912 the outward call at Mahé was cancelled, and in 1918, as a result of heavy losses during the war, the Messageries Maritimes ended the service completely. The last liner to call at Seychelles was the *Bosphore,* on 15 June 1918.[15]

13

Saving the Tortoise
1888 -1903

Seychelles is Seychelles.
Colonial Office, confronted with
yet another irregularity, August 1912

Seychelles made further constitutional progress during the 1880s, the most important advance occurring in December 1888, when the Board of Civil Commissioners was dissolved.

Since the granting of wider powers to the Board in 1882 it had been recognised that a smaller executive body was needed. The Board was therefore scrapped, and the Administrator (a title supplanting that of Chief Civil Commissioner) henceforth presided over two separate bodies: an Executive Council, made up of the District Judge, Treasurer, and Legal Adviser, and a Legislative Council composed of the Executive Council members plus the former Board's three nominated Unofficial members. Given that the Administrator chaired both Councils, and possessed almost the same powers as a colonial governor, there was little chance of serious disagreement between the two bodies.

It was this denial of democratic process that prompted a group of inhabitants in September 1892 to petition the Secretary of State, Lord Ripon, requesting that in future the three Unofficials in the Legislative Council be elected, a proposal apparently so preposterous that it was dismissed as verging on "Offenbachian burlesque". The elective principle had recently been introduced in Mauritius, but the Lieutenant-Governor was opposed to "entrusting the inhabitants of Seychelles ... with so weighty and unfamiliar a responsibility". The Colonial Office agreed, noting that although Pope

173

Hennessy would have given the people of Seychelles a greater say in their affairs, "the reasons for the decision then taken, that Seychelles was quite unfitted for such a constitution, still holds good".

The petitioners' declared aim was admirable: to "ensure the better development of ... these fertile islands and ... open a new era of prosperity and happiness to all classes of the inhabitants". They pointed out that the three Unofficial members had no mandate to speak for the people and, to make matters worse, that laws were being passed by the Legislative Council "without having first been published for general information". Two laws particularly, one prohibiting the carrying of vanilla samples to town without a police permit[1] and the other relating to the traditional sharecropper system called *moitié*, were described as vexatious. The petitioners also complained that salaries in government service (other than that of the Administrator) were too low, that the police were inefficient, and that money allocated for roads and education was not spent as directed.

The sixty inhabitants who signed the petition could hardly be described as unbiased, yet the document has the familiar ring of justified grievance. Most of the signatories were lawyers, small merchants and traders, along with several large landowners, and a handful of expatriates.[2] The guiding hand appears to have been Hollier Griffiths, the former police chief who had stood in as Chief Civil Commissioner during the absence of Barkly. Griffiths had subsequently been criticised, some said unfairly, by an inquiry into his administration, and as a result he had retired and was now in trade. He was not prospering, and was a bitter man.

Despite some differences of opinion, all the petitioners were united in wanting the removal from the Executive and Legislative Councils of the District Judge, Robert Myles Brown, whose behaviour had long been a cause of resentment. Only recently Brown had acted as Administrator, for the second time, and his domineering ways were not forgotten. The powers of the District Judge "are perhaps greater than are possessed by any man in a civilised country", or so thought US consul Thomas Prentice. Since then more power had been given to the Judge, including that of trying capital cases, sitting with assessors.[3] "His word is law," noted Ada Edwards, a shrewd observer of the Seychelles scene. Mrs Edwards liked neither Brown nor the Administrator, Risely Griffith, which was understandable given that her planter husband had been consistently turned down for government appointments. She accused the Administrator of being stingy, and spending all his time in Government House writing dispatches, "without troubling to make himself acquainted with the geography of the country, the requirements of the inhabitants or the manner in which sums voted by Council are expended". The people, she claimed, were hoping for "the advent of a more courteous and enlightened head of the Government".

As for Brown, Mrs Edwards admitted that he was "an upright and painstaking individual". Unfortunately his judgements, when eventually delivered, were "exhaustive, if not always lucid". And in the Council Chamber he was "subservient to no other ... and greater than he has to bow his head". She deplored the cost of the 1888 constitutional changes, and noted that Griffith had had his personal emoluments raised to R.13,500, plus duty-free concessions, whereas a Chief Civil Commissioner's salary had only been R.3,800, with no concessions.

She also thought it improper that the three nominated Unofficial members were allowed to hold government appointments.[4] She estimated that the administration cost Seychelles R.121,845 just in salaries, adding that this "large sum would be cheerfully paid, provided the country received a *quid pro quo*, but when the universal feeling is that all that is being done is done badly, the taxpayer naturally resents what on the face of it, appears an unnecessary imposition". Britain needed to be more alive to the importance of the islands "and not foist government officials upon them, whose career has been a failure elsewhere", she concluded.

Similar opinions had been expressed often enough in the past. In London, this latest Seychelles petition excited scant interest. The Colonial Office agreed that draft ordinances should be published in the *Government Gazette*. "They might not be read by anyone", noted one official, "but publication would remove the grievance." To other complaints the Secretary of State was advised to give a non-committal reply, saying the petitioners' views had been noted, and when there were funds the government would do its best to implement improvements. When that would be, it was unable to say.

Despite substantial export earnings from coconut oil, copra, and vanilla, it was indicative of the state of the economy that the New Oriental Bank, which had opened in Victoria in 1887, closed in 1892.[5] Two years later the government attempted to generate savings by opening its own Savings Bank, but that made little progress, and by 1896 the bank had only 125 accounts on its books.

Coconut had been hit some years earlier by beetle blight,[6] which was now affecting exports. This and the falling price of coconut oil was being aggravated by a depreciation of the Indian rupee (Seychelles had switched from sterling to the rupee in 1876). At the same time vanilla, on which so many hopes were pinned — for it was ideally suited to the small-scale producer — was proving an uncertain source of wealth, and Griffith, who predicted that the current diminution of trade would persist, was proposing to raise taxes on imports.

In this depressive atmosphere some questioned the wisdom of Seychelles cutting its remaining ties with Mauritius. The administration had by now almost complete financial, legislative, and judicial control, yet it was intent on adding more privileges and prerogatives associated with a Crown colony. In 1890 Griffith introduced Seychelles' own postage stamps;[7] in 1896 his successor, Cockburn Stewart, sent off to the Colonial Office the late General Gordon's design for a Seychelles flag. A year later he was arranging for a gallows to be ready to carry out any death sentences the Seychelles High Court might impose. Finally, with further enhancement of his powers, Stewart was Governor in all but name. To his great disappointment, however, he was still "His Honour the Administrator" rather than "His Excellency".

These advances involved not only Seychelles cutting its ties with Mauritius, but also strengthening its claim to administer the other smaller island dependencies of the western Indian Ocean. Since the days of the French the Amirantes had been under Seychelles jurisdiction, but in 1879 the Board of Civil Commissioners petitioned for additional islands to "be made to form part of the Seychelles Government and proportionally contribute to its charges". These included the Cosmoledo group of Astove, Assumption and Aldabra, as well as Providence, St Pierre, Jean de Nove (or the Farquhar islands), and even lonely Tromelin island, off the eastern coast of Madagascar. "The Glorioso islands are also included in the petition but it is, to say the least, doubtful whether they are dependencies of Mauritius," noted the Colonial Office. Later Napier Broome was to find that the Alphonse group, which included Bijoutier and St François, was in administrative limbo, being neither under Mauritius nor Seychelles. As a result he proposed that Alphonse "be taken and considered to be, for all intents and purposes, part of and belonging to the Islands and Archipelago of the Seychelles".

Britain's tardiness in formalising its administration of the smaller islands had encouraged France to stake its own claims, at first tentatively, then more openly as Madagascar came increasingly under French domination. Attention had focussed for several years on the Glorioso (or Glorieuses) islands,[8] which lie about one hundred miles south of Astove, between Madagascar and the Comoro islands. Here Pierre Ohier, a French resident of Seychelles, had been established since 1873 fishing and hunting turtle, after being told by the Mayotte commandant that he could settle there at his own risk. Later, word came that Mauritius intended to lease the Glorieuses to an Englishman, prompting inconclusive discussions between Paris and London on the status of the islands.

When Ohier abandoned the islands in 1880, France gave the lease to another Seychelles resident, Hippolyte Caltaux. At the same time Louis Deltel, also of Seychelles, wrote to Mayotte asking to lease the islands of Aldabra, Assumption, Astove, as well as Europa and Juan de Nova in the Mozambique channel. If he could not have them all, he would like at least Aldabra. "I think that the French government would prefer to lease these islands to French nationals, rather than allow them to be occupied by foreigners," he commented. But France was not prepared to push its claims quite so far, and when, in 1888, yet another Seychelles resident, Jules Minier, sought leases of Aldabra, Cosmoledo, Assumption and Astove, he was turned down. "There is no cause to grant a concession over these islands, which could not fail to prompt a lively protest from the British government," commented an official at the Ministry of Marine in Paris. Neither government wanted a confrontation over islands "*sans grande valeur*", and when, in 1892, France eventually annexed the Glorieuses no

177

protest was made by Britain. Rather more fuss was made when it was disclosed that the French government had been promising for some years to lease Aldabra and Cosmoledo to a French resident of Seychelles, Henri Gaston Payet. The deal fell through when Payet died in January 1882 without being able to raise the purchase money, but Britain was annoyed to learn of reports circulated by France that Aldabra was not a British possession.[9] Griffith first heard of this on his return from leave in May 1892 when he received a letter from Admiral Kennedy, C-in-C East Indies, suggesting that (he) Griffith confirm formal possession of the Aldabra atoll in order to avoid future misunderstanding with France. HMS *Redbreast* was at his disposal, but in any event the ship would sail for Aldabra to show the flag. Griffith was concerned that this demonstration, contrary to what was intended, might throw doubt on the validity of Britain's claim to the atoll, but he decided anyway to take passage in the *Redbreast*, putting an appropriate advance notice of his visit in the *Government Gazette*. He took with him a new flagstaff and two Union flags.

After a three-day crossing Griffith arrived off Aldabra, where he was met by the lessee, James Spurs (the same who had welcomed Harriet Allen to Diego Garcia in 1870). Spurs had a five-year lease on Aldabra, Cosmoledo, Astove and Assumption, from where he sent mangrove poles, salted fish, and turtle to Mahé. According to Griffith, Spurs was "losing heart" and would have liked to dispose of the lease. He said there was little rain on Aldabra, and although water was available it was not located in an area suitable for settlement, making the growing of crops difficult. (This statement contradicts a report of 1878 which said there was good spring water on the main island, and that maize, sweet potatoes, and other produce could be grown). Griffith saw little advantage from Aldabra, an atoll almost as large in land mass as Mahé, but he believed "the French would lay claims to them (Aldabra and the other islands of the group) if they thought there was the slightest chance of securing them", and so he formally raised one of the two Union Jacks he had brought with him on the new flagstaff.

Although Spurs had spent eighteen years on Diego Garcia plus another five on Farquhar, before transferring to Aldabra, he was far from being the typical island manager. Described by

178

Henry Morton Stanley

General Charles Gordon

Kabarega of Bunyoro

Nicholas Pike

Rear-Admiral Edmund Drummond (seated, extreme left), C-in-C East Indies, with officers and crew members of HMS Bonaventure on Praslin island, June 1896. Top: The Bonaventure, a cruiser of 4,360 tons, at Colombo.

Governor Walter Davidson and Monsigneur Hudrisier, Bishop of Port-Victoria, with the C-in-C East Indies, Rear Admiral Edmund Poë, during a visit by the flagship HMS Hyacinth in 1907.

The steam launch Alexandra, which was built at Bombay in 1901 for the Seychelles government. It replaced the sailing vessel Wave.

'Be proud to belong to the British Empire.' So urged the Governor of Seychelles, Lieut.-Colonel Charles O'Brien (left), in an appeal to the patriotic spirit of the people during World War 1. Over a thousand men volunteered to serve in East Africa, where many died from disease and neglect. The two officers in the contingent were Francis Whiting and France LeMarchand.

Below: Graves of some of the Seychelles Carrier Corps volunteers at Mont Fleuri cemetery, Victoria.

2/Lieut. Francis Whiting

2/Lieut. France LeMarchand

Griffith as observant, and a lover of nature, he showed a special respect for the "gigantic tortoise". During the early settlement of the Seychelles the tortoises there had been wantonly slaughtered for food and oil, provoking the navigator Bougainville to warn that if destruction continued unabated "this important and nutritious commodity" would soon disappear. By the early 1800s this was virtually what happened; only on Aldabra, too isolated from the usual shipping routes, did the giant tortoise survive in any number.

Griffith knew that Spurs would observe the regulations the government had introduced to protect these creatures[10] following an appeal by the naturalist Charles Darwin. Darwin had studied the giant tortoises of the Galapagos islands during his voyage in the *Beagle* (1832-36), and in 1874 he and a number of other scientists had written to the Mauritius governor stressing "the great scientific interest" attached to these prehistoric animals.

General Gordon had also been impressed by the size and longevity of the giant tortoises, and during his visit to Seychelles in 1881 he had purchased two with the intention of taking them back to England. When this proved difficult he presented them to Government House, where they were kept in a walled enclosure. Griffith described them as two fine specimens, and made efforts to increase the herd. Although many inhabitants on Mahé kept tortoises as pets and for food, the numbers were relatively small. In 1892 and again in 1895 Griffith increased the government's holding — twenty-three of the tortoises were acquired for "the ridiculously small sum" of R.103. The campaign for preservation was to gain a further fillip from the giant tortoise featured in Gordon's design for a new Seychelles coat of arms.

Today there are estimated to be more than 150,000 tortoises on Aldabra. Yet a hundred years ago it was not unusual for visiting ships to report seeing only one or two, sometimes none. Spurs believed rightly that they were still numerous, explaining that from May to September the tortoises concealed themselves in the scrub. It was, he thought, only on Picard island that they had disappeared, most of them killed by sailors. Making his own contribution to conservation, Spurs moved eleven tortoises to Picard after having cleared the island of rats, which preyed on the young. Griffith considered

179

Spurs was overestimating their numbers, and when a scientist[11] from the British Museum advised moving some of the tortoises to the granitic islands for protection, Griffith suggested Curieuse as a suitable site. Darwin's warnings were at least being heard, and in 1901 the government issued an Ordinance to protect, as "a natural object of interest", the Gigantic Tortoise of Aldabra.[12]

Unfortunately the same concern was not shown to Seychelles' marine turtles. Although Spurs was aware of the need to maintain stocks by conserving females and the young, he estimated that he could export about 12,000 green (edible) turtles from Aldabra each year. He deplored the great diminution in the number of hawksbill turtles (or caret), which were speared indiscriminately by harpooners (presumably whalemen), who were unable to see in the disturbed water whether the creatures were large or small. Because the head of the harpoon opened after entry, it had to be cut out of the turtle, resulting in the death of many young. "If the laws are not amended and enforced, before ten years turtles will be no more," Spurs warned in his report to Griffith, who forwarded it to Kew and the Admiralty.[13]

The coral islands of the Amirantes were particularly suited for the cultivation of coconuts, on account of the sandy soil and the absence of destructive pests. Coconuts, including coconut oil and the products of the soap factory in Victoria, were still the main pillar of the Seychelles economy. Only vanilla could seriously challenge its pre-eminence, which it began to do in 1896 when for the first time the value of vanilla exports was almost double that of the combined export value of copra, coconut oil, and soap. But vanilla was a capricious producer, as Griffith had known when he suggested to Mauritius that a botanical station be set up to encourage and assist planters in developing new crops. He pointed out that without vanilla and the coconut Seychelles would have little else left to export; neither coffee, cocoa, nor cloves had yet become major crops, nor, in his opinion, were they ever likely to. Griffith wanted to establish the botanical station on the former Church Mission land at Capucin (the Forêt Noire road was by then under construction), but there was opposition to the project, and it was not until 1901 that the botanical station was opened in Victoria.[14]

Vanilla would eventually collapse as a major export, but only after several more prosperous years, culminating in a record figure of R.1,338,720 rupees in 1899. In contrast the value of all coconut-based exports fell more or less steadily. In 1901, with vanilla exports again exceeding one million rupees, coconut products had a value of only R.205,321, attributable, according to Administrator Ernest Sweet-Escott, to neglect of existing plantations. Sweet-Escott, who had succeeded Stewart in 1899, warned that whereas the danger of over-production of coconut was slight, "in the case of vanilla, which, so far, is only used for flavouring purposes ... the danger ... is considerable". He added: "There is a capriciousness about the yield of vanilla, and even a greater capriciousness about its price, which renders it desirable that planters should have some other products of economic value to rely on." By 1902 the bottom had fallen out of the European vanilla market, the natural product being largely replaced by vanillin, an artificial substitute twenty times cheaper.

Those worst affected by the collapse were not the large plantation owners, who had their copra to fall back on, but small producers who grew their vines on others' land and shared the proceeds with the proprietor. "There are now few estates where it [the *moitié* system] does not exist," Stewart had noted in 1898. Having put everything they had into vanilla, such people were forced back into poverty or casual labour; or, if they were so inclined, they could go as contract labourers to one of the outer islands where Mahé's relative prosperity was being matched by increased economic activity.

One of the most prominent traders to exploit the resources of the outer islands was a blind but wealthy Persian, Abdool Rassool, who had extensive business interests in Mauritius. He had been trading in Seychelles for some years under the name Said & Co, with coconut plantations and other property on Mahé and La Digue. He acquired a half share in Denis and Providence islands, and on the death of the owner also leased Poivre, D'Arros, and Desroches. In 1892 he offered to take the remaining islands of the Amirantes, including Rémire, African Banks, Desnoeufs, Étoile, Marie Louise, and Boudeuse. Production of the islands included turtles, salted fish, and sea birds eggs. Island trade had previously been in Mauritian hands, but immigrants from the Indian sub-continent like Oliaji and Jivan Jetha were now strong competitors. Active in import-export, they provided in the absence of a proper banking system much needed credit facilities, although the result was a constant drain of specie to Bombay, a situation not rectified until the introduction of local banknotes in 1914.

The turn of the century was also marked by extensive exploitation of guano deposits,[15] an industry that had begun in a small way on Bird Island. Much of it went as fertiliser to the sugar-cane fields of Mauritius, which previously had imported high-grade guano from Peru.

As always, a shortage of labour was the main obstacle to all economic activity in Seychelles. A coir factory that had been established in Victoria in the 1870s by a Frenchman, Pallu de la Barrière, had to close down in 1880 because of lack of labour. The company's agent, Bonnetard, who had sought permission to recruit Indians from Mauritius, complained that although the company offered higher wages than anyone else it could not attract sufficient Seychellois. "Notwithstanding the inducements, as soon as a workman saves ... a small amount ... he leaves, perhaps for three months, perhaps altogether". More successful was the soap factory established in 1885 by another Frenchman, Paul-Louis Guérard, on the 'Pallu' site.

Salmon thought that bringing in Indian labour "might have an awakening effect on the people here", but steady, continuous employment, especially in the confines of a factory, was not the desired lifestyle of the Seychellois. As long as he could survive on fishing, vegetable gardening, and casual labour, he preferred his idleness. It was a way of life that the *moitié* system encouraged, and although the government made several attempts to discourage it, including a stricter law on vagrancy, it continued to be the norm.

The theft of coconuts and vanilla were also subject to new laws, as was *bacca*, the traditional brew of fermented sugar-cane. Regulating the latter was not easy. *Bacca* was so simple to produce, and although by licensing distilleries the government could generate revenue, it was concerned at the incidence of drunkenness, especially if the drink came from an unlicensed source.[16] The problem was compounded by the invidious system under which workers, especially those on the smaller islands, were paid with *bons*, or vouchers, which could be used

182

only in the employer's store to purchase food, or *bacca*. Despite protests by proprietors, Salmon in 1876 banned the use of *bons*, claiming that wages should be paid in cash. His directive seems to have been ignored, for *bons* continued well into the next century.

There was by now little to differentiate "the new population" of Africans and the Creole majority. Reports from the estates where the former worked were generally satisfactory, and in a report to Mauritius in 1892 Brown considered that the Africans no longer needed special protection. He cautioned, however, that "proprietors and managers of estates should feel that they are under some supervision". The planters earlier called for the introduction of more Africans to meet "the present agricultural requirements of and further development of this Dependency". The Secretary of State, Lord Knutsford, agreed. He had received reports that the Africans were well treated, and considered it "a mercy to save any of them from the slavery in the French islands". He promised to ask the Navy to do what it could to help, but nothing came of this initiative.

While employers appreciated the physical strength of the African worker, some also noted his ability to learn new skills. "They are a fine race," declared Ada Edwards, who found them intelligent, and "with great power of reason and capacity of knowledge". She attributed this to a close association with Whites and the teaching given by the Roman Catholic mission. They particularly made good carpenters and masons, and she noted that they were keen to send their children to school. They also delighted in dressing up and holding frequent fêtes. Unfortunately their lack of ambition bred indolence, for as long as they could earn enough to meet their basic needs they were satisfied. "The majority of them are content to dwell in a leaf shanty, provided it be watertight, and to subsist on the coarsest fare, simply a few roots of the manioc plant and a morsel of fish, with but little variation." Only when they fell sick was there any *misère*.

But Africans made indifferent domestic servants, according to Mrs Edwards. Having learned the meaning of freedom, they wanted to assert their independence, and would frequently absent themselves for days. She found them honest and faithful, "to a limited extent". She acknowledged that financial considerations made them reluctant to marry, their love of show and display making the cost of marriage clothes and the wedding feast prohibitive.

Unfortunately we know little of what the Africans themselves thought of their condition. In the early days of their 'freedom' they had been forced to work on the plantations as apprentices, and undoubtedly suffered from abuses despite the authorities' efforts to ensure they were properly treated. Later things improved, to the extent that one could argue their lives were now much superior to anything they would otherwise have experienced in Africa. "I know of few, if any, of his race who are better or more comfortably situated than is the liberated African of Seychelles," wrote Barkly in 1883. He was probably right.

The children especially had benefited from the rudimentary schooling given by the Roman Catholic and CMS missions. Now mature men and women, they and their elders officially expressed in June 1897 their gratitude for having been liberated from slavery and allowed to settle in Seychelles. The occasion was the diamond jubilee of Queen Victoria's Accession. About two thousand liberated Africans went to Government House, where the Administrator, Cockburn Stewart, waited to greet them. They were grouped by tribes, and marched behind a Union Jack embroidered with the words "the Flag that set us free". An address they had drafted in Creole was read out in English, and replied to by Stewart in Creole. Three cheers were then given, and they retired. "This demonstration was quite spontaneous," claimed Stewart to the Secretary of State.

The jubilee celebrations continued for the rest of the week, with an official dinner at Government House, the firing of a 60-gun salute by HMS *Eclipse*, the flagship of Admiral Drummond, a firework display (the first to be seen in Seychelles), the lighting of bonfires on the mountains, and children's sports on Gordon Square. There were also thanksgiving services at the Roman Catholic cathedral and St Paul's Anglican church. The celebrations cost over R.5,000, and another R.1,000 was voted by the Legislative Council towards the erection of a public drinking fountain in Victoria.[17] The jubilee was the high spot of Cockburn Stewart's career. He had put back his leave in order to be present, but with so

184

many pressing matters before him he continued to delay his departure. He knew that before long Seychelles would be declared a full colony, although there was little chance of his being named the first Governor and Commander-in-Chief.[18] Anyway, he was due for retirement.

In May 1899 Stewart left Seychelles for the last time. He died at sea on the way home. Later, in a report of his death, the newspaper *Le Réveil* commented: "We have too much respect for the dead to speak today about his administration. Let us therefore forget the past, and talk of the present, or rather the future. It certainly cannot be said that we have had much luck with our past administrators, and we hope this run of misfortune will not continue." The newspaper went on to criticise those administrators who knew little or nothing about Seychelles, and who were unable to take advice. It suggested that Brown, now acting Administrator for the third time, should be confirmed in the post.[19]

Whatever his faults, Stewart had been among the first to advocate that the islands be made a separate colony. He realised that there could be no substantial progress without a good road-building programme. His determination to push this through made him unpopular with some, for many landowners objected to roads crossing their property; they also objected to paying taxes to meet the cost.

In his first report to the Secretary of State in 1895 Stewart had remarked on the "deplorable state of repair" of the roads. Beyond the first four miles of the road south from Victoria there were only "shreds and patches" unfit for carriage or cart traffic, and difficult even for pedestrians. He had come across obstructions such as coconut trees blocking roads which landowners refused to move, claiming they were not obliged to under the law, and once he had to go personally to have some rocks blasted to clear the way for a road. On Praslin and La Digue there were no roads at all.

In the 1896 estimates, Stewart proposed revising the local rate to meet the cost of new roads. "I regret to say that the evasion of the tax by the richer inhabitants is notorious," he added, promising to ensure better collection in future. Stewart said that the Baie Lazare and Forêt Noire road works, which had been suspended before his arrival in Seychelles, would be resumed. He also mentioned the state of Government House, which he described as "quite unsuited to the requirements of an English family". Victoria generally was now much cleaner, after the residents had been forbidden to keep pigs in town and public latrines had been provided. There was need of a slaughter house, however, as people still killed livestock in their backyard.

Stewart visualised great economic benefits from vanilla cultivation. "Nothing pays better than vanilla," he claimed, adding that an area of 5,000 acres at Mare aux Cochons, where a new road was expected, would be ideal for its cultivation. "I cannot help thinking that if the scores of young Englishmen who leave the mother country year after year for other lands knew of it they would give preference to an English colony which offers advantages not to be met with elsewhere for the investment of small capital, say £1,000." Stewart appears to have spread the word about the prospects for vanilla in Seychelles, for he later remarked that he had received several letters of inquiry, although "only two gentlemen have taken the practical step of coming out here to judge for themselves".

Most agricultural produce still had to go to Victoria by pirogue, which caused waste and delay, and was one reason why fruit growing was unsuccessful. Stewart did succeed in interesting the Secretary of State in his roads project, and an engineer was sent from Ceylon to make a survey. Subsequently a loan not exceeding £20,000 was approved, and Stewart set about finding the necessary labour. He tried first to get coolies from India, and also suggested employing workmen from Aberdeen who were familiar with granite. "Here we have neither tools nor appliances for breaking up granite and no one who knows anything about it," he complained.

Meanwhile another engineer, who was to supervise the road works, arrived from Ceylon. He upset Stewart when he judged that the work would cost over R.7,000, or double that of his colleague's estimate. "I must confess that I am much disappointed to find two officers of the Public Works Department of Ceylon so widely disagreeing as to the cost of these works," he informed the Secretary of State." I had looked forward to opening up the country in a thorough and satisfactory manner, but if Mr Waddell is correct, the work to be done for the money must be seriously curtailed."

He added that the only thing to do would be to create paths

instead of roads in some areas. Five months later in October 1898, Waddell returned from Bombay with 320 labourers to continue work on the roads. Unfortunately the labourers were to prove unsuitable, and the whole of the roads programme had to be restarted after Stewart's departure from Seychelles. It was an unfortunate interruption to a project that had appeared so promising.

During his administration Stewart paid several visits to the outlying islands. To make the trips, the only government vessel available was the seven-ton, undecked cutter *Wave*, which had been in service for about fifty years. Like Barkly, Stewart suggested to London that Seychelles purchase a gunboat to aid communication between the islands. He had noted in the *Navy List* that two such craft were for sale, but his proposal was rejected. It was not until December 1901 that the steam launch *Alexandra*, built at the Royal India Marine Dockyard, arrived in Seychelles to replace the *Wave*. Henceforth government officials would not be subject to the vagaries of the wind when going around the islands.

* *

Britain had not forgotten Seychelles' usefulness as a place of exile. Almost everything about the islands was ideal. Detainees did not need close supervision, for there was little chance of escaping. The Seychellois seemed not to object to their islands being used as an open prison, and if the climate was sometimes oppressive it was healthy enough for a lengthy, enforced residence.

Five years had passed since the departure of ex-Sultan Abdullah of Perak, but as Joseph Chamberlain was still Secretary of State for the Colonies it was perhaps natural that he should think of Seychelles when faced with the problem of what to do with the large number of Boer prisoners captured in South Africa. Britain had been at war with the Boer republics since October 1899, and of the thousands of prisoners taken some had already been sent to Ascension island. On 19 April 1900, Chamberlain cabled Seychelles to inquire if the Dependency could also take some prisoners. Sweet-Escott had recently taken up the post of Administrator, and was eager to oblige. Félicité Island, where some of the Malay deportees had lived for a time, was available. Lessee

187

Harold Bergne offered to put it at the government's disposal for R.100 a month. PWD superintendent Sébert Baty confirmed that huts with corrugated iron roofs could be built for R.150, with leaf verandas. Leaf huts would be cheaper, but would take longer to make. He suggested putting 2,000 prisoners on Curieuse and 500 on Félicité.

Dr Robert Denman, the medical officer, agreed it was possible to accommodate that number on Curieuse if the leper and pauper camps were moved. The camp sites would have to be cleared and burned. He suggested sending the paupers to the old African camp at Mont Fleuri, and the lepers to Anse Marie Louise. Sweet-Escott cabled Chamberlain the same day to say Seychelles would be ready to accept the prisoners, but by June the Secretary of State had changed his mind. However, Sweet-Escott favoured the idea of removing the lepers from Curieuse, and within months he had both them and the paupers moved to Round island, off Praslin.[20] Meanwhile Chamberlain had informed Sweet-Escott that he should prepare for the arrival of a rather different guest, namely King Prempeh of Ashanti.[21]

The Ashantis had a long history of resistance to European encroachment in West Africa. They had once defeated the British in 1825, and they continued to raid and enslave other tribes and disrupt the trade of the Gold Coast. In 1875, a British-led punitive expedition captured the Ashanti capital, Kumasi. There followed a peace treaty, involving a British presence in Kumasi and the paying of an indemnity, but dissension within the tribe continued. After years of unrest the young chief Prempeh, then aged 16, was declared king with the support of the Gold Coast governor.

Years later, in a petition seeking his release from Seychelles, Prempeh described his fall from power. "A couple of months after I was proclaimed [king], the Governor sent another officer to Kumasi to announce that as his Excellency himself had set a King on the throne, he will make the King as a planted tree which is being watered and had grown up favourably." The British wanted to introduce schools into Kumasi, "but I the King and all the inhabitants not knowing that it was for our own good refused to accept same," admitted Prempeh. When the British insisted, offering to pay subsidies to the Ashanti and protect them from their foes, "we allowed ourselves to be deceived by our mischievous and refused to accept same." He admitted that there were other faults "which we have done to Government and which we confess." Having reflected on what he described as the good deeds of the English, they thought of surrendering, but changed their minds and continued resistance "to make matters worst".[22]

The result was the capture of Prempeh and several of his chiefs, and their removal to Freetown in Sierra Leone. In Ashanti other chiefs, including the 80-year-old Queen Mother of Egisu, commander of the rebel forces, continued to wage guerrilla warfare. "They were also captured," recalled Prempeh in his petition, "and since we are here [in Seychelles] we sympathise greatly for our misdeeds; but we blessed our Sovereign King George V for the kind treatment and supervision we still receiving in His Majesty's hands".

On behalf of himself and the others Prempeh asked for forgiveness and permission "to return to our country where we promise that no similar error will be ever heard of us any more". The contrite, obsequious wording of the petition is understandable; Prempeh, now aged 40, had by then been a prisoner in Seychelles for thirteen years, during which time he and the other detainees had several times petitioned the British government for their release. All of them were ready to make whatever submissions were necessary to be freed.

Prempeh and his followers, numbering fifty-six, including wives and children, had arrived at Mahé from Sierra Leone on 11 September 1900. Sweet-Escott had been advised to use the same procedure as that for the detention of the Malay sultans in 1877, namely to issue an Ordinance under which he, as Administrator, and "with the advice and consent of the Legislative Council", conferred on himself necessary powers for the detention of certain political prisoners from West Africa. The ordinance stipulated that detainees attempting to escape were liable to two years' imprisonment, and anyone aiding their escape also two years, with or without hard labour.

A property of about 17 acres at Le Rocher, with a good wooden house of six rooms and a separate dining room, had been leased from Jean-Louis Adam at a rent of R.80 per month.[23] Here Prempeh and Yakyed Assibi, ex-king of Koku, other chiefs and their families were accommodated. Deltel Brothers & Co. supplied furniture, crockery, cutlery, and bedding. The prisoners thought the cooking pots were not large enough, and the mattresses had to be specially made. The rest of the party occupied huts at the African camp, near La Misère crossroads.

Sweet-Escott received Prempeh and the others at Government House, and also visited them at Le Rocher. From existing photographs Prempeh appears the typical African king, dressed in a voluminous robe, with head-dress and decorated sandals, and in one photograph with an umbrella held over him. Forwarding this picture to the Secretary of State in February 1901, Sweet-Escott noted that the ex-Queen Mother Elizabeth Ya Etchia was "a lady of considerable character", while ex-King Assibi "appears to be fast losing in the congenial climate of Mahé the truculent look which I noticed ... last year". Also in the photograph was Prempeh's son and heir, "a smart little boy", who was receiving good reports from the headmaster of Victoria School. Meanwhile some of the Ashantis were working as labourers or servants in town, and Sweet-Escott wondered whether it would be possible to recruit others from the Gold Coast to work on the vanilla estates.

Four months later the second group of Ashanti prisoners arrived in Seychelles. This included the formidable Queen Mother of Egisu, several of the most warlike chiefs, and the chief executioner of Kumasi. They were all accommodated at the African Camp. In a letter forwarded to Sweet-Escott, the British Resident at Kumasi, Captain Donald Stewart, warned that the latest arrivals were different from Prempeh and the first batch. "These last are men who stirred up and led a rebellion against the Government, and several of them would have been tried for murder and hung if it had not been for officers commanding columns having offered them their lives if they gave themselves up." The Queen Mother had been particularly prominent in waging war against the British.

In November 1901, just over a year after their arrival, Prempeh and some of the Ashanti chiefs petitioned Chamberlain for permission to return home. In a covering letter Sweet-Escott said that except for "indications of intemperance" he had no complaints about their behaviour. He had now forbidden them spirits, but "only recently ex-King Prempeh and some of the chiefs endeavoured to satisfy with

190

ginger beer their cravings for drink. The result was not satisfactory, and the lesson of moderation in the consumption even of non-alcoholic drinks appears to have been learnt". Prempeh's petition was refused, Chamberlain expressing regret "that it is not possible for me to hold out any hope that they will be allowed to return to Ashanti at an early date". A similar reply, to another petition, was made in November 1902.

Despite these setbacks Prempeh never lost heart, remaining cheerful, learning to speak Creole and English, and doing his best to integrate into Seychelles society. Dr John Bradley, a recent arrival in Seychelles, was impressed by the Ashanti king's striking personality, and noted that among his followers his word was law. When Prempeh held court to listen to complaints, his executioner stood behind him with an axe, and "he was quite surprised, when for a very serious offence by one of his own slaves, he [was informed] the death penalty ... could not be carried out". According to Bradley, Prempeh instead introduced a system of fines, to be paid in bottles of rum.

Prempeh was puzzled by the existence of two rival Christian religions in Seychelles. He is reported to have elected to become an Anglican only when told that this was the religion of King Edward VII. Prempeh's three wives were an obvious obstacle to his baptism, and he had to be persuaded to send two of them back home. They left Seychelles, together with a maid and eleven children, accompanied by Bradley, who saw them as far as Marseilles. Subsequently Prempeh was received into the Church of England by the Bishop of Mauritius. He was given the name Edward, and became a regular worshipper at St Paul's church in Victoria.[24] "The spectacle of Prempeh, the Queen Mother and the two ex-Kings of Uganda, Mwanga and Kabarega, sitting side by side in Church is not devoid of interest," Sweet-Escott had earlier remarked in a letter to Chamberlain.

The presence of Kabarega and Mwanga, who had arrived in Seychelles about a year after Prempeh, was a further indication of Seychelles' new role as a place of detention. Originally Sweet-Escott had planned to accommodate Kabarega and Mwanga separately, at Anse Royale and Baie Ste Anne, Praslin, in order to keep them apart from each other and also from Prempeh. He thought the three chiefs might get along very well together, but did not want to take any chances. "I am prepared to deal with any disturbance should it arise, but there is no object in taking a step which might provoke a disturbance," he explained. In the end, Kabarega and Mwanga were both lodged in a house leased from Mr Gendron at Pointe Conan.[25] They expressed satisfaction with their quarters; all they asked was for an additional cookhouse and latrine as they were two separate families. The twelve soldiers of the East African Rifles who had escorted the prisoners to Seychelles were accommodated in the police barracks until they could return home.

The two African rulers, whose adjoining kingdoms straddled the headwaters of the Nile, had for years opposed the advance from the north and east of European explorers, Arab slavers and Christian missionaries. However by the end of the 1890s they had finally been defeated and captured, and the kingdoms of Bunyoro and Buganda incorporated into the new British protectorate of Uganda. At first the ex-kings had been sent to Kismayu, on the Somali coast, but in January 1901 the British commissioner for Uganda, Sir Harry Johnston, wrote to London urging that they be transferred "to some place like the Seychelles Islands" where they would be unable to communicate with their supporters.

Mwanga's infant son Daudi Chwa had already been proclaimed Kabaka (king) of Buganda, and Johnston said it was the regents' wish that Mwanga should never be allowed to return. "Mwanga ... being a nominal Roman Catholic while the little King is being brought up as Protestant, there is occasionally a hint of a movement being set on foot by the French priests of great sympathy being felt for the exiled King — a sympathy, if it exists at all, of their own manufacture." He noted that recently he had been approached indirectly by these missionaries to see whether a deputation might visit Mwanga in Kismayu, a proposal he had rejected. If Mwanga could be sent to Seychelles it would put an end to such intrigues.

The bitter rivalry between the Catholic and Protestant missions in Buganda, represented by the White Fathers and the CMS respectively, had succeeded in converting large numbers of Baganda to Christianity, and at the same time bequeathing a legacy of religious animosity that was to colour Ugandan politics for years to come. Mwanga had originally

192

favoured the Catholic, or French party, though he feared and suspected all groups, including the Arab Muslims, and, like his father Mutesa, he indulged himself in playing one against the other.

"None can fail to see that he is fitful and fickle, and, I fear, revengeful. One vice to which he is addicted is the smoking of bhang," noted the CMS representative. "Under the influence of the narcotic he is capable of the wildest unpremeditated action." These words were to be prophetic. Shortly after his accession Mwanga, angered by the refusal of several young pages who had embraced Christianity to submit to sodomy, ordered three of them to be tortured and killed. A year later, in 1886, at an assembly of pages, Mwanga ordered the Christians among them to step forward and renounce their faith. When they refused, some thirty were taken away to be horribly mutilated and then burned to death.[26]

Unlike Mwanga, the former ruler of Bunyoro, Kabarega, although described as "treacherous and cruel", had some redeeming qualities, not least his courage and determination. As a young warrior he had been present when Speke and Grant had marched through his father's capital near Masindi on their way to discover the source of the Nile. He had later fought successively the European explorers Baker, Gordon, Stanley and Lugard (creator of modern Uganda), as well as the kings of Buganda. Invariably defeated and driven from his capital he never gave up, deserving the description of "the most resourceful guerrilla leader in Central Africa".

Mwanga did not long survive in Seychelles. In October 1902 Sweet-Escott reported to London that he was dangerously ill, and had refused the operation advised by the chief medical officer and Dr Addison. Seven months later the former ruler of Buganda died, and was buried in the cemetery at Mont Fleuri. His body was returned to Uganda in 1910. Kabarega lived on in exile, a large, dignified figure in formal European dress. He was released in 1923 when aged 80, but died on the journey home. However warlike he may have been in his youth, Kabarega spent his final years peacefully in Seychelles.

As for Prempeh, also mellowed by his long years of exile, he was released the following year, and returned to the Gold Coast, together with most of his followers.[27] In a letter written for publication in the newspaper *Le Petit Seychellois*, he thanked the British monarch for allowing the Ashantis to return home, and expressed appreciation of "the unfailing courtesy and respect shown to me by all classes of the population" in Seychelles.

14

The New Colony
1903 - 1913

C'est fête. Sous les cocotiers
Passent en robes blanches
Les négresses aux belle hanches
Dans l'ombre des sentiers

Paul-Jean Toulet
Vers Inédits, 1936

After more than a century as a dependency of Mauritius, Seychelles was at last to become a Crown colony. Henceforth all ties with the mother colony would be severed, the only remaining link being a right of appeal in certain cases to the Mauritius Supreme Court. The Letters Patent and Royal Instructions had been promulgated by Order in Council on 31 August 1903. The formal proclamation of the new Colony of Seychelles[1] would be made on 9 November, the birthday of King Edward VII.

The occasion was a personal triumph for Sweet-Escott. He had suggested that Seychelles be declared a separate colony two months after becoming Administrator in December 1899, and although the Secretary of State demurred, Sweet-Escott had refused to be discouraged. Now here he was, on the appointed day, taking the oath of office as Governor before the Judge, restyled Chief Justice, Mr Alfred Herchenroder, while in the harbour a British cruiser, HMS *Pearl*,[2] fired a 17-gun salute. A similar salute followed from a visiting French warship, the *Gueydon*.

If Sweet-Escott had worked hard to separate Seychelles from Mauritius, its governor, Sir Charles Bruce, had tried almost as hard to prevent it. Bruce claimed that had Sweet-

Escott been frank with him he would have given his proposals for separating Seychelles from Mauritius "impartial, friendly and even favorable consideration". Instead the Seychelles administrator had gone behind his back, exploiting differences between Seychelles and Mauritius over issues such as the treatment of labourers on Farquhar island and the appointment of Mauritian officials to Seychelles. When Bruce sought clarification on some point, he was told that "the Secretary of State decides, and not the Governor of Mauritius, whether suggestions made by the Administrator of Seychelles ... shall be adopted or not". The one-time classics master of Royal College was not prepared to accept interference from the college's former Rector.

Sweet-Escott assured London that he had no personal interest in obtaining full colony status for Seychelles, only an "honest conviction" that it was the right thing to do. He argued that the constitutional changes approved in 1897, which gave the Administrator the powers of a governor, were flawed, "for clearly there cannot be at the same time two Governors and Commanders-in-Chief of these islands".

When the Colonial Office insisted that Sweet-Escott could not claim the powers of an independent governor, and must obey instructions from the Governor of Mauritius unless they conflicted with rules issued by the Crown, he retorted that the word 'lawful' should have been inserted before 'instructions', adding that if the Governor of Mauritius could instruct the Administrator of Seychelles without knowing anything about the islands or the correspondence that had passed between the latter and the Secretary of State, then it was high time Seychelles was separated.

By now Sweet-Escott was being labelled "impertinent and insubordinate", and an irritated Secretary of State warned him that no definite decision on separation had yet been reached. As a result it was not until November 1903, with the impending retirement of the Mauritius governor, that Seychelles was declared a separate colony.

Bruce was still smouldering with resentment when he called briefly at Mahé on his way back to England and, whether by oversight or design, he was unable to stay long enough to witness the swearing-in of Sweet-Escott.[3] He had sent the obligatory message, in which he regretted that the ties binding

Seychelles to Mauritius for so long had finally been severed. In contrast, Sweet-Escott's speech stressed the disadvantages Seychelles had suffered as a dependency, and called on the inhabitants to give him their support and understanding to ensure the future prosperity of the islands. He then called for three cheers, which were echoed outside the Court House as he and Mrs Sweet-Escott returned to Government House, passing the clocktower he had unveiled "in loving memory" of Queen Victoria six months earlier.

Everyone was proud of *lorloz*, as it was called. One of a series of clocktowers made by a Croydon firm, the model ordered by Sweet-Escott as a memorial to the Queen — she had died on 22 January 1901 — was a replica of the clocktower erected in 1892 outside London's Victoria Station.[4] The eleven cases carrying the clock parts did not arrive in Seychelles until early 1903, and there was further delay after one of the crates containing the 60lb movement weights dropped into the sea during unloading. The Public Works Department succeeded in making a duplicate weight, and the clocktower was eventually unveiled on 1 April 1903.

Reporting this to London, Sweet-Escott noted that it stood in a "commanding position where four roads met, and has much improved the appearance of the centre of the town". All memorials run the risk of losing their relevance, and the Victoria Clocktower was no exception. As the crowds gathered round it to celebrate Seychelles being declared a separate colony, it must have seemed to many less an object of reverence to a past queen than visible testimony to a people's progress.[5]

Exactly six months after being sworn in as governor, Sweet-Escott left Seychelles to take up the post of governor of British Honduras. At the Colonial Office some doubted his suitability for what was regarded as a more exacting job. He had proved in Seychelles that he was industrious and painstaking, but some felt he lacked originality. He was also accused of worrying over trifles, and taking offence too readily when overruled.[6]

During most of his time in Seychelles, Sweet-Escott had been favoured by a buoyant economy, with vanilla, despite fluctuations in price, remaining the mainstay of the economy.[7] Government revenue, more than half of which came from customs duties, had continued to increase, the figure of

R.399,311 collected in 1900 being the highest ever recorded. In addition to vanilla, other principal exports were coconut oil, copra, turtle shell, soap, guano, and vacoa bags,[8] with efforts being made to diversify into other crops, including coffee, cloves, and pepper. The botanic station, which had opened in 1901, was experimenting with tobacco and rubber.[9] In the same year Seychelles held its first agricultural show.[10]

Immigration from Britain, which had always been minimal, increased in the latter part of the 19th century, adding names such as Butler, Young, Green, Stevenson, and Dingwall to the more common French names. "For a man of energy, perseverance, and temperate habits Seychelles affords as good an opening as any other tropical colony," advised *The Times*, adding that an immigrant should possess sufficient capital to buy land outright and to wait until the crops gave a return. Nor should he rely "as many planters do, on the somewhat capricious return which a vanilla plantation gives, but endeavour to plant up his estate with other tropical products for which the climate and soil of Seychelles are well suited". *The Times* did not mention the shortage of labourers, nor the fact that out of a population of 19,000 three-quarters could be termed as non-productive

Dr Bradley, medical officer for South Mahé, were struck by the extravagant living of the white proprietors, who "were well dressed, gave good and expensive luncheons, and entertained in a lavish manner". It was a life style imitated to a lesser degree by all classes. "The improvidence of the people as a whole, and the easy way in which they fall into the hands of money lenders" meant that none was prepared when the crash came in 1904, due mainly to the failure of the vanilla crop. "People that seemed opulent were now paupers," wrote Bradley. Unable to repay loans suddenly called in by Indian shopkeepers and mortgage agents their properties were seized and sold.

When Sweet-Escott's successor, Walter Davidson, took over he described the financial situation as grave, and proposed several retrenchment measures, including not filling vacancies in the public service, cutting the police force by one-third (dependent on his finding an efficient police chief), and making economies in the medical department. He also wanted cuts in staff at the government-run Victoria School, suggesting that if the school head, currently on leave, was posted elsewhere, the acting head, George Mackay, could take over. "This gentleman is a Scotchman of tenacity of purpose and patience. He has strength of will enough not to be discouraged and to stick to the job."

As a former teacher Sweet-Escott had taken a keen interest in the standard of schooling in Seychelles, especially at Victoria School, the name given to the non-denominational school set up by the government in 1891. He firmly believed that nothing could beat an English education, and he disapproved of the St Louis College, with its exclusive French instruction by the Marist Brothers, frequent catechism, and lack of compulsory games. Under the Education Ordinance of 1900 he had taken firmer control of education by transferring responsibility from the Legislative to the Executive Council. He had also imposed a policy that English would be used wherever possible, in the hope that, by promoting the learning of English he would induce a sense of loyalty in the Seychellois, and give pupils of African origin "the opportunity of improving their position by reaping the full benefits of such education as we can bring within their reach".

The Administrator had been instrumental in securing two scholarships of R.600 each for boys to study at Royal College, Mauritius, or at a school in Britain. He was tactful enough to insist that the scholarships should not be confined to boys of Victoria School. What he did not envisage was that St Louis College would invariably win the scholarship race. Within a few years the open scholarship scheme was abandoned. Like others before and after him, Sweet-Escott attributed poor performance at school to the use of two languages, French and English, both of which had to be acquired as foreign languages as most of the children knew only Creole, "which is too restricted and rude to be a medium of learning". He considered that as Seychelles was a British colony the medium of instruction should be English. Secretary of State Joseph Chamberlain was not so sure. He thought parents should have a choice of English or French, but his views reached Sweet-Escott too late. He had already opted for English.

According to a 1902 report English teaching was by then receiving more attention, although it was still impossible to conduct an examination solely in that language. As for French,

199

the spelling was poor, "no doubt ... from confusion with Creole". Five years later, another report claimed that 80 per cent of the population could neither read nor write, while less than 5 per cent could "speak English of any kind".

Bishop Hudrisier, since 1892 the first Bishop of the new Roman Catholic diocese of Port-Victoria, cooperated with the government by introducing English into the mission schools; his main difficulty was to find sufficient teachers. At the convent, where Irish Sisters of St Joseph de Cluny had been teaching English as a foreign language since 1864, more were brought in to take charge of the enlarged English classes. Bradley did not favour giving too much schooling to ordinary folk, as they then disliked manual work "and want to be clerks, office boys, or [be in] some employment where they can wear boots, and have collars and ties". Looking ahead, he envisaged "a composite language" emerging in Seychelles, where French and English words would be mixed in with Creole.

Undoubtedly the main obstacle to the Seychellois learning to speak English or French was the overwhelming influence of what Sweet-Escott called that "debased French patois". Product of a predominantly African slave society, Creole was firmly rooted in the consciousness of the people. As such it was a barrier rather than a bridge to the learning of French. The promotion of English faced a different challenge, that of the French connection. French was the language of the propertied classes, of the Church, and of the Mauritians whose influence extended throughout the public and private sector, and it would not be easily supplanted. Privately, Sweet-Escott regretted the adherence of Mauritians to the French language, and considered them indifferent British subjects, "never entirely loyal", some, in his opinion, almost as bad as Irish Nationalists. He also thought they lacked the grit and backbone that for him epitomised the average Englishman.

In 1911, in a further attempt to promote English, the government set up a secondary school, King's College, with facilities for boarders. Planned on the lines of an English public school, it had at first only a handful of pupils, but to attract parents away from St Louis College Davidson introduced a number of scholarships. He also split Victoria School into separate paying and non-paying schools, to reassure white parents that their children need not mix with those from the labouring classes. The latter henceforth would be accommodated in what was known as the Government Free School.

Although these developments were unwelcome to the Roman Catholic mission — they were seen as diverting funds from the hard-pressed grant-aided schools — its influence over all aspects of education remained unshaken. "The Roman Catholic Church is hard working ... and does all in its power to advance and get the people to its churches and schools," noted Bradley, who forecast a continuing decline in the Church of England. In 1902, there were twenty Catholic schools in Seychelles, with a total of 2,195 pupils, while the number attending the four Anglican schools was 267. Ten years later the total school population was 2,692, with most of the increase at the Catholic schools. For girls, secondary education had been provided at the convent's paying school since 1904. Bishop Clark, who succeeded Hudrisier on the latter's death in 1910, successfully resisted attempts by Davidson to downgrade St Louis College in order to leave King's College as the sole secondary school for boys.

The government's intervention in education was to prove a mistake. It was costly, it did not greatly advance English teaching,[11] and for the Catholic Church it was a constant source of suspicion and mistrust, as instanced by the row over boarders at King's taking their morning bath without clothes. Word of this had reached Father Justin de Gumy (one of the first Swiss priests to be sent to Seychelles, who later became Bishop of Port-Victoria). He wrote to the principal, George Mackay, pointing out that naked bathing was "opposed to good morals and to the virtue of purity". He asked that Catholic boys be allowed to wear clothing. Mackay wrote to the parents, all of whom except one thought the priest should not interfere. Father Justin replied that it did not matter what the parents thought, and that he would withhold Communion from the boys. The matter eventually reached the Governor, and the priest's threat was withdrawn.[12]

In 1914 Mackay, who was also inspector of schools, applied for a similar post at Mauritius. His departure, and that of several teachers who went off to war, seems to have been a fatal blow. In 1919 King's College closed. For some, the failure to improve education in Seychelles lay solely with the parish priest, who "has no desire to see education on liberal lines ... and is in his heart in direct opposition to the British government and its supervision of his schools". So wrote Mackay's successor, D.W. McLeod, who criticised the priests for not only keeping French influence alive but in maintaining a backward, "mechanical and useless proficiency" in the classroom.[13]   McLeod claimed that even the Sisters of St Joseph de Cluny, although they did not dare say so, would have welcomed the arrival in the country of English priests. Four years after the closure of King's College, the government handed over Victoria School to the missions. Thus ended the government's attempt to run its own schools, an experiment that would not be tried again until 1944.

In a move intended to remove Catholic ill-feeling over the education reforms of 1910, Davidson sought approval to put R.10,000 of public funds towards the rebuilding of the Roman Catholic Cathedral, which was reported to be "tumbling to pieces". A refurbished cathedral, he argued, would add to the sense of municipal pride, already awakened by the new Government House,[14] construction of which had started in 1911, and the Carnegie Library,[15] which he had formally opened earlier that year. The Colonial Office was not impressed; it suggested that if Seychelles had money to spare it should spend it on roads and drainage.

Davidson also encouraged the growing overseas interest in Seychelles that had been stimulated by the writings and lectures of Darwin and General Gordon. In 1905 he welcomed the arrival of an Indian Ocean expedition led by the British naturalist J. Stanley Gardiner,[16] who spent several weeks on the islands examining land and marine organisms. Gardiner also interested himself in the tales of pirate treasure in Seychelles, and concluded that "where a legend is universally spread, experience leads us to believe that it rests on a basis of truth".[17] Despite the legends only one instance of treasure trove was to be officially recorded, that of a large quantity of silver coin and other articles uncovered in 1911 on Astove island.[18]

Davidson was also behind the publication in 1909 of a volume of documents relating to the French discovery and early settlement of Seychelles collected by a former inspector of the Messageries Maritimes shipping line, Albert-Auguste

Fauvel. Davidson wrote an introductory chapter to the book, and paid for the printing of what is still a core reference for those researching the history of Seychelles.

He gave backing to local initiatives such as the Society for the Protection of Animals. Formed in July 1912 by an eccentric Englishwoman, Miss Emma Wardlaw Best, the society had as its patron Mrs Davidson, while the Governor arranged for the society's notices to be put in the *Government Gazette* free of charge. Miss Best, a trained nurse, had arrived in Seychelles while on the way home from India with an ailing father, and decided to stay on when her father died. In 1899 she purchased Moyenne island, where she lived along with an increasing number of stray dogs.[19]

The notion that animals needed to be protected from cruelty was utterly foreign to most Seychellois, and in December 1915 Miss Best is found complaining to Davidson's successor that someone had left a dog hanging from a wire round its neck, at the side of the Bel Air road. Miss Best rescued the dog, but despite the urgings of the Governor the police were unable to find the culprit.

Economically, Seychelles had been slow to recover from the effects of the 1904 slump. The government offered loans to planters as they switched from vanilla back to coconuts, but although some officials assured themselves that "the planters and their labourers can never actually starve" there was extensive hardship. In 1907 a highly unpopular income tax was replaced by a new scheme of direct taxation, with surtaxes on certain imports and licences, and to meet a shortage of labour the government arranged for Indians, both men and women, to be brought in. Over a hundred arrived from Madras early in 1904, a movement that continued until, in 1909, official fears were being expressed at the influence and amount of property Indians were acquiring.[20] Despite a number of bankruptcies in 1911 the economy continued showing signs of revival, both copra and guano fetching high prices right up to the outbreak of war in 1914. Planters were also diversifying into other products.[21]

However, communications with Europe, India, and the Far East were still far from satisfactory. The return of the MM steamers in 1902 had been widely welcomed, but the French line's rates were high despite a heavy Seychelles subsidy, and while its steamers would assure the quick dispatch of small quantities of vanilla to Europe, they refused to load with copra because of its bulk and unpleasant smell.[22] On the other hand, British India ships were calling at Seychelles only if there was sufficient inducement, a situation that persisted until a few years before the outbreak of war, when the BI liners resumed calling at Mahé on a regular monthly basis. Fortunately, there were some newcomers among the shipping lines, notably the Deutsche Öst-Afrika Linie, which, with a brief interruption, maintained a service up to the outbreak of war. A Scandinavian shipping company also began calling at Mahé.

There had been a brief return of American whalers to Seychelles during the early years of the century. In 1904 the 366-ton whaler *Josephine* (Captain H.D. Smith) caught eighty-three whales off Bird island. There was a return visit by Smith in 1906, after he and another whaler were driven by bad weather northward from the Crozet islands, where they had been hunting right whales. In 1912 the New Bedford barque *Charles W. Morgan*[23] was hunting sperm whales off Bird island, which was a novel enough sight for the island's inhabitants to sail out in a schooner to view the captured whales. Later the *Morgan* called at Mahé, where it spent several days carrying out repairs and giving shore leave to the crew. It sailed again on 16 August, having paid Seychelles its only direct benefit, R.15 in harbour dues.

Davidson feared that the *Morgan*'s visit presaged not the return of individual whaleships as previously, but an invasion of Seychelles waters by flotillas of steam trawlers, serviced by a large depot ship. "These steam flotillas have devastated all seas which they have visited," he wrote. "The 'right' whales are greatly reduced in number ... so now attention is being turned to the sperm whales. In my opinion, one visit of a steam flotilla will wipe out the sperm whales on the Seychelles Bank ... the greed of the capitalists who have embarked capital in such a flotilla will override any idea of ultimate advantage accruing from the preservation of the whales." He pointed out that, unlike the Falklands, Seychelles was not just a station on the migratory route of whales but a place where they congregated all the year round. He urged that the government introduce licences for whalers in order to limit the damage to sperm whale stocks. This was duly done by Davidson's successor,

Lieut.-Colonel Charles O'Brien. The first licence was granted to the St Abbs Whaling Company, which in 1913 sent the motor vessel *St Ebba*, under Captain Harald Henricksen, to begin whaling off the Seychelles. It met with fair success, and Henricksen returned to Scotland to arrange more capital. The result was the amalgamation of the St Abbs company with the Mossel Bay Company of South Africa. Two more whaling vessels were sent out, and the company set up a land base on St Anne, which consisted of a factory for oil and another for the production of whale guano.

The base was visited by O'Brien, who witnessed the first small whale being towed in and hauled on to the platform for cutting in. "We witnessed the interesting process of cutting off the fat, the obtaining of sperm from the head and the preparation of the flesh for reduction to oil in the boilers," he wrote, adding that he had been told the small whale would give about twenty-five barrels of oil.

O'Brien was convinced that with careful management there were good prospects for whaling, but he was to be disappointed. The total number of whales caught between October 1914 and July 1915 was 122, a number that would have been greater had the factory been sited nearer the whaling ground off Denis and Bird islands. This, plus the high cost of Norwegian personnel and the generally inefficient management resulted in the failure of the enterprise, the company going into liquidation in October 1915. Although the government tried to interest others, and continued discussions off and on with various companies up to 1934, nothing came of their efforts.

* *

On a chilly November day in 1913, the Judicial Committee of the Privy Council[24] met in London to advise on an appeal by a Mahé businessman against his conviction by the Seychelles Supreme Court two years previously. Although Rex v. Lanier was a relatively minor matter of alleged embezzlement, the standing of the main protagonists was such that it had quickly become a *cause célèbre*. Central to the affair was Louis Édouard Lanier, a Franco-Mauritian whose energy and enterprise had made him one of the colony's most powerful traders. Lanier, a member of Legislative Council, French consul in Seychelles and agent for the Messageries Maritimes shipping line, was also trustee for the guardian of the Lablache minors, natural sons of the late Alfred d'Emmerez de Charmoy. Among Lanier's trading rivals were d'Emmerez de Charmoy's son Adolphe and the money-lender Mamode Hossen, who since the death in 1896 of his father-in-law, Abdool Rassool, controlled the affairs of Said & Co.

Lanier's downfall began with the failure of one of his overseas ventures, prompting "a vindictive combination" of d'Emmerez and Hossen to have him declared bankrupt, thus raising concern over the administration of the Lablache minors' money invested in Lanier's company. At a family council meeting, presided over by the Seychelles acting Chief Justice, Alexander Williamson, Lanier offered a guarantee for the Lablache funds, together with a suitable mortgage. This was unanimously accepted.

"One would have thought that everything was now satisfactorily arranged and ended," commented the Privy Council. "The minors' interests were completely protected. Sharply as the appellant (Lanier) had been pulled up, he had answered the call; the council were satisfied; and the guarantee and mortgage were put up on record." It therefore appeared "incredible ... that ... after all this ... criminal proceedings were instituted against the appellant under the Seychelles Penal Code."

The person behind these 'incredible' proceedings — and the subsequent grave miscarriage of justice — was the same who had chaired the family council, acting Chief Justice Williamson. Described as "an astute, unscrupulous man whose hand is against everyone", Williamson was known for the arrogant and dubious manner in which he administered justice, as well as for his scandalous behaviour outside the courtroom. Among the many widely held accusations against him was that he shared not only a house but also his wife with the Civil Chaplain, the Rev. Ernest Newton. According to rumour, personal rivalry in the pursuit of sexual favours had led to the mutual antagonism between Williamson and Lanier.[25] Even so, given the occasional notoriety of the Seychelles judiciary, all this might have passed without official censure had the Lanier appeal and another case involving Williamson and prominent members of the Seychelles Club not alerted London that things were far from satisfactory in the Colony.[26] Williamson's hand was certainly seen to be against Lanier when the latter appeared in the Supreme Court on 5 July 1911 to answer the charge of having "wilfully, fraudulently, and feloniously" embezzled the funds of the Lablache minors. First, Williamson refused a week's adjournment to allow Lanier's counsel to arrive from Mauritius. The trial went ahead, and although — as the Crown counsel at the Privy Council hearing admitted — no jury would have convicted Lanier, he was found guilty by the acting Chief Justice and sentenced to eighteen months' hard labour.

Harsh as this was, the length of the sentence was just too short for an appeal to be made to the Mauritius Supreme Court. Williamson refused a request by defence counsel to increase the sentence to make it appealable. Lanier's counsel then tried another tack to involve the Mauritius court, but was unsuccessful. Fortunately for Lanier he was released after serving less than six months of his sentence, three doctors having agreed that his life was endangered if he remained in prison.[27]

Davidson, on his return from leave, considered that justice and expediency demanded that Lanier's application to appeal to His Majesty in Council should be allowed. The company Mahé Syndicate offered the necessary £300 security for the appeal, but this was eventually waived by the government. As a result of these lengthy legal proceedings it was not until October 1913 that the Privy Council's Judicial Committee heard counsel's argument on the Lanier appeal. By that time a question had been raised in Parliament about the state of affairs in Seychelles,[28] and Williamson, faced with the prospect of an official inquiry, had resigned from government service.

In its findings the Privy Council held that it was unnecessary for it to consider the rushed manner of the trial, or the harshness of the sentence, "for, in their Lordships' view, even although the proceedings were taken to have been unobjectionable in form, justice had gravely and injuriously miscarried". Describing the sentence on Lanier as "an invasion of liberty" and "a denial of his just rights as a citizen", the Privy Council declared him not guilty. Sentence and conviction were quashed. The Crown had to pay costs of the appeal and return the costs awarded against Lanier by the Seychelles court. The total charges amounted to £828 18s 8d.[29] "This is awful ... we cannot do anything but pay," someone wrote in a Colonial Office file. The *Law Times* referred to the administration of criminal law in some parts of the Empire as being "far from satisfactory", and expressed the hope that "the whole matter ... be probed to the bottom".

* *

Although Lanier could henceforth portray himself as the innocent victim of a gross miscarriage of justice, he was to be exposed to a less favourable light some years later, when summoned to appear in court to confirm that he did indeed pay his labourers "in whole or in part by the drink he himself manufactures". The question was put to him by police magistrate Arthur Brooke, who had just fined one of Lanier's labourers R.3 for being drunk and disorderly. Brooke wanted to highlight the evils of paying workers with *bons*. Not surprisingly, Lanier was indignant at being interrogated about a system which, he claimed, was general practice among the planters. He protested to the Governor.

O'Brien attempted to smooth things over. He had little time for Brooke, whom he considered a misfit indulging a sense of justice and compassion not provided for in Colonial regulations, and he must have been doubly irritated on learning that the Colonial Office viewed Brooke's zeal favourably. "We have ourselves had to draw attention ... to the unsatisfactory state of wages [in Seychelles]," noted one official, "and the system of payment by *bons* is vicious".

In the end, however, it was the system that triumphed, and Brooke committed suicide. "Is this not a strange Colony!", he had once remarked. The words could serve as his epitaph.

15

Scourge of War
1914 - 1919

Tell the people to be calm, and to be proud
to belong to the British Empire.
Lieut.-Col. O'Brien, Governor, 8 December 1916

News of the outbreak of war in August 1914 "dropped like a bomb" on South Mahé. Traders closed their shops, many people ran off to the hills, and each night thieves raided backyards for pigs, fowls, and tortoises. According to Bradley, an earthquake could not have produced more consternation. Almost everyone envisaged German fleets bombarding the coast and sacking their homes. Bradley attributed the panic to the Creole mind, but Governor O'Brien thought Bradley had himself contributed to the "ignorant excitement", which may well have been true given that the doctor was clearly enjoying himself.

As justice of the peace he had eagerly assumed the duties of civil defence supremo, and in his first General Order to the region had set up a chain of look-out posts to search for any sign of the enemy. "I expect all men to be on the *qui vive*," he told the sentries, warning them that if anyone was found asleep at his post punishment would be "extremely severe".

On the day after the outbreak of war one of the sentries reporting seeing a man-of-war fifty miles off Port Glaud, sailing south. This turned out to be a false alarm, the nervous sentry having mistaken a cloud on the horizon for the smoke of an enemy raider, but unfortunately Bradley had already sent off the report to the Governor.

Two weeks later Bradley dispatched another report

concerning the possible movement of German warships. The messenger left Anse Royale for Victoria at 9 pm on the 19 August, arriving at Government House at 2.30 the following morning. An angry O'Brien informed Bradley that his note was useless. "Further, the sending of a dispatch messenger at that hour can only cause unnecessary excitement and unrest, and finally the messenger took so long in the journey that had the message been of first importance it would have been of no purpose." Nor was that all. "We are not playing soldiers," Bradley was reminded. "I have pointed out to you several times the necessity of using discretion and doing nothing to unnecessarily alarm or excite people." Also, sending such messages made a farce of the Colony's intelligence gathering.

However, the possibility of a German attack was real enough, and was particularly worrying after the cable links to Mauritius and Zanzibar were accidentally cut, leaving the islands completely isolated. The German light cruiser *Emden* was known to be active in the Indian Ocean, as was the cruiser *Königsberg*, the largest, fastest, and most powerful vessel in the region.

The Seychelles learned later that the *Königsberg* had anchored off Aldabra at the end of August for a brief rendez-vous with a collier. The manager of the settlement, unaware that war had broken out, hailed the ship but was told to clear off as there was smallpox on board. Immediately after coaling, the cruiser sailed. Fears of attack remained acute in Seychelles until it was confirmed that the *Königsberg* had sought refuge in the Rufiji river on the East African coast.[1] By then the Zanzibar cable had been repaired, although it was not until November 1914 that the link with Mauritius was restored. In the same month the *Emden* clashed with the Australian cruiser *Sydney*, and now lay wrecked on the Cocos islands. In April the following year a naval party and two Marconi engineers arrived in Seychelles to erect a wireless station at Bel Ombre, ensuring an additional line of communication for the island.

On the outbreak of war the Governor had formed a defence committee, which discussed matters such as price control, internal order, the planting of additional food crops like sweet potatoes, maize, and manioc. Among other measures it took were the training of the police in firearms and the formation of an Emergency Citizens' Corps, drawn from members of the

Miniature Rifle Club. On a given signal they were to parade outside the Carnegie Library, with rifle and ten rounds of ammunition.² A similar force was planned for Praslin, but after the island's justice of the peace, Dr N.P. Jewell, advised against arming anyone on Praslin or La Digue, the force of selected men were given staves and truncheons. Twenty-eight members of the Colony's civil service and other citizens were sworn in as special constables, including two members of the Prempeh family.³

Fund-raising for the Red Cross was organised, and Bradley reported that a total of R.600 was raised in South Mahé, along with contributions of clothing and bedding. "The sympathy of the Creole population is with our army," he noted, which was "in marked contrast to the demeanour of the people during the Boer War, when every presumed victory of the Boers was hailed with acclamation, and the slightest English reverse was received with joy." Undoubtedly he was right to attribute the change of attitude to the French being allies in the war, although he thought that the slow spread of the English language also played a part. There was, too, the effect of the Colony celebrating each year Empire Day, which Bradley considered helped to teach the children that they were "part and parcel of the British Empire".

Feelings of Anglo-French solidarity received a boost in November 1914 with the arrival at Mahé of a contingent of officers of the French colonial army on their way to Madagascar. Governor O'Brien was host to the senior officers at Government House, while others found ready hospitality in private homes or were accommodated at the Carnegie Hall. With two weeks to wait for a ship to take them to Madagascar, the French were able to make the most of their visit, and at a review of the contingent on Gordon Square, the Governor expressed the people's pleasure at the visit of their French allies. Before leaving the visitors donated over R.2,400 to a Prince of Wales fund for the exclusive use of British sick and wounded servicemen. It was, for everyone, a brief, bright respite from the anxieties of the war.

Unemployment on Mahé had become a serious problem. With little shipping space available and a drastic drop in demand for the traditional produce of copra and guano, hundreds of labourers normally employed on the outer islands

211

were no longer needed. So when a call came for Seychelles to supply men for the Allied war effort in East Africa, it seemed a convenient way of cutting unemployment.[4] No-one in authority seems to have considered how the Seychellois would stand up to the harsh climate of the malaria-ridden East African coast. O'Brien was away on leave. If the acting governor, Ewen Logan, had any misgivings he put these aside, and government notices went out inviting labourers to serve with the military in East Africa.

Over one thousand men volunteered for what was to become the Seychelles Carrier Corps. Almost all were from Mahé. Many failed the medical, and others were rejected on account of having a police record. Although General Smuts, C-in-C of the East African forces,[5] had asked in his original cable for five thousand labourers and porters — and had assumed an error in transmission when Seychelles offered five hundred — the government in the end managed to form a first contingent of 670 labourers, with twenty-seven overseers. They embarked on 19 December 1916, in the *Berwick Castle*. Sailing with the men were two newly commissioned officers, 2/Lieutenant France LeMarchand and 2/Lieutenant Francis Whiting, the latter having returned from the outlying islands just in time to join the ship. There were also seven NCOs: Vossary d'Unienville, Charles Moulinié, James Frichot, Louis Desaubins, Napoléon Bristol, Alphonse Hoareau, and Charles Lubin.

Even before the ship sailed there were indications of the challenge the Seychellois would pose to the military mind. Captain C. Tomkinson, sent by East Africa GHQ to accompany the Seychelles contingent to Kilwa Kisiwani, on the German East Africa coast, was dismayed at the amount of luggage being taken on board, but was warned that any attempt to reduce the baggage might lead to mass desertion. Tomkinson was also surprised to see that some of the NCOs were dark-skinned, while several white men appeared among the labourers. When he questioned "the desirability of whites messing with blacks", his assumptions were quickly corrected. Later Logan described the "quite black" Charles Lubin as "probably the most useful man" in the whole contingent.

Before the ship sailed many men went on sick parade, and were found to have venereal disease. Tomkinson attributed this to their having received two months' pay in advance, which he supposed they had spent on a last fling in Victoria. Unfortunately there was no time for further medical examination of the whole contingent before departure. A priest, Father Jérémie, sought to accompany the men, but the Bishop refused him permission. Given the large number that were soon to die, a priest would have been a reassuring presence.

Although the military in East Africa later complained that many of the men were of poor physique, it was not so much the physical condition of the volunteers but the fact that their diet was unsuitable that brought about the Seychelles contingent's rapid collapse. This is clear from the numbers who contracted, often with fatal consequences, the vitamen-deficiency disease beri-beri, which had been all but eradicated in Seychelles.[6]

A scale of rations drawn up in Mahé for the men was largely ignored by the East African authorities, who thought that "these Seychellois porters will be very well done if they get the ordinary porter scale". Logan, who realised it would be impossible for the men to have their usual diet of fish, had proposed meat every alternate day, with lentils and vegetable on the other. Little attention was paid to his request. As a result meat or biltong was issued every day, with dates given as a substitute. The meat was often bad and, as the Seychelles medical officer later pointed out, the men did not know what to do with the biltong, while to them dates were not proper food.

For a time these dietary problems were overshadowed by the question of whether the Seychellois should have early-morning tea and biscuits. In a letter to Smuts on the day before the *Berwick Castle* sailed, Logan warned that without a cup of tea and a biscuit first thing in the morning "I do not think it will be possible to get good work out of them". The biscuit he had in mind was the *gros biscuit salé*, large, round, and rock-hard, which requires a good soaking before it can be eaten. It was, and in some homes may still be, an essential ingredient to starting the Seychelles day.

The question of whether or not to supply the Seychellois with biscuits was to produce a lengthy and heated exchange of cables between the military after the receipt of a garbled

213

message from Seychelles informing supply officers in East Africa that each Seychellois required ten biscuits every morning.

Director of Military Labour (DML), Dar es Salaam, to Assistant Director of Supplies (ADS), GHQ, Dar es Salaam, 16 December 1916: I understand this is the flat biscuit costing about 5 cents in Zanzibar. It seems very doubtful whether they could eat 10 of them...

Director of Supplies and Transport (D of S & T), EA Force, to DA & DMG, EA Force, 16 December: ... Biscuits are quite out of the question ...

DA & QMG to DML, 16 December: I believe you have some Seychellites in your office. The above [porters] ration ought to be all right, do you agree? Note that biscuits cannot be provided.

DML to DA & QMG, 17 December: I think we can begin on the ordinary porter ration and see how they take it.

ADS, Dar es Salaam, to DST, Dar es Salaam, 6 January 1917: I have no objection to issuing Cape boys scale of ration to the Seychelles porters ...

DADML, Kilwa, to DML and ADS, Dar es Salaam, 8 January 1917: Seychelles receiving full porter rations plus tea and sugar as sanctioned ... Will not eat beans. Supplies willing issue 4oz bread or biscuit in lieu if sanctioned. Recommend. Reply.

ADS to DML, 11 January: The local supply officer does not know what the general supply of biscuits in the country are ...The stock in Kilwa of biscuits has been laid in for certain people and if issued to the Seychelles porters would mean that the others would have to go without.

This was the final word, and for the Seychellois their last biscuit with early morning tea was that arranged by Lieutenant LeMarchand on the morning the *Berwick Castle* arrived at Kilwa Kisiwani. Appropriately, it was Christmas Eve.

Within days of arriving in East Africa, men began to fall sick. On 9 January Cupidon Labiche died of dysentery, the first in a rapidly accelerating death toll, news of which was cabled back to Mahé. On 26 February, when more than twenty had died, Logan sought assurances from Smuts. The deaths, he warned the South African commander, were having an adverse effect on further recruitment. The death toll continued to rise. In March the total was eighty-one. April was worse; one hundred died, mainly from dysentery and malaria. Only by mid-May, after a further fifty had expired, did the number of deaths ease off.

Reports of the deaths were not the only deterrent to further recruitment. Word had gone round Mahé that Seychellois volunteers would be under the same discipline as soldiers of the King's African Rifles, whose punishments included flogging.[7] Logan advised Smuts that flogging was not allowed under Seychelles law, but he rather weakly failed to forbid it, requesting only that any punishment be imposed "under adequate safeguards". Nevertheless, a further eighty-one labourers and three oversees left Mahé on 28 February for East Africa. There were no officers in the party, which was commanded by Corporal Charles Cosgrow.

It was a miserable journey, in the steamship *Tabora*. Cosgrow reported that they were fed with inferior quality rice and dhall curry by "the Mohamedan Bazaar man". As a result most of the men were soon suffering from diarrhoea. At Zanzibar, they transferred to another ship for Dar es Salaam. Again there was trouble with food, and by the time the ship docked at Dar es Salaam on 15 March many of Cosgrow's men were on the sick list.

The decision to land the second Seychelles contingent at Dar es Salaam instead of Kilwa reflected the belated realisation that the men from the islands were unsuited to the Coast climate. At Kilwa, where the Seychellois had been employed loading and unloading ships, and moving goods up to the front, dysentery was rife, and as quinine had been issued only after the men's arrival in Africa, there were soon several cases of malaria. An outbreak of measles in February had pushed the sick list even higher. In that month twenty-eight men, mainly overseers, were repatriated via Bombay, and early in March the South African medical officer at Kilwa Kisiwani recommended that all be sent home "owing to their bad state of health, poor physique, and inability to stand service on the Coast". At first it was decided to transfer them north to

Mombasa, to see if they fared better there. On 7 April the South African doctor and LeMarchand listed 295 men as being fit to travel. Another twenty-eight would have to go by hospital ship, and eleven were considered too ill to be moved. In the end, all but four dying porters were put aboard the hospital ship *Palamcotta*. As predicted by the doctor, several died before the ship reached Mombasa.

On 7 May Smuts sent a cable to Mahé saying that the Seychelles Carrier Corps had suffered "very much from sickness", and that he was expediting its repatriation. On 11 May, 353 labourers, with five overseers and one NCO (Cosgrow once more in command), embarked at Mombasa on the hospital ship *Guildford Castle* for Seychelles. The following month another 123 porters and several NCOs left Mombasa for home in the hospital transport *Barunga*. The two officers, LeMarchand and Whiting, stayed on for a time in East Africa, as did the remainder of the NCOs.

Although the Seychelles authorities were prepared for a large number of sick — the quarantine station on Longue island had been extended in readiness — the report by the chief medical officer, Dr Joseph Addison,[8] indicates that their condition was even worse than he had imagined. Of the 350 or so landed from the *Guildford Castle*, fewer than forty were capable of doing any work. Addison found that there were at least sixty urgent cases suffering variously from bacillary dysentery,[9] malaria, and pneumonia (in some instances, all three). The first two diseases had up to then been unknown in Seychelles. About seventy men had beri-beri — a disease the East African authorities had apparently not diagnosed — with about fifty cases in the ultimate, paralytic stages of the disease. Worse perhaps, and indicative of the treatment the men had received, most were in rags, their bodies dirty, with open, suppurating sores on legs and feet. Many were infested with lice. Several had died on the ship, and more were to succumb at the quarantine station, and later at Victoria Hospital.

It was fortunate for Addison that the former Praslin doctor, Jewell, now an officer in the East African Medical Service, was in Seychelles on sick leave. He was able to take over general duties, allowing Addison to concentrate on the sick at Longue island, where he was assisted by the matron of the maternity home, Miss M.G. Halkett.[10] Jewell was highly critical of the

216

Seychelles authorities for having sent the men to East Africa in the first place, and attributed the cases of beri-beri to the lack of a proper diet. Despite the care given to them, twenty-five of the patients died at the quarantine station. After a fortnight, fifteen were still seriously ill and were transferred to Victoria Hospital. The others were allowed home. The government issued a directive that all should receive medical treatment free. Fortunately medical services in Seychelles had greatly improved since the opening of a public hospital at Mont Fleuri in 1875. In 1897 a new ward, known as Victoria Ward, had been added, as well as a public paying dispensary. The hospital continued in use until the opening in 1924 of the present Victoria Hospital.

O'Brien returned to Seychelles in August 1917, to see for himself the full extent of the catastrophe. Of the 791 men of the colony who had gone to East Africa, 314 were dead and eleven missing, a loss of over 40 per cent of the total force. Feeling it imperative to answer accusations that the returning men had been badly treated, O'Brien set up a committee of "independent-minded gentlemen" to look into the grievances. The committee subsequently reported that the Seychellois had suffered "nothing more than the inevitable discomforts and hardships consequent on their voluntary entry into a theatre where war was in progress". The dysentery among the men was attributed to lack of care over drinking water. Little was said about the food, except that the spread of beri-beri might have been less had Indian rather than Saigon or Rangoon rice been given.

The report seemed to satisfy O'Brien, who in a note to London expressed regret that the dispatch of the force had not been a success, and explained that "the absence of serious epidemic or endemic disease, and the easy way in which life can be sustained in this colony, renders our people liable to contract any disease and they appear to have little power of resistance".

That might have been the end of the matter, had it not been for the high losses through disease in most of the units in the East African campaign. The Army Council ordered a full-scale inquiry, which was undertaken by the Surgeon-General, Dr M. W. Pike. His conclusion on the Seychellois contingent was much the same as O'Brien's: that the fault lay with the men themselves, physically and morally, as well as the conditions in which they had to work. Pike also concluded that the medical examination on recruitment had been faulty, which, taken together with poor physique and "being non-immune to malaria and dysentery", made the Seychellois unfit for service on the East African coast. As for the incidence of beri-beri, Pike considered that this had been "possibly aggravated by probable infection by *Ankylostomiasis* (hookworm),[11] said to be endemic in Seychelles and very debilitating".

Pike's report drew an angry reaction from Addison, who defended the standard of the medical examination of the recruits, pointing to the numbers that had been turned down. He accused Pike and others of trying to shift the blame on to the Seychelles medical authorities. He referred again to the men's unsuitable diet, to the fact that no proof of tubercular disease had been offered, and suggested that the beri-beri had not been diagnosed, as it was not recorded for any of the deaths in East Africa. He rejected the claim that the Seychellois had poor physique, and referred to reports by ship captains who had said that the Seychellois worked well when they were fit.

In September 1918, with the Great War rapidly drawing to a close, the people of Seychelles were still living with bitter memories of the war. Not all of the survivors had regained their health, and poverty would continue to be the lot of many.[12] At Mont Fleuri cemetery, forty-eight graves — all unmarked except for those of Charles Leveilleux and Rodolphe Hoareau, whose families had erected headstones — would remain as mute testimony to the lives of Seychellois sacrificed, some would say unnecessarily, in the Allied cause.

It had been "an entirely new experiment", explained Logan to the Secretary of State in a lengthy report in September 1918. He regretted the deaths among the Seychellois, but pointed out that all units in the East African campaign had suffered heavy losses from disease, the only exception being the West Africans. That Logan felt it necessary to justify the government's actions so late in the day indicates that not all were satisfied with earlier explanations of why so many Seychellois had died. The South African military easily persuaded themselves that the blame lay solely with Seychelles, both the authorities and the volunteers. Had not Smuts asked specifically for the NCOs to be European? Logan retorted that the men had been selected according to their ability, not the shade of their skin. He defended the pay advances given before they left Seychelles (blamed for the late disclosure of venereal disease among the men), and pointed out that the volunteers needed to make provision for their families. He explained also that it had been impossible to hold a final medical examination before the ship sailed as many of the men might have changed their minds about going.

"No-one who does not know the Seychellois and their utter lack of discipline ... can appreciate the immense difficulty of the task," he argued. "The Seychellois ... are, I should say, much more difficult people to manage in the mass than raw natives who are accustomed to tribal authority." After reading Logan's report, the British government pronounced itself satisfied that all reasonable precautions had been taken "in the difficult business of dispatching labourers to East Africa". The blame, it seemed, could be conveniently laid at the door of the Seychellois.

In March and June 1919 O'Brien's successor, Sir Eustace Twisleton-Wyckham-Fiennes, bt, asked the Secretary of State if Seychelles could have a war trophy, such as a field gun or a machine-gun,[13] which "would be most welcome and would greatly please the inhabitants". Indeed, he would like to have two field guns, one for Gordon Square, the other for Government House. Fiennes pointed out that Seychellois had served not only in East Africa but also in France, Mesopotamia, and at sea, although the only organised body had been the Carrier Corps. The Colony had suffered greatly during the war, and a gun would "serve as a fitting memorial".

After a lengthy correspondence, Fiennes was informed in February 1920 by the administrator in East Africa that the town bell of Wilhelmstal (Lushoto, in Tanzania), along with a pair of brass shell cases used by guns salvaged from the cruiser *Königsberg* would be sent to Seychelles. He regretted that so many souvenirs such as bells, statues, and large bronze German eagles had "mysteriously disappeared in directions which cannot be traced".

The Wilhelmstal bell was the only one remaining, and this was duly delivered, as were the two shell cases and, from Woolwich, several helmets, two trench mortars, and nine machine-guns. The trophies were stored at Victoria School, but in August 1921 the director of education asked for them to be removed. He suggested the helmets and the shell cases be placed in Carnegie Hall, and the machine-guns sent to the police station.[14]

On Armistice Day 1928, the tenth anniversary of the ending of the war, the Seychelles governor, Montagu George de Symons Honey, unveiled at Mont Fleuri cemetery a war memorial. Constructed of coral blocks by the PWD for the Imperial War Graves Commission in London, the central plaque carries the inscription: "To the Glory of God and in Memory of these Men of the Seychelles Carrier Corps who risked and lost their lives for King and Country in East Africa in the years of the Great War and whose graves are not known." On the four side panels the individual names of those who died are recorded.

Two years later, the War Graves Commission provided simple granite headstones for the forty-six unmarked graves. Maintained by the commission, the graves today form a neat and dignified cluster in the cemetery's north-east corner. A memorial stone was also erected by the family of Lieutenant LeMarchand, who died at Bombay in 1919 from illness contracted during his service in East Africa. An annual pension of £75 was granted to LeMarchand's widow, with additional allowances for the maintenance and education of his four children.

LeMarchand's case was an exception, and for many years it was a regular complaint among Carrier Corps veterans that the government had failed to keep a promise on compensation. Commenting on the Armistice Day ceremonies held in 1936, the newspaper *L'Impartial* described as "a black spot" the government's failure to recognise adequately the war services of the Seychellois. After the wreath-laying held on that day, the former volunteers were asked to gather at Gordon Square. It was an invitation that aroused hopes among many of something more than what in fact materialised: a voucher that each man could exchange for a pint of *bacca* at M. Confait's tavern.

There was, it seemed, no end to hard times in Paradise.

SEYCHELLES ROLL-CALL

The following notes include biographies of officials responsible for the British administration of Seychelles up to 1921; omitted are Harrison and Wilson, on whom little information has been found, and some others who served only briefly in an acting capacity. Governors of Mauritius have been listed sparingly. They include the first and last governors responsible for Seychelles as a dependency of Mauritius, namely, Sir Robert Farquhar, bt, and Sir Charles Bruce. Sources include: Dictionary of National Biography, Dictionary of Mauritian Biography, Who was Who, Marshall's Royal Navy Biography, Colonial Office List, 'Figures du Passé', by Guy Lionnet (L'Echo des îles), and private archives.

BARKLY: Arthur Cecil Stuart Barkly. Chief Civil Commissioner, Seychelles, 1882-85 and 1887-88. b. 1843, son of Sir Henry Barkly, Governor of Mauritius, 1863-70; ed. Harrow; served in 3rd Carabiniers, 1862-65; private secretary to father in Mauritius and Cape Colony, 1866-70; resident magistrate, Basutoland, 1879-80; CCC Seychelles, 1882-85; acting Lieutenant-Governor, Falkland Islands, 1886-87; CCC Seychelles, 1887-88; last British Governor of Heligoland, 1888; died, 1890. Married to Fanny, daughter of Bishop of Mauritius, who was author of two travel books: *Among Boers and Basutos* (London, 1893) and *From the Tropics to the North Sea*, including 'Five Years in the Seychelles' (London, 1897).

BELCHER: Captain Sir Edward Belcher. British naval officer. Entered Navy in 1812. Made round-the-world voyage of scientific research in HMS *Sulphur*, 1836-42, during which he visited Seychelles in February 1842. His description of the voyage was published in two volumes, 1843. Belcher commanded the *Sulphur* in first China war; knighted, 1842; took part in Arctic search for explorer Sir John Franklin, and was court-martialled for abandoning his ships; acquitted, but saw no more active service. Admiral, 1872; died, 1877. According to W.L. Clowes, *The Royal Navy* (1897), Belcher made 'a hell afloat' of every ship he commanded. Lady Belcher, step-daughter of one of the mutineers of HMS *Bounty,* gained some notoriety by accusing her husband in court of having given her venereal disease.

BENEZET: Antoine Bénézet. French settler. b. 1786, at Bordeaux. Served as soldier under First Republic; taken prisoner, and while at Plymouth, England, learned the art of plaiting and dyeing straw. Arrived in Seychelles about 1815, where he was clerk to notary Jean Remy d'Argent; later was clerk to *juge de paix* Guillaume Fressanges. Bénézet was responsible in the 1830s for introducing a new cottage industry based on the plaiting and weaving of coco de mer fibre into hats, baskets, boxes, and other articles. So successful was the industry, that the government had to take measures to prevent the wholesale cutting of coco de mer leaves. He is also credited with being first to effect artificial pollination of the coco de mer. A bachelor, he died in 1842. A street in Victoria is named after him.

221

BLUNT: Captain Francis Theophilus Blunt. Chief Civil Commissioner, Seychelles, October 1880 to February 1881. b. 1837, son of clergyman; entered army in 1854, and served in Crimea and Indian Mutiny with the 12th Lancers (1854-61), and the 7th Dragoon Guards. Joined Colonial Service in 1869; acting Inspector-General of Police, Mauritius, 1871-72, and Inspector of Immigrants from September 1872. British consul at Réunion. Left Mauritius on leave of absence in September 1878. Applied from England for CCC post; died at Seychelles, from dysentery, February 1881. Survived by wife and three children. One son, who became Bishop of Bradford, was a notable critic of King Edward VIII in the abdication crisis of 1936.

BRADLEY: Dr John Thomas Bradley. Chief Medical Officer of Health, Seychelles, 1924-34. b. 1872, Ireland. Arts undergraduate, Royal University of Ireland; prizeman in medicine, midwifery, and women's diseases, Queen's College, Belfast, 1897-98; MD, School of Tropical Medicine, Brussels, 1901; assistant medical officer, Glamorgan County Asylum, 1901; appointed assistant medical officer, Seychelles, 1901; justice of peace, South Mahé, and chairman of local Health Board; medical superintendent, Lunatic Asylum, 1907; Emeritus physician, Seychelles Government Hospital; Officer of the Order of the British Empire (OBE), 1933; Knight of the Order of Pope Pius IX and Knight of the Order of the Crown of Italy. Bradley was a substantial property owner in Seychelles. On retirement he founded and edited the *Seychelles Clarion* newspaper; author of *The History of Seychelles*, (Victoria, 1940). He had two daughters. Died at Victoria, 1942.

BROWN: Richard Myles Brown. District Judge, 1884-1900, and on three separate occasions acting Administrator, Seychelles. b. 1848, Mauritius. ed. Royal College and Liverpool Collegiate Institution. Studied law at Middle Temple; called to Bar, 1869. Served as Legal Adviser to Seychelles government, 1872-77; resumed legal practice at Mauritus, 1877. In 1884 returned to Seychelles as District Judge. For several months in 1891, 1895, and 1899, was acting Administrator. In 1900 appointed puisne Judge at Mauritius; retired 1913; died at Lausanne, 1928.

BRUCE: Sir Charles Bruce. Governor of Mauritius, 1897-1903. b. 1837; ed. Harrow. Sanskrit scholar; texts published by Imperial Academy of St Petersburg, 1862; poems, 1866. Assistant librarian, British Museum, 1863; Professor of Sanskrit, King's College, 1865; Rector, Royal College, Mauritius, 1868; Director of Public Instruction, Ceylon, 1878; Colonial Secretary, Mauritius, 1882; Lieutenant-Governor, British Guiana, 1885; Governor, Windward Islands, 1893; Governor of Mauritius, 1897, until retirement in 1903.

CLARK: Father Bernardin (Thomas Edward) Clark. Bishop of Port-Victoria, 1910-15. b. Hackney, London, 1856, into a Protestant family; converted to Roman Catholicism, 1870; studied at London, and at Jesuit College, Turnhout, Belgium. In 1873 began novitiate with Capuchins at Le

Mans; priest, 1882 at Cork, Ireland; the following year he was sent to Seychelles, where he spent the next eighteen years. Apostolic Vicar, Aden. Returned to Seychelles as Bishop, 1910. Died, 1915. Succeeded by Mgr Jean Damascene Lachavanne (1916-20), who was the last Savoyard Bishop of Seychelles.

COLEBROOKE: Major William Colebrooke. British army officer and administrator. b.1787; first lieutenant, Royal Artillery, 1803; served in India and Java, returning to England with rank of major in 1821. Appointed, with Mr William Blair, to the Commission of Eastern Enquiry, 1822; visited Seychelles in 1829 to examine condition of slaves. Governor of Bahamas, 1834; of Leeward Islands, 1837; of New Brunswick, 1841; and of Barbados and Windward Islands, 1847; colonel, 1836; Knight of the Order of the Bath (KB), 1837; major-general, 1854; retired, 1856; general, 1865; died near Slough, Berkshire, 1870.

DACRE: Admiral James Dacre. British naval officer. Entered navy, 1796, in the *Sceptre* (64), commanded by his father, Captain (later Vice-Admiral James Dacre). Served in Mediterranean and West Indies during Napoleonic wars. In the War of 1812, while commanding the frigate *Guerrière* (48), fought an unequal contest with the USS *Constitution* (56). Dacre, who was severely wounded, had fifteen men killed and sixty-three wounded. At a subsequent court-martial Dacre was honourably acquitted of having lost his ship. In 1845 he was appointed C-in-C at the Cape, with his flag in HMS *President* (50). The following year Dacre was involved in an incident with the French consul at Mauritius, which for a time threatened relations between Britain and France. Dacre visited Seychelles in October 1847 and appears to have had a row with the Civil Chaplain, Delafontaine. Dacre disliked by planters in Mauritius and Réunion on account of his squadron's interruption of commerce with Madagascar. Admiral, 1870; retired, 1875.

DAVIDSON: Walter Edward Davidson. Governor of Seychelles, 1904-12. b. 1859, son of late James Davidson, of Kellyleagh, County Down, Northern Ireland; m. (1) 1882, d. of John Baker MD, of London, one son; (2) 1907, Margaret Agnes, two daughters. Went to Cambridge on scholarship, and entered Ceylon Civil Service, 1880; Mayor of Colombo, 1898; Colonial Secretary, Transvaal, 1902. After term as Governor of Seychelles, he was appointed Governor of Newfoundland, 1912, and of New South Wales, 1918; created Knight Commander of the Order of St Michael and St George (KCMG), 1914. Davidson published two books on Ceylon, as well as, at his own expense, *Unpublished documents on the history of the Seychelles anterior to 1810*, by A.A. Fauvel. Reporting his death in September 1923, *The Times* described him as 'a kindly and courteous English gentleman of the best type'.

DELAFONTAINE: Rev. George Ferdinand Delafontaine. Civil Chaplain, Seychelles, 1843-53. b. 1811, at Geneva, Switzerland, son of François Delafontaine, inhabitant of Corsier, canton of Vaud, and Louise Marie *née*

Grand. Lived at Marennes, Charente, France, 1836, and married Louise Marie Dilly, daughter of pastor; six children. Delafontaine returned to Switzerland from Seychelles in 1853, and served as pastor at Rolle (1853), Sainte-Croiy (1856-61), and Rolle (1861-79). Died at Rolle, 1879. Three of Delafontaine's children were born at Mahé, including George Charles Émile (b. 1846), who returned to Seychelles in 1878. Served as lay preacher at St James's Anglican chapel, Cerf Island, 1901. Died at Seychelles, 1934.

DES AVANCHERS: Father Léon (Michel Golliet) des Avanchers. b.1825, at Avanchers, diocese of Tarentaise, Duchy of Savoy; educated St Pierre d'Abigny seminary; entered Capuchin monastery, Chambéry, 1842; ordained priest, 1848; left France in 1849 for Ethiopia, but delayed at Aden; controversial mission to Seychelles, 1851; at Agra, India, 1852-53; apostolic vice-prefect, Seychelles, 1854-55; return to East Africa, 1857; in Ethiopia from 1859; died at Afallo, 1879, probably poisoned by the Queen of Ghera. His remains found in 1928 by Italian explorer Enrico Cerulli.

DUMONT D'URVILLE: Captain Jules Sébastien César Dumont d'Urville. French naval officer, noted for his exploratory voyages in Pacific and Antarctica. b. 1790, Condé-sur-Noireau, Normandy; entered navy 1808; *lieutenant de vaisseau*, 1821; discovered wreckage from the La Pérouse expedition at Vanikoro, Solomon Islands, 1828; *capitaine de frégate*, 1829. In 1830 Dumont d'Urville visited Seychelles, noting in *Voyage Pittoresque autour du Monde* (Paris 1834), that *"les familles qui habitent Mahé sont encore aujourd'hui françaises par l'origine et par le coeur. Un compatriote est toujours le bien-venu chez elles".* He found that his week in Seychelles completely restored his health. In 1837 he left Toulon on a three-year, round-the-world voyage in the *Astrolabe*, discovering the French Antarctic territory of Terre Adélie (named after his wife). On 8 May 1842 Dumont d'Urville, his wife, and young son were killed in a train crash on the recently opened Paris-Versailles railway.

DUPONT: Paul Evenor Rivalz Dupont. Curator of Botanic Station and Commissioner of Crown Lands, Seychelles, 1902-21; Director of Agriculture and member of Seychelles Executive and Legislative Councils, 1924. b. 1870, at Curepipe, Mauritius, s. of Eugène Dupont and Pauline d'Emmerez de Charmoy; ed. Mauritius and Agricultural College, Grignon, France. Diploma in Agriculture. Chemist, Benares sugar estate, Mauritius, 1894; Assistant Director of Agricultural Station, Mauritius, 1899; sent on special mission to Seychelles in 1900. Travelled widely in Far East and gained renown for his scientific research. Appointed Assistant Director of Agriculture, Mauritius, 1921, but had to resign due to ill health. Returned to Seychelles in 1924. On retirement returned to Mauritius; died at Rose Hill, 1938.

FARQUHAR: Sir Robert Farquhar, bt. First British governor of Mauritius and its Dependencies. b. 1776, 2nd son of Sir Walter Farquhar, bt, physician to the Prince of Wales. East India Company agent at Amboyna and later lieutenant-governor of Pulo Penang; commissioner for adjusting

British claims in Moluccas and returning islands to the Dutch after the Peace of Amiens, 1802; Governor of Bourbon, July-December 1810; Governor-General of Mauritius and Bourbon, 1811; Governor of Mauritius, 1815-17 and 1820-23; adopted policy of conciliation towards French settlers. Concluded treaties against slave trade with Radama of Madagascar and Imam of Muscat. On voyage home in 1823 visited Madagascar and received by chiefs in recognition of efforts against slave trade. Elected to Parliament, 1825, for Hythe constituency, 1826 to 1830. Married, 1809, daughter of J. France-Louis Latour, of Madras. Died 1830; succeeded by son, Walter Minto Farquhar, MP. The most southerly islands of the Seychelles, the Farquhar group, are named after him.

FAUVEL: Albert-Auguste Fauvel. French shipping line official, sinologist, historian, and scientist. b. 1851, at Cherbourg; son of naval officer. Poor eyesight prevented him from joining the navy; studied Mandarin and entered Chinese customs service, 1872; m. 1884, returning with his wife to China; left service after French naval bombardment of Foochow, 1884. Appointed Inspector, Messageries Maritimes, 1885, and visited Seychelles several times. Retired, 1908. In addition to his *Unpublished Documents on the history of the Seychelles Islands anterior to 1810* (Victoria, 1909), Fauvel's writings include several studies of Seychelles flora and fauna. Discovered the *Alligator Sinensis*, a hitherto unknown Asiatic species of a creature thought special to America. Correspondent of the Natural History Museum of Paris. Died, 1909, at Cherbourg.

FIENNES: Sir Eustace Edward Twisleton-Wykeham-Fiennes, bt, Governor of Seychelles, 1918-21. b. 1864, second son of Baron Saye and Sele; ed. Malvern College; major, Oxfordshire Imperial Yeomanry and honorary lieutenant, army. Served Riel Rebellion (north-west Canada), Egypt, 1888-89; Mashonaland expedition; South African War, 1900-02; twice mentioned in dispatches.; World War I, with Oxfordshire Yeomanry, in France, 1914; with Royal Navy Division as Intelligence Officer, Antwerp and Dardanelles, 1915; DAAQMG, Plymouth, 1916-18; mentioned in dispatches. MP for Banbury, 1906-18; Parliamentary Private Secretary to First Lord of Admiralty, 1912; Governor of Seychelles, 1918-21; and of Leeward Islands, 1921-29. m. 1894, Florence Agnes, d. of John Rathfelde, of Constantia, South Africa; two sons, both killed in war. Died, 1943. Grandson, Sir Ranulph Twisleton-Wykeham-Fiennes, bt, former SAS officer, writer, and Polar explorer, made first crossing of Antarctica and longest Polar journey, 1992-93. The name Fiennes continues in Seychelles, with the Fiennes Institute for old people and the Fiennes Esplanade in Victoria.

FRANKLYN: William Hales Franklyn. Civil Commissioner, Seychelles, from 1869, and Chief Civil Commissioner from 1872 to 1874. b. 1816, in Kent. Master mariner; m. Margaret Elspeth Dickson, at St Helena, 1840; one daughter. In Crimea War, commanded the steam transport *Tonning*, and honoured by ship-owners for services in gale at Balaklava, November 1854. Arrived Victoria, British Columbia, 1859; stipendiary magistrate at

Esquimault and Nanaimo, Vancouver Island. Left on merging of the two colonies. Died at Seychelles, 3 April 1874, when about to go to England on leave. Wife died at Victoria, British Columbia, 1899.

FREY: Henri Nicolas Frey. French general, who attempted to remove and transport to Paris the Seychelles Stone of Possession, 1894. b. 1847, Corsica; St Cyr, second lieutenant, 1868; served in Senegal, 1869-74; captain, 1874; aide de camp to Maritime Prefect, Brest, 1879; commanded battalion of Senegalese native infantry, 1884; colonel, 1887; at Tonkin, 1889-91, and noted for his campaign against the *Pavillons Noirs* guerrillas; on return to France promoted to general; commanded *5ème Régiment de l'Infanterie de la Marine*. In 1894 sent on inspection tour of New Caledonia, Réunion and Diego Suarez; in Senegal, 1897, and Cochin China, 1898-1900. Divisional general, 1900; Deputy Inspector-General of colonial troops; Grand Officer of the *Légion d'Honneur*, 1906; Reserve list, 1911. Died at Menton, 1932.

GOMM: Sir William Maynard Gomm. Governor of Mauritius, 1842-49. b. 1784, at Barbados; entered army, 1794, served in Europe throughout Napoleonic wars; lieutenant-colonel, 1812; major-general, 1837; officer commanding troops, Jamaica, 1839; governor of Mauritius, 1842-49; appointed Commander-in-Chief, India, in 1849 by royal patronage, but because of opposition did not assume command until 1850; remained in India until 1855; field marshal, 1868; Constable of Tower of London, 1872. Married, 1830, Elizabeth, daughter of Lord Robert Kerr. Died, 1875.

GORDON: Sir Arthur Hamilton Gordon, 1st Baron Stanmore. Governor of Mauritius, 1871-74. b. 1829, London, fourth son of 4th Earl of Aberdeen; private secretary to his father, when Prime Minister, from 1852 to 1859; Member of Parliament for Beverley, 1854-57; secretary, Corfu mission, 1858-59; Governor of Mauritius, 1871-74; of Fiji, 1875-80; New Zealand, 1880-82; High Commissioner and Consul-General, Southern Pacific, 1877-82; Governor of Ceylon, 1883-90. As Governor of Mauritius, Gordon was behind the increased powers given to Seychelles in 1872. Knight Commander of the Order of St Michael and St George (KCMG), 1871; Grand Cross (GCMG), 1878; died 1912.

GORDON: Lieut-Colonel Charles George Gordon. British army officer and administrator. b. 1833, at Woolwich, son of artillery officer; commissioned Royal Engineers, 1852; served with distinction in Crimea; captain, 1859. Joined British forces fighting Chinese in 'Arrow War'; directed burning of Summer Palace at Peking, 1860; commander of 'Ever Victorious Army' of Chinese peasants raised to defend Shanghai during Taiping Rebellion. Returned to England 1865; commander of Royal Engineers at Gravesend for five years, during which he developed his own unorthodox brand of Christianity; Governor of Equatoria province, Sudan, 1874-76; later Governor-General at Khartoum; returned to England in ill health, 1880; subsequently served in India, China, Mauritius, and Cape Colony; visited Seychelles, 1881, and developed theory that the islands were the Garden of Eden; major-general, 1882. Sent to the Sudan in 1884 to evacuate Egyptian garrisons threatened by the Mahdi uprising; held out in besieged Khartoum for nearly a year; killed when city fell to Mahdi's army in January 1885.

GRIFFITH: Thomas Risely Griffith. Administrator, Seychelles, 1889-95. Entered colonial banking, 1869, serving in London, Barbados, and St Vincent; auditor, Grenada, 1872-78; private secretary to Governor of Windward Islands, 1875; Treasurer, Gold Coast, 1878; Colonial Secretary, Sierra Leone, 1879; Administrator, Seychelles, 1889-95. Commander of the Order of St Michael and St George (CMG), 1893. On leaving Seychelles Griffith became Administrator, St Kitts.

GRIFFITHS: William Harrison Hollier Griffiths. British trader and magistrate. b. Camberwell, Kent, 1792; married Anne Schmidt, 1825, at Bordeaux; arrived Mauritius 1831. Founded, with Paul Huet de Froberville, the company of Froberville Griffiths & Cie; president of Mauritius Chamber of Commerce, 1827; instrumental in setting up, with Scots trader James Blyth, the Mauritius Commercial Bank, which opened in 1839; US consular agent, 1839; retired from business in 1854, and was named district magistrate at Rivière du Rempart; transferred to Seychelles in 1856; acting Civil Commissioner, 1856; died, 1857.

GRIFFITHS: George Harrison Hollier Griffiths. Acting Chief Civil Commissioner, Seychelles, 1884-86. b. 1840, at Mauritius, son of William Harrison Hollier Griffiths (see above). Entered government service, 1866; Chief of Police, Inspector of Immigrants, Inspector of Nuisances, and Inspector of Liberated Africans at Seychelles, 1881. Griffiths was criticised by an official inquiry after his term as acting CCC. Inspector of Police, Mauritius, 1887; Acting Chief of Police, Seychelles, 1889; Inspector of Roads and Joint Conservator of Crown Lands, 1896; Town Surveyor, 1900; Treasurer and Collector of Customs, 1901; Companion of the Imperial Service Order, 1903; died at Seychelles, 1911.

GUMY: Father Justinien (Ludovic) Gumy. Swiss Capuchin priest. b. 1869, at Avry-sur-Matran, Switzerland; ordained, 1892; teacher of theology; sent to Seychelles, 1903, returning in 1913. Left again in 1920 for Seychelles, where he became Bishop of Port-Victoria the following year. Retired, 1934, and returned to Switzerland; died, Fribourg, 1941.

HAVELOCK: Captain Arthur Havelock. Chief Civil Commissioner, Seychelles, 1879-80; b. 1844, third son of Lieut.-Colonel W. Havelock; married, 1871, Anne Grace, only daughter of Chief Justice of Ceylon. Entered 32nd Regiment (Duke of Cornwall's Light Infantry), 1862; captain, 1873; retired from army 1877; aide to Officer administering Mauritius, 1873 to January 1874; Acting Chief Civil Commissioner, Seychelles, April 1874 to February 1875; Colonial Secretary, Fiji, 1875-76; President, Nevis, 1877-78; Administrator, St Lucia, 1878-79; CCC, Seychelles, 1879-80; Governor of West Africa Settlements, 1881; Governor of Trinidad, 1884;

of Natal, 1885-89; of Ceylon, 1890-95, of Madras, 1895-1900; of Tasmania, 1901-04. Knight Commander of the Order of St Michael and St George (KCMG), 1884; Knight Grand Commander of Order of Star of India (GCSI), 1901. Died 1908, at Bath, where he had gone to take the waters. Lady Havelock died, 1908.

HEATON: Sir John Henniker Heaton, bt. Postal reformer. b. 1848, at Rochester, son of army colonel. At 16 he went to Australia; married in 1873, daughter of an Australian businessman; returned to live in England in 1885, when he was elected MP for Canterbury; held seat until dissolution of Parliament in 1910. Spoke mainly on postal matters and was instrumental in getting penny post introduced in the Empire. It is probable that Henniker Heaton first met the ex-Sultan of Perak in 1885 when his ship called at Seychelles on the way back from Australia. He thereafter took up his cause in Parliament and accompanied the ex-Sultan from Seychelles to Britain in 1894, shortly before his release. Baronet, 1912; died, 1914, at Geneva. *The Times* described him as 'prophet of cheap communication'.

HENNESSY: Sir John Pope Hennessy, Governor of Mauritius, 1883-89. b.1834, at Cork; studied medicine at Cork and London; gave up medicine and became barrister; elected Conservative MP for King's County, 1859; took silk, 1861; lost seat to Liberals, 1865. Through support of Disraeli was offered governorship of Labuan, an island off north-west Borneo; served there until 1871; m. Kitty Low, part-Malay daughter of Colonial Treasurer; Governor of West African settlements, 1872; of Bahamas, 1873-76; of Hong Kong, 1877-82. Became first Catholic Governor of Mauritius, 1883; remembered for his concern for the poor and disputes with planters; instrumental in introducing elective franchise in colony; inquiry held into his governorship. Suspended, but returned to Mauritius, 1888, remaining there until December 1889. Returned to England due to ill health; MP for North Kilkenny; died near Cork, 1991. A statue of Pope Hennessy is in the Place d'Armes at Port Louis, and many streets in Mauritius are named after him.

HERCHENRODER: Furcy Alfred Herchenroder. Chief Justice of Seychelles, 1903-06. b. 1865 at Mauritius, descendant of an officer of the Île de France Regiment; ed. Royal College; called to Bar of Middle Temple, 1888; m. Eleanor Alice Vinton the same year; five sons, four daughters. Crown Prosecutor, Mauritius, 1893, Magistrate, Seychelles, 1898; District Judge and then, in 1903, Chief Justice; introduced a Penal Code for Seychelles. Governor Sweet-Escott praised him for 'skill and patience whereby the code of laws has been systematised and consolidated'. King's Counsel, 1905; Procurator and Advocate-General, Mauritius, 1906; revised Mauritius Legal Code; Chief Justice of Mauritius, 1913; knighted, 1914; retired 1929; died 1932, at Paris.

HIGGINSON: James Macaulay Higginson. Governor of Mauritius, 1851-57. b. 1805. Entered Indian Army, and served until 1839, first as aide to the Governor-General, Lord William Bentinck, and then as private secretary to Lord Metcalfe. Retired from Indian army, 1840; Governor of Antigua and Leeward Islands, 1846-50. In his final year as Governor of Mauritius, 1857, he inaugurated, jointly with the Governor of Réunion, a regular steamship service between Mauritius and Aden, with a call at Seychelles. This Anglo-French venture lasted only fourteen months. Higginson was said to be *'peu populaire'* in Mauritius. Knighted, 1859, and retired to Ireland. Higginson was married twice. Died, 1885.

HODOUL: François Hodoul. Seychellois businessman, administrator, and politician. b. 1824, at Mahé, grandson of Jean-François Hodoul (see below), and ardent defender of French and Catholic traditions. Educated at Royal College, Mauritius, followed by travel in Europe and India. Member of Board of Civil Commissioners, 1871; acting Inspector of Schools, 1873-1881; Unofficial member of Legislative Council, 1888; created Companion of the Order of St Michael and St George (CMG), 1901; Papal knight. Died, 1909.

HODOUL: Jean-François Hodoul. French privateer, and Seychelles planter and businessman. b. 1765, at La Ciotat, near Marseilles; qualified as a sea captain before he was 25. Arriving in the Indian Ocean in the early 1790s, he carried out several trading and slaving voyages between the Île de France and Madagascar, also calling at Seychelles where he married, in 1794, Marie Corantine Olivette Jorre de St Jorre, the daughter of a settler. Hodoul embarked on his career as a privateer two years later. He returned to Seychelles after the Peace of Amiens in 1802, built a house at Les Mamelles, south of present-day Victoria, and established a plantation on Silhouette island. Over the years Hodoul enlarged and developed his various properties, which, according to Holman, "he cultivates with great assiduity and success, especially cocoa, which has only lately been introduced into these islands". Hodoul bought Desroches island in 1825, and in 1829 set up a ship-repair establishment on an island in Victoria harbour, known today as Hodoul island. Hodoul died on 10 January 1835. According to oral family history (recorded by Shaun and Patricia Mitchell, of Coorparoo, Queensland, Australia) Hodoul had been out riding on his estate, Ma Constance, when he apparently had a heart attack. His body was found after his horse returned without him. He was buried at Bel Air cemetery, his tomb inscribed with the words *Il fut juste.* Hodoul's wife, who died in 1856, was buried beside him.

HORNE: John Horne. Scottish botanist and horticulturist. b. 1835, at Lethendy, Perthshire. Worked at Kew from 1859 until appointed head gardener of Royal Botanical Gardens, Pamplemousses, Mauritius; Assistant Director, 1866; also Guardian of Woods and Forests from 1876. In 1871 and 1874 visited Seychelles, and was the first to make a comprehensive study of the indigenous vegetation. Described the destruction of the coco de mer as 'an outrage on science and a disgrace to civilisation'. Fellow of Linnaean Society, 1873. In 1877 went to Fiji. married, 1886, Margaret, daughter of Reuben Browning, half-brother of poet Robert Browning.

229

Retired to Channel Islands; died 1905.

HUDRISIER: Marc (Michel) Hudrisier, Bishop of Port-Victoria, 1892-1910. b. 1848, at Faverges, Haute-Savoie. Entered Capuchin order, 1867; ordained at Annecy, 1873; served in Seychelles, 1875-76; transferred to Lahore; chaplain to British troops during Afghanistan campaign, 1878-80; Rector of St Thomas College, Punjab, 1881; Administrator, Diocese of Lahore, 1886, and Vicar-General to Mgr Mouard. In 1890 named titular Bishop of Theos and Apostolic Vicar of Seychelles; Bishop of Port-Victoria on Seychelles becoming a separate diocese, 1892. Increased number of parishes and improved Church finances; instrumental in bringing first Swiss missionaries to Seychelles, 1904. Suffered a stroke in August 1909, and returned to France. Governor Davidson, writing to the Secretary of State, referred to Hudrisier's 'long military service and his capacity to understand and sympathise with English ways of thinking, which he used to the full measure of his opportunities'. Hudrisier died in 1910.

IGNATIUS: Father Ignatius or Ignace (Jean-Pierre) Galfione. Apostolic Prefect of Seychelles, 1864-80, and Apostolic Vicar, 1880-81. b. Villafranca, Piedmont, 1815; took vows at Roche-sur-Foron, Savoy, 1833; ordained as priest, 1838. Arrived Seychelles in October 1864. Completed construction of the Church of the Immaculate Conception, Victoria, in 1874; noted for his expansion of the mission and achieving government salaries for priests; arranged with the Brothers of Christian Schools to open St Louis College, 1867. Titular Bishop of Aureliopolis, 1880; named first Apostolic Vicar of Seychelles, 1880; died, 1881.

JEHENNE: Captain Aimable-Constant Jehenne. French naval officer and hydrographer. b. 1799, at St Malo de la Lande (Manche). Began career in the Marine at Paris; *enseigne de vaisseau,* decorated for his conduct during Algiers expedition, 1830; *capitaine de corvette,* 1840; commanded the store ship *Prévoyante,* 1838-48; carried out voyage in western Indian Ocean to confirm existence and position of various islands, visiting Seychelles in October 1841; *capitaine de vaisseau,* 1848. Published 'Hydrographic Description of Nossi-Bé and Mayotte' (Paris, 1850); rear-admiral, 1855; Préfet Maritime, Lorient. Commanded squadron off coast of Syria, 1860-61. Grand Officer of *Légion d'Honneur;* Grand Cross of Order of St Stanislas of Russia; Commander of the Order of Medjidié, and of the Order of Savoie. Died 1865, at Brest.

JEREMIAH: Father Jeremiah (Giantommaso). b. 1820 at Paglietta, in Abruzzo, Kingdom of Naples (incorporated into newly created Kingdom of Italy in 1860); novice priest 1836; entered College of St Fidèle, Rome, 1845. Arrived at Mahé in September 1853 along with Father Théophile Pollar of Châteauneuf, Savoy, as Seychelles' first Apostolic Prefect (1852-64). Founded the Parish of Victoria. Narrowly escaped death during the cyclone and landslide of October 1862. Instrumental in rebuilding the convent of St Joseph de Cluny. On leaving Seychelles in 1864, Father Jeremiah served in Chile, before returning to Paris. Died of smallpox,

1871. Father Théophile stayed on in Seychelles as a parish priest. He died in 1889 at Victoria.

KEATE: Robert William Keate. Civil Commissioner, 1850-52. Studied at Lincoln's Inn; called to Bar, 1844; joined Colonial Service; after service at Mauritius and Seychelles, appointed Lieutenant-Governor, Grenada, 1853-56; Governor of Trinidad, 1856; Governor of Natal, 1872, and of West Africa; died, 1873, at Cape Coast Castle.

LAPLACE: Captain Cyrille-Pierre-Théodore Laplace. French naval officer. b. 1793, in American ship in Caribbean; entered navy as cabin boy, 1809; served in Indian Ocean and was at capture of British frigate *Africaine* off Grand Port, Mauritius, 1810; in *Marengo*, 1810-11; fought with a naval detachment in Belgium towards end of Empire; service in North America, Caribbean, and West Africa, 1816-18; *lieutenant de vaisseau*, 1819; *capitaine de frégate*, 1827. The following year took command of the *Favorite* (24), for scientific voyage around the world, 1829-32, of which he published an account in 1833-34; *capitaine de vaisseau*, 1834, and appointed to command of the *Artémise* (52). Sailing from Toulon in December 1837, Laplace completed another round-the-world voyage, during which he signed treaties with Polynesian chiefs, paving the way for French protectorate over Tahiti and the other Society islands; published in 1842 an account of the voyage of the *Artémise,* 1837-1840; rear-admiral, 1841; commanding Antilles squadron, 1844; Préfet Maritime at Rochefort, 1848; vice-admiral, 1853; member of the *Conseil d'Amirauté*, 1854; Préfet Maritime at Brest, 1855; retired, 1856; president of the French Geographical Society; died at Brest, 1875.

LATHAM: Lieutenant John Latham. British army officer. b. 1791, at Liverpool, of Irish stock. Entered Lancashire Militia as ensign at 17; transferred to 82nd Regiment (Prince of Wales's Volunteers), 1809; lieutenant, 1812; served under Wellington in Peninsular War, 1812-14, and in Upper Canada, under Sir Gordon Drummond; wounded at siege of Fort Erie, and received one year's pay as compensation and, from 1816, a yearly pension of £70 (about £5,000 today); served in army of occupation in France until January 1816, when regiment was transferred to Ireland; in January 1819 embarked at Cork for Mauritius; captain (without purchase), 1830; retired by sale of commission, April 1833; m. 1824, Nancy Robles (d. 1830), of Mauritius; one daughter. Latham commanded a detachment at Seychelles, 1827-28; left Mauritius with his regiment for England in 1831, accompanied by daughter, Ann Elizabeth. Retired to Roscrea, Tipperary; died 1837.

LEMARCHAND: Louis Joseph France LeMarchand. Landowner. b. 1888, at Mahé, third son of Louis and Rosalie LeMarchand (Athénas). m. 1911, Marie Médélisse Hodoul, two sons, two daughters. Working as estate clerk at St Pierre island, 1914. Served in World War I as lieutenant with Seychelles Carrier Corps in East Africa. Died as result of war service in India, date uncertain. Pension granted to widow and children, 1919.

LESAGE: Lieutenant Bibye Lesage. British army officer. Civil Agent, Seychelles, 1813-15. b. 1779, London. Lieutenant, 22nd Foot (later the Cheshire Regiment); was at capture of Ile de France (Mauritius), 1810; In 1815 granted concession of Denis Island and, later, Desroches. Sent by Governor Farquhar to Madagascar in 1815 to negotiate a treaty with Radama I. In 1819 Lesage was a passenger in the ill-fated *Six Soeurs* (Captain Raymond Hodoul) from Seychelles, and was among survivors from the burning ship who reached La Digue after ten days in an open boat. Lesage continued to live in Mauritius as a commercial agent.

LOGAN: Ewen Reginald Logan. Chief Justice, Seychelles, 1914-1919. ed. Charterhouse and Exeter College, BA 1891, MA 1897; called to Bar of Inner Temple, 1899; served Boer War in Imperial Yeomanry, 1901; assistant resident magistrate, Transvaal, 1902; magistrate, East African Protectorate, 1905; as Chief Justice of Seychelles was officer administering the government from July 1916 to March 1917, and from May to October 1917; drafted, in conjunction with barrister Alfred Gellé, code of civil procedure for Seychelles. Puisne Judge, Gold Coast, 1920; Chief Justice, Bahamas, 1925; puisne judge, Northern Rhodesia, 1927; knighted 1928; retired 1931.

MacGREGOR: William MacGregor. British medical practitioner and colonial administrator. Medical officer in charge of leper colony, Seychelles, 1873-75. b. 1846, at Knowhead, Donside, son of Aberdeenshire crofter; m. Mary Thomson, 1868; one son. Studied medicine at Glasgow and Aberdeen; medical assistant at Royal Lunatic Asylum, Aberdeen, before his appointment to Seychelles in 1873. In addition to being in charge of the Curieuse Island leper camp, MacGregor was also at various times Medical Officer for Praslin, Inspector of Schools and Liberated Africans, Civil Status Officer, and Sub-collector of Taxes at Praslin. MacGregor took a lease on Curieuse Island, building a house there for his wife and first daughter, Helen (known as the Doctor's House, it was completely restored in 1997 with funds from the French government). MacGregor developed a close friendship with the Governor of Mauritius, Sir Arthur Gordon, which lasted until Gordon's death in 1912. MacGregor followed Gordon to Fiji, where he became after ten years Colonial Secretary and acting Governor. He was subsequently Governor of British New Guinea, Lagos, Newfoundland, and, lastly, Queensland. After the death of his wife in Fiji, he married for a second time in 1883. He retired to Scotland in 1914, and died at Aberdeen in 1919. MacGregor was the first crofter's son to become a colonial governor and, in his lifetime, the only doctor to do so.

MADGE: Edward Madge. British army officer. Civil Agent, Seychelles, 1815-26; b. 1776; commissioned 1794; lieutenant, 19th Foot (Green Howards); captain, 1802. Assistant Registrar of Slaves at Mauritius, 1826; removed from government service as result of parliamentary inquiry, 1828; died at Pondicherry, 1850. Group of rocks near Praslin formerly named Madge Rocks.

232

MORESBY: Captain Fairfax Moresby. British naval officer. b. 1786. Calcutta. s. of army officer; entered navy 1799 as seaman; midshipman with Nelson in West Indies; lieutenant, 1806; commander 1811; post-captain, 1814. For service in Adriatic and on land with Austrian troops awarded Imperial Order of Maria Theresa, 1814; Companion of the Order of the Bath (CB), 1815. Appointed to command of *Menai* (24), and proceeded as senior officer at Cape of Good Hope. In February 1821 assumed chief command at Mauritius for suppression of slave trade, and visited Seychelles; on behalf of Governor Farquhar concluded treaty on slave trade with Imam of Muscat. Returned to England with Farquhar, 1823. Various sea commands, 1837-1845; rear-admiral, 1849; C-in-C, Pacific, 1850-53; vice-admiral, 1856; admiral, 1862; Admiral of the Fleet, 1870; died, 1877. Married at Malta, 1814, Eliza Louisa, of Bakewell, Derbyshire; three sons, two daughters.

MOUARD: Father Symphorien (Charles-Jacques) Mouard, Apostolic Vicar of Seychelles, 1882-89. b. 1828, at Sombernon, Seine-Maritime, France; ordained, 1854. Mouard went to India in 1859, serving at Agra, latterly as Director of Schools. He was named Apostolic Vicar (titular Bishop of Sidonia) by Pope Leon XIII on 18 September 1882, and arrived in Seychelles the following December. In April 1883 Mouard consecrated the chapel of Sacré Coeur at Beauvoir, which later became the focus of an annual pilgrimage. In November 1884 he was formally recognised as Bishop by the government, with equal precedence in Seychelles with the Anglican Bishop of Mauritius. Mouard left Seychelles in February 1889 to take up a post at Lahore, were he died in July 1890.

MYLIUS: Charles Augustus Mylius. Civil Commissioner, Seychelles, 1839-50. b. 1795, at Zell, Germany; s. of Baron Frederic Henri Mylius; entered Colonial Service as assistant secretary, 1812; chief clerk, Mauritius, 1819; assistant Collector of Customs, 1820; Deputy Auditor-General, 1825; Registrar of Slaves, 1832; retired in 1850 after his service in Seychelles; died, in England, about 1860.

NICOLAY: Major-General Sir William Nicolay. Governor of Mauritus, 1833-40. b. 1771, into Saxe-Gotha family settled in England. Served with army in India (at Seringapatam, 1792, and Pondicherry, 1793), in West Indies, and in Europe (at Corunna and Waterloo); major-general, 1819; governor of Dominica, 1824, and subsequently of Antigua, St Kitts, and Nevis; governor of Mauritius, 1833-40; lieutenant-general, 1837; died at Cheltenham, England, 1842.

NORTH: Marianne North, traveller and painter. b. 1830, at Hastings; elder daughter of Frederick North, MP for Hastings, and descendant of Lord North of Kirtling. Her widowed father encouraged her interest in botany and painting, and she often travelled with him in Europe and the Middle East until his death in 1869. In 1871 she began a series of journeys around the world which occupied the next 16 years of her life, and was to produce a collection of over 800 paintings, mainly of tropical plants and

233

flowers. One of her last journeys was to Seychelles in 1883-84. She died at Alderley, Gloucestershire, in 1890. Her paintings are on permanent display at the Marianne North Gallery at Kew Gardens. Her memoirs were published posthumously under the title *Recollections of a Happy Life.*

O'BRIEN: Lieut.-Colonel Charles Richard Mackey O'Brien. Governor of Seychelles, 1912-18. b. 1860, s. of Lt.-Col. Sir Terence O'Brien, Governor of Heligoland and Newfoundland. m. (1) Christian Mary (d. 1899), two sons, one daughter; (2) 1902, Selina Beatrice, d. of Sir Howard Elphinstone, bt., two daughters. ed. Felsted, Sandhurst; 2nd Lieut. 30th Cambridgeshire Regiment, 1878; captain, lst Bn. East Lancashire Regiment, 1887; major, 1897; lieut.-colonel, 1902; served South African War, 1899-1902; twice mentioned in dispatches; president, Military Tribunal, Johannesburg; retired from army, 1903; acting Commissioner of Police, Transvaal, 1903; Colonial Secretary, Gambia, 1910. On leaving Seychelles O'Brien was appointed Governor of Barbados, 1918-25, and Special Commissioner, Sierra Leone, 1926. Created Knight Commander of the Order of St Michael and St George (KCMG), 1920; died, 1935.

OWEN: Captain William Owen. British naval officer. b. 1774; son of naval captain and younger brother of Admiral Sir Edward Owen, C-in-C, West Indies (1822-25). Entered navy, 1788; appointed to command of brig *Seaflower*, 1803; visited Seychelles in squadron under command of Captain John Ferrier; discovered Seaflower channel off Sumatra. Taken prisoner by French, September 1808, and held at the Île de France (Mauritius) until exchanged in June 1810; in charge of transports at Madras for seizure of Île de France. Returned to England, 1815. Survey of Canadian lakes, 1815-16. In 1821 appointed to the *Leven* and *Barracouta* to carry out survey of African and Arabian coasts. Attempted to force Imam of Muscat to tighten anti-slaving measures by raising British flag over Mombasa (1823-26) at invitation of dissident sultan, leaving naval officer Lieutenant Reitz as governor, a move eventually repudiated by Britain. Visited Seychelles in 1824 and left description of islands in published memoirs. Founded a colony on Fernando Po, West Africa, 1827, and served in southern Africa until 1831; retired to estate at Campobello, New Brunswick, in 1835; died at St John, 1847.

PELLY: Colonel Lewis Pelly. British army officer and administrator. b. 1825, Stroud, Gloucestershire. Ensign, Bombay Army, 1841; captain 1856; lieutenant-colonel, 1863; *chargé d'affaires*, Teheran Legation, 1860; special mission to Afghanistan and Baluchistan; returned to India, 1861; mission to Comoro Islands; Political Agent and Consul, Zanzibar, 1862; witnessed cyclone and landslide at Seychelles, 1862; Political Resident, Persian Gulf, 1863; negotiated with Sultan of Muscat on slavery, 1865-71; colonel, 1871; Chief Commissioner of Rajputana states, 1874; Knight Commander of the Star of India (KCSI), 1874; sent on mission to Afghanistan, 1876; retired, 1877. Declined to administer Congo Free State for King Leopold II of Belgium; major-general, 1882; lieutenant-general, 1887; MP for North Hackney, 1885; died at Falmouth, 1892.

PHAYRE: Major-General Sir Arthur Purves Phayre. Governor of Mauritius, 1874-78. Served in Bengal infantry. Chief Commissioner, Burma; returned to England 1867; major-general, 1871. As Governor of Mauritius, Phayre was sympathetic to plight of Indian immigrants. Visited Seychelles in October 1875 and approved Venn's Town site.

PIKE: Nicholas Pike. American author and naturalist. U.S. consul at Mauritius, 1867-73; visited Seychelles with Governor Gordon, 1871. b. 1818 at Newburyport, Massachusetts; went to New York, 1839. probably as a clerk. In 1849 elected president of Brooklyn Natural History Society. In 1852 a friend secured him the post of consul at Oporto. Rewarded by Portuguese government for discovering that sulphur cured a grape fungus. Returned to US and served in Civil War with rank of lieutenant-colonel. Appointed consul at Mauritius, 1867. Wrote extensively on natural history of Mauritius; left nearly 500 drawings and paintings of Mauritius fish. His main work, *Sub-Tropical Rambles in the Land of the Aphanapteryx*, was published in 1873. Returned to US, 1874, and lived for many years in Brooklyn. Died 1905.

SALMON: Charles S. Salmon. Chief Civil Commissioner, Seychelles, 1874-79, the first Roman Catholic appointed to that post. Sub-collector and justice of peace, Sherbro Island, Sierra Leone, 1866; manager of British Sherbro, 1866-68; Collector of Customs, Gold Coast, 1869; Chief magistrate, Gold Coast, 1870; acting Administrator, Gold Coast, 1871. After five years as CCC, Seychelles, Salmon was appointed President of Nevis, 1880-85.

SAVY: Charles Dorothée Savy. French settler. The Savys were among the first French families from Bourbon to settle in Seychelles. Charles Savy is reported to have arrived in 1785, and was probably the brother of the Savy of whom the Seychelles commandant, Gillot, wrote in 1783: *J'ai l'honneur de vous donner avis que nous avons Mr Savi pour habitant avec l'agrément de Mr le Vicomte de Souillac; il est arrivé avec un de ses fils et un noir ... Ce Mr Savi que j'ai connu dans l'Inde, dans l'autre guerre, est un galant homme, bien éloigner de la troupe des autres habitans. Il attend sa famille dans le courant de l'année.'* In 1806 Charles Savy, who was noted for his great height, was appointed by Quéau de Quinssy a member of the *conseil de commune,* which supervised the upkeep of roads and the conditions and disciplining of slaves. He married Joséphine St Jorre, of Mauritius. The family name of Savy appears on the list of those incarcerated in the Conciergerie prison in Paris, and subsequently executed, during the French Revolution, .

STANLEY: Henry Morton Stanley. British-American explorer and journalist. b. 1841, as John Rowlands, at Denbigh, North Wales; sailed as cabin boy to New Orleans, 1859, where he was befriended by a merchant, Henry Stanley, whose name he took; soldier in Civil War; seaman and sailor in US navy; became a journalist and offered services to *New York Herald* to cover war in Ethiopia; reported fall of Magdala, 1868. In 1869 undertook relief of Livingstone; visited Seychelles while on his way home to report finding Livingstone at Ujiji, on Lake Tanganyika; received Royal Geographical Society Gold Medal. He returned to Africa after Livingstone's death and explored the region of the Congo; entered service of King Leopold II of the Belgians to help create the Congo Free State. Married, 1890, and regained British nationality in 1892; MP for Lambeth North, 1895-1900; Knight Grand Cross of the Bath (KGCB), 1899; died in London, 1904.

STEVENSON: Sir William Stevenson. Governor of Mauritius, 1857-1863. b. 1805, in Jamaica, son of a planter. Called to Bar, 1837; assistant judge, Jamaica Supreme Court, 1841; Superintendent, Honduras, 1854; Knight Commander of the Order of the Bath (KCB), 1862. Although referred to by Sir Arthur Gordon as "anti-Catholic Stevenson", others have described Stevenson as an excellent governor. He carried through many improvements during his five years in Mauritius, although his pro-Indian policies were not popular. In 1883, Pope Hennessy spoke of him as "one of the ablest of my predecessors". His health undermined by dysentery, Stevenson died at Le Réduit on 9 January 1863.

STEWART: Henry Cockburn Stewart. Acting Chief Civil Commissioner, Seychelles, March-November 1881, and Administrator, 1895-99. b.1844, eldest son of Rev. Robert Walter Stewart and grandson of Lord Blantyre; educated Edinburgh Academy and abroad; married May Dorothy Neville-Rolfe. Private secretary to Lord Rosmead, Governor of Ceylon, 1865-72; Assistant Colonial Secretary, Mauritius, later Colonial Secretary. Died at Aden, shortly after leaving Seychelles, June 1899.

SWEET-ESCOTT: Ernest Bickham Sweet-Escott. Administrator, 1899-1903, and Governor of Seychelles, 1903-04. b. 1857, at Bath; younger son of Rev. Hay Sweet-Escott; m. 1881, Mary Wingfield (d. 1935). ed. Bath, Balliol College, Oxford; BA, 2nd and 3rd class honours, Classics and History, 1880; MA, 1911. Entered Colonial Service as Classics professor, Royal College, Mauritius, 1881; Assistant Colonial Secretary, 1886; Colonial Secretary, British Honduras, 1893; senior clerk, Colonial Office, 1898. After his service in Seychelles, appointed Governor of British Honduras, 1904, and made a Knight Commander of the Order of St Michael and St George (KCMG). Governor of Leeward Islands, 1906; of Fiji and Consul-General, Western Pacific, 1912. Retired at own request, 1918. President, Pedestrians' Association, Worthing. Died, 1941.

THOMASSET: Hans Paul Thomasset. Naturalist and rubber planter; director of Seychelles Coconut and Rubber Company. Of South African origin; arrived in Seychelles with the Percy Sladen Expedition, 1905; went to Aldabra, 1907; several Seychelles plants and animals named after him; founded *Le Petit Seychellois* newspaper.

WADE: Captain George Thompson Wade. Civil Commissioner, Seychelles, 1852-61. Served with the 13th Foot (Somerset Light Infantry) during the First Afghan War (1838-1842). This ill-conceived and badly executed campaign was to thwart Russian ambitions in the region. Although initially successful, the joint British-Indian force of 20,000 was besieged in Kabul and other Afghan towns, and ultimately had to withdraw with heavy losses. Wade, as Civil Commissioner, welcomed the first Roman Catholic Apostolic Prefect, Father Jeremiah, to Seychelles in 1853, and did much to improve relations with the Roman Catholics. Died of dysentery, in September 1861.

WARD: Swinburne Ward. Civil Commissioner, Seychelles, 1862-68. b. 1830, presumed son of Sir Henry George Ward (former Secretary to Admiralty). First cousin of the poet Swinburne. Entered Admiralty, 1847, and was private secretary to father and his successor. In 1855 transferred to Ceylon and Madras, in both places father was governor. Auditor-General, Mauritius, from 1868. Career in Seychelles undistinguished, and one of last acts of Mauritius Governor Sir Arthur Gordon was to order examination of Ward's accounts. Returned to England, 1876; died in London, 1885.

WHITING: Francis Arthur Whiting. British settler. b. 1870, at Epsom, Surrey; s. of Clifton Whiting, stockbroker, and Minna Whiting (Hackblock). Arrived Seychelles, 1893; one of founders of Seychelles Club, 1894; m. (1) Hélène Button, who died aged 21, one son; (2) Elisa Button, two sons, one daughter; (3) Edith d'Unienville, of Mauritius. Worked for a time at Felicité island. Served as lieutenant with Seychelles Carrier Corps in East Africa in World War I. After the war went to Majunga, where he worked in a meat factory. Joined there by his wife Edith and family. In the 1920s worked on Railways in Kenya; died, 1921. Some family members returned to Seychelles.

WILLIAMSON: Scots lawyer and administrator. ed. Edinburgh University, MA, 1893; called to Scottish Bar, 1897; lecturer in Jurisprudence, 1897; author of *John Law of Lauriston*, and other books of historical and antiquarian interest. Legal Adviser, Crown Prosecutor, and Police Magistrate, Seychelles, 1908; acting Chief Justice, May-August 1909. Resigned Colonial Service, 1912, while awaiting outcome of appeal to Privy Council against his judgement in the Lanier case.

WRIGHT: Edward Perceval Wright. Irish doctor and botanist; in 1867 made a six-month visit to Seychelles, after an expedition he was to have made to Iceland was postponed; the result was his comprehensive study of the flora and fauna of Seychelles. Wright was appointed a temporary medical officer in Seychelles, and, among other duties, was responsible for the leper camp on Curieuse island. b. Dublin, 1834; ed. Trinity College, Dublin; Professor of Botany and Keeper of Herbarium, Trinity College, 1869-1904; died, 1910.

YOUNG: Alfred Karney Young. Chief Justice of Seychelles, 1909-13. ed. Magdalene College, Oxford, BA: called to the Bar, Middle Temple, 1889. Held various posts in British Honduras, 1890-99; Crown Prosecutor and

Legal Adviser, Seychelles, 1903; Attorney-General, Central Africa protectorate, 1906; magistrate, Trinidad, 1908; Chief Justice of Seychelles from 1909.

OFFICERS ADMINISTERING SEYCHELLES, 1813-1921 *

<u>Dependency of Mauritius</u>

1813 - 1815	BIBYE LESAGE	Government Agent
1815 - 1826	EDWARD MADGE	
1826 - 1837	GEORGE HARRISON (acting)	
1837 - 1839	ARTHUR WILSON (acting)	
1839 - 1850	CHARLES MYLIUS	Civil Commissioner
1850 - 1852	ROBERT KEATE	
1852 - 1861	GEORGE WADE	
1862 - 1868	SWINBURNE WARD	
1869 - 1872	WILLIAM FRANKLYN	
1872 - 1874	WILLIAM FRANKLYN	Chief Civil Commissioner
1874 - 1879	CHARLES SALMON	
1879 - 1880	ARTHUR HAVELOCK	
1880 - 1881	FRANCIS BLUNT	
1881	H. COCKBURN STEWART (acting)	
1882 - 1885	ARTHUR BARKLY	
1885 - 1886	G. HOLLIER GRIFFITHS (acting)	
1887 - 1888	ARTHUR BARKLY	
1889 - 1895	T. RISLEY GRIFFITH	Administrator
1895 - 1899	H. COCKBURN STEWART	
1899 - 1903	E. SWEET-ESCOTT	

<u>Crown Colony of Seychelles</u>

1903 - 1904	E. SWEET-ESCOTT	Governor
1904 - 1912	WALTER DAVIDSON	
1912 - 1918	CHARLES H. O'BRIEN	
1916 - 1917	EWART LOGAN (acting)	
1918 - 1921	Sir E. T.-WICKHAM-FIENNES, bt	

Brief acting appointments have been omitted.

239

SOURCES AND NOTES

Seychelles National Archives	SNA	Bibliothèque Nationale, Paris	BN
Archives de France, Paris	AF	Public Record Office, London	PRO
Ministry of Foreign Affairs, Paris	FAP	US National Archives, Washington	NAW
Ministry of Foreign Affairs, Nantes	FAN	Kendall Whaling Museum, Mass.	KWM
Mauritius Archives	MA	Church Mission Society, London	CMS

CHAPTER ONE

Source material for this chapter comes from SNA B/29 and PRO CO 167/154; in addition, reports and related correspondence of the Commission of Enquiry into the Slave Trade are found in Parliamentary Papers XXV 292 and in PRO CO 145/1 and SNA B/3. The reference to Latham taking away two domestic slaves is in Mauritius to Harrison, 19 December 1829 (SNA B/6), and allegations of the *Zenga* punishment appear in Wilson to Mauritius, 2 May 1835, with enclosures (SNA B/10). The Babette Loizeau affair is treated in SNA B/6, B/8, and B/29. Published works consulted included Moses D.E. Nwulia, *The History of Slavery in Mauritius and the Seychelles, 1810-1875* (East Brunswick, NY, 1981), and 'Historical Miscellanea', collected by A.W.T. Webb and H.J. MacGaw (Seychelles Archives).

1   Inconclusive conflict between Britain and the United States arising from Britain's oppressive maritime blockade of Europe and the Royal Navy's impressment of sailors from American ships. There was also an underlying US wish to expel Britain from Canada. War was declared by President James Madison on 18 June 1812. Most military activity took place along the Canadian border. A notable occurrence was the burning by the British of public buildings in Washington. The war ended with Treaty of Ghent, in December 1814.

2   The 82nd Regiment of Foot, also known as the Prince of Wales's Volunteers, was raised in 1793; amalgamated with the 40th Foot in 1881 to form the 2nd Battalion, South Lancashire Regiment; with further amalgamations became, in 1970, the Queen's Lancashire Regiment; headquarters at Warrington, Cheshire. A detachment of the 82nd Foot was stationed in Seychelles from 1827 to 1829.

3   James Holman, British naval officer, blinded in action in 1810 while serving in the *Guerrière* frigate on the North American station. Naval knight of Windsor. During a voyage round the world he visited Seychelles in 1829, aboard HM sloop *Jaseur* (Captain Lyons). His four-volume account of the voyage was published in London, in 1834.

4   Between 1815 and 1825 Seychelles exported to Mauritius about 1,500 bags of cotton each year. – *Notes Statistiques sur les Îles Seychelles*, 1850, anonymous, quoted by J.P.G. Lionnet, *Journal of the Seychelles Society*, October 1962.

5   The colonial dollar was issued in 1820 by Colonial Office for Mauritius and its dependencies, replacing the Spanish dollar or piastre. It had a value of four shillings in British currency. In 1860 it was replaced by the pound sterling, which, in turn, was replaced in 1876 by the Indian rupee. In 1914 emergency currency notes

of R.5 and R.10 were introduced. In 1939 Indian and Mauritian coins of 10 cents and above were replaced by Seychelles coins. In 1945, all Mauritian and Indian notes and coins, except small copper coins that had been legal tender in Seychelles before 1901, were demonetized. Throughout the text, the $ sign indicates the US dollar.

6   Other points in Harrison's report included: 1) complaint about criminal cases being judged at Mauritius through depositions made before a *juge de paix*; as a result accused might stay in prison for up to a year awaiting verdict; 2) suggestion that Government Agent should have authority to allow movement of slaves between islands; 3) the only common fruits in Seychelles were plantains, bananas, and pineapples; 4) green turtles selling for three and a half dollars; tortoises brought over from Aldabra; 5) crocodiles not seen for many years; 6) there were from eighty to 100 homes in the town, with several good shops and two or three billiard rooms; 7) a causeway has been built, leading to a builder's yard which can take vessels of up to 300 tonnes; ships can also be repaired at Hodoul Island (where permission was given to Hodoul in November 1829 to erect 'a marine establishment'); 8) ship materials and provisions in short supply; 9) about fifteen vessels, amounting to 1,350 tons, built since January 1817; a ship of 200 tons ready to be launched at Praslin, but shipbuilding not profitable; 10) three footpaths going over mountains; horses and mules used for transport, also hammocks or palaquins. In a covering letter to Secretary of State, 16 March 1831, Mauritius governor Sir Charles Colville described Harrison as 'a most fit person for the situation he holds'. (PRO CO 167/154).

7   *'Mahé conserve toujours son cachet français'.* — Erique Guilloteaux, *Madagascar et la Côte des Somalis, Sainte Marie, et les Seychelles: Leur rôle et leur avenir* (Paris, 1922).

8   The suspect schooner was the *Victor* (Captain Eugène Dubois Duniclac), said to be sailing from Bombay to Bourbon. It anchored some way off the island, and no-one went on board to investigate its cargo. Proprietors of D'Arros island at the time were Lefèvre and François Savy. — Harrison to Mauritius, 24 April 1828 (SNA B/29).

9   Among settlers anxious to amend details of slaves being transferred to Mauritius was Madam Paton, a widow thought to have made many mistakes in her returns. — Harrison to Mauritius, 27 August 1827 (SNA B/29). *Madanm Paton* is the Creole name for the cattle egret, a bird commonly seen in Seychelles. Origin of the name is uncertain.

10   Like his predecessors, Harrison obtained the concessions of several islands (in his case, Providence, Des Noeufs, and Boudeuse), and would have required slaves to work on them. — 'Historical Miscellanea', Vol. III (SNA).

11   Separating families was particularly cruel, as it denied to slaves the capacity of showing affection. Harrison refers to a slave who had been purchased by the government in 1829 from the company Crook and Naz. The man was due to be shipped to Mauritius but he attempted to delay for as long as possible his separation 'from a Negress with whom he had lived for many years back [and] to whom he appears greatly attached' (SNA B/29).

12   A proclamation by Governor Farquhar in 1817 forbade the export of Seychelles produce except through Mauritius. The Commissioners of Eastern Enquiry advocated the repeal of this restriction, and on 1 March 1831 Mauritius authorised export to India of a limited quantity of sugar. Earlier, Harrison had received a petition from twenty-five inhabitants asking for sugar to be shipped to India in the brig *Sans Pareil* (Captain Charles Marcy) in return for rice. If allowed, 'it would be a great relief to all classes of the inhabitants'. — Harrison to Mauritius (PRO CO 167/154).

13   The medical report reads: '*Les deux fesses couvertes de blessures non fente, les unes plus récentes que les autres, se prolongeant vers les flancs et paraissant être le résultat de plusieurs administrations successives récentes de coups de fouet. La fesse gauche présentant dans sa partie moyenne une plaie à peu pres circulaire d'environ 8 pouces de circonférence recouverte de croûtes comme les autres plaies particulières. La fesse droite présentant dans sa partie moyenne une plaie de forme ovalaire d'environ trois pouces de long sur deux de large dans son milieu également recouvert de croûtes'* (SNA B/29).

14   In the early years of British administration in Seychelles cases of murder were sent to Mauritius for trial and execution of sentence. This generally was the procedure under French rule, with one notable exception. In 1809, the commandant Quéau de Quinssy sought and received permission to carry out death sentences on the spot. The following year a slave named Pompée was convicted of the murder of Pierre Michel Inard, a white overseer, and sentenced to death. As there was no executioner available to carry out the beheading, the tribunal unanimously ruled that the convicted man should be burned. This took place on a beach near the Moussa river, at half-past three in the morning of 15 August 1810 (SNA A/23/5 & 6).

15   One of the youngest infantry regiments in the British army, the 99th Foot was raised in Glasgow in 1824 by Major-General Gage John Hall, who had been governor of Mauritius from November 1817 to December 1818. In 1825 the regiment sailed to Mauritius, where it remained for twelve years. In 1832 the Queen bestowed on the 99th the name The Lanarkshire Regiment, but it lost its Scottish connection in 1881 when it was re-formed as the 2nd Battalion, the Wiltshire Regiment. In 1959, in a further amalgamation, it became, along with the Royal Berkshire Regiment, the Duke of Edinburgh's Royal Regiment, with headquarters at Salisbury, Wiltshire. In 1994, the Royal Regiment amalgamated with the Gloucestershire Regiment to form the Royal Gloucestershire, Berkshire and Wiltshire Regiment. The 99th Foot provided a military detachment in Seychelles on two occasions, from 1829 to 1832, and again from 1835 to 1837.

CHAPTER TWO

This chapter is based on published works by Captain Laplace, namely *Voyage autour du Monde par les Mers de l'Inde et de Chine sur la Corvette de l'État La Favorite pendant les Années 1830, 1831, et 1832* (Paris, 1833), and *Campagne de Circumnavigation de la Frégate l'Artémise, 1837-40* (Paris, 1842); also referred to is an undated report by Laplace to the Minister (AF 5 JJ 1103). The remark by the anti-slavery MP Thomas Buxton is quoted in F.A. Hoyos, *Barbados: A History from the*

Amerindians to Independence (London, 1978). Also consulted was G.S. Graham, *Great Britain in the Indian Ocean* (London, 1967). The correspondence dealing with the treatment of slaves and granting of land concessions on the outer islands is in SNA B/6 and B/7 respectively. Complaints by the Seychelles medical officer is found in SNA B/12.

1   Naval action at Navarino Bay, off south-west Greece, where a Turco-Egyptian fleet was totally destroyed in 1827 by a combined French, British, and Russian force. Described as 'an untoward event' by the Duke of Wellington, the Battle of Navarino resulted two years later in the emergence of an independent Greece. Echoes of the Greek revolt against Turkey reached as far as Seychelles, where Harrison was confronted at breakfast one morning by an angry Greek sea captain named Chiefala protesting that his English partner had reneged on a scheme to buy a ship in Seychelles and fit it out as a privateer against Turkish shipping. In a note to Mauritius about this 'ridiculous affair', Harrison said that had Chiefala not been Greek he would have treated him far less courteously. He warned him and his partner against attempting to carry out their scheme, and alerted Mauritius to the possible arrival there of the would-be privateers. – Harrison to F.E. Vitet, private secretary to Governor, 26 August 1828 (SNA B/29).

2   '*Les cartes de l'archipel qui se trouve au N de l'Île-de-France laissent encore beaucoup à désirer, malgré les travaux d'un grand nombre de navigateurs. Beaucoup d'îles et de bancs y sont mal placés, et les incertitudes sont d'une telle nature qu'il faudrait, pour les lever, faire de la reconnaissance de ce seul archipel l'objet d'une mission spéciale.*' – Chief Hydrographer's advice to Laplace, quoted in *Voyage Autour du Monde.*

3   Jean-Baptiste Lislet Geoffroy, a former French engineer officer and surveyor at the Île de France, carried out a complete survey of Mahé in 1793. The remarks quoted here are contained in his '*Mémoire sur la Nouvelle Carte de l'Archipel du nord-est de Madagascar'*, Port Louis, 5 November 1817 (AF 3 JJ 358).

4   Moresby expressed the hope 'that those who follow me may navigate in their neighbourhood with greater confidence than heretofore, and those that are bound to India will find that the route by the eastern coast of Madagascar is not studded with so many dangers as has been supposed'. Moresby, in HMS *Menai,* visited Mahé, where he purchased 150 head of cattle, rice, and refreshment for his sick. He found the inhabitants hospitable and, unlike some other visitors, he considered their moral character to be good, except for their inclination to trade in slaves. – From an article in *Nautical Magazine and Naval Chronicle*, undated (SNA).

5   '*Cette réserve froide et cérémonieuse des dames anglaises avec les étrangers en fut bannie, et nous jouîmes tout à fait au privilège des voyageurs dont le séjour doit être court.*' As for the Seychellois, Laplace found that *'leur caractère est généralement bon, affable et hospitalier; presque tous marins, ils ont l'esprit hardi et entrepenant du métier. Quoique disséminés dans l'île sur leurs habitations, les colons aiment la société et les plaisirs'.*' – Laplace [op. cit.].

6   Few crocodile remains have been found in Seychelles. In 1966 Swiss herpetologist René Honegger photographed a crocodile skull, which is now preserved in the Natural History Museum, Victoria. Until recently it was thought that the skull was that of a Nile crocodile (*Crocodylus niloticus*), but recent

research suggests Seychelles was inhabited by the even larger Indopacific estuarine or saltwater crocodile (*Crocodylus porosus*). — J. Gerlach and K.L. Canning, 'On the Crocodiles of the Western Indian Ocean' (*Phelsuma*, Vol. 2, 1994).

7   In contrast to her husband, Radama, whom she succeeded on his death in 1828, Queen Ranavalona I bitterly opposed European expansion, although she employed French and British advisers, notably Jean Laborde and James Cameron. In 1835 she outlawed Christianity and expelled all missionaries. Four years before her death in 1861 she exiled all Europeans, including her closest advisers.

8   Farquhar's instructions in November 1815 were that he should administer Madagascar's European settlements 'as dependencies of Mauritius'. However, the following year he was ordered to restore any settlements France had held before January 1792. Farquhar seems to have been reluctant to do so, telling the Bourbon governor that it was impossible to know what the French had held, and that the ports were open equally to both nations. The French replied that if Madagascar territories had been temporarily ceded to Britain, how was it possible to reverse the argument and say they did not exist: *'Il me semble que l'Angleterre plus que toute autre nation, a un grand intérêt à maintenir dans toute sa intégrité, ce principe généralement reconnu par toutes les puissances maritimes, que l'acte de prise de possession constitue la souveraineté sur les côtes habitées par des peuples hors de la civilisation européene'.* — quoted by Graham [op. cit.].

9   Son of the Merina ruler Andrianampoinimerina, Radama I consolidated his father's power throughout Madagascar. He admired Europeans, and was anxious to obtain their help in building Madagascar into a modern state. In 1816 he sent his two young brothers to be schooled in Mauritius. He tried to adopt an even-handed policy towards the British and French. By the time of his death in 1828 almost the whole of Madagascar was under Merina rule. He was succeeded by his widow, Ranavalona (note 7).

10   Sir Thomas Fowell Buxton, bt. British philanthropist, politician, and administrator. b. 1827, son of Sir Edward North Buxton, bt; ed. Harrow and Trinity College, Cambridge; succeeded to baronetcy, 1840; president of British and Foreign Anti-Slavery Society; Governor of South Australia, 1895-98. m., 1862, Lady Victoria Noel, d. of Earl of Gainsborough, five sons, five daughters; died 1915. One of the districts of Victoria, capital of Seychelles, is named Mont Buxton.

11   William Wilberforce. British politician. b. 1758; entered politics, 1780; came under evangelical influence and helped to outlaw the slave trade, 1807; spent rest of life trying to secure the complete abolition of slavery. In 1825 sponsored the foundation of the Anti-Slavery Society; died 1833.

12   James Dowland. British administrator. b. 1805, Nottingham, England. Writer in Mauritius service, 1826; Seychelles Sub-Agent and Assistant Registrar of Slaves, 1828; Chief of Inland Revenue, Mauritius, 1838; acting Colonial Secretary, 1854. Dowland was held responsible for the cholera outbreaks in Mauritius in 1854 and 1856, but was permitted to retire before publication of the inquiry's report. Died at Bristol, 1903.

13   Reprimanding Dowland, Registrar of Slaves Patrick Salter told him he wanted an explanation whenever descriptions of slaves did not tally, and not Dowland's 'implied wishes for confiscation'. — Salter to Dowland, 27 May 1830 (SNA B/6).

14   The Order in Council of June 1829 'repealed, abolished and annulled' all laws that created disabilities for subjects of free condition of African or Indian birth or descent. This measure had been proposed by the Commissioners of Eastern Enquiry in July 1828. The free coloured population of Mauritius numbered about 18,000, compared with 8,000 Whites and 65,000 slaves. The British had inherited from the French the island's strict racial divisions (relaxed during the Revolution, but restored under Napoleon). Births, marriages, and deaths were registered separately, and although many Coloureds had substantial land holdings and were a respected community, discrimination, both official and unofficial, meant there were no mixed cemeteries, Coloureds could not marry Whites (forbidden under the *Code Noir*), and at the theatre only the gallery was available to them. Except for one elementary school, established in 1814 by the London Missionary Society, and a free school opened in 1823 with the support of the government, education of the coloured class was a matter for themselves. When the Royal College was opened to coloured children in 1832, white parents boycotted it until 1839. – Report by Commissioners of Eastern Enquiry (PRO CO 167/143) and Nwulia [op. cit.].

15   A French parliamentary committee report recommending rejection of the petition was approved by the Chamber of Deputies on 2 March 1833. It was pointed out that under Article 8 of the Treaty of Paris of 1814 Mauritius had been transferred to Britain without conditions, and that therefore the capitulation was no longer valid. One deputy questioned the petitioners' motives, saying the aim of the British government was to 'establish those measures of humanity that we ourselves would like to see prevail in our own colonies'. *Le Moniteur* of 4 March 1833 reported the debate. Recently historians have again raised the question of whether the Treaty of Paris cancelled the special conditions of the capitulation whereby the Mauritius inhabitants retained rights of language, customs, religion, and civil law.

16   The 29th (Worcestershire) Regiment, which was raised during the war with France in 1694 as Thomas Farrington's Regiment, was stationed at Mauritius from 1826 to 1838. The regimental journal notes that on 28 October 1830 the regiment was inspected at Mahébourg by the Governor, Sir Charles Colville, and that among musicians on parade were 'three blacks, the remnant of a corps of black drummers, authorized in the regiment'. In 1970 the Worcestershire Regiment amalgamated with the Sherwood Foresters, to form the Worcestershire and Sherwood Foresters Regiment, part of the Prince of Wales's Division. The 29th maintained a detachment in Seychelles from 1831 to 1833.

17   Seychelles' first newspaper did not appear until 1840, when the Mauritius governor approved an application by one Mamin to publish a journal at Mahé. The Governor had doubts about 'the advantage of a free press, where there are no means of punishing its licentiousness'. – Mauritius to Mylius, 28 May 1840 (SNA).

18   The Reform Bill was a notable political advance for Britain, giving a larger share of power to the growing commercial and industrial classes. Unrepresentative 'rotten' boroughs were abolished, and the franchise was extended to those paying yearly rental of £10 in towns and £40 in counties. Artisans were no longer tied to their employer, and workmen could combine to obtain better wages. In the same year as colonial slavery was abolished, employment of children under nine in Britain was prohibited. A start was made in reducing the number of capital offences, which fell from 223 to seven in 1837. Previous to the Reform Act, Parliament had repealed laws that discriminated against Catholics and non-Conformists .

245

19   Louis-Philippe I. b. 1772, of the House of Orléans; fought with distinction in Revolutionary Army at Valmy and Jemappes (1792); lived abroad until Restoration of Louis XVIII; proclaimed King of the French after Revolution of 1830, abdicated during Revolution of 1848; died in England, 1850.

CHAPTER THREE

Sources include the logs of the American whalers *Georgia* (343 tons), of New London, Connecticut, and the *William Lee* (311 tons), of Newport, Rhode Island, filed under OLOG 15 and MR 172 respectively, at the Mystic Seaport Museum, Mystic, Connecticut. Also consulted were Alexander Starbuck's *History of the American Whale Fishery* (Secaucus, New Jersey, reprinted 1989), and 'Historical Whaling Records from the Western Indian Ocean', a document prepared by Phoebe Wray and Kenneth R. Martin for the Seychelles delegation at the International Whaling Commission meeting, 1980 (SNA IWC/SC 32/08). This document quotes from Charles Nordoff, *Whales and Fishing* (Cincinnati, 1856). Harrison's reference to whaling ships putting in at Mahé is given in a report to the C-in-C East Indies, forwarded by Commander William Barrow, of HM sloop *Rose*, April 1837 (SNA B/12). It was also published in *The Nautical Magazine and Naval Chronicle*, 1839. The deposition by boatsteerer Thomas Smith is in the Seychelles National Archives under B/29. Harrison's query on whether slaves should be employed on whalers is filed under B/3, and the incident involving the Savy family under B/9. The stabbing of Captain Howard is in B/11, and the affair of Captain Cross in B/9 and B/10. Correspondence on Anjouan envoys taking passage in American whalers is found at SNA B/11 and PRO CO 1/5495.

1   The sperm whale is the largest of the toothed cetaceans; others in this group include the bottlenose whale, the killer whale, or orca, the pilot whale, the dolphin, and the porpoise. Sperm whales, which are widely distributed around the world, are commonly found in the area of Seychelles during the breeding season. The humpback is one of the smaller baleen whales, the type characterised by the plates of 'whalebone' (or baleen) in the mouth, through which it strains out the small sea creatures, or krill, on which it feeds. The largest animal in the world is the baleen Blue whale.

2   Spermaceti was highly prized, one of its uses being in the manufacture of fine, scented candles. Another valuable by-product of the sperm whale is ambergris, sometimes found on the beach, and thought to be the undigested parts of the giant squid on which the sperm whale is thought to feed. Ambergris is said to have medicinal properties; it is also used in the manufacture of expensive perfumes. The ornamental carving of whale's teeth, a shipboard pastime known as scrimshaw, remains a popular art form for collectors.

3   Lost on the Blanchisseuses (Madge Rocks), between Les Mamelles and Cousine islands, 17 December 1828 (SNA B/29).

4   American whaleships operated independently of a land base. They brought the whale carcases alongside for cutting in, before rendering the blubber into oil

(trying out), and storing it in barrels below decks. Several writers have wrongly identified the remains of a whaling station on Sainte Anne as evidence of an American land base, reportedly from 1832. See 'American trade in the Indian Ocean, 1795-1815', a paper by George Bindley Davidson, read to the Seychelles Society, 1 February 1963 (SNA F2.13), as well as a paper prepared in 1981 for the International Whaling Commission (SNA IWC/31/8).

5   Among whaleships that came to grief was the *Greenwich*, owned by Messrs Bennett & Son, of Rotherhithe, which was wrecked on Denis island in February 1833. Captain Joseph Foosey had to resort to 'apprentices and Portuguais and hired Blacks' to salvage most of the whale oil and ship's provisions, as his crew refused to assist. Among the *Greenwich's* crew who had earlier left the ship was William Whitehead, alias Martin. In 1831 he had been put ashore on Denis, too ill to work. Described as having 'a red face and red nose', and known as 'Bill in the Bunk', Martin claimed his sickness, diagnosed by the doctor as venereal disease, was caused by wounds received at Navarino. Inquiries by his family as to his whereabouts elicited the information that in April 1838 Martin was still living at Mahé. – Foosey to Harrison, 28 February 1833 [given wrongly as 1832] (SNA B/8), and Mauritius to Wilson, 31 January 1838, with affidavit sworn before Wilson by Allan Keast, policeman and former second mate of the *Greenwich*, 17 April 1838 (SNA B/12).

6   The *Thomas Blyth*, completed in 1837 at a cost of £2,000 for James Blyth, of Mauritius, was named after his father. It was the first of a large fleet of ships – nicknamed pea-soupers on account of the colour of their hulls – that Blyth operated between Mauritius and London. Like the *Thomas Blyth*, many were barques, which carry a fore-and-aft sail on the mizzen mast.

7   In January 1834 Captain Joseph Abbott of the whaler *Princess Mary* offered passages to England. If whales were scarce, the voyage was estimated to last about seven months; otherwise, passengers might be at sea for 18 months. (SNA B/9).

8   Samuel Tripp Braley. American whaling captain. b. 1817 at Rochester, near New Bedford, Mass. First whaling voyage in Atlantic, 1834; sailed for Indian Ocean in the *Gideon Barstow*, of Rochester; in 1838 wrecked on Cocos Islands. Sailed as third, second, and then first mate of the 276-ton whaling barque *Arab*, of Fairhaven, on two voyages in Indian Ocean; master of the *Arab*, 1845; m. Mary Ann King, 1845. Second voyage as master of the *Arab* to Indian Ocean, 1849-53. From 1854 to 1857 was master of the *Harrison* (371 tons), of New Bedford. Worked for some years on father's farm before returning to sperm whaling as master of the *Benjamin Franklin*, in the North Atlantic and Indian Ocean. Last voyage to Indian Ocean in the *Sea Fox* (166 tons), of Westport, Mass. (1869-70); died at Mahé on 16 August 1870, and was buried in the Bel Air cemetery. Mary Ann's grave in Rochester records her husband's death at Seychelles. Their son, Henry, a lawyer, was mayor of Fall City, 1882-84.

CHAPTER FOUR

References to the abolition of slavery, petitions by slave-owners, and condition of apprentices appear in SNA B/10 and B/12. Estimating the value of slaves is in correspondence from Commissioners of Compensation to Harrison (SNA B/9). The habit of liberated female slaves showing off their shoes is mentioned by Nwulia [op. cit.]. Issuing of sabres and muskets to police, and petition for a military detachment are in SNA B/12. The observer of disturbances in Mauritius was probably US consul Nicholas Pike (NAW). The Governor's 'sincere appreciation' at the way apprentices celebrated their freedom is in SNA B/13. Praise by Governor of Harrison's 'judicious and prudent' action, and subsequent development of leper colony on Curieuse, including surgeon's report, filed severally under PRO CO 167/154 and SNA B/6, B/12, and B/29. Correspondence relating to Petit Jean and others included in B/6 and B/8. Bourbon governor's application to send prisoners to Seychelles is filed in B/12, and Harrison's police recruits in B/7. Published material includes Captain Sir Edward Belcher, *Narrative of a Voyage Round the World in HM ship Sulphur, during the years 1836-1842, Vol. II* (London, 1843).

1   Mauritius returns do not indicate the total amount of compensation paid to Seychelles slave-owners. A document in the Seychelles National Archives lists payments to the following, as at 1 February 1835: Mme Henriette Petit, now wife of J.B. Remi d'Argent, £100 for one male slave; Charles Mahé Quincy, £710 for four males and five females; M. Meistre, £120 for one male; Leonard Beaufay, £810 for three males and eight females; Jupin Fondaumière £130 for one male; Chérimont Gontier, £420 for five males; Widow La Bucle, £530 for one male and five females; Pierre Leperre, £800 for six males and five females; Widow Pierre-Marie Larue, £100 for two males and one female; Adrienne Lemerle, £440 for three males and four females; Louis-Marie Tirant and Jupin Fondaumière, £5,260 for 42 males and 13 females. Total amount paid for 110 slaves, £9,420 (equivalent to approximately £750,000 today). (SNA B/84).

2   The troops withdrawn were from the 99th Foot, which in 1833 had relieved men of the 29th, the second time the regiment had provided a detachment in Seychelles. By 1836 indiscipline was so bad that the Governor decided it was 'absolutely necessary' for the 99th to be withdrawn. — Mauritius to Harrison, and subsequent correspondence, 19 May to 5 October 1836 (SNA B/11 and B/30).

3   The 35th (Royal Sussex) Regiment was raised in 1701 as the Earl of Donegall's Regiment, and nicknamed the Orange Lilies. It was first affiliated to the county of Dorset, before switching to Sussex in 1804. In 1832 William IV granted the Royal prefix to the 35th, which, after amalgamation with the 3rd Regiment of Bengal European Infantry, was re-formed in 1881 as the Royal Sussex Regiment. In 1966 the regiment became the 3rd Battalion The Queen's Regiment. In 1992 the Queen's and the Royal Hampshires were amalgamated to form The Princess of Wales's Royal Regiment, with headquarters at Canterbury, Kent. A detachment of the 35th was stationed at Seychelles for most of 1839.

4   Charles Savy of Sainte Anne took with him to Mauritius three orphan children, for whom he was formally acting as guardian, although they were little better than servants. He was allowed to take them only on condition that he produced them before a Mauritius court. When he failed to do so, Seychelles had them returned. — Mylius to Mauritius, 30 August 1843 (MA TA 45).

5   Quoted in 1977 Census Report (Victoria, April 1978). Harrison had described this situation in his 1830 report (PRO CO 167/154).

6   Harrison seems to have been the first British administrator to propose action to preserve the coco de mer palm, which was being heavily cut to provide straw for the new industry of basket and hat-making introduced by the Frenchman Antoine Bénézet. 'I am decidedly of ... [the] opinion as to the probability of this magnificent Palm tree becoming extinct, in course of time, unless some measure be adopted for its preservation'. — Harrison to Mauritius, 21 October 1828 (SNA B/29).

CHAPTER FIVE

Mylius's correspondence with Mauritius and related dispatches to London are filed under PRO CO 167/212 and SNA B/31. The naming of Victoria is referred to in MA TA/43 and TA/44. Slave-owners' correspondence with Mylius is in SNA B/73A. Harrison's opinion of clergyman Morton and subsequent comment by Governor Colville are in PRO CO 167/154 and CO 167/212 respectively. The latter file also includes complaints by Mylius, and Treasury report on costs of Seychelles. Banks' report is at PRO CO 167/228; his comments are also quoted by Charles Pridham, *England's Colonial Empire: an Historical, Political and Statistical Account* (London, 1846). Mylius's comment on the Clarkes is in SNA B/11, and his criticism of Delafontaine in B/31. Private sources and the archives of the Society for the Propagation of the Gospel in Foreign Parts (SPG) in London were consulted for Delafontaine's correspondence. Keate on Seychelles' needs is filed under B/31, while the petition to the Mauritius governor on immigration is in PRO CO 167/315. Immigration matters are also contained in SNA B/7 and B/18. The French deal with Sultan of Zanzibar on purchase of slaves is referred to in Select Committee Report on Slave Trade, 1871, quoted by William Law Mathieson, *Great Britain and the Slave Trade, 1839-1865* (London, 1929). The petition by Napoléon Savy is in PRO CO 167/344. Reaction by French consuls to incidents at Mauritius is found at FAP, *Correspondance Politique: Consuls* Vol. 20. Ending of slavery at Réunion is described by Sudel Fuma, in *'Un Conflit de Civilisation: Immigrants Indiens et Société Coloniale de l'île Bourbon, 1838-48'* (*Le Mouvement des Idées dans l'Océan Indien Occidental,* published by Association Historique Internationale de l'Océan Indien, St Denis, Réunion, June 1982).

1   Mauritius colonial secretary George Dick informed Mylius that the Governor had noticed in his correspondence the frequent use of the word 'Colony', adding: 'His Excellency apprehends that this is not correct and that these Islands cannot be so designated, being only Dependencies of Mauritius'. — 24 September 1839 (SNA B/13).

2   Queen Victoria, of Great Britain and Ireland (1837-1901) and Empress of India (1876-1901). b. Kensington Palace, London, 24 May 1819; d. of Edward, Duke of Kent, and grand-daughter of George III. Succeeded to throne, 20 June 1837, on death of her uncle, William IV; coronation, 28 June 1838. In February 1840, she married her cousin, Prince Albert of Saxe-Coburg-Gotha, with whom she had several children. Albert died in 1861, his widow continuing to mourn him for many years. She died at Osborne, Isle of Wight, 1901.

3   'The French inhabitants affect to be dissatisfied at the change of the name of the port to that of our beloved Queen.' — Belcher [op. cit.].

4   Ordinance No. 12 of 1841 reads in part: 'Whereas the principal inhabitants of the Island of Mahé, one of the Seychelles Islands, have, in a petition to the Governor, expressed their desire that the Town and Port of the Island, which have not as yet received a special designation, should bear the name of Her Majesty ... the Town of the Island of Mahé shall bear the name of "Victoria" and the Port that of "Port Victoria".' (*Laws of Seychelles, Vol. I,* p. 75; Herchenroder edition.)

5   A note received by Mylius in June 1839 from a M. Dubois warned him: *'Les apprentis sont désordonnés; si vous m'accordez la surveillance sur eux je vous ferois un raport [sic] exact sur le désordre qu'il se passe'* (SNA B/72A).

6   With the final withdrawal of British troops, the Seychelles police assumed responsibility for the islands' security. On his visit three years later, Belcher [op. cit.] noted that the police wore army coats and black beaver hats, 'quite *à la militaire'.* The police clothing sent from Mauritius included two yards of gold lace for the sergeant-major's uniform. — Police Dept. to Mylius, 1 July 1840 (SNA B/73A).

7   Mylius and the stipendiary magistrate Clément appear to have got off on the wrong foot from the start. A dispute over accommodation was followed by a complaint from Clément that he had been deprived of a desk used by the previous magistrate, causing him 'serious inconvenience and [which] will oblige me to close my court, and adjourn the hearing of the cases that were to come before me today'. — 6 and 11 March 1839 (SNA B/72A). A month later Clément, returning from a trip to the Amirantes in the schooner *Emancipation,* landed at North West Bay without going through quarantine. He later protested to Mylius over the subsequent prosecution of the schooner captain and crew, and suggested the matter should be referred to the Governor. — 27 April 1839 (SNA B/72A). When news of the affair reached Mauritius, Mylius earned a mild rebuke, the Governor expressing 'surprise and regret at seeing so little harmony among the few public officers at Seychelles, and so much evidence of personal animosity among them'. He recommended that the schooner captain and crew be pardoned. — Mauritius to Seychelles, 20 September 1839 (SNA B/13). Mylius also upset the officer commanding the military detachment, Lieut. James Tedlie, by apparently repeating an allegation that Tedlie had concealed himself in the schooner on its arrival back at Mahé. 'Your informant has made you a false report,' Tedlie wrote, 'and I have to request that you will make yourself better informed before you repeat anything concerning me'. — 23 May 1839 (SNA B/72A). At the same time Tedlie sent an invitation to Mylius to attend a *feu de joie* in the barracks square the following day in honour of the Queen's birthday.

8   Mylius had no authority to incur expenditure, and on occasion he paid for projects out of his own pocket. To a request for an advance of £700, he was told that past experience showed that £300 would be sufficient. — 3 September 1839 (SNA B/13). Many of his decisions, such as closing the billiard room on Sundays and religious holidays, were overturned — 15 April 1841 (SNA B/17). There were frequent complaints from Mauritius about the lateness of his financial returns, and refunds of personal expenditure were generally refused. Mylius had hoped for the concession of Felicité island, in the manner of his predecessors Madge, Lesage, and Harrison, all of whom were given concessions, but he was informed on 1 May 1843 that the Secretary of State had directed that all Crown land had to be disposed of by

public sale (SNA B/18). Later Mylius criticised the way Crown land had been allocated to private individuals, attributing it to 'petticoat influence'. — 21 September 1848 (MA TB 32).

9   In 1839 Cauvin and Hodoul agreed to put up half the money for a market if they were refunded. The market was built, but the condition of reimbursement does not seem to been honoured (SNA B/31). In July 1869, the land known as Terrain du Bazar was ceded by the Michaud heirs for use as a public market. In the 1950s Victoria Market was named after the Governor Sir Selwyn Selwyn-Clarke (1947-50), a name that was preserved when a new town market opened in 1999.

10   Among those impressed by the Civil Commissioner's undertaking of religious duties was Captain Aimable-Constant Jehenne, commanding the French naval vessel *Prévoyante*, who visited Seychelles in October 1841. Jehenne noted in a report to the Minister of Marine and Colonies: '*De cette manière, il s'est en quelque sorte intronisé dans toutes les familles, est obéi et respecté par la population noire*' (SNA F/2.282).

11   Mylius was to remind Mauritius that he had urged appointing a Catholic priest on 29 May 1840, and again on 18 May 1848. — 10 January 1849 (SNA B/31).

12   The Society for the Propagation of the Gospel in Foreign Parts was founded in 1701 by English evangelist Thomas Bray, who had earlier formed the Society for the Promotion of Christian Knowledge (SPCK). Main aims of the SPG were to minister to British people overseas and to evangelise non-Christian races in British colonies. The society merged in 1965 with the Universities Mission to Central Africa (founded in 1859) to form the United Society for the Propagation of the Gospel. The London Missionary Society was founded in 1795 by a group of Congregationalists, Anglicans, Presbyterians, and Wesleyans to promote Christian missions to the heathen. Its first twenty-nine missionaries went to Tahiti in 1796. Active in China, India, Africa, and the South Seas, the society has since 1966 been the responsibility of the Congregational Council for World Mission.

13   The Mico Charity was founded with money from the legacy of Lady Mico (formerly Jane Robinson), who died in 1670, leaving 'the moiety of a sum of £2,000 to redeem poor [that is, Christian] slaves from Barbary states'. As by 1816 this purpose was no longer relevant, the money was left to accumulate until, in 1834, with capital totalling over £115,000, the trustees decided to use it for the education of newly liberated negro slaves. They were persuaded in this by the prominent anti-slaving campaigner and successor to Wilberforce, Sir Thomas Fowell Buxton, bt. The Mico Charity worked mainly in the West Indies, but eventually concentrated on the training of teachers in Jamaica. Today the Mico College in Jamaica, operating under the Mico Foundation, has more than 1,200 resident students. The Lady Mico Charity in England continues to make annual and specific grants to the Jamaica college. The name Mico is virtually unknown in Seychelles today.

14   'There are only three private schools,' wrote Banks, 'one for the better class held by a Mr Collie, who has about twenty pupils; the other two are of the character of Dame schools, and have only from 7 to 10 children.' [James Moses Collie, teacher from Aberdeen, Scotland; married, 1830, to Virginie Courtois; held several different government posts; died at Seychelles, 1872]. Another of the schools was run by the 'Demoiselles D'Offay', two spinster sisters, Rosalia and Germance. Born

251

in Mahé, they lived in the early 1840s with their brother at Anse Déjeuner. They jointly owned a property between Royal Street and St Joseph's Street in Victoria, which they sold in 1885. It may have been here that their school was located. They died at Mont Fleuri, Germance in 1888 and Rosalia in 1899. – 'People in Seychelles History', *Regar* newspaper, Victoria, 1996.

15   An application in 1835 by Mme Mein, widow, to have a son educated at Royal College at government expense was refused. – Mauritius to Seychelles, 21 December 1835 (SNA B/10). Five years later the governor approved a place for a Master Mein. – Mylius to Mauritius, 4 July 1840 (MA TA 43).

16   This comment, initialled JR, appears in the margin of a memorandum on Seychelles drawn up at the Colonial Office for the Secretary of State, Lord John Russell, 21 January 1840 (PRO CO 167/212).

17   Referring to the expected arrival of British troops, Delafontaine confided: *Je désire pouvoir leur offrir mes services spirituels et célébrer le culte en leur langue; mon maître me dit, pour m'encourager sans doute, que dans peu de temps je serai capable de faire assez bien le service divin; je ne demande pas mieux, parce que ce sera un nouveau moyen de me rendre utile'.* – Delafontaine to Rev. E. Hawkins, of the SPG, 19 Pall Mall, London, 25 June 1845 (private collection).

18   There were thirty boys and thirty-three girls in 1852, compared with fifty-six and forty-six in 1839. Figures quoted by Keate, 2 February 1853 (SNA).

19   Delafontaine seems to have scored a minor victory over Mylius, for he informed the SPG: 'It appears he [Mylius] has received a reprimand from the Governor, for these two or three months he has remained quiet and inoffensive, yet I think it prudent to keep a good look-out.' He asked for some French Bibles to be sent for a lending library he was setting up, and requested Hawkins to remember him in his prayers. – Delafontaine to Rev. E. Hawkins, of the SPG, 24 March 1846 (private collection).

20   The remark was made by Dr William Ford, to Mauritius, 5 July 1850 (SNA B/31). Captain Jehenne of the *Prévoyante* also praised Mylius as '*un homme actif, honorable, d'un aspect éclairé, ayant à coeur la prosperité de la petite colonie.*'

21   '*Le sol reste sans culture et ne produit que les fruits qui n'exigent qu'un facile travail. Tandis que la nature cultivée pourrait enrichir les habitants, par son étonnante fertilité, elle y est couverte de ronces, et les fruits qu'elle produit sans culture et malgré la paresse des propriétaires, restent et pourrissent sur les plantes qui en sont chargées. La misère la plus désespérante règne dans presque toutes les demeures; et cette situation, jointe à la dépravation des moeurs, font de ces îles le point le plus désolé de la terre.'* – Delafontaine to Hawkins, 25 June 1845.

22   The figure of 1,000 was presumably a slip of the pen. Captain Corneille Nicolas Morphey, who claimed the Isle de Séchelles for the King of France and the Compagnie des Indes in 1756, estimated that the main anchorage, then named Port Royal, could accommodate 200 ships.

23   Situated off Madagascar's north-west coast, the island of Nossi-Bé was a Sakalava stronghold in the 1830s. Threatened by a Merina invasion in 1838, Queen Tsiomeko appealed to the Sultan of Zanzibar for assistance. He made only a token

gesture of support, and the Queen then turned first to the British in Mauritius and then to the French, to whom she eventually ceded the island, which became a French colony in 1841. The same year the Sultan of Mayotte, fearful of being acquired by Madagascar or Zanzibar, offered his island to France in return for a generous settlement. Admiral de Hell, governor of Réunion, accepted, and in 1843 the island was annexed to the colony of Nossi-Bé. In 1845 the capital of the colony was moved from Hell Ville to Dzaoudzi, on Mayotte, but eight years later Nossi-Bé and Sainte Marie were detached and Mayotte was again a separate entity.

24   While Europe had agreed on keeping Muhammad Ali's ambitions in check, his continuing aggression against the Sultan of Turkey, his titular overlord, eventually caused differences between the Powers. France, swayed by a vociferous public opinion, found itself in 1839 sole supporter of the Egyptian pasha. and for a while the peace of Europe was threatened. In the end the problem was resolved, with a pact that gave Turkey back the territory it had lost, while leaving Muhammad Ali secure in Egypt. Relations between London and Paris were to remain cool.

25   The trouble began when the *Isère* strung out various national flags to dry, with the Union Jack, by chance or design, below the others. Captain Driver of the *Greenlaw* retaliated by lowering the Tricolour under his bowsprit. An officer from the French ship protested, but Driver refused to remove the flag until ordered to do so by the Governor, Maj.-Gen. Sir William Nicolay. The captains of the *Isère* and the accompanying French brig the *Lancier* (16) demanded reparation. Subsequently Driver formally apologised before the Governor, and it was agreed that the *Greenlaw* would fly the French flag at its masthead throughout the following Sunday. This was done, but the French claimed that the gesture had lacked due solemnity, and insisted the flag be flown once more. According to Bourbon governor Hell the matter would have ended there had not others influenced *l'aspect faible et incertain'* of Nicolay, who belatedly demanded an equivalent gesture of apology by Captain Le Barbier de Tinan, of the *Isère*. The French consul suggested a compromise, whereby the *Isère* would raise the Union flag and fire a salute and, at the same time, the *Greenlaw* would hoist the French flag, and a salute would be fired by the shore batteries, but Le Barbier de Tinan and the captain of the *Lancier*, Baron de la Roque de Chanfray, rejected this. In his letter to the Secretary of State, Nicolay claimed that the two officers had been exciting pro-French feeling in Mauritius, and he had therefore decided, if there was any threat to 'the peace and tranquillity of this town', to send troops to take forcible possession of the French ships. He consequently moved up guns to cover an advance of boats. In the end the French ships sailed without making the usual compliments on passing the forts. The incident boosted, if anything, the careers of Le Barbier de Tinan and Baron de la Roque de Chanfray, who eventually attained the rank of vice-admiral and rear-admiral respectively. – Nicolay to Secretary of State, 21 September 1839 (PRO CO 167/212); Hell to Minister of Foreign Affairs, Paris, 25 September 1839 (AF BB/4/593); and *The Times,* 4 January 1840.

CHAPTER SIX

Sources for the Des Avanchers mission to Seychelles include: *'Papiers d'Abbadie: Mission du Pays des Gallas'* (BN naf 23851);   *'Notice géographique et historique sur les Îles Séchelle par le Révérend Père Léon des Avanchers, capucin, 1857'* (SNA   F/2.409); and correspondence of Civil Commissioners Keate and Wade (SNA B/31, PRO   CO 167/328, and MA T53); also Des Avanchers' report to the Congregation, 24 November 1855 (Archives des Capucins, Annecy). Published works consulted included Father Louis Dayer, *Les îles Seychelles* (Sion, Switzerland, 1967), Father Paul Hinder, *La Croix sur les Îles* (Fribourg, Switzerland, undated), Dr J.T. Bradley, *The History of Seychelles* (Victoria, 1940), and *l'Echo des Îles* newspaper, May 1992. The Adolphe Loizeau affair is in PRO CO 167/366, SNA B/31, and MA TA 42. The scandal of Campbell's magistracy is also in B/31, and in PRO CO 167/35 and MA T 52. Governor Higginson's address to Seychelles planters is filed in SNA A/2.20; accusations against Wade and defence testimony in PRO CO 167/35, and letters by François Savy *père*, in Mauritius *Commercial Gazette*, October and November 1854. The *Blackwood's Magazine* article on the loss of the *St Abbs* and subsequent events is reproduced in 'Historical Miscellanea', Vol. IX (SNA F/2.14). The account of the Poiret mystery is based on notarial minutes and death certificate at the Seychelles National Archives; a letter by Father Théophile to Apostolic Vicar of Trebizonde, Turkey (Archives de Savoie); an article in *Le Gaullois*, reprinted in *Réveil de Mahé* (editor, Numa Morel), 26 October 1906; and readers' letters in *The Times* of London, August 1936. The published work of E. de Lagrange, *Louis XVII aux Seychelles* (Rennes, 1954) was also consulted. A report on the findings of French historian Jacques Rivière appeared in *Seychelles Weekend Nation* of 10 November 1998.

1   The second largest ethnic group in Ethiopia, the Gallas are distinct from the Christian Amharic and Tigray people of the Abyssinian highlands. Monsignor Gulielmus Massaïa, preceptor to the House of Savoy; was appointed Apostolic Vicar to the Gallas in 1846, but was unable to enter the country until 1851; he stayed there for thirty-five years. Cardinal in 1884; died 1889.

2   Mules and donkeys were common beasts of burden in Seychelles. Twelve donkeys were among the animals lost on Mahé during the 1862 cyclone. There are also references to camels being at one time on the island.

3   Antoine d'Abbadie was of Irish origin. He and his brother Arnaud-Michel were celebrated for their extensive travels in Ethiopia (1834-1846). Des Avanchers corresponded regularly with both.

4.   Keate reminded the Governor that in September 1850 he had asked for a portion of the Delorié land to be reserved for a church, a proposal that had been made earlier by Mylius. Although £605 had been raised by public subscription for the building, Keate wanted the government to meet a small outstanding balance. Delafontaine had estimated that the church would cost £2,000.

5   'I am of the opinion that before venturing on such a course [allowing a priest to reside in Seychelles] it would be advisable to wait till the effects of the measure I have proposed for the extension of religion and education shall have been seen ...' — Keate to Mauritius, 29 August 1850 (SNA B/31). Two months before the arrival of Des Avanchers, Charles Savy of Sainte Anne had written to the Governor accusing him of leaving the people without moral instruction, and claiming that they were forced to bury their dead like animals. Quoted by Dayer [op. cit.].

6   Dayer suggests that divine power, independent of man's will, guided the Catholic missionary to Seychelles. In an article in *l'Echo des îles* (September 1992), Father René Metral describes Des Avanchers' arrival in Seychelles as '*pur hazard*'.

7   The Capuchins, or Order of Friars Minor Capuchina (OFM Cap), are a branch of the Franciscans. The order was founded as a reform movement in 1525 by Matteo da Bascio, who wanted to return to literal observance of the rules of St Francis of Assisi. He designed the habit with pointed hood (capuccino), from which the order takes its name. Members are engaged in missionary and social work.

8   '*Les chefs de famille me prièrent de dire la Sainte Messe et mirent à ma disposition un local où les personnes de race blanche vinrent en foule pour y voir un prêtre du culte catholique. Ce même jour, je commençai à baptiser un grand nombre d'enfants, et dès ce jour, je fis journellement le catéchisme. Ce peuple, qui jusqu'alors avait résisté à toutes les suggestions du ministre protestant, venait en foule entendre la parole de Dieu et l'écoutait avec avidité.*' — Hinder [op. cit.].

9   'Immediately on his landing the Reverend Gentleman [Des Avanchers] called on me and informed me personally of the object of his visit, venturing at the same time to threaten me, if I did not accede to all his demands, with the displeasure of the population, with whom he had then had no intercourse, but which he did not appear subsequently disinclined to excite. Reflection however, and probably the advice of less imprudent persons appear to have demonstrated to him the error of this course, as they afterwards induced him to recall a circular he had issued on the following day announcing his arrival, and calling upon the faithful to protect him from the persecutions of the Government, and to confess in his subsequent letter to me that he had acted too abruptly.' — Keate to Mauritius, 19 March 1851. The letter Des Avanchers handed to Keate referred to the Bishop of Port Louis being unable to send a priest to Seychelles. As a result the Vicar Apostolic to the Gallas, Gulielmus Massaïa, had been charged by the Sacred Congregation for Propagation of the Faith to send Father Léon des Avanchers ... 'to reside at the Seychelles Islands to exercise and fulfil the mission' with which he had been entrusted. An assurance was given that there would be no cost to the government .

10   Keate was employing double standards by insisting Des Avanchers go first to Mauritius. Some months earlier he had allowed into Seychelles Mr. Duverné Pothin, who arrived with his family from Réunion in the brig *Espoir* (Captain Mellon) without having called at Mauritius to seek permission to reside in Seychelles. Keate described Pothin as industrious, his sons were tutors to some families, and he recommended they be allowed to stay. He similarly recommended a Mr De Leïpêque, who had arrived in the same ship. The latter held a certificate of *officier de santé* from Réunion, although Keate doubted whether this would entitle him to practise medicine in Seychelles.

11   Although born and educated in the Duchy of Savoy, which was not incorporated finally into France until 1860, Des Avanchers claimed French nationality. — Letter to Civil Commissioner Keate, 7 March 1851 (PRO CO 167/328).

12   Among those signing the petition were: C. Cayol, Nageon, Mellon, Savy de Ste Anne, D. St Jorre, Le Clerc, F. Hodoul, and C. Jouanis. This and Governor's reply (PRO CO 167/328).

13   Bishop William Collier was English and a Benedictine, which may explain his attitude to Des Avanchers. Born in 1802, near Richmond, Collier was educated at Ampleforth, Yorkshire, and Douai, northern France. Ordained, 1826; Superior, Douai College; Benedictine representative to Holy See, 1834; Apostolic Vicar, Mauritius, 1840; first Bishop of Port Louis, 1847; left Mauritius in 1862 because of ill health; retired to Coventry, England; died, 1890.

14   The Sacred Congregation for Propagation of the Faith collects and distributes funds for Roman Catholic missions throughout the world. Originally a lay society formed in Lyon in 1822 to raise money for the Louisiana mission, it merged and adopted the fund-raising methods of Pauline Jaricot, who had been collecting for missions since 1818. Pope Leo XIII later designated Jaricot the official founder of the society. Its headquarters moved in 1922 to Rome, where it became the main fund-raising agency for RC missions.

15   'Pendant mon dernier séjour, j'ai baptisé 1,300 personnes, béni 200 mariages, célébré 100 premier communions, ouvert deux églises et une chapelle, non comprise celle de Port Victoria, qui a été agrandie, restaurée et placée sous le vocable de l'Immaculate Conception.' So wrote Des Avanchers, quoted by Hinder [op. cit.], who also refers to Des Avanchers erecting a cross at Pointe Larue, a place noted for shipwrecks. Tradition has it that after that there were no more wrecks.

16   Until handing over the school, Wade had spent more than £77 in supporting it, a sum that the Society for the Propagation of the Gospel refunded. — Wade to Fallett, 2 October 1855 (SNA B/31) and SPG minutes, 19 December 1856, quoted by Ian R. Stone, 'Education in Seychelles: The Government and the Missions, 1839-1944', a dissertation for B.Phil. degree (Open University, 1977). Unlike his predecessor Delafontaine, Fallett seems to have made no attempt to learn English. A CMS missionary who visited Seychelles in August 1864 described him as 'a very nice old man', adding: 'As he is not acquainted with English, we are obliged to converse with him in broken French.' (Journal of Rev. Thomas Campbell, CMS Archives, University of Birmingham, C MA 0.9).

17   Bishop Ryan sailed to Seychelles in HM gunboat *Lynx* (Captain Barkley) to consecrate St Paul's church in Victoria. Wade was away on leave at the time, and his place at the consecration was taken by Telfair. Also present were Ferdinand Savy (contractor), Théodore Loizeau (notary), and Stanislas Butler (surveyor). During his visit the Bishop also consecrated the Anglican church at Grand'Anse, Praslin, and licensed a chapel on La Digue. Nominated to the new diocese of Mauritius in 1854, Dr Vincent Ryan was noted for his energy and tact. He had previously been principal of Highbury Training College for Schoolmasters in London.

18   Des Avanchers referred to negotiating with the Pasquières heirs in Réunion the sale of their land in Victoria, where it was intended that a convent and school be established. 'À Bourbon, j'ai vu les héritiers de M. Pasquières et ils m'ont vendu pour la somme de 400 piastres la maison et l'emplacement qu'ils ont à Mahé. Cet emplacement est destiné pour les réligieuses qui doivent aller à Mahé.' — Des Avanchers to M. Paris Le Clerc, 9 October 1855 (private collection).

19   Forwarding a petition from Loizeau to the Governor on 8 July 1853, Wade referred to the deplorable state of Seychelles society, the high social position of Loizeau, and the gravity of his offence. 'His Excellency may better judge whether this case is deserving of mercy, or whether a severe lesson to one of the principle

[sic] inhabitants may not have a beneficial effect on the whole population.' — Wade to Governor, 8 July 1853. On 19 July Loizeau was released on a temporary basis (SNA B/31). The Mauritius attorney-general held that the charge should have been one of disturbing the public peace and not of instigating rebellion. — 15 October 1853 (MA TA 52).

20   Dashwood Watts Rickets. Acting Civil Commissioner, Seychelles, December 1852 to July 1853. b. 1804, at Calcutta; second cousin of the Earl of Liverpool (Prime Minister, 1812-27); ed. Charterhouse and Cambridge; entered Colonial Service at Mauritius; married twice; died 1887.

21   Campbell denied enforcing English in the courtroom. In a letter to Ricketts (15 March 1853) he said pleadings and examination of witnesses were in the language of the parties, with French, Creole, and Hindustani all tolerated. He considered that promoting French would be 'prejudicial to the progress which the present generation of the Seychelles are making in civilisation ... It is a remarkable fact that English is more generally spoken here by the lower classes than in the Mauritius'. He attributed this to their mixing with American whalers and to the instructions they received at Delafontaine's school. Campbell referred to the old people's 'morbid hatred' of the English language, but believed that progress would come from its use (PRO CO 167/350). In 1841 English had been declared the language for official government correspondence, and after 1848 no-one was to be eligible for a new appointment in government service without a competent knowledge of English (SNA C/SS/36 Vol. 1).

22   The leper colony was not removed from Curieuse until 1900, when the inmates were transferred to Round Island, off Praslin.

23   The Long Pier, a feature of Victoria harbour until major land reclamation changed the face of the town in the 1970s, was constructed by stages under a number of different civil commissioners. In 1850 Mylius, in a letter acknowledging permission to repair a bridge over the St Louis river at a cost of £50, complained to Mauritius that he had almost broken a leg on the bridge, and had as a result built a causeway further down at his own expense (SNA B/31). It appears that from this there resulted in what was to be known as the Mylius wharf (Webb, in 'The Seychelles Story', refers to Mylius receiving a grant of £50 to build a pier). Nicholas Pike, US consul at Mauritius, who visited Seychelles in 1871, said the pier was started under Civil Commissioner Swinburne Ward (1862-68), when 100 feet were completed. Work was restarted in March 1870, under the personal supervision of Chief Civil Commissioner William Franklyn (1868-74).

24   The Peninsular Steam Navigation Company (Oriental was added later) was formed in 1834, with sailings from London to Portuguese and Spanish ports. In 1837 it won a contract to carry mail to the Iberian peninsula, previously a monopoly of the Post Office and Admiralty. In 1840, received royal charter, and began service from Suez via Aden to Calcutta and Madras (the East India Company refusing at first to surrender the Bombay route). By 1850, with 23 steamships, P & O was sailing to Australia, via Bombay. In 1857 the company's ships began calling occasionally at Mahé, developing this into a monthly service from 1860 to 1866.

25   The prisoner, Chérimond Gautier, had been convicted of breaking into a room occupied by a female prisoner, Marie Daline Vidot, a married woman, and 'co-habiting with her'. He was sentenced to three days' solitary confinement after the

Prisons Committee refused to sanction a flogging. When Wade sought reasons for the discrepancy in punishments, the Committee did not reply.

26   Signatories to the petition, dated 24 October 1854, were: J. M. Collie, E. Dubois, Mathiot, F. Hermitte, N. Loizeau, J. Loizeau, C. St Ange, F. Hodoul, A.J. Jacques, N. Quessy, J. Courtois, A. Dubois, G. Courtois, C. Carnot, C. Vadet, A. Germain, A. Dupuy, J.Barallon, Julienne, V. Poultin, C. Delorié. D. Calais, Christin, and A. Renaud. Expressing satisfaction with the island's administration, they commented: *'Cette Dépendence a trop souffert par les faits d'une coterie qui n'a à son cœur que ses propres intérêts et ne songe nullement à ceux de la patrie'.* (PRO CO 167/366).

27   The Mauritius inquiry held that most charges against Wade were not proven, but it criticised the Civil Commissioner for allowing the prison building to deteriorate (£510 had been voted for its repair but not used), and for sanctioning the flogging of an Irish seaman, William Mitchell, ostensibly for having escaped from prison. Evidence was given that flogging was to dissuade prisoners from attempting to escape. Mitchell had complained that the flogging had been unduly severe. The inquiry disagreed with Wade that Mitchell had been 'most justly punished and that no cruelty was perpetrated'. The Governor accepted most of the inquiry's findings, but rejected its view that Mitchell's punishment was improper. The complainants were Savy, Philinte, Jouanis, Cayol, Petit, and several others (PRO CO 167/366).

28   Several death threats were made against various British administrators in Seychelles. Mylius believed that a Captain Payet had been behind the 'atrocious murder' of his favourite servant in 1848. He was convinced that he was to be the next target. Mylius also claimed that $1,000 had been put on his head after he had ordered the town billiard room closed during church services. — Mylius to Mauritius, 5 October 1848 (MA TA 49). In 1913 Governor Davidson was told by Police Inspector Louis Tonnet that R.500 had been offered to a Mauritian to attack him while he was taking his morning ride near Pointe Conan. The potential assassin had demanded R.1,000.

29   The remark was made by Major-General Charles Murray Hay, officer commanding the Mauritius garrison and acting governor, in a dispatch to the Secretary of State, 26 March 1855 (PRO CO 167/367). As a captain in the Coldstream Guards, Hay had earlier served in Mauritius as aide to the governor.

30   Consisting of nine islands, covering an area of eight square kilometres, Jean de Nove was named by its discoverer, the Portuguese navigator João de Nova; it was later renamed Farquhar islands after the first British governor of Mauritius. The largest islands are North Island and South Island. Today there is an airstrip and settlement on North Island. The Farquhar group consists of the atoll, and the islands of Providence and St Pierre. They remained dependencies of Mauritius when Seychelles became a colony in 1903, but were transferred to Seychelles in 1921. Copra, cattle, fishing, and charcoal production are the main activities. There is a small island in the Mozambique Channel, held by France, which is also named after the Portuguese navigator.

31   Edward Charles Ross. British soldier and administrator. Served throughout the Indian Mutiny in the Central India Frontier Force. Appointed Consul-General for Fars and the Persian Gulf; knighted, 1892; died 1913, at age of 77.

32   This seems an exaggerated description, and one wonders whether Father Théophile actually witnessed the funeral. He is clearly uncertain about Poiret's identity, wrongly describing him as being among those deported by Napoleon to Seychelles. The relevant paragraph in the letter to the Apostolic Vicar of Trebizonde (where Father Théophile had served as a young priest) reads: *'Parmi les Français que nous avons administré à l'heure suprême, il faut citer Mr Louis Poiret Flammand. Il était au nombre des déportés septembriseurs relegués aux Seychelles. Il parait aux yeux des Seychellois pour être Louis XVII. Toujours est-il qu'il avait, ainsi que ses enfants que nous avons baptisés, le vrai type des Bourbons; la fille ainée Marie-Antoinette ressemble parfaitement l'infortunée princesse son homosynome. Louis XVII reçoit les derniers sacremens et meurt en 1856 à Port Victoria. Ses funerailles ont été celles d'un prince'* (Archives de Savoie). According to Dayer [op. cit.], the last rites were administered to Poiret by Father Jeremiah.

33   The DNA tests, announced in Paris on 19 April 2000 by Prince Louis de Bourbon, were carried out by Professor Jean-Jacques Cassiman, of the University of Louvain, Belgium, and Professor Bernd Brinkman, of Münster University, Germany. The heart that was used for genetic comparison with hair samples from Marie-Antoinette and other members (both living and dead) of the Hapsburg dynasty, was reportedly removed by one of six doctors who carried out the autopsy in the Temple prison in 1795. Concealed and preserved in alcohol, it passed through several hands before being consigned, in 1895, to one of the Pretenders to the French throne, Don Carlos, Duke of Madrid. In 1975 it was presented by the Duke's grand-daughters to the Prince Louis de Bourbon, who deposited it in the vaults of the French kings at St Denis. The DNA results were immediately contested by the Institut Louis XVII, which supports the claim by descendents of Karl Wilhelm Naundorff (see below). The Institute demanded a more independent examination. Exhumations carried out in 1846, 1894, and 1979 at the Paris cemetery where the Dauphin was presumably buried all failed to establish conclusively the identity of the corpse.

34   The most prominent claimant was Karl Wilhelm Naundorff (1787-1845), a German clockmaker, who called himself Duc de Normandie and published two works trying to prove his claims. He died at Delft, in the Netherlands. His tomb carries the inscription 'Louis XVII, King of France and Navarre'. The Duchesse d'Angoulême. the Dauphin's sister (freed from the Temple in exchange for French prisoners held by the Austrians), always refused to receive any of the pretenders. In 1998 DNA tests by Professor Jean-Jaques Cassiman using bones from Naundorff's grave and hair samples of Marie-Antoinette failed to show any genetic match.

35   Although Poiret's letter is addressed to *'Cher Mon Oncle'*, the Archduke Charles (1771-1847) was the third son of Archduke Leopold II, elder brother of Marie-Antoinette, and therefore the Dauphin's cousin. However, given the Archduke Charles's seniority and their relative positions, Poiret's use of *mon oncle* is not surprising.

36   Addressing a conference at Mahé in November 1998, French historian Jacques Rivière said that after four years of research he was 90 per cent. sure that Louis Poiret and Louis XVII were the same person. Rivière, president of the *Société d'Études Scientifiques de la Réunion*, reported having followed a trail of documentary evidence from Dunkirk to Mauritius, by way of England, Scotland, and Spain, which showed how Poiret had eventually reached Seychelles. He said there was evidence that his escape from France was engineered by Louis Poiret, an

official of the National Convention and an English spy. Rivière stated that samples of Marie-Antoinette's hair had been taken to Réunion by a confidante of the Princesse de Lamballe, a friend of the Queen. These would be scientifically compared with hair from Poiret descendants in Seychelles, a test which he believed would confirm his findings. — *Seychelles Nation*, 10 and 14 November 1998.

37   Schmoderer reportedly arrived in the French steamer *Emirne*, which left Mauritius on 23 September 1864, inaugurating a new monthly service by the Messageries Impériales between Mauritius and Suez. The priest, Father Ignatius Galfione (Apostolic Vice-Prefect of Seychelles, 1864-1880) arrived at Mahé on 30 October 1864. The article in *Le Gaullois* was reprinted in the *Réveil de Mahé* (editor, Numa Morel), 26 October 1906.

38   There is at the Seychelles National Archives a death certificate dated 21 March 1863 for Louis Poiret, son of Poiret and Marie Edesse, who died of a wasting disease. He was unmarried.

39   In addition to the letter from Isabelle Stirling, published in *The Times* of 8 August 1936, there is in the same issue a letter concerning Poiret from J.A.F. Ozanne (formerly Archdeacon in Seychelles). The other *Times* correspondents were: Brian Walsh (former private secretary to the Governor of Seychelles), 3 August; W.R.H. Trowbridge, 12 August; and Guy Cooper (former Legal Adviser, Seychelles), 15 August. A report on this correspondence appeared in the Seychelles newspaper *L'Impartial,* 24 October 1936.

40   An indicator of Seychelles' economic revival was the rise in population. In 1840 this had fallen to 4,369 on Mahé, but by 1850 the total population was 6,500, rising to 7,500 just before the influx of liberated Africans began in 1861. With the extension of coconut plantations, the value of oil and copra exports rose in 1865 to £20,133, or 73 per cent. of total exports.

CHAPTER SEVEN

Correspondence relating to the arrival of liberated slaves in Seychelles is found in PRO CO 167/439, CO 167/442, CO 167/560, and CO 170/54. The log of HMS *Lyra* is in PRO ADM 53/7044 and 53/7045. Related published works are W.C. Devereux, *A Cruise in the Gorgon* (London, 1869), G.L. Sulivan, *Dhow Chasing in Zanzibar Waters* (London, 1873, reprinted, 1968), and R.W. Beachey, *The Slave Trade in Eastern Africa* (London, 1976). Also consulted was J.M. Filliot, *Histoire des Seychelles* (Paris, 1983). French reaction to British efforts to end the Zanzibar slave trade is set out in FAP *Correspondance Politique: Consuls* Vol. 39. Selected correspondence over the French fishing vessel *l'Espoir* is in SNA C/AM/1, and in FAP *Correspondance Politique: Consuls* Vol.42, and *Mémoires et Documents: Afrique* Vol. 70; while assessments of public opinion in Mauritius are in PRO CO 167/535 and FAP *Correspondance Politique: Consuls* Vol. 38 and 73. US consul Pike's comment on stagnation of trade, in NAW Microfilm M462, reel 4.

1   A graphic description of conditions in a captured dhow was given by Captain G.L. Sulivan [op. cit.]: 'On the bottom of the dhow was a pile of stones as ballast,

and on these stones, without even a mat, were twenty-three women huddled together — one or two with infants in their arms — these women were literally doubled up, there being no room to sit erect; on the bamboo deck, about three feet above the keel, were forty-eight men, crowded together in the same way, and on another deck above this were fifty-three children. Some of the slaves were in the last stages of starvation and dysentery. On getting the vessel alongside and clearing her out, a woman came up, having an infant about a month or six weeks old in her arms, with one side of its forehead crushed in. On asking how it was done, she told us that just before our boat came alongside the dhow, the child began to cry, and one of the Arabs, fearing the English would hear it, took up a stone, and struck it. A few hours after this the poor thing died, and the woman was too weak and ill to be able to point out the monster who had done it, from amongst the ten or dozen Arabs on board'. Sulivan noted, however, that because of their greater marketable value, women and children were usually reasonably looked after. Despite the horrors of the passage to Arabia, slaves in an Arab household were generally treated better than those owned by Europeans or Africans. The Koran enjoins Muslims to treat their slaves well.

2   HMS *Lyra*. Steam sloop, 485 tons; armed with nine 32-pounders; built in 1857. Crew of 73, with seventeen officers and ten marines. In 1866, while under the command of Commander R. A. Parr, the *Lyra* landed 300 Africans at Seychelles. A front-page report and picture of the ship were published in the *Illustrated London News* on 5 January 1867. Before joining the anti-slaving patrol in the Indian Ocean, the *Lyra* had taken part in the suppression of piracy in the Persian Gulf, 1857-61. The ship was broken up in 1876.

3   The Church Missionary Society was founded in 1799, under the name of Society for Missions in Africa and the East. Thomas Scott, author of a Biblical commentary, was secretary. It became the Church of England's most effective organisation for mission work overseas, with, in 1969, about 900 missionaries in forty-nine dioceses world-wide, and an annual income of over £1mn. It was renamed the Church Mission Society, in keeping with its changing role in the post-colonial era. The Society's headquarters are in Waterloo Road, London.

4   Governor Stevenson denied a claim by the Zanzibar consul, Colonel C.P. Rigby, that Mauritius had a fatal climate. — Stevenson to Duke of Newcastle, 27 May 1862 (PRO CO 167/439).

5   Rigby recommended Seychelles for the landing of liberated slaves shortly after his arrival in Zanzibar in 1858, according to Beachey [op, cit.].

6   Commander Oldfield recorded receiving, presumably from Wade, three copies of Naval Regulations and Instructions, along with an Admiralty letter dated 25 March 1861. He passed one copy of the Instructions to Commander Stirling of HMS *Wasp* (the officer quoted in *The Times* correspondence of 1936 on the mystery of Louis XVII). On 24 May the *Wasp* and the *Ariel,* dressed overall, fired a royal salute in honour of the Queen's birthday. The *Lyra* was still undergoing a refit and clean-up at the time.

7   The Mauritius Council's finance committee had warned that unless immediate steps were taken to balance the Seychelles budget, the Secretary of State should be told of the 'injustice of allowing a distant dependency like that of Seychelles, from which we derive little or no advantage, continuing any longer a

burthen on Mauritius'. – Proceedings of Council of Government, 1862 (PRO CO 167/59), quoted by Nwulia [op. cit.].

8   H.Nicholas Duverger Beyts. b. 1820, son of assistant collector of customs at Bombay. Teacher, then district clerk, Mauritius, 1852; district magistrate, 1858; acting Protector of Immigrants, 1859; member, Mauritius Legislative Council, 1867; Census Commissioner, 1871; member, Executive Council, 1873; Receiver-General, 1877; acting Colonial Secretary, Mauritius, 1881; Companion of the Order of St Michael and St George (CMG), 1881.

9   Of the 100 labourers requested by Seychelles, sixty were for Praslin. Some proprietors, like Napoléon and Théodore Loizeau, asked for only one labourer each. Governor Stevenson commented that the numbers would not have freighted a third of an ordinary immigrant ship. – Beyts to Mauritius, 16 October 1860, and Stevenson to Duke of Newcastle, 2 March 1861 and 27 May 1862 (PRO CO 167/427 and CO 167/439).

10   The term Mozambique, or 'native of Mozambique', was used generally for Africans from the mainland. Death certificates issued in Seychelles between 1856 and 1862 show that 'natives of Mozambique' represented a sizeable proportion of the population even before the landings of liberated Africans. Today, it is insulting in Seychelles to describe someone as a *Mazanbik*.

11   The Anglican chaplain was Adolphe Vaudin, of Sark, one of the Channel Islands. He succeeded Fallet in October 1865 and remained as Civil Chaplain until May 1875.

12   The Treaty takes its name from Lieut.-Colonel. Atkins Hamerton, who persuaded the Sultan to restrict the movement of slaves. Hamerton was Britain's first Agent and Consul-General at Zanzibar from 1841. He died there in 1857.

13   'Off Pangani river ... Captain went in whaler chasing dhows. On 22nd (March 1861), off (Waseen); whaler returned and said captain had gone south. On 23rd dhow came up, had been captured by captain previous night; had 90 slaves on board ... 25th returned to Zanzibar.' Log of HMS *Lyra* (PRO ADM 53/7044).

14   War of Secession (1861-66), between the southern, slave-owning states (the Confederacy) and the northern states of the USA. It was one of the longest and most bitter wars of the century.

15   Conditions of immigrant labour in Réunion were much worse than in Mauritius, and labourers who went back to India on completing their contracts never returned. In November and December 1868 there were outbreaks of rioting by immigrants in St Denis. The Indian government stopped further export of labourers to Réunion in 1882.

16   The War, between Russia and an alliance of Britain, France, and Turkey, was fought mainly in the Crimea (1853-56); the allies had the support of a Sardinia-Piedmont army from 1855. Cause of war was rivalry in Middle East, sparked by Russian demands to exercise protection over Orthodox subjects of Sultan; also dispute between Russia and France over privileges of Russian Orthodox and Roman Catholic Churches in Holy Land.

17   The French consul's reaction is noted in C.E.B. Russell, *General Rigby, Zanzibar and the Slave Trade* (London, 1935), and quoted by Kenneth Ingham, *A History of East Africa* (London, 1962). War between Sultan Seyyid's successors had been widely expected. Writing to his brother in April 1852 while his ship *Indefatigable* was at Mahé, a French naval doctor forecast that as Sultan Seyyid had no legitimate successor, *'son empire sera partagé ...entre ses fils illégitimes, qui se feront la guerre'.* — Charles Coquerel, *Lettres d'un marin à sa famille* (Paris, 1870).

18   The remark was made by the US consul in Mauritius, George Fairfield. Consul from 1856 to 1862, Fairfield frequently complained to Washington about lack of funds, noting that on his arrival there was no sign of there ever having been a US consulate at Port Louis. A similar complaint was made by Fairfield's successor, who was annoyed at having to provide furniture, for 'there was not a desk, table or chair belonging to the US consulate' (NAW T-118 and microfilm M462).

19   Sir Henry Barkly. Governor of Mauritius, 1862-1870. Had previously been Governor of British Guiana, Jamaica, and Victoria (Australia). Barkly's son, Arthur Cecil Stuart Barkly, who was private secretary to his father, was appointed Chief Civil Commissioner of Seychelles in 1881.

20   Although the Mauritian Press was often anti-British, French consul Fourcaud did not consider this the general feeling among the people. *'La génération actuelle née sous pavillon anglais a peut-être conservé des sympathies pour la nationalité des ses ancêtres, mais pas au point de faire craindre de sa part quelques actes propres à la reconquérir. Du reste, l'insouciance et la mollesse du caractère créole sont trop connus du gouvernement local pour lui permettre une pareille supposition.'* — Consul to Minister, 5 May 1849 (FAP *Correspondance politique: Consuls* Vol. 24).

21   In August 1880, the Governor, Sir George Bowen, had to choose between Beyts, an Eurasian, and a British-born official, Cockburn Stewart, for the post of assistant colonial secretary during his absence on leave. Stating that both men were qualified for the post, Bowen added: 'I am strongly of opinion that men of all races and complexions in the British Empire should be encouraged to distinguish themselves in the Imperial service of the Crown.' However, the commander of troops, Maj.-General Murray, had reservations about Beyts, as in the event of acting Governor Napier-Broome dying, Beyts would become acting governor and commander-in-chief. — Bowen to Kimberley, 13 August 1880 (PRO CO 167/589). In 1892, Seychelles Administrator Risely Griffith showed his racial basis when Mauritius district cashier Louis Albert Célestin was recommended to him as a replacement for Inspector of Schools James Brodie. 'I hope Mr Célestin is better [than Brodie] and that he is not a coloured man,' was his response. Célestin was not appointed (PRO CO 167/671).

22   In March 1862 Rigby had warned that French feelings were being fostered in Seychelles by frequent visits of French warships. — Stevenson to Duke of Newcastle, 27 May 1862 (PRO CO 167/439). During 1869 six British warships called at Seychelles, compared with twenty French during the same period. — Consul Atwood to US Secretary of State Hamilton Fish, 31 December 1869 (NAW microfilm M462, reel 4).

23   The capitulation of Napoleon III at Sedan effectively ended the Second Empire. There followed the siege of Paris and the conclusion of the Franco-Prussian War, ushering in the Third French Republic.

24   With the Cape as Britain's main base in the western Indian Ocean, London had largely left it to Mauritius to develop its own shipping links. In 1836 the Mauritius Steam Navigation Company was formed, with James Blyth as director. It purchased the British-built steamer *Madagascar,* which was used mainly to transport cattle from Madagascar. The company, however, ran into difficulties and sold out to the government. Another company, Barron Frères et Cie, started a steamer service between Mauritius and Réunion in 1858, but this also failed.

25   The inaugural voyage was by the *Emirne,* of 650 tons, which left Mauritius in the evening of 17 September 1864, calling first at Réunion. On the way to Mahé it lost two hours at Platte island because of currents, arriving Port Victoria at 2.40 pm on 23 September. It left at 7.15 the same day for Suez, arriving there on the 29th. The voyage had lasted eleven full days. In his report the captain commented: '*L'Emirne remplit admirablement les conditions de navigabilité et de vitesse d'un bon paquebot ... C'est un navire parfaitement réussi. Il me reste encore à le juger, marchant à la vapeur, avec du gros temps contraire.*' The other ship on the route was the *Mozambique.* Until 1869 the MM steamers did not call at Mahé on the outward voyage during the adverse monsoon (June to August) until a report by Commandant Dupleix showed that it occasioned no loss of time, nor burning of extra coal. From the start the company was determined to offer passengers a better service than P & O, including the provision of second-class cabins for '*voyageurs qui, pour être moins favorisés par la fortune, n'en sont pas moins des gens bien élevés*'. Fares were fixed as low as F.1,500 for first class, and F.1,200 for second. The French consul in Mauritius believed that the new service would enjoy '*un cachet particulier*', adding: '*Outre sa nouveauté, son aspect plus démocratique devait la singulariser auprès des compagnies anglaises. Ajoutons enfin que la rencontre d'un service français et d'îles Seychelles et Maurice, où demeure une population francophone sous administration coloniale anglaise, constitue une chance de succès supplémentaire au plan psychologique.*' — AF, *Fonds Réunion*, Carton 306, quoted in '*Les Îles de l'Océan Indien Occidental et le Bateau: Communication des Hommes et des Idées, à travers les Archives de la Compagnie des Messageries Maritimes (1864-1920)*', doctoral thesis by Mlle Danielle Barret for the University of Paris VII; also documents in the Messageries Maritimes archives, Marseilles (copies in SNA A/32).

26   Despite France's prime position on the Suez to Mauritius route, it remained largely dependent on foreign shipping for links with the East African coast and the smaller islands of the Indian Ocean. Captain Robert Playfair, who succeeded as consul at Zanzibar in 1863, had at his disposition a small steamship given by the Sultan for carrying mail from Zanzibar to Seychelles. Playfair timed the ship's arrival at Mahé so that it linked with the homeward-bound P&O or Messageries Impériales liners. Later the French consul complained that France had not itself developed a steamship link between Seychelles, Zanzibar, and the French outposts of Mayotte and Mohéli. '*Je prie Votre Excellence de remarquer qu'un aviso de la Marine Impériale prend à Mahé le courrier pour Mayotte. Si ce petit bâtiment en retournant à Mahé s'écartait de sa route pour toucher à Zanzibar, il pourrait aussi s'arrêter à Mohéli et, reliant entre ces différentes stations, unir dans la même pensée les actes de la station à la Réunion, du commandant supérior à Mayotte, et du consul à Zanzibar.*' — Consul to Minister, 20 May 1863 and 26 August 1869 (FAN Zanzibar Carton 1). In 1873 the British India Steam Navigation Company secured a contract to carry French mails between Zanzibar, Mayotte, and Nossi-Bé.

27   This was a branch of the Mauritius Post Office, which used Mauritius stamps

until the appearance of the first Seychelles stamp in 1890. Before December 1861 an agent in Seychelles was responsible for forwarding letters to Mauritius, a duty that was scarcely arduous. Incomplete records for the years 1851 to 1853 suggest that there was on average only four letters a month from Seychelles. For the period 1854 to 1861 annual receipts from ship letters at Mahé averaged £6.12s. Postal rates to Europe in 1861 were sixpence per letter (round the Cape) and one shilling (via Marseilles, reduced to 10 pence in 1869). From about 1877 all mail went via Marseilles, at a cost of 6½ pence. (Rates and figures extracted from data supplied by Sue Hopson, of the Indian Ocean Study Circle).

CHAPTER EIGHT

Accounts of the 1862 cyclone are from the log of HMS *Orestes* (PRO ADM 53/8290); letters from the Mauritius governor to Secretary of State, 18 October and 3 November 1862 (PRO CO 167/443) and report by Swinburne Ward to Mauritius, March 1863 (MA TA 62); Press cuttings in 'Historical Miscellanea' by Webb and McGaw (SNA F.2/14); and two articles 'On the Island of Mahi, Seychelles' by Lieut.-Colonel Lewis Pelly, *Royal Geographical Society Journal* (London, 1865) and 'The Cyclone and Avalanche of 1862: Causes, Impacts and Possible Future Trends', by Nirmal Jivan Shah and Kantilal Jivan Shah. Sir Arthur Gordon's account of his visits to Seychelles are in *Mauritius: Records of Private and Public Life 1871-74* (Edinburgh, 1894) and in correspondence with the Secretary of State (PRO CO 167/535). US consul Atwater's comments are in NAW microfilm M462 reel 4, and Pike's remarks on the Long Pier are contained in a letter to the Royal Society of Arts and Sciences, Mauritius. Defence measures at Réunion were discussed by the *Conseil d'Amirauté* (AF BB/8/900). Quotations by William MacGregor are from R.B. Joyce, *Sir William MacGregor* (1971). MacGregor is also quoted by Civil Commissioner Franklyn in a letter to Mauritius (PRO CO 167/553). Details of HMS *Columbine*'s mission are in letters from Lieut. A.K. Harene, RN, to his sisters Freddy and Edie, 12 Strathmore Gardens, Kensington (private collection). H.M. Stanley's account of his visit to Seychelles is from *Travels, Adventures, and Discoveries in Central Africa* (London, 1872). Anglican concern over state of education in Seychelles can be found in CMS Archives, University of Birmingham, C MA 0 6, and in Ven. Ghislain Emmanuel, *Diocese of Mauritius 1810-73* (Port Louis, 1975). Havelock's memorandum on African minors' wages and subsequent correspondence, 29 March and 30 June 1874 (PRO CO 167/560). Gordon's list of qualities required by a Seychelles governor is in a letter to Earl of Caernarvon, 1 May 1874 (PRO CO 167/560).

1   Whaling ship *Charles Carroll*, 412 tons, of New London, Connecticut (Captain Smith). Out 14 May 1859; condemned at Mahé, 1862; sent back 1,000 barrels of whale oil. — Starbuck [op. cit.].

2   The Sisters of St Joseph de Cluny is a world-wide congregation of missionary nuns, founded in France about 1808 by Anne Marie Javouhey. Her first aim was to care for poor children in Paris, but at the request of the Governor of Bourbon four

Sisters were sent to the Indian Ocean island in 1817 as teachers. Activities of the congregation spread to Madagascar and India. In 1861, three Sisters were sent from Bourbon to Seychelles, arriving there on 12 February.

3   Pelly has left us a description of Victoria before the Avalanche. 'Port Victoria is the chief town of Mahi [sic], a neat township picturesquely dotted among underwood immediately above the line of sea beach and along the lowest swellings of a background of hills. It possesses a creditable stone-masonry church, and the Government House peeps out prettily from its English-looking grounds and shrubberies. A clear boulder-strewn stream rushes down between the Commissioner's lawn and the main street of the town. The houses in general are built of wood upon coral foundations, and have the high roofs, gables, and general character of the little chateaux and farmsteads of Normandie.'

4   In the chapel of the Convent of St Joseph de Cluny, which was renovated and rebuilt in 1996, there is a stained glass window depicting the nuns tending the injured woman.

5   Buried at the foot of the altar, the bodies of the two nuns were reinterred near the Communion Table during the paving of the Cathedral floor in 1923. – Dayer [op. cit.].

6   The Anglican church had to be closed for repairs to the tower. Henry Watley Estridge, *Six Years in Seychelles* (1885), wrote: 'The English church is not a very fine building – though quite large enough for its present congregation. It once had a tower and a clock; but the former becoming unsafe it was pulled down, and the clock – the property of the inhabitants – transferred to the Roman Catholic church as the most prominent place in the town for it being seen.' Estridge was appointed Collector of Dues and Customs in 1879. He had previously served in India, in the Bombay Marine and as an ensign with the 46th Regiment. The artist Marianne North stayed with Estridge and his wife for several weeks during her visit to Seychelles, 1883-84. Estridge, who left Seychelles in 1885 on appointment as Examiner of Accounts, British Bechuanaland, is reputed to have been the first to climb Seychelles' highest mountain, the 905-metre Morne Seychellois (2,972 ft). He later became Accountant-General in Bechuanaland, and retired from government service in 1889.

7   The total number of deaths varies. The highest figure, of eighty dead or missing, is quoted by Nirmal and Kantilal Jivan Shah [op. cit.]. According to the official police report at the time the total was seventy-five.

8   Dupuy paid tribute to the captain of HMS *Orestes,* 'whose men worked as hard as possible and without shrinking, side by side with the prisoners and such other men I could have, in the mud, either in search of dead bodies or in making drains in the streets'. He also praised the police, especially their commander, Brunton, 'for his intelligence, energy and his humanity'. – Dupuy to Stevenson, 15 October 1862 (PRO CO 167/443).

9   The *Avalasse* was not quickly forgotten, and people referred to events having occurred before or after the disaster. The word also entered their vocabulary with the expression *'Laisse l'Avalasse traîne moi!', indicating* despair or resignation.

10   Speaking to the author on 22 May 1997, senior meteorologist Micky Belle

estimated that, 'with the type of weather changes we are getting', the chance of a cyclone hitting Mahé was between 20 and 30 per cent. He said that in recent years he had noted 'quite an alarming warming rate' in the air temperature over Mahé, which would lead to a huge amount of evaporation, increasing the possibility of tropical storms.

11   The Institute of the Brothers of Christian Schools was founded by St Jean-Baptiste de la Salle at Rheims in 1684 for the education of boys, especially from poor families. It is now established world-wide, and provides administrative staff colleges, agricultural schools, corrective and trade institutions. There is a similar body of Brothers, founded at Waterford, Ireland, in 1802. The Brothers of Christian Schools were present in Seychelles from 1867 to 1875.

12   Derence Atwater. US consul at Mahé, from February 1869 to October 1870. Previous to Atwater's appointment there was only a consular agent at Seychelles. Atwater, from Torryville, Connecticut, arrived at Zanzibar in January 1869, where he was offered a free passage to Seychelles in a French naval steam packet the *Régent*. Rent for the consulate office was $150 a year. Writing to the US Secretary of State (1 April 1869), Atwater referred to the scarcity of timber in Seychelles and 'exorbitant prices of every article of consumption'. He left Seychelles on 27 October 1870 to take up a post at Tahiti. In a letter to Secretary of State Hamilton Fish (20 October 1870) he thanked him 'for this change to what I believe will be a more suitable place for my health'. (NAW microfilm M462, reel 4).

13   'There is a coaling station here at which the best Cardiff coals and patent fuel can be obtained in any quantity.' — Atwater to US Secretary of State, 31 December 1869. With no coal east of Suez, supplies had to be shipped out, usually by sailing colliers round the Cape. Atwater reported that three or four colliers arrived at Mahé each year. They normally carried a few tons of merchandise. — Annual report, 30 September 1870 (NAW microfilm M462).

14   Gordon forecast that the pier would give Seychelles 'an importance far more considerable than it has yet possessed'. HMS *Forte* had brought light rails and waggons for the new pier, and divers from the ship blew up an inconvenient rock in the inner harbour. Expressing appreciation to Admiral Cockburn for having removed the harbour's 'only blemish', Gordon noted that at low tide there was now 28 ft of water where the rock was located. — Gordon to Kimberley, 21 September 1871 (PRO CO 167/535) and *Records of Private and Public Life* [op. cit.].

15   Whaling ship *Herald,* 300 tons, of New Bedford, Massachusetts (Captain John R. Sturgis). Out, 14 August 1869; arrived back, 23 August 1872, with 1,180 barrels of sperm oil, 80 barrels of whale oil, and 300lb. of whalebone. Altered from barque to ship, 1869; sold to London, 1873. — Starbuck [op. cit.].

16   Gordon asked the Secretary of State for four months leave on account of his rapidly declining health. This was refused, and he was told that if necessary someone else would be appointed to his post. No more was heard from Gordon on this subject. — Gordon to Kimberley, 22 September 1871, and reply (PRO CO167/535).

17   In Seychelles in recent years poachers of hawksbill turtle (or *caret*) have been known to sell or eat the flesh, despite warnings by the government.

18   'I don't like the people — that is the swells — and they don't like me, for they resent my efforts to improve the condition of the coolies.' — Gordon, Stanmore Papers, quoted by Joyce [op. cit.].

19   The reference here is probably to Charles Dupuy (no relation, apparently, to magistrate Eugène Dupuy), who was appointed US consular agent in 1862. There was subsequently some controversy over this appointment. Defending Dupuy, W. R.G. Mellen (US consul at Port Louis, 1863-66) forwarded to Washington statements attesting to Dupuy's fitness for the post, denying that he was coloured, and asserting that, although he was the keeper of a hotel licensed to sell spirits, it was kept in a quiet and orderly way. Pike thought otherwise, and on his becoming consul at Mauritius he got rid of Dupuy. He later explained that he had been mortified at being represented by 'a low vulgar colored man and keeper of a dram shop over whose door the arms of the United States had been emblazoned for the last three years'. — Mellen to US Secretary of State, July 1863 and December 1864; and Pike to US Secretary of State, 15 June 1868 (NAW microfilm M462, reel 4).

20   Formed in Mahé in 1869 by a Paris-born printer and photographer, Paul Pascal de Giovanni, the Union Sincère was successor to an earlier Masonic lodge, which closed in 1851. Giovanni was elected first Worshipful Master, with Charles Jouanis and Henri Houareau as 1st and 2nd wardens. In August 1871 the following were inducted as masters: André Jorre de St Jorre, public notary, and Thomas Lyle Horner, Royal Navy surgeon, living at Mahé. English names, many of naval officers, were to predominate among the first members, while financial and other problems beset the lodge's early years. On 24 August 1871 Giovanni wrote to the president of the Supreme Council of the Grand Orient de France explaining the situation: *'Vous ne sauriez vous faire une idée de la désorganisation qui a frappé notre Réunion Sincère à propos de calomnies répandues par un de nos membres et semant pourtant le ridicule et même le mépris sur la Réunion Sincère, dont j'ai la faveur d'être le Vénérable Maître. Joignez à cela une mortalité inaccoutumée et le départ imprévu de cinq des mes officiers dignitaires, et vous avez une idée de la position critique que je viens de traverser pendant sept mois.'* Giovanni added that some members had wanted to suspend the lodge, but he opposed this. In 1874 Giovanni left Seychelles, and was replaced by Alphonse Emmanuel Nageon de l'Étang (1st warden), Charles Dupuy (2nd warden), and F.A. Jouanis (3rd warden). Before his departure, the lodge moved its meeting place to Rue Royale, described by Giovanni as *'la plus jolie rue du pays'.* The rent was higher than before, but the lodge was by now considering building its own temple. Total membership was about twenty-five (BN Manuscrits FM² 863). In 1877 the decision of the Grand Orient to suppress the obligation of belief in God (which until then had figured in the constitution) led to a break between the French and English lodges. In the same year the present Seychelles Lodge No 8789 was formed at Mahé under the auspices of the United Grand Lodge of England. — *Dictionnaire de la Franc-Maçonnerie* (Paris, 1891).

21   Felix Pool. b. 1830, at Savognin, a Romansch-speaking area of Switzerland near St Moritz; a baker by trade, he lived in South Mahé, where he ran a general store with the sign *'Pauvre Diable'.* He died in October 1894. Pool family descendants in Switzerland were unaware of their Seychelles branch until a chance visit to Savognin by Georges J. Pool and his wife, Jeanne, in 1989. 'Jeanne decided to cash some travellers cheques at the local bank,' Georges recalled. 'When she presented her cheque, she was asked if she was a Pool from the district ... it turned out that the banker's mother-in-law was a Pool.' Only two descendants of Felix Pool's brothers still live in Savognin. Felix's younger brother emigrated to Cuba,

where he died aged 40. All that was known of Felix in Savognin was that he had emigrated to an unknown country. Pool is a common name in Seychelles, with fifty-six Pools and two Pooles listed in the 1997 telephone directory. Georges Pool, a great-grandson of Felix Pool, has for many years lived in Australia.

22   A bacterial infectious disease, leprosy is believed to be transmitted via the upper respiratory tract, although entry through contaminated skin still remains a possibility. The source of the disease, *Mycobacterium leprae*, was discovered in 1873 by a Norwegian, G.H.A. Hansen. Leprosy causes chronic inflammation of the skin, peripheral nerves, upper respiratory tract, eyes, bone, and testes. Associated with overcrowding and poor living conditions, it was once common in Europe, but is now mostly found in Central Africa and Asia. Uncertainty about how to deal with leprosy was common among officials in the early 1870s. The Secretary of State Lord Kimberley noted in September 1871: 'I have ... no faith in the dicta of the medical profession on this subject. Opinions as to contagine and infection are constantly changing and what was confidently maintained a few years ago, is now in some cases as confidently given up (PRO CO 167/535).

23   Gordon did not agree with MacGregor, commenting that 'to a gentleman whose ideas of propriety are founded on the habits of a Scotch city the light clothing commonly worn by labourers all over the tropics is no doubt startling'. Quoted in Franklyn to Mauritius, 2 June 1873 (PRO CO 167/553).

24   Franklyn's predecessor, Swinburne Ward, had noted that former slaves incapacitated by age or infirmity risked being chased away, sometimes to 'perish miserably from hunger and neglect within a short distance of the huts in which they had lived for so many years'. Influenced by such barbarous example, Africans themselves rarely showed any consideration for the old and sick. Earlier, Wade had cited the case of an old woman who fell into a hole two miles from town. The Creole property owner did nothing until the police came to remove her. They put her into a hut, but when the police returned the following morning they found she had been moved outside, and was lying on the ground barely clothed and covered with flies. The police took her to the prison, when she died. Wade asked for the introduction of some form of Poor Law. — Wade to Mauritius, 16 March and 28 August 1863 (MA TA 62).

25   Difficulty in finding proper employment for liberated Africans is given as the reason for the Admiralty deciding in July 1869 that no more freed slaves be landed in Seychelles. — Raymond Howell, *The Royal Navy and the Slave Trade* (London, 1987).

26   David Livingstone. Explorer and missionary. b. 1813, at Blantyre, Scotland educated himself while working in a cotton factory. Studied medicine at Glasgow, and joined the London Missionary Society; embarked for South Africa, 1840; married, 1845, daughter of missionary Robert Moffat, who shared some of his travels into interior of East and Central Africa; crossed the continent to Luanda and back, 1852-56; consul at Quelimane, 1858-64; wife died in Africa, 1862, and eldest son, Robert, killed in American Civil War, 1864. Livingstone started on expedition to solve question of Nile basin, 1865; reached Ujiji, 1869; famous meeting with H. M. Stanley, 10 November 1871; died at Chitambo, Barotseland (now Zambia), May 1873; his body carried to Coast by two servants, Susi and Chuma; buried at Westminster Abbey, London, 1874. His accounts of the activities of slavers in Africa did much to abolish the trade.

27   Commenting on Oswald Livingstone, Stanley wrote: 'Mr Livingstone exhibited many amiable traits of character, and proved himself to be a studious, thoughtful, earnest man.'

28   Rev. Peter Sorensen Royston. Served at Madras; secretary to East Africa mission, at Mauritius, 1864-66; returned to India; Bishop of Mauritius, 1872-90; visited Seychelles five times between 1876-88. – Eugene Stock, *History of the Church Missionary Society* (London, 1899) and Ven. Ghislain Emmanuel [op. cit.].

29   Captain Sulivan [op. cit.] noted that 'the clergyman there, does all that he can for a few of the children, but it is almost as much as he can do to attend to the old population or residents ... I have heard from his own lips how anxious he is to extend his labours so as to include the slaves, but, with the exception of the few children who have been received in the schools, he is unable to do anything for them for want of assistance'. Vaudin was replaced as chaplain by the Rev. John Gallienne Bichard, who after twenty-one months was invalided back to Mauritius.

30   The mission was named after a former governor of Bombay, Sir Bartle Frere, who was sent to Zanzibar to urge the Sultan to close down all slave markets. He had also been asked by the CMS to recommend a site on the East African coast where liberated Africans might be settled.

31   The last reported capture of a slave dhow was in 1899, although the traffic was not completely abolished in Zanzibar until 1907, and in Tanganyika in 1922.

32   Rev. William Bartlett Chancellor. Entered CMS college, 1870; ordained, 1873; in same year appointed to Mombasa mission. Transferred to Seychelles in 1875, and founded Venn's Town. Returned home on account of eye problems in 1879; died at Ramsgate, Kent, 1887.

CHAPTER NINE

Alexander Starbuck's *History of the American Whale Fishery* (Secaucus, NJ, 1989, first published 1877) is again the source for information on voyages of American whalers. Harriet Allen's diary (1868-71) and that of her daughter Nellie (1870-71) are filed at the Kendall Whaling Museum, Sharon, Mass., under Log 402/401. The description of Jane Worth by the *Gazelle*'s fourth mate is quoted by Joan Druett, *Petticoat Whalers* (1991). US consuls' reports are at the US National Archives, Washington. Iain Walker, *The Complete Guide to the Southwest Indian Ocean* (France, 1993), was consulted for some of the information on Diego Garcia.

1   Whaling barque *Merlin*, 246 tons, of New Bedford, Mass. (Captain David E. Allen). Out, 23 June 1868; returned, 3 April 1872. – Starbuck [op. cit.].

2   Whaling barque *Platina*, 266 tons, of Westport, Mass. (Captain David E. Allen). Out, August 1860; returned, December 1863. Allen also captained the *Platina* on two earlier voyages to the Indian Ocean, October 1853 to February 1857, and June 1857 to April 1860. He was later captain of the *Sea Fox* (1865-67), the ship commanded by Samuel Braley at the time of his death at Mahé in 1870. – Starbuck [op. cit.].

270

3   Whaling barque *Annie Ann,* 220 tons, of New Bedford, Mass. (Captain John C. Pierce; managing owner John W. Pierce). Out, 24 June 1869, originally for the Pacific. Sent home 495 barrels of sperm; condemned at Mauritius, November 1871. – Starbuck [op. cit.].

4   Crew's testimony claimed that throughout voyage they had been kept short of food; all had been attacked by scurvy, and could hardly walk. The mate persuaded Pierce to put in at Rodrigues, where they stayed seventeen days. 'The captain has also treated many of the crew with great cruelty, knocking men down and then kicking them brutally,' the testimony continued. 'On one occasion while Denis Shay, seaman, was at the wheel Captain Pierce kicked him in the side, knocking him down and while down striking him with his fist, cutting his head badly, and bruising his eyes in a terrible manner. Shay was so frightened that he attempted to jump overboard but the 2nd officer Mr C. Pierce seized him by the collar and took him to the forecastle where his wounds were washed and dressed, and it was four days before he could do duty.' The testimony was signed by the first officer and crew.

5   On 5 December 1872 the *Boston Advertiser* reported that the *Pioneer,* 208 tons, arrived without papers after being held up for ten months at Mauritius through disagreement with the US consul. The authorities allowed it to enter port. It carried over 300 barrels of sperm, 173 barrels of whale oil, and 900 lb of whalebone, and had earlier sent home 232 barrels of sperm.

6   Pike urged Washington to make an example of both captains, who had 'behaved in a most disgraceful manner, dishonouring the Flag that protects them'. – Pike to Asst Secretary of State, 9 January 1872 (NAW).

7   Instancing the case of seaman John Brown, of the New Bedford whaling barque *Oceola 2nd* (master, Jonathan Chase), Pike told the Asst. Secretary of State: 'I think measures should be at once adopted to put a stop to brutalities worthy only of the darkest ages of the world, and a standing disgrace to our country.' Brown, who had impressed Pike with his simple and straightforward account of cruelties suffered at the hands of Captain Chase, deserted his ship at Praslin. Later he was taken to Mahé, where he was sentenced to seven days' labour on the roads. He then worked his passage to Mauritius, and gave himself up. – Pike to Washington, 3 May 1872 (NAW). The *Oceola 2nd,* which sent home 718 barrels of sperm, was condemned at Mahé in October 1872. – Starbuck [op. cit.].

8   'Few islands in a similar state of civilization are more beautiful and attractive in appearance [than Seychelles]. The inhabitants appear to lead an easy going life and existence seems free from the incessant struggle and hardship men usually meet with in the world. This is the idea too often presented to men fresh from recollections and toils of a lengthened cruise, and desertion is too often the result.' – US consul Prentice to Secretary of State, 17 December 1878 (NAW).

9   Several months after leaving Anjouan a near-tragedy occurred. 'We had a dreadful fright last evening,' Harriet wrote on 22 November 1871. 'It was soon after tea. D. and I were in the house playing backgammon. One watch below eating their suppers. The officers scattered about. Steward and Henry busy in the pantry. Suddenly the man at the wheel (the French Creole) rushed forward to the door saying something in French in an excited manner. I caught the words ... and knew Nellie was overboard. Just then Joe at masthead caught sight of her and shouted.

271

Everybody rushed aft and all was confusion.' Nellie, while fishing, had tripped on a rope and fallen into the sea. She later recalled seeing a crowd on the stern, and was sure she would be saved, but after a while she tired, and went under a couple of times. Harriet realised that the boat that had been lowered would not reach her in time. Fortunately Charlie, a Kanaka, and Frank, from Fayul, dived in and caught hold of her. The steward, who had also dived in, almost drowned before the boat pulled him in. 'It has taught me a good lesson,' Nellie admitted.

10   Diego Garcia is the largest atoll of the Chagos archipelago, which includes the Perhos Banhos and Salomon atolls as well as other scattered islands around the Great Chagos Bank. The British formed a settlement on Diego Garcia in 1784, but on their withdrawal the archipelago was claimed by France. The French in Mauritius began exploiting the fishery and coconut resources of the islands, and this continued under British rule. Diego Garcia and the other islands today form the British Indian Ocean Territory (Aldabra, Farquhar, and Desroches islands, previously part of the BIOT, were restored to Seychelles in 1976). The United States maintains a large naval and air base on Diego Garcia under lease from Britain.

11   James Spurs was the son of Thomas Spurs, chief mate (acting captain) of the *Tiger*, of Liverpool, which was wrecked on Astove island in August 1836. The ship was bound for Bombay with a cargo of manufactured and other goods worth £80,000, much of which went missing during the salvage operation. Mylius described the cargo as having been 'most unlawfully, if not piratically, dealt which'. He regretted it was impossible to prove anything. (MA TA 44). Pointe Marianne, where Harriet Allen landed, was situated on the western arm of Diego Garcia, and according to a recent guide book has probably disappeared under the US air base.

12   There was a resurgence of whaling after the American Civil War (1861-65), a conflict that cost the industry dear in ships lost to Confederate raiders, but the general decline persisted and by the 1870s the number of whaleships at sea never went above double figures. The decline was particularly noticeable in the Indian Ocean. which thereafter never represented more than 5 per cent. of all American whaling, compared with 25 per cent. during the 1840s. At the industry's peak, in 1851, 300 American whaling vessels cleared New England ports.

13   The harpoon was designed by a Norwegian, Svend Foyn. It had an explosive head and a pivoted crosspiece which, released on discharge of the explosive, prevented the harpoon being withdrawn. The idea of a harpoon gun, however, was not new. The New Bedford *Whalemen's Shipping List* of 17 August 1847, quoting from the *Nantucket Inquirer*, reported on 'a very curious contrivance for killing whales', describing it as a short gun, weighing about 25 lb, 'from which a harpoon is to be fired into the animal'. The newspaper added: 'The whole apparatus is very ingenious. Whether or not it is really an improvement on the present mode of killing whales is more than we are able to say' (KWM).

14   Prentice's successor as consul, Evelyn Mussey, pointed out that only a limited number of inhabitants wore footwear of any kind. Mainly cheap cloth shoes were on sale, and only 78 dozen pairs were imported in 1884. — Mussey to Washington, 15 July 1885 (NAW).

15   A possible clue to the ownership of the whaler *Diamantina* is Dr James Brooks' wife, whose name was Diamantina. Brooks, the former government

medical officer, was actively engaged in various forms of business..

16   George Franklyn Church was master of the New Bedford whaler *Laetitia*, 208 tons, which sailed for the Indian Ocean in 1875, and was condemned at Mauritius in November 1879, Church having by then been replaced, probably at Seychelles. Church seems to have remained at Seychelles as a trader and master of the ship *Venezuela*, which is mentioned as having brought coconut oil from Poivre island in March 1882. Between 1885 and at least 1886, Church was master of the whaler *Diamantina*. In 1890 he became acting government pilot at Victoria, retiring in December 1893. Church Street in Victoria, although also known as Rue de l'Eglise, is said to be where Captain Church lived, and to have been named after him. — Log of the *Mermaid*, 1884-90 (KWM); Starbuck [op. cit.]; and Griffith to Mauritius, 12 November 1892 (PRO CO 167/650).

CHAPTER TEN

Much of this chapter is based on letters from the Rev. Richard Chancellor to the CMS in London (filed under C MA 0 10 in the CMS Archives at Birmingham University) and reports published in the *Church Missionary Gleaner*, of April and October 1876. Correspondence by Chancellor's successor at Venn's Town, Henry Warry, is filed under C MA 0 20. A report by Edwin Luckock and extracts from the diary of Louisa Frances Royston appear in the *Gleaner* Vol. XV, 1888, and Vol. XVI, 1889. Material has also been included from Ian Rodney Stone, 'Education in Seychelles: The Government and the Missions 1839-1944' (The Open University, 1977). Chief Civil Commissioner Salmon's correspondence with Mauritius is found in SNA B/36 and B/37, and that of Griffith in B/41. French consul Cheyron's remarks are in FAP *Correspondance Politique* No. 80. Comment on Salmon's unsuitability is in PRO CO 167/586, and Governor Bowen's reference to 'troublesome little dependency' in PRO CO 167/592. Documents relating to deportation of ex-Sultan Abdullah of Perak are in PRO CO 167/574 and in SNA C/SS/2, B/37, and B/42.

1   Henry Venn. English evangelist. b. 1796, son of Henry Venn, central figure in group of religious philanthropists known as the Clapham sect. Educated at Cambridge; deacon of Ely, 1819; returned to Cambridge as lecturer, 1824. Resigned living of St John's, Holloway, to devote himself full-time to Church Missionary Society; honorary secretary, 1841-73. During his tenure as secretary, almost 500 clergymen were sent abroad. Promoted trade as way to end slavery, and brought Africans to England to learn new methods of growing cotton, palm oil, and other crops. Served on two Royal Commissions. Died at Mortlake, Surrey, 1873.

2   The inspectors were E. Lasserre and J. Comber-Browne. In an unusual criticism of the Convent, the inspectors claimed that the nuns took into the orphanage only Roman Catholic children and made 'servitors' of them. They also alleged colour prejudice. Salmon retorted that the nuns 'gave sound notions on chastity and modesty' and that there was much less colour prejudice in Seychelles than in Mauritius, and none at the school. It was the first and last time that Mauritius inspected schools in Seychelles.

3   Seychelles had been raised from apostolic prefecture to apostolic vicariate in August 1880. The former Vice-Prefect, Father Ignatius Galfione, as titular Bishop of Aureliopolis, became the first Apostolic Vicar in a ceremony at the Capuchin monastery at Chambéry. He returned to Seychelles in December 1880, but died a year later. His successor was Father Symphorien (Charles-Jacques) Mouard, who was named Apostolic Vicar (titular Bishop of Sidonia) by Pope Leon XIII on 18 September 1882. He arrived in Seychelles the following year.

4   *En somme la mission fait beaucoup de bien ici, et ses ressources sont des plus limitées. L'orphélinat contient déjà de nombreux enfants qui constituent une lourde charge pour la mission. Tout nouveau subsidence doive être bien placé entre les mains de Mgr Mouard, qui a beaucoup fait depuis son arrivée ici et qui ne demand que les moyens de faire plus encore.'* — Cheyron to Nicault, 23 March 1887 (FAP *Correspondance Politque* No. 80). At least one donation of F.500 was made to Seychelles schools by the Alliance Française in Mauritius.

5   James Brodie, from Scotland, was appointed Inspector of Schools in 1881. Before that BCC member François Hodoul had acted as Inspector, with an allowance of £50 a year. In addition to being Inspector of Schools, Brodie was also Audit Examiner, clerk to the BCC, clerk to the Board of Health, and clerk to the Board of Education. At first he worked well, and was praised by Chief Civil Commissioner Barkly for the efficient performance of his duties. — Barkly to Mauritius, 26 May 1883 (SNA B/39). In 1885 a change occurred, and he began to give concern to his superiors by failing to turn in reports on time. In January 1891 he was suspended from duty, but reinstated in March. He was again suspended for a time in December. His tardiness and slack behaviour continued in the first part of 1892, to the dismay of schools which, if not inspected, were unable to get their grants. Mauritius suggested that Brodie should either be brought before the Executive Council with a view to dismissal or transferred to a third class clerkship in Mauritius. The Colonial Office directed that he should go before the Council, but before the order arrived Brodie had been given three months' leave to visit his wife, seriously hurt in a cyclone in Mauritius. In September 1892 he apologised to the Executive Council, citing ill health as excuse. The Colonial Office approved his suspension, but did not bar his being given a subordinate post in Mauritius. Brodie's case, like that of George Barrow (note 7) illustrates the difficulty small colonies faced from idle or incompetent officials.

6   Rev. John Francis Grandjean, a Belgian national, was frequently involved in acrimonious exchanges with the Roman Catholic mission. He accused nurses at the hospital, including the chief nurse, Sister Marie Saint Landri, of proselytising Protestant patients. The accusations were held to be unfounded. Formerly a Roman Catholic priest, Grandjean had married in the Anglican Church, a fact that did not endear him to Bishop Mouard. In August 1887 another Anglican minister, Joseph François Bossy, also a former priest, announced that he was to marry a Roman Catholic widow. Protesting to Mauritius, Mouard pointed to the danger of unfrocked priests 'finding in Seychelles wives and comforts unavailable to them in their own countries'. He claimed that the Bossy marriage would prolong the religious strife 'which has disturbed the peace of the quiet inhabitants of this archipelago since priests who gave up their sacred calling have been admitted here as Protestant ministers'. Mouard had a notice condemning the marriage read in all churches. In it he referred to Britain's guarantee of 1810 to maintain the Catholic religion *'dans toute son intégrité',* which, he claimed, included priests being prevented from marrying. Mauritius eventually held that the Bossy marriage was not

illegal, and that it could not interfere (SNA C/AM/2). Bossy, who came from Marseilles, became a British subject and lived at Anse Royale until his death in 1909. Sister St Landri, b. 1840 as Mary Caroll, at Castlehill, Ireland, arrived in Seychelles in 1872 and was appointed matron of Victoria Hospital in 1876. In 1901 she was made an honorary serving Sister of the Order of St John of Jerusalem. She retired as matron in 1911, and lived at St Joseph's Convent, where she died in 1919. On the opening of the new Victoria Hospital in 1924, a room was named after her.

7   As Collector of Dues and Taxes, George Barrow was charged in December 1878 with delay in taking legal proceedings against trade licence offenders. He had a record of insubordination over a period of two to three years, and was believed by Salmon to have been, along with Dr Brooks, instigator of a petition accusing the Chief Civil Commissioner, two other Commissioners (LeMarchand and Hodoul), the District Judge and others of dishonest and dishonourable conduct, and calling for their dismissal. Salmon claimed that there were two versions of the petition, one in English, the other French, and that many did not know what they were signing. The Colonial Office eventually approved Barrow's dismissal (PRO CO 167/591). In September 1880 he sought re-employment, but the Colonial Office refused, saying that 'if Barrow's history had been known he would never have been appointed'. In his youth Barrow had suffered transportation to Australia for forgery.

8   Final approval was given by the Secretary of State, Lord Kimberley, in December 1880. In a memorandum to the Governor, Kimberley stated: 'In view of the distance between Mauritius and the Seychelles, and the consequent hindrance to the effective administration of the latter which is entailed by the necessity of a reference on matters of ordinary administration to the Governor of Mauritius, it is in my opinion desirable that the local executive of the Seychelles should have greater freedom of action though still remaining subject to the control of Mauritius, and that the Chief Civil Commissioner should hold the same relative position to the Governor as the Presidents of the Leeward islands, other than Antigua, hold to the Governor in Chief of those Islands.' Kimberley added that the reforms should help diminish 'the disputes with subordinate officers which of late years inflicted on the Governor of Mauritius and the Secretary of State voluminous correspondence about trifling matters' (PRO CO 167/ 586, 167/589, and 167/596).

9   Desmarais had been named co-respondent in a divorce case brought in the Mauritius Supreme Court by a clerk at Seychelles, Berthier, against his 18-year-old wife. According to the Bishop of Mauritius, Desmarais had 'cruelly seduced this poor young girl under circumstances the most revolting'. She had admitted her sin. He asked that Berthier be given a posting away from Seychelles. Acting Governor Frederick Napier-Broome reported that many thought Desmarais innocent, suggesting that Berthier was 'an excitable, jealous man who has persecuted his wife into a confession of criminality'. The court case seems in the end to have been dropped, and Desmarais, who was to have been transferred to Mauritius, was allowed to return to Seychelles. – Napier-Broome to Colonial Office, with enclosures, 22 March 1881, 31 October 1881, 7 August 1882 (PRO CO 167/592, 596, and 602).

10   Signatories included Rosamond Gontier, D.J. St Jorre, Jean Héreau, and Denys Calais. In addition to the falling price of coconut oil, the petition referred to the difficulty in changing to other crops, such as Liberian coffee and vanilla. 'Vanilla hitherto has not proved itself in this clime to be a yearly producing plant,' it said, 'and Liberian coffee is still on its trial, and as nascent industries they cannot hold

out to the owners of the soil any return save in a distant future, even if their present efforts proved successful – nor, even in such case, can Your Petitioners foresee the prospect of a return to the times of their former prosperity.' In the margin, someone had noted: 'What former prosperity?'

11   Little Brothers of Mary, a congregation of teaching brothers founded at Lyons in 1817 by Marcellin Champagnat for the Christian education of French youth. In 1836 first Marist brothers were sent on mission to South Pacific. Since then more than a hundred schools of all types have been opened in twenty-three mission territories. The Marist Brothers were present in Seychelles from 1884 to 1946.

12   Chief Civil Commissioner Barkly considered Warry too weak to maintain discipline, and turned down a suggestion that instead of sending juvenile offenders to prison they should go to Venn's Town. His recommendation was that the boys should receive 'fifteen stokes with a cane or birch rod ... administered by the parent or guardian of the boy himself, if such parent or guardian desires it, but of course in the presence of the prison authorities so as to ensure necessary severity'.– Barkly to Mauritius, 18 August 1882 (SNA B/39).

13   Having given up the lease at Capucins the CMS was obliged to remove the Venn's Town buildings after the government decided not to purchase them for a botanical station. Today only a few stone ruins remain at the site. – *Buswell Intelligencer*, CMS, 1915, and Griffith to Mauritius, 14 March 1893 (PRO CO 167/650).

14   In fairness, the opinion of George Mackay, principal of King's College and Inspector of Schools, should be recorded In a report dated August 1902, he described Venn's Town as perhaps the most practically successful example of education in the Colony. The boys and girls had a knowledge of field and domestic work, and they could also speak English. Unfortunately they were too few in numbers (SNA C/AM/17).

15   Archbishop Makarios of Cyprus from 1950, and President of Cyprus, 1959-77; b. Paphos, 1913, son of farmer; educated at Nicosia, Athens, and Boston. Bishop of Kitium (Larnaca), 1948 (while still a student at Boston); supported armed struggle against British, led by National Organisation of Cypriot Fighters (EOKA), 1955-59; deported to Seychelles, 1956; released the following year on condition he did not return to Cyprus. Signed London agreements in 1959, renouncing *Enosis*, or union with Greece. The same year Makarios was elected President of an independent Cyprus. Re-elected in 1968 and 1973. Survived four assassination attempts; died, 1977, of heart attack.

16   The British Press was largely critical of the Perak war. *The Times* said those in authority in the Straits Settlements should have realised they could not establish orderly government in Perak purely by moral means. 'If ... we conclude that it is our duty to govern and civilise Perak we must make adequate provisions for the contingencies of our rule,' the newspaper commented. *The Times* also criticised the hasty and ill-prepared response by the military. There had been substantial casualties – one British regiment lost two officers and fifteen men killed, with ten times that number affected by disease – and rockets fired at insurgent positions had sometimes proved faulty. 'If we are to maintain the tradition of our invincibility among these semi-civilised races we cannot afford to adopt a slovenly manner either of making war or of keeping the peace in our relations with them,' admonished *The Times*. Another commentator deplored the fact that Parliament had ignored the

services of soldiers fighting in 'an unfashionable war', pointing out that it was the first time Gurkhas had been on active service abroad.

17   Ex-Sultan Abdullah's correspondence, published by Prof. Cheah Boon Keng in the *Journal of the Malaysian branch of the Royal Asiatic Society* (Vol. LXIV, 1991), strongly supports his case, and shows that the decision by the Straits Settlements Executive Council to banish him to Seychelles was decided by only one vote. Abdullah argued in a letter to the Queen, written on 13 August 1880, that he and Birch were prime targets of the Upper Perak chiefs, who intended to implicate Abdullah in Birch's murder because they considered him responsible for the Pangkor Treaty, which had brought the British into Perak. They wanted to have Sultan Ismail reinstated. Abdullah claimed that he had told Birch to delay putting up notices in districts under the control of Maharajah Lelah and Ismail. 'I warned him that we had no friends in that quarter, and further requested the said Mr Birch to postpone his ideas until the following day, and that I would gladly accompany him with ample assistance.'

18   Tony Beamish, author of *Aldabra Alone*, was a member of the Malaysian national anthem committee. He had suggested the song *Terang Bulan*, but it was thought by the committee to be too frivolous. An international competition was then organised, but none of the entries was selected. Beamish was then asked to produce an orchestrated version of *Terang Bulan*, and this was played by the Malaya Police Band before the Cabinet, and unanimously adopted.

CHAPTER ELEVEN

The visit to Seychelles by the future General Gordon is based on several sources, including papers at the archives of the Royal Botanic Gardens, Kew. Also consulted were the correspondence of Salmon, Cockburn Stewart, Barkly, and Griffith relating to the protection of the coco de mer, filed in SNA under B/35, B/39, B/43, and PRO CO 167/596. Documents relating to the defence of Seychelles and the development of submarine cables are found in SNA CC/SS/47 Vol. I, and in PRO CO 167/592; and in FAP *Correspondance Politique* Vol. 80 (1887) and Vol. 97 (1891).

1   Sir Frederick Napier Broome. b. 1842, in Canada, son of a missionary; educated England; emigrated in 1857 to New Zealand, engaged in sheep farming. Returned to England, 1869; Colonial secretary, Natal, 1875; Colonial secretary, Mauritius, 1877; administered Mauritius, 1878-79 and, as Lieutenant-governor, 1880-83; knighted 1884; Governor of Western Australia, 1885; Governor of Trinidad, 1891; died 1896, in London.

2   Scientific society which preserves manuscripts and collections of Swedish botanist and explorer Carol Linnaeus (1707-78), who was the first to create a uniform system of defining and naming different genera and species. In a report to Washington (December 1878), US consul Thomas Prentice referred to Linnaean Society protesting to the British government at continued cutting of coco de mer leaves. Prentice's predecessor in Seychelles, Derence Atwater, also referred to the destruction, and warned that the palm could become extinct. 'It is much regretted that this unique and remarkable palm has been destroyed with the same improvident thoughtlessness as the forest in Mahé,' he wrote in December 1869.

3   Gordon was not the first British officer to report on the defence of Seychelles. Lieutenant A.B. Fyers, of the Royal Engineers, visited Mahé in September 1853. He recommended defending Victoria with heavy guns sited behind a parapet, and concluded that if the enemy could be prevented from entering the harbour for a time 'reinforcements would in all probability arrive'. The report was dismissed by the War Office as 'not quite intelligible'. Fyers also proposed a coaling station on Sainte Anne and the setting up of a meteorological station to study the effects of 'rotatory storms' of the Indian Ocean, and help 'clear off the mist which hangs around ... these awful phenomena' (PRO WO 1/518).

4   Frank Brodie, brother of Schools Inspector James Brodie, was among those who accompanied Gordon to Praslin. In a letter written in 1923, Brodie described Gordon's party disembarking at Ecole de Pickwood (the Anglican school at Grand' Anse). They crossed the stream at Nouvelle Découverte, where Gordon took off his shoes and rolled up his trousers. Brodie saw on Gordon's leg a scar he had received in the China wars. – quoted by Guy Lionnet (*Seychelles Weekend Nation*, 1 August 1987).

5   Guy Lionnet, in *The Romance of a Palm* (Seychelles 1970, reprinted Mauritius, 1986), writes: 'Several copies of the manuscript are known to exist. They all contain variations: Gordon, who was a prolific writer, thus appears to have expounded his theory several times. One of the manuscripts is reported to be at the Pamplemousses Botanical Garden, in Mauritius. Another is at the Gordon's Boy School, at Woking, in England. At least two other copies are known to be privately owned. Sprinkled with numerous short quotations from the Scripture, the text of these manuscripts gives the impression of a feverish, "inspired" writing, rather than that of a logical study. In spite of obvious naïvetés it makes fascinating reading.'

6   Given the nut's suggestive shape, it is not surprising that the finely textured jelly of the immature nut should be regarded as an aphrodisiac. In previous years this jelly was frequently served with liqueur as a dessert. Today the sale of all coco de mer nuts, whether from private or government-owned land, must go through the government. Strict penalties apply for possession of an unregistered nut.

7   On 30 April 1896 Cockburn Stewart sent to the Colonial Office Library notes by Gordon on Seychelles and a design for the flag incorporating the coco de mer palm and giant tortoise. – 17 April 1896 (SNA B/44).

8   Muhammad Ahmed Ibn al-Sayyid Abdullah, the Mahdi, or Chosen One. Sudanese religious leader, b. Dongola province, 1844. In 1881 declared holy war against Egyptian rule, and in January 1885, after a long siege, captured Khartoum. The Mahdi died five months later, and was succeeded by the Khalifa Abdullah. In 1898 an Anglo-Egyptian army under General Kitchener retook Khartoum. A year later the Khalifa Abdullah, who had fled the city, was killed in an ambush.

9   The name *Lodoicea sechellarum* was given to the coco de mer palm by the French naturalist Jacques-Julien de La Billardière in 1801. However, in 1917, this was changed to *Lodoicea maldivica* to accord with the international convention on botanic nomenclature which recognises the name given first, in this case, by the Dutch botanist Rumphius, who named the nut *Cocus maldivica* at a time when the origin of the palm was unknown, although nuts had been found in the Maldives islands. The generic name *Lodoicea* was proposed by the naturalist Philibert Commerson, from the Latin name for Louis, King of France. – Guy Lionnet, *The Romance of a Palm*.

10   The most famous coco de mer forest on Praslin, the Vallée de Mai, did not become Crown Land until 1948, although a government report had recommended its purchase as early as 1908. The ravine is sometimes said, incorrectly, to have been given its name by former owner France Jumeau when he bought the land in 1928. The Vallée de Mai, which is today managed by the Seychelles Island Foundation, was declared a World Heritage Site in 1983. A similar designation was earlier accorded to the Aldabra atoll.

11   A three-member committee assembled at Mahé on 11 September 1881 on the order of Rear-Admiral William Gore-Jones, C-in-C East Indies, to make recommendations on Seychelles defence. The members were Lieut.-Col. Charles Gordon, R.E.; Capt. Richard King, RN, senior naval officer at Mauritius; and Lieut. Reginald Rogers, RN (T). (PRO CO 167/596). Their report, dated 15 September 1881, is found in SNA C/SS/47 Vol.I.

12   The White Tower was situated on the north-east coast, between the town of Victoria and Pointe Conan. The feature appears on early maps of Mahé, but the author has been unable to confirm its exact location or purpose.

13   The previous year the Orient shipping line had offered to establish a coaling station at Diego Garcia which could be used by naval ships, but the Admiralty showed little interest (PRO CO 167/591). In 1887 the Admiralty changed its mind, and put both Mahé and Diego Garcia on its list of coaling stations. It expressed concern to the Colonial Office that the agent for the French shipping line Messageries Maritimes and French consul at Seychelles, Félix Cheyron, had a monopoly of the coaling wharves on Mahé. 'My Lords [of the Admiralty] are of opinion that it is to the disadvantage of this country that a coaling monopoly under foreign guidance and control should exist in British Territory, such as these islands.' In a letter to the Chief Civil Commissioner, dated 9 August 1887, Cheyron protested his loyalty and unbiased service (SNA C/AM/2).

14   The British consul at Tamatave had complained that many lower-class Mauritians were arriving in Madagascar without resources. Many fell sick and died; others had become vagabonds and had to be repatriated. Other Mauritians tried to recruit labour. They ill-treated the natives and had been causing disorder. – Foreign Office to Under-Secretary of State for Colonies, 12 June 1880, with enclosure (PRO CO 167/591). The following year Mauritius banned the emigration of Indians and liberated Africans to any foreign country with which Britain had no labour convention, such as Madagascar (PRO CO 167/592).

15   While in Seychelles Gordon had witnessed the arrival from Réunion of the 350-ton French barque *Francis* with 395 Indian labourers, who were being returned home. The vessel was badly leaking. Most of the labourers were in a poor state, and several had died. They were landed at the quarantine station on Longue island, where several more died. Cockburn Stewart provided the labourers with medicine and met other expenses the French refused to meet. The surviving coolies were later taken by two other ships to India. Subsequently India banned further emigration of workers to Réunion. – Cockburn Stewart to Mauritius, 8 October 1881, and Desmarais to Mauritius, 28 November 1881 and 19 January 1882 (SNA B/38).

16   A Royal Commission presented three reports on Imperial Defence between 1879 and 1882. In March 1884, the War Office proposed defence works for Singapore, Hong Kong, Aden, Colombo, and Mauritius. The cost of fortifications and armaments at Mauritius was put at £89,000, with Mauritius contributing

£55,000. The work went slowly, however, and it was not until 1888 that French consul Drouin alerted Paris that he hoped to send a map showing the location of the new defences. He also said the garrison in Mauritius was to be increased to 1,400 men. — Drouin to Minister of Foreign Affairs, 26 July 1888 (FAP *Correspondance Politique: Consuls* Vol. 97).

17   Confidential memorandum 'Telegraphic communication with stations from the point of view of Imperial Defence', to Seychelles Administrator, 18 June 1887, updated 9 August 1889 (SNA CC/SS/47 Vol. I).

18   The first marine cable was laid between Britain and France in 1850. The Atlantic was spanned between Ireland and Newfoundland eight years later, but the insulation failed and it was not until 1866 that a cable was laid successfully.

19   In a letter to the Minister of Foreign Affairs, dated 11 March 1891, Consul Drouin referred to the unlikelihood of Britain accepting a cable that crossed French territory. He added: *Je ne crois pas inutile à ce propos de faire connaître confidentiellement à Votre Excellence que, si je suis bien informé, le gouvernement britannique se serait persuadé que plusieurs dépêches du gouvernement du Maurice, une notamment contenant des plans de fortifications, auraient été ouvertes à bord des paquebots français, et ce serait même le véritable motif de la subvention donné depuis un an à la British India Co. pour un service postal de Colombo à Port Louis; presque toutes les dépêches officielles empruntent aujourd'hui cette voie bien que plus longue d'un tiers que celle des M.M.'* On 21 August 1891, Drouin informed the Minister that Britain had rejected the French proposal (FAP *Correspondance Politique* Vol. 97).

20   On 16 November 1893, four days after installation of the cable, Secretary of State the Marquis of Ripon transmitted his congratulations to Griffith, expressing the hope that the telegraphic link would promote the prosperity of Seychelles. There had at first been some uncertainty as to where the cable should be brought ashore. A representative of the Eastern and South African Telegraph Company, who visited Seychelles in January 1893, had proposed that one or both of the cables should be landed at North West Bay, from where they would cross the island to Victoria, and in April tenders were invited for digging a trench along the side of the St Louis road into Victoria. However, this proposal was scrapped, and both cables were landed at the Long Pier. No further submarine cables seem to have been laid at Seychelles until 1922, when the Colony was connected directly with Colombo and Aden. These cables also came in at the Long Pier, and then crossed to the Turtle Pond, near where the Cable and Wireless offices are today situated. The last telegraphic submarine cable was abandoned at Seychelles in 1971. — Public notice, *Government Gazette,* 25 April 1893; Griffith to Ripon, 4 May and 11 November 1893 (SNA B/43).

21   Capital of New Caledonia, a mountainous Melanesian island, 900 miles off the east coast of Australia. Indigenous people known as Kanakas. Discovered by Cook, 1774; claimed by France in 1860; penal settlement, closed in 1898. Kanaka uprisings, 1884; military government replaced by civilian rule, 1946; Overseas French Territory since 1984; strong movement for independence since 1980s.
22   The Administrator was Cockburn Stewart, who had returned to Seychelles in 1895 to replace Griffith. The situation could have been worse had British India not decided that year to open a new service between India and Africa, calling at Mahé. The service was hardly appreciated by the Seychellois, many of whom believed that

280

if BI was driven away the MM steamers would return. As for the mail service with Mauritius, Seychelles letters were now dependent on the occasional schooner.

23   The stone, carved with the royal arms of France and the inscription I. DE SECHELLES (badly defaced, possibly at the time of the French Revolution), was left on Mahé as a symbol of sovereignty on 1 November 1756 by Captain Corneille Nicolas Morphey, of the frigate *Le Cerf*. After the theft and return of the stone in 1894, it stood for many years in the grounds of Government House. It is now housed in the National History Museum in Victoria. The French left stones or cairns indicating right of possession on some of the other islands of Seychelles, but none has been found.

24   Russian designs on Afghanistan, and Britain's chronic trouble with France over Egypt, sharpened in 1894 with the signing of a Franco-Russian alliance and a visit by the Russian fleet to Toulon. Admiral Sir John Fisher, Third Sea Lord of the Admiralty, expressed British fears in a note to the First Lord in December 1894: 'The French, no doubt, sincerely desire peace with England, provided they can replace England in Egypt, and the Nile Basin, and elsewhere. To obtain peace on these terms they would not shrink from trying a fall with England, if they thought there was a fair chance of success.' – quoted by Arthur Narder, *The Anatomy of British Sea Power* (London, 1964).

CHAPTER TWELVE

Material from the MM Archives, quoted by Danielle Barret for her doctoral thesis *'Les Îles de l'Océan Indien Occidental et le Bateau: Communication des Hommes et des Idées, à travers les Archives de la Compagnie des Messageries Maritimes (1864-1920)'*, University of Paris VII, was consulted extensively, as was unpublished research into MM shipping schedules by Sue Hopson, of the Indian Ocean Study Circle, and Guy Lionnet. Seychelles' dissatisfaction over the BI steamship service is recorded in SNA B/44. The Denis island lighthouse is the subject of several documents in PRO CO 167/650, SNA B/42, and the Blue Book for 1872 in SNA D/1. The lighthouse was described as indispensable by Captain Maubeuge, of the *Godavéry*, December 1882, and French workers throwing their tools into the sea is mentioned by Guy Lionnet, *'L'Histoire d'un Phare',* in *Seychelles-Culture*, No 18, May 1974. The smallpox epidemic and subsequent quarantine problems are recorded in dispatches by Barkly (SNA B/39), Hollier Griffiths (PRO CO 167/650), Cockburn Stewart (SNA B/44), and notices in the *Government Gazette*, 1885 and 1886. The epidemic is described by Fanny Barkly, in *From the Tropics to the North Sea* (London, 1883).

1   Several inhabitants could not accept that the Messageries Maritimes was to withdraw. *'Les regrets que laisse notre départ ne peuvent s'expliquer. Partout on ne peut y croire et l'évidence sera pénible pour ceux qui veulent encore se faire illusion.'* So wrote the MM agent at Mahé in his annual report. – MM Archives, quoted by Barret [op. cit.].

2   Among those who visited Seychelles in 1891, and again in 1893, was the artist Paul Gaugin, travelling to Tahiti via Nouméa. – Guy Lionnet, 'The French Steam

Navigation Company Messageries Maritimes in the Western Indian Ocean in the 19th and 20th Centuries', a paper read at the International Conference on Indian Ocean Studies, Canberra, 1979.

3   Fanny Barkly, who arrived in Seychelles on the MM steamer *Yarra*, observed: 'The vessels of this line are fitted with the latest improvements, they are lighted throughout with electric light, the cuisine is excellent, and in fact, the comfort of the passengers is as carefully studied as in a first class hotel'. — Barkly [op. cit.].

4   Despite being described by *Le Réveil* newspaper as *'une ligne boîteuse'*, the BI company was to provide Seychelles with a reliable steamship service for more than 70 years. Formed in 1861 by William Mackinnon (1823-1893) from an earlier Calcutta-based coasting service, the British India Steam Navigation Company operated at first exclusively in eastern waters. In 1874 BI liners began to sail to London, and from 1890 the company's links with Africa were strengthened with a regular service from London to Zanzibar, which connected with the Mombasa-Bombay steamers that called at Mahé. In 1914 BI amalgamated with the P & O company, although it retained a high degree of autonomy, becoming in 1922 the largest single merchant fleet in the world, with a total of 158 vessels. The independence of India and Pakistan after World War II led to withdrawal of the Indian coasting trade, and closer cooperation with P & O resulted in the eventual disappearance of the British India line. The last of the company's steamers to call at Mahé was the *Karanja*, in September 1972.

5   The French vice-consul also blamed incessant quarantines for the company's difficulties: *'Cette question des quarantaines en étant encore une des grosses difficultés du service ... les habitants de ce pays sont trop hostiles à tout progrès de ce genre pour me laisser espérer de grandes modifications."* — MM Archives, quoted by Barret [op. cit.].

6   Although the lighthouse tower collapsed two months before Barkly's arrival in Seychelles, the Chief Civil Commissioner must bear some responsibility for the subsequent delay before a solid, permanent light was erected on Denis Island. The conservator of Crown lands, Charles Button, appointed to inquire into the inital collapse, found there had been a lack of supervision, use of improper building materials such as blocks of sun-dried lime and sand instead of genuine coral, use of salt water in preparing the mortar, over-haste, and neglect of safety precautions, criticisms that pointed directly at the superintendent of public works, Mr Cauvin, who also faced charges of having unlawfully flogged some of the prisoners employed on the project. Despite this, Barkly decided to retain Cauvin, and had all but one of the eleven charges of assault against him dismissed, advancing him money to pay the fine on the remaining charge. Barkly then appointed Button, who had some knowledge of engineering, to be in charge of rebuilding the tower, under the general supervision of Cauvin. With the latter resentful over the inquiry's findings and jealous of Button, it proved to be an ill-judged decision. Determined to push ahead, Barkly had 80 tons of stone sent from Curieuse to form the foundations of the new tower, but the Board of Civil Commissioners intervened and decided that no further attempt should be made to build the tower until reference had been made to Mauritius. Barkly had to admit to the Governor that he had misled him about the state of the project, but insisted that a safe and durable lighthouse could be built; all that was required was proper supervision. Unfortunately that supervision was missing. Cauvin was constantly occupied with the management of his own property and other private business, he was frequently insurbordinate, and

eventually Barkly wrote to Mauritius asking if he could be dismissed. In January 1883 Cauvin resigned, and Button was left in sole charge of the project. — Desmarais to Mauritius, 27 December 1881; Barkly to Governor, 6 October 1882; Barkly to Mauritius, 1 December 1882 (SNA B/38 and B/39).

7   HM schooner *Undine,* 267 tons, 1 gun, commissioned at Portsmouth, January 1882; on Mozambique station, commanded by Lieutenant W.B. Ponsford, RN. A full report on the consequences of the *Undine's* passenger, D. Bouquié, being landed at Seychelles was made by Mauritius governor Pope Hennessy to the Secretary of State for the Colonies, the Earl of Derby, 15 April 1884 (PRO CO 167/612).

8   Dr James Henry Brooks, medical officer, Seychelles, 1858-79. b. Henley-on-Thames, Oxfordshire; son of a surgeon. Described by Fanny Barkly as 'a very clever man' who seemed to have discovered the secret of perpetual youth, and by CC Board member François Hodoul as a person who had spent 'the best years of his life to earn a fortune for himself'. In addition to medical duties, Brooks involved himself in various businesses, including shipping, cotton, soda water manufacture, and retail trade. His monopoly over the supply of coal (for which he had the lease of Hodoul Island) brought him into a long-running conflict with the Messageries Maritimes agent Cheyron, prompting questions in London on whether government officers should engage in trade (PRO CO 167/561). In 1898 Brooks was appointed German consul. Died 1920, aged 89.

9   'You will only die from chickenpox if you are unfortunate enough to have a serious complication of pneumonia, nephritis, or encephalitis, or if a secondary infection occurs in debility due to other diseases and/or malnutrition.' — Dr Maureen Kirkpatrick, in an interview with the author, 15 March 1998.

10   The tortoise that was eaten was not one of the two left behind by General Gordon, who had asked the Barklys 'to take care of my tortoise'. — Fanny Barkly [op. cit.].

11   Among those quarantined on Longue island was the painter Marianne North, who arrived in Seychelles at the height of the smallpox epidemic. This does not seem to have troubled her until she came to leave in early 1884, and found she could not get away on the MM steamer unless she spent about two weeks in quarantine. For the first ten days on the island she spent most of her time painting, but her health was breaking down and she began to imagine that the inhabitants of Longue island were going to murder her. — Marianne North, *Recollections of a Happy Life* (1893).

12   There are similarities between chickenpox and smallpox, but smallpox lesions are deeper and denser and appear together; they are distributed more around the head and outer limbs. Chickenpox is rather superficial and manifests itself more on the trunk than the face and hands; also the lesions come in crops over a period of time. If looking for an excuse for Dr Lepper one could say only that 'it might have been a very light dose of smallpox, or else he may have not seen any smallpox before, or he was influenced in his diagnosis by his planned trip to Mauritius'. — Dr Maureen Kirkpatrick, in interview with author.

13   Unable to leave Seychelles by the regular MM service because of the smallpox

epidemic, Barkly and his family sailed to Colombo in HMS *Osprey*. They were to be absent from Seychelles for almost two years, as a result of extensions to his leave and a brief, temporary appointment as acting governor of the Falkland Islands. Fanny Barkly makes clear that her husband was not happy at having to return to Seychelles. As a result of the epidemic he was sued for damages by a Mrs Petit. His appeal that, as representative of the Queen he was not liable, was rejected. Dr Lepper, who was also sued, resigned the service (PRO CO 167/618).

14   Further relaxation of quarantine restrictions were effected by Ordinance No. 20 of 1900, which established a Quarantine Committee, separate from the Board of Health. A government statement said that easing of the restrictions had made Seychelles' 'unfortunate notoriety' in matters of health a thing of the past.

15   The Messageries Maritimes provided steamship services to Seychelles for over fifty years. From 1864 to 1882, its steamers called at Mahé on their regular monthly run between Marseilles and Réunion/Mauritius (after the opening of the Suez Canal this service involved transfer at Aden). From 1882 to 1896 Mahé was a port of call on the fast Marseilles-Australia-Nouméa route; at the same time the company maintained a regular Seychelles link with Mauritius and Réunion and (from 1888) with Madagascar ports. After the return of MM steamers to Seychelles in 1901, Mahé remained regularly linked with Europe and the islands of the western Indian Ocean until 1918.

CHAPTER THIRTEEN

The petition of 1892 for constitutional reforms and subsequent correspondence are in PRO CO 167/671. Mrs Edwards' comments appear in her book *Seychelles Archipelago*, 1893. Griffith's proposal to raise taxes is in PRO CO 167/650, and petition on additional islands for Seychelles in CO 167/592. French claims to the Glorieuses islands are in FAP *Mémoires et Documents: Afrique* Vol. 70, and *Correspondance Politique: Consuls* Vol. 73. Griffith's views on a botanic station are filed in PRO CO 167/650, and Sweet-Escott's warning on vanilla in 'Colonial Reports: Seychelles, 1901.' Cockburn Stewart's reference to the *moitié* system in SNA B/44, and Bonnetard's and Salmon's complaints regarding supply of labour in B/35. In the same file is Salmon's ban on paying by *bons*. References to liberated Africans are in PRO CO 167/650, SNA B/39, B/42, and B/44. Deportation of Prempeh, Kabarega, and Mwanga is recorded in SNA C/SS/2. Mwanga was described as 'fitful and fickle' by Scots missionary Alexander Mackay, quoted in J.F. Faupel, *African Holocaust: The Story of the Uganda Martyrs* (London, 1965). Kabarega's qualities as a guerrilla leader were noted by Alan Moorehead, *The White Nile* (London, 1960).

1   To prevent vanilla theft, planters were required to have a police permit to take samples to the market. An employee could be sent with the permit and a letter, but this meant a loss to the planter of one day's labour. Planters complained that the police were uneducated and could not read the permits. 'That some of the police cannot read or write is no fault of the government,' responded the Chief Civil Commissioner.

2   The signatories (with remarks added by the Chief Civil Commissioner)

included: George Hollier Griffiths (proprietor and shopkeeper), E. Savy (attorney and proprietor), André Nageon de Lestang (notary), G. Butler (landowner), E. Lanier, A. Moulinié, E. St Jorre (scrap merchant), Armand Georges, A. Gendron (landowner), C. Lemarchand, A. Deltel (proprietor), E. Delorié, A. Westergreen (alien), V. Westergreen (possessing nothing; is an alien), J.B. Adam (proprietor), O. Pothin (alien), H. Chenard (clerk), W.H. Walker (chemist), C. Savy (public writer and attorney's clerk), Henri Tirant (has nothing), J. Hodoul (clerk), F. Houareau (vanilla preparer), L. Hodoul (manager of Barbarons), H. Houareau (planter), W. H. McGaw (planter of La Digue), and A. Pothin (no means). According to Griffith the petitioners formed 'a very small and insignificant body of the taxpayers'. (PRO CO 167/671).

3   The Seychelles Capital Offences Order in Council, 6 February 1892 (promulgated in Seychelles on 30 April) created a Court of Assize, consisting of the District Judge as president, sitting with four to eight assessors. The assessors had to be British, male, resident in Seychelles, with annual income of R.500 or personal estate (or the husband of a woman with personal estate) of R.5,000. Early in 1897, with a murder case before the Court, the Administrator, Cockburn Stewart, wrote to Mauritius asking for a plan of a gallows. The three men accused of murder were found guilty and sentenced to death. However, the gallows was not needed, as the Executive Council later commuted the sentences to penal servitude for life. — Stewart to Mauritius and Secretary of State, 23 January, 20 February, and 1 October 1897 (SNA, B/44).

4   The three Unofficial members, and their appointments in government, were: Eugène Serret (Magistrate), François Hodoul (Inspector of Schools), and Noël Jouanis (Registrar of Mortgages).

5   Several months before the closure of the New Oriental Bank, the manager called for a change in the bankruptcy law to prevent debtors absconding. He referred to two Arab traders openly leaving on an MM steamer although they were deeply in debt to the bank. He suggested that the shipping company should in future close its passenger list earlier and send a copy to the police. — Brown to Mauritius, 12 January 1892 (PRO CO 167/650). The bank building was acquired by the government, which partially leased it as offices. Griffith described the building as 'needlessly expensive, unnecessarily durable, ugly in shape, and not altogether fitted for that amalgamation of public offices which the government would secure if it erected buildings for itself'. He considered that the real loss to the shareholders was the original outlay, and not in the realisation of their assets, offered at a quarter of the sum expended. — Griffith to Mauritius, 11 February 1893 (PRO CO 167/650). Mrs Edwards, who was ready to offer an opinion on anything, described the side view of the bank as resembling 'a pig's ear'. Today the building accommodates the Seychelles High Court and Judicial Department. In 1911 a branch of the Commercial Bank of Mauritius opened in Seychelles, but closed four years later. Seychelles had then to wait until 1959 for another bank to open. This was Barclays DCO, now Barclays Bank International.

6   The *Melittomma* beetle first appeared in Seychelles in the 1860s, but it was only in 1881 that its destructive activities were reported to be widespread, about one-third of estates being affected. A committee set up to inquire into the disease reported that a borer insect was responsible. — Stewart to Mauritius, 17 June 1881 (SNA B/38). In February 1895 the Legislative Council decided more time was needed to consider what action should be taken. — Note, 2 February 1895 (PRO

CO 167/691). Damage to the palm is in fact caused not by the beetle but by the larva, which on hatching bores into the bole of the palm and feeds on its sap. After about a year the beetle emerges, but dies shortly after mating and laying. Repeated infestation results in the coconut palm becoming hollow at the base and eventually falling. Although the cause of the disease was identified in 1903, it was only in the 1950s that serious attention was given to the problem.

7 The first Seychelles postage stamps were issued in April 1890. A proposal that the Dependency should have its own stamps, instead of using those of Mauritius, had been put to the Governor the previous year by Griffith, who thought this would be to the material advantage of Seychelles and consistent with its 'recently extended constitutional condition'. He informed the government that according to De La Rue & Co. of London the cost for eight varieties of stamps would be £96, but that sales to collectors abroad would 'in a few months recoup this Government for the original outlay'. He enclosed in his letter to the Governor three designs suggested by De La Rue. – Griffith to Pope Hennessy, 4 July 1889 (PRO CO 167/650). In 1893 an inland postal service was started in Seychelles on a trial basis, with letter boxes at police stations at Anse Royale, Anse Boileau, Port Glaud, Praslin, and La Digue. The police were responsible for the collection and distribution of mail. The service was discontinued after nine months because it did not pay. Griffith remarked that it was not really surprising 'when it is remembered how small a proportion of the population can write, how few that can write have any inclination or necessity for doing so, whilst those who have business transactions invariably send their own messengers to town, directing them to wait for and return with a reply'. – Griffith to Mauritius, 12 July 1894 (SNA B/43).

8 The Glorieuses, named after the French ship the *Glorieux*, in which D'Après de Mannevillette surveyed the coast of Madagascar in 1753, were included as dependencies of Mauritius in a list published in 1880, on the flimsy grounds that they had been described as such in an English geography book of 1849 and in the Mauritius surveyor-general's report of 1863-64. In 1892 Commandant Richard, in the *Primauguet*, took possession of the islands for France.

9 Britain had been stung by a report in a French pamphlet suggesting that Aldabra belonged to France. In March 1890 the British ambassador told the French government that the atoll was British. However, the Prime Minister, Lord Salisbury, decided 'some act of sovereignty, such ... as a visit from the Administrator of Seychelles, should be performed as a proof of British rights'. The whole affair was embarrassing to Mauritius, where the acting colonial secretary, H.N.D. Beyts, denied in a Press statement that he had ever told the French consul that Aldabra was not British. He suggested the confusion had arisen over whether Mauritius or Seychelles administered Aldabra, adding that the French consul may have thought that as Aldabra was not administered by Mauritius it was not British. – Confidential dispatch to Secretary of State, 12 June 1893 (SNA C/SS/73), and Jerningham to Secretary of State, 22 October 1892 (PRO CO 167/671).

10 Spurs was later to fall out of favour. In May 1901, when his lease came up for renewal, Chamberlain decided it should go to Baty, Bergne & Co., because their offer was better and because of 'the well-known interest' of the Hon. Lionel Walter Rothschild, MP, of Tring Park, trustee of the British Museum and a keen amateur zoologist. The Secretary of State also quoted unsubstantiated claims that Spurs had sold large numbers of tortoises to visiting ships. Although these reports were almost certainly untrue, he refused Sweet-Escott's request to clear Spurs' name, 'since the

statements about him [Spurs] were communicated to you in a confidential dispatch intended for your private information'. In December 1903 the lease on Aldabra was transferred to Adolphe d'Emmerez de Charmoy, who employed Spurs as manager. He subsequently sold it to W. & J. Biggerstaff, who wanted to develop the atoll. In 1922 it was purchased by the Seychelles Guano Company, but little guano was mined (SNA C/SS/73 and B/37). Spurs died at Mahé in 1928.

11   The scientist was Dr A. Günther, of the Natural History Department at the British Museum. He had been associated with Darwin's campaign to save the giant tortoise, and had published in 1877 an authoritative work on the different species of giant tortoise. Writing to Lord Ripon in February 1893, Günther expressed doubts about Spurs' estimate of their numbers on Aldabra, recalling that full grown specimens were so scarce in the 1870s that the trustees of the British Museum had to pay a Seychelles planter £60 for one. In August 1878 Aldabra had been visited by HM surveying ship *Fawn,* under the command of Captain William Wharton (later the Navy's Hydrographer), who 'was able to find one tortoise only, and [that] not fully grown' (SNA C/SS/73). In 1909 the British naturalist J. Stanley Gardiner visited Aldabra. He reported that giant tortoises were plentiful in some parts, and concluded that they were not in danger of extinction.

12   The tortoises Griffith sent to Curieuse were some years later sent back to the herd at Government House, which in 1904 consisted of forty-four adults, including one called Gordon and another Spurs. There were also seventeen young tortoises. In 1910 Governor Davidson decided to reduce the Government House herd, and sent forty-nine to Longue island. The herd was finally dispersed in 1921, five or six being sent to Britain, some to the Botanical Gardens in Victoria, and a large number to Longue island. Those sent to Britain are now dead. The fate of those sent to Longue island is unknown. – Justin Gerlach, *Famous Tortoises* (Cambridge, 1998). Günther may have been the first to identify some of the tortoises in Seychelles as survivors of a breed previously thought to have disappeared from Mahé. – Davidson to Secretary of State, 20 August 1909 (SNA C/AM/10).

13   Hunting has reduced the number of green and hawksbill turtles around the main granitic islands of Seychelles to negligible numbers. In 1994 the Seychelles government banned the sale of turtle shell articles, and introduced new regulations for the protection of the green turtle.

14   In 1895 the director of the Royal Gardens at Kew, Thistleton Dyer, was asked to advise on the setting up of a Botanic Station in Seychelles. His proposals were rejected by the Legislative Council as being too costly. Griffith reminded Mauritius that he had originally wanted the station to be self-supporting, by growing vanilla and coffee, both of which were present at the abandoned CMS mission site. He added: 'Let a good crop of vanilla be upon the vines and an indication become apparent of the present tightness and depression being removed, and I have no doubt that the veiled opposition will vanish.' It was not until 1901 that the Botanic Station finally opened, with Paul Rivalz Dupont of Mauritius as curator. In 1902 he was also appointed Commissioner of Crown Lands. Dupont, who had previously been assistant director of the agricultural station in Mauritius and who returned there for a while as Director of Agriculture, gained prominence for his scientific research. His work was not universally appreciated in Seychelles, however. In a report to the Colonial Office in 1904, Governor Davidson claimed 'he has no system, no large ideas, and is not strong enough ... to make others follow him.' The Governor added that he would not be sorry if Dupont was tempted away to Mauritius, as he

could run the botanic station with a gardener (PRO CO 167 and SNA C/AM/18).

15   The extraction of guano began on Bird island in 1895, with the export that year of 390 tons (valued at R.9,650). Later the Amirantes islands were also exploited, and guano exports steadily rose. In 1901 the amount was 5,598 tons, valued at R.54,000. By 1913 production had risen to 35,000 tons, but the war affected exports and the industry never fully recovered. The harmful effect of guano extraction has been most noticeable on Assumption island and St Pierre.

16   In 1880 the Board of Civil Commissioners restricted the sale of *bacca* to licensed dealers. The following year it became illegal to possess without a licence fermented liquor made from the juice of sugar-cane, pineapple, coconut, or jamrosa. The regulation also covered the possession of brewing implements. In 1893 Brown, then acting Administrator, moved to suppress completely 'a practice prejudicial alike to public order and to the revenue' by prohibiting the crushing of sugar-cane or extraction of juice except by sugar manufacturers or licensed distillers. Possession of juice whether fermented or not became an offence, with fines of up to R.500. The making or possession of *calou* or other juice susceptible of fermentation was also prohibited. This regulation caused great discontent, but remained in force until 1896, when it was disallowed by the Secretary of State, and the regulation of 1881 was renewed. In 1909 large-scale production of *bacca* began and consumption rapidly increased. It was considered by many that *bacca* was no more harmful than cider and less so than rum. The law recognised the greater harm to poor people if induced to give up *bacca* in favour of concoctions such as *la purée*. The sale of *bacca* continued to be restricted to licensed premises, but householders could have up to four litres of fermented juice on their premises.

17   The jubilee fountain, surmounted by a miniature statue of Queen Victoria, was unveiled by the Administrator, Sweet-Escott, on 5 January 1900. Reporting the occasion, the newspaper *Le Réveil* likened the fountain to a funerary monument. It complained that when the fountain button was pushed, only a thin stream of water appeared, *'une mince filet d'eau ... comme un regret — l'on dirait un pleur dans une cuvette inférieure, une véritable lavemain'.* The newspaper added that at a cost of over R.1,422, one could surely have done better. The fountain, no longer operable, stands outside the High Court building. The statue was removed in 1977, but a replica, donated by the British government, was placed on the fountain in June 1993. The original statue is on display in the National History Museum in Victoria.

18   Described by one official as 'an unscrupulous and impecunious man', Stewart was often in financial trouble. He borrowed money at high rates of interest, and his cheques were frequently dishonoured (PRO CO 167/624). Bradley [op. cit.] suggests that his roads programme in Seychelles was mismanaged, and that there were unexplained shortfalls in his accounts.

19   In March 1897 Stewart complained to Chamberlain about the District Judge, Brown. 'Mr Brown's contention appears to be that I should not communicate with you without first consulting him, a claim that might entail serious disadvantages and ... is in any case at variance with the usual procedure in other colonies,' he wrote. Although Stewart claimed to be on 'perfectly good terms' with the Judge, there was obviously jealousy and resentment between the two men. Twice (in 1895 and 1897) Stewart strongly recommended Brown for a position of puisne Judge at the Mauritius High Court, saying it was objectionable to keep a judge in Seychelles for so long. But Brown remained until 1900, by which time Stewart had left. The

Administrator also quarrelled with the Civil Chaplain, Rev. G.E. Walters, over the latter's insistence that he should have the same privileges at Government House as the Roman Catholic Bishop, members of the Executive and Legislative Councils, and foreign consuls. Stewart considered Walters' status that of head of department, and refused. The Chaplain also objected to his wife not receiving due precedence at an official function, when she was sent into dinner after the wife of the medical officer. He wrote to Stewart demanding 'a full and unreserved apology'. In lengthy correspondence with the Secretary of State, Stewart claimed Walters was being used by certain malcontents to cause mischief. He referred to a series of petitions got up by Walters and others, and named particularly Philip Boustead, who had created 'an anti-government clique', and Dr Brooks, who 'has kept the place in a ferment for the last 25 years'. On Walters, Stewart noted that he could not speak a word of French and many of his congregation could not understand a word of English. – Stewart to Chamberlain, June-July 1898 (SNA B/44). In March 1900 Walters went on sick leave and did not return.

20   The paupers and lepers, segregated on different sides of the island, lived on Round Island until 1917, when the paupers were transferred to the newly opened Fiennes Institute, Victoria. In 1920 the lepers were sent to Round Island, off Mahé, where they stayed until 1929, when male lepers were returned to Round Island, Praslin. Female lepers, then numbering six, were to follow, but never did, although their numbers greatly increased. Conditions on the two small islands were unsatisfactory, and in 1937 a new settlement was established on Curieuse island, to where the lepers were returned. They remained there until 1965, when all were transferred to Anse Louis, Mahé. Since 1943 chemotherapy has contained the disease, and as patients are now regularly cured the eradication of the disease world-wide has become a real possibility. Leprosy is still occasionally diagnosed in Seychelles.

21   Chamberlain did not completely give up the idea of sending Boer prisoners of war to Seychelles. In May 1901 Sweet-Escott was obliged to tell him that Seychelles was unable to accommodate any large number of prisoners. Six months later, on 16 November, about 1,000 Boer prisoners called at Seychelles in HM transport *Armenia*. Although available documents do not indicate the ship's destination, it is probable that the prisoners were on their way to Ceylon. The following year Sweet-Escott appears to have agreed to take a number of Boer rebels from Cape Colony who had been sentenced to penal servitude. An army officer from Aden, Captain A. W. Martyn, arrived in Seychelles in February 1902 to report on its suitability. Baty and Bergne, lessees of Felicité, offered to provide food for 200 prisoners and guards, but because of a scarcity of labour, the whole proposal appears to have been dropped.

22   The Ashanti war provided plenty of ammunition for Liberal MPs to attack the government. The member for Caernarvon, Lloyd George, scoffed at Chamberlain's claim that the war was to halt slavery and human sacrifice, and said the real reason was the Gold Coast governor's desire to seize the Golden Stool, symbol of authority among the Ashanti. There would have been no war if it had been a wooden stool, said another. When a Conservative member described Prempeh as 'the most cruel and heartless man the world ever produced', John Redmond, Irish Nationalist, retorted: 'Oh, you said the same about Kruger [the Boer leader].' The motion against the government was defeated. – *The Times*, 19 March 1901.

23   The house where Prempeh lived at Le Rocher is still the property of the

Adam family. A large burn mark on the veranda floor is said to be where Prempeh rested the bowl of his pipe.

24   The Bishop persuaded Prempeh to allow one of his nephews to return with him to Mauritius to study at St Paul's Theological College. John Boateng Aquassi Prempeh, born in Seychelles in 1903 and educated at the Anglican school, was ordained in Mauritius in 1928. At his father's request he went to Gold Coast in 1930, where he served as a missionary in Accra until his early death in 1941.

25   The house at Pointe Conan was used for several years as offices by the Seychelles Institute of Management. In 1998 it was demolished to make way for a new Institute building.

26   Altogether twenty-two Catholics and twelve Protestants were burned to death in Buganda between 1885 and 1887. Most of the executions were carried out at Namugongo, near Kampala. In 1920 the Catholic martyrs were beatified by Pope Benedict XV, and subsequently canonised, on 18 October 1964, by Pope Paul VI. The feast day of St Charles Lwanga and the Ugandan martyrs is 3 June.

27   One of Prempeh's grand-daughters, Princess Huguette, told the author in an interview in 1998 that she vaguely remembered being taken by her mother to see her grandfather. Her mother, who was Seychelloise, stayed behind after Prempeh was released in 1924, although her father, James, returned to the Gold Coast.. 'At that time people were afraid that if you go among these people ... all sorts of things would happen to you,' she said. At the age of 29, Princess Huguette did go to Kumasi, where she stayed for some twenty years. She later married an Italian and went to Italy. In 1970 she returned alone to Seychelles. Her children all live in Ghana.

CHAPTER FOURTEEN

Official correspondence on the separation of Seychelles from Mauritius is in PRO CO 167/753, Sweet-Escott's remark on the Clocktower in SNA B/47. Dr Bradley's report on South Mahé, 1913, with Governor O'Brien's covering letter of February 1914, is in CO 530/22, and Governor Davidson's retrenchment measures in SNA C/AM/18. Controversy over the language for schools is in 'Colonial Reports: Seychelles 1903', PRO CO 167/753, SNA C/88/36, and B/40. Sweet-Escott's description of Mauritians as indifferent subjects is in PRO CO 167/761. Correspondence regarding Miss Best and protection of animals is in SNA C/AM/17 and C/AM/20. Also consulted on Miss Best, Brendon Grimshaw, *A Grain of Sand: The Story of One Man and an Island* (Nairobi 1996). The claim that settlers could never actually starve is found in 'Colonial Reports: Seychelles 1903'. Davidson's paper on whaling is in SNA C/88/14. Additional references to the Lanier case are in PRO CO 530/20 and 530/21. The affair of magistrate Brooke is in PRO CO 530/33.

1   Sweet-Escott had proposed that the Colony be named 'Seychelles' instead of 'The Seychelles'. The Colony comprised 89 islands, Coëtivy and the Farquhar

islands remaining under Mauritius administration until 1908 and 1922 respectively.

2   HMS *Pearl*, 2,575 tons, light cruiser of third class (Captain Edward Ashe); armed with eight 4.7in. guns, and six three-pounders. Commissioned in December 1901. Arrived Mahé, 3 November 1903, from Diego Garcia. On 9 November ship dressed overall in honour of King's birthday. At 10.25 HMS *Pearl* saluted the Governor of Seychelles with 17 guns, and at noon fired a Royal Salute. It sailed for Desroches island on 15 November (PRO ADM 53/24717).

3   After the swearing-in, a crowded levée was held, 'attended by all sections of the population', according to a report in *The Times,* 11 November 1903. Later there was a luncheon at Government House, when toasts were proposed to the King, the Governor, and the Colony. A sports meeting took place in the afternoon, and 'an African saga [sic] dance was performed in the evening in the open air'.

4   Stephen Coombes, managing director of the Croydon firm of clock manufacturers Gillett & Johnston, told the author that a series of clocktowers, in three different sizes, were erected in several English towns, where they conveniently disguised the ventilation shafts of newly constructed underground toilets. He estimated that there were probably about twenty still in existence. The clocktower outside Victoria Station, at the junction of Vauxhall Bridge Road and Victoria Street, was the first to be erected in London, in 1892. Reporting its unveiling, *The Times* (15 March) considered that it would have been better sited at Piccadilly or Holborn Circus, as it was dwarfed by the height of the buildings in Victoria Street. Called Little Ben, it was removed 'temporarily' in 1964 for a street-widening scheme, and was not re-erected until 1981, after a £35,000 refit. Its restoration was financed by Elf Aquitaine UK to commemorate the wedding of Prince Charles and Lady Diana Spencer, and as a gesture of Franco-British friendship. The Seychelles clocktower is listed as an historic monument. It is 25 feet high, weighs five tons, and its four dials are 2½ feet in diameter. In 1999 the clock mechanism, which had to be wound manually every week, was replaced by a modern quartz masterclock.

5   The Air Seychelles in-flight magazine *Silhouette* (Vol. 9, No. 2) states that the 'miniature' clocktower 'commemorates the declaration in 1903 of Seychelles as a Crown colony'.

6   Sweet-Escott applied on 23 January 1903 for the governorship of British Honduras, where he had previously served as colonial secretary. Comments in the Colonial Office on his application were mixed. One official conceded that he had done well in routine administration, but added: 'I cannot say whether he has enough originality to devise plans for opening up an undeveloped colony, which I understand is wanted in British Honduras.' Another, noting that Sweet-Escott had done excellent work in Seychelles and deserved promotion, added that unfortunately he resented being overruled, 'and is apt to see slights where no slight is intended'. Only one official thought that Sweet-Escott was fitted to be governor (PRO CO 167/761). Whatever the views expressed at the Colonial Office, Sweet-Escott was popular in Seychelles. *The Times* reported that on his departure from the Colony in May 1904 there was 'an enthusiastic crowd on the jetty to bid him farewell'.

7   In 1900 the price of vanilla reached a record high of R.33.06 per kg, but by 1903 it had dropped to R.8.50. Although the price was to rise again, the abnormal drought in Seychelles in 1904 reduced both quantity and quality. Thereafter vanilla continued to decline as planters looked to alternative products.

8   The vacoa bag industry did not survive the competition of gunny bags from Calcutta, and by 1905 was practically dead. Like the vanilla and cinnamon bark industries, it depended largely on female labour, described by one visitor as 'the mainspring of life' in Seychelles. This he attributed to the climate, which 'being hot naturally imparts ardour and strength to the women, but leaves the men weakened and less energetic'. – Mathew Murat, *Gordon's Eden, or the Seychelles Archipelago* (Mauritius, 1900).

9   'I really do not see that there is any industry better adapted to the soil and climate of Seychelles than the culture of Para rubber,' wrote the director of the Botanic Station, Rivalz Dupont, in his report for 1904. Dupont had introduced rubber seedlings into Seychelles from various regions, but found that Para rubber (from the *Hevea Brasiliensis* plant) grew best and was more resistant to drought. The newly formed Rubber and Coconut Estates Co. bought up several plantations and began a programme of extensive planting. In 1911 Seychelles exported its first quantity of rubber (132kg). The following year rubber exports were valued at R.2,265. The hopes for the industry were not realised, however. Many planters were reluctant to invest in rubber and, unable to compete with the Malay product, the industry did not long survive the end of World War I. The name rubber was coined by an English chemist, Joseph Priestly, in 1770 when he found that the elastic substance secreted by certain tropical plants rubbed out pencil marks. Rubber did not become commercially important until the early 1840s, after Charles Goodyear discovered the process of vulcanisation (which prevents rubber becoming sticky or brittle with change of temperature).

10   Sweet-Escott put on a second agricultural show in October 1903. Although more successful than the first, the lack of public response was disappointing. Sweet-Escott attributed this 'to the want of sufficiently strong sporting and English elements in these Islands'. He was convinced people did not exhibit because they were afraid they would not win a prize, and added: 'It is also partly due to that strange *incuria rerum* which in a tropical Colony like Seychelles it is so desperately difficult to overcome.' If only the native planters could be awakened from their lethargy, and relied on their own efforts instead of *'Le Bon Dieu'*, he was sure there would be some progress.

11   However, Governor O'Brien noticed 'a considerable difference in the manliness of the youngsters' when he invited a group of boarders of King's College to tea at Government House. He also found that 'they spoke English more naturally and less parrot-like'. – O'Brien to Secretary of State, 8 January 1914 (PRO CO 530/19).

12   The nine boarders at King's College on 31 January 1913 were: R. Bestel, A. Deltel, P. Savy, E. de St Jorre, two Whiting boys, J. Tregarthen, F. Finniss, and R. Button (PRO CO 530/23).

13   In his report McLeod praised the 'sterling personal influence of the Sisters', but he doubted whether many of them were trained teachers. As to the 'mechanical and useless proficiency' he found generally in the classroom, he instanced 'pupils who could read their textbook upside down as rapidly and correctly as in the ordinary position', while others could define a mountain or a river, but 'assured me there were neither mountains nor rivers on Mahé'. McLeod criticised the system of giving grants to schools according to examination results, and suggested their

performance should be gauged by the inspector's report. McLeod's own report was dated August 1914, but it 'remained so long in the drawer of Mr d'Unienville' that it was not until February 1916 that it came to the notice of Governor O'Brien (SNA C/AM/19).

14   Government House was built by the Public Works Department at a cost of R.77,000 (£5,133), Although said to have been designed by the wife of the Governor, Mrs Davidson (who apparently forgot in her plan to allow for a staircase), the official architects were W.M. Vaudin (Superintendent, PWD) and his assistant, L. Le Vieux. Work started in November 1910, but the Davidsons had left Seychelles before the building was completed, and it was not until August 1913 that Governor O'Brien and his family took up residence. An official report said it was a handsome building 'far in advance of anything previously attempted'. The central hall had parquet flooring and the three main reception rooms were panelled in local wood.   An adjoining area of 22 acres, known as Terrain Dugand, was acquired for R.6,036, and added to the existing grounds. Offices for Sweet-Escott and his staff had previously been built near the entrance to Government House grounds.   This building is today the National History Museum. The remains of the old Government House, built in 1851, were demolished in 1959.

15   The Carnegie Library building (now the National Museum of Natural History) resulted from a gift of £2,000 to Seychelles from the Scots-American businessman and philanthropist, Andrew Carnegie. The lending library was opened by Governor Davidson on 22 January 1910. Over 3,000 books were purchased by a special vote of the Legislative Council. From its opening the library recorded some 300 readers a month. The upper storey of the building was used as a public hall .

16   J. Stanley Gardiner. b. 1872, at Belfast. Emeritus Professor of Zoology at Cambridge, 1909-37. Leader of the Percy Sladen Expedition to the Indian Ocean in HMS *Sealark*, 1905, and a subsequent expedition in 1908. The purpose was to complement the oceanographic research carried out by the Admiralty and Royal Society in HMS *Challenger*, 1872-76, this having omitted Indian Ocean. Gardiner wrote and lectured on his visits to Seychelles (*Nature*, 1905-06, and *Geographical Journal*, 1906); awarded Darwin Medal of the Royal Society, 1944; died 1946.

17   One of the earliest accounts of pirate treasure was given by a member of the Natural History Society of Mauritius, Elisée Liénard, who visited Frégate island in the 1830s. He described being shown a hole where a large trunk filled with coin, crockery, and swords had been found. He also visited various ruins which suggested early European occupation. He noted that the first inhabitants of the island had discovered the remains of a blacksmith's forge and a lead channel that conveyed water from a nearby spring. 'On a rock ... one can distinguish, without being able to decipher it, an inscription which appears to have been cut in the stone by means of a chisel.' There were also, standing on a height, three tombs made in coral, on which were laid sword hilts. According to what the inhabitants told Liénard, the pirates took away most of their treasure when they left. They were later captured and hanged, except for one, who was spared on account of his youth. 'On his death bed he gave one of his friends a note which contained an indication of the place where the [remaining] treasure had been hidden.' Liénard added: 'I have seen this note, and I had no doubts about the authenticity of the preceding facts.' Unfortunately, a subsequent search revealed no treasure.

18   The lessee of Astove, Adolphe d'Emmerez de Charmoy, acquired half of the

treasure, the other half going to the government. Two years later the government reported that four coins, a silver spoon, buckle, and silver bosun's whistle had been stolen from a safe. The missing articles were never found. In 1961, a search of Government House and the Treasury vault confirmed that all the remaining articles had also disappeared (SNA C/SS/13). The longest treasure hunt in Seychelles history has been that by an Englishman, the late Reginald Cruise-Wilkins, who, in the late 1940s, began a search at Bel Ombre, Mahé, for the supposed treasure of the French pirate Olivier Le Vasseur, alias La Buze. The search has continued intermittently, under Cruise-Wilkins' son John.

19   The stone and coral ruins of Miss Best's 'House of Dogs' still stand on Moyenne island, where a plaque was erected in her memory by the present owner of the island, Brendon Grimshaw. It is believed that local fishermen stole dogs for the purpose of taking them to Miss Best, who gave them a small present. There were forty dogs in all in 1915 when Miss Best went to live on Mahé, presumably taking her dogs with her. When she died in 1919 the dogs numbered about seventy. They were, according to one report, all destroyed. The society she founded succumbed to neglect, until re-formed some forty years later by Brigadier T. Dodd as the Seychelles branch of the RSPCA (SNA C/AM/17). The branch was subsequently dissolved, since when efforts to form a similar society have been unsuccessful.

20   While recognising the benefits from Indian and Chinese immigration, a report in 1909 by W.L. Rind, Clerk to the Governor, noted that most of the valuable town property was in the hands of Indians, 'and the chief danger lies in the possibility of the spread of their operations to estates in the country'. He added that, in general, 'the Indian of the class found in the Colony is quite incapable of estate management', and he feared they would tend to exhaust the land for a quick profit, before returning to India. The role of the Chinese in the expansion of the economy was noted by Murat [op. cit.]. He described them as redoubtable rivals of the Indian merchants, one of the wealthiest being 'a China-man by the name of Affoi, who has a sailing vessel which trades between Mauritius and the dependency'.

21   The Imperial Institute, South Kensington, noted that although in 1910 Seychelles' export earnings, at R.2,242,730, were approximately the same as in 1907, there was a considerable decrease in vanilla exports, which occupied third place after copra and guano. Essential oils (cinnamon bark, clove leaves, ylang-ylang, lemon grass, and citronella) amounted to 486 litres (worth over R.2,000), but this was capable of expansion. Calipee, an essential ingredient of turtle soup, had assumed some importance, with 12.5 tons (worth R.42,000) exported.

22   The Messageries Maritimes returned to Seychelles on very advantageous terms. Although its ships would at first not accept cargo such as coconut oil, copra, or coir rope yarn because of offensive odours or carrying capacity, the company received a 2,000 franc subsidy for each call made at Mahé. MM ships were also exempt from port and harbour dues and, with no contract, were free of any penalties.

23   The *Charles W. Morgan* is the most famous surviving whaleship in the United States. Built in 1841, it made thirty-seven voyages before ceasing whaling in 1921. It is now moored at the Mystic Seaport Museum, in Connecticut, and is a popular tourist attraction.

24   The Privy Council originated in medieval times in England as the King's Council, consisting of the chief ministers of state, bishops, peers, and household officials. As the king's executive arm, it was closely involved in colonial matters. Its judicial functions, including trying cases of treason and rebellion, were abolished in the 17th century, leaving only appeals from the colonies and dependencies. In 1834 the judicial proceedings of the Council were formalised by the creation of the Judicial Committee, which still functions as the supreme court of appeal for British dependencies and some former colonies. Membership of the Privy Council is conferred on Cabinet Ministers and others in recognition of political services.

25   Mrs Williamson's liaison with the Civil Chaplain, the Rev. Ernest Newton, is referred to by O'Brien in a letter to the Secretary of State. It reads, in part: 'The Williamson-cum-Archdeacon *ménage à trois* continues to cause some scandal. Archdeacon Newton is pleasant enough but I would not trust him far, and yet he has the full support of his Bishop. – O'Brien to Sir George Fiddes, 20 April 1913 (PRO CO 530/23). O'Brien also referred to Lanier's character being 'somewhat vitiated by a fondness for the ladies' giving as his source W.F. Stephens, local manager of the Mahé Syndicate. – O'Brien to Secretary of State, 3 March 1914 (PRO CO 530/23). Among Williamson's critics was the owner of Moyenne island, Miss Best. In a letter to the Secretary of State, she urged an investigation into the activities of the acting Chief Justice, accusing Williamson of imprisoning people out of personal spite, and of frequenting prostitutes in Hangard Street. She also charged him with spying on women with their skirts rucked up to the waist as they washed clothes in a nearby stream. An outspoken feminist, with advanced ideas on sex and society, Miss Best also criticised the sexual repression of white women in Seychelles. 'Whilst men in honourable positions let loose the vilest passions, they – ready for that motherhood which they are told is their only *raison d'être* – are not allowed a reasonable and decent outlet for natural human desires. If they are unfortunate enough to 'fall' ... they can commit suicide or leave a country too small to hide in.' The negress, she thought, was happier – 'often a good and loving mother and proud ... of her half white child'. – Miss Best to Secretary of State, 6 May 1912. Referring to Miss Best's letter, Davidson assured London that 'no importance need to be attached to communications from this lady, who has spent many years struggling against constituted authority'. After several years' campaigning against police abuses in Sydney, 'she has again settled in Seychelles to devote her energies to reform administration'. He added: 'I question whether her allegations against him [Williamson] have any basis of fact.' – Davidson to Secretary of State, 29 May 1912, with enc. (PRO   CO 530/19). Sweet-Escott had earlier formed a similar opinion of Miss Best, informing the Secretary of State that he had heard there was lunacy in her family. Referring to a pamphlet distributed by her, entitled 'A marriage protest and free union declaration', Sweet-Escott claimed her mode of living would not stand investigation. As to accusations she had made against him over his removal in 1901 of the lepers and paupers camp from Curieuse island to Round island, off Praslin, he commented: 'I do not understand in what sense it can be said that I have broken faith with these unfortunate persons, or disregarded the public safety.' – Sweet-Escott to Secretary of State, 21 June 1902 (PRO CO 169/754).

26   The case involving Williamson and the Seychelles Club arose out of a proposed lantern slide show at the club of paintings, mostly of female nudes, from some of France's principal museums. The club committee arranged that a screen would be erected on the night of the show (1 September 1911) to prevent a crowd gathering in Gordon Square to watch. At the last moment the Civil Chaplain,

Newton, protested about the forthcoming show to the acting Governor, Chief Justice Alfred Young, who sent a note to the club committee warning it against displaying potentially offensive pictures. Young sent police to the club on the night, and no nudes were shown. Subsequently the committee demanded Newton's resignation for having informed Young. When he refused, his name was removed from the club membership. Newton sued the club for defamation of character, and the case came before the acting Chief Justice, Williamson. In the dock were members of a newly elected club committee, the previous committee having resigned in protest at Young's actions. The committee insisted that the pictures were well-known works of art, and denied the Judge's claim that the show had been arranged 'to gloat over nude figures of white women'. But Williamson found them all guilty, and imposed hefty fines. The trial was later described at the Colonial Office as a gross miscarriage of justice, and Young was told he had been unwise to make his warning public. The action of Newton was seen as 'an impudent hypocrisy' in view of some previous misbehaviour that had forced him to cut short his career in India. In the end the fines imposed by Williamson were returned, and an apology offered to the committee members. It was recommended that Williamson should not act as Chief Justice again (PRO CO 530/16 and CO 530/19). As for Newton, he later resigned, and O'Brien urged the Church to ensure that his successor was 'a suitable gentleman'. The Colonial Office agreed, stressing that whoever was appointed should not have 'primitive notions of sexual morality'. It warned that if another scandal occurred, the post of Civil Chaplain might be abolished. – O'Brien to Bishop's commissary, 26 August 1913, and Colonial Office comments (PRO CO 530/22). The Anglican Church was unfortunate at times in its choice of representative in Seychelles. One of Newton's predecessors, the Rev. E.R. Ward, was sent home immediately after his arrival, when several witnesses, including the captain of the ship in which he had travelled, testified to his immorality, drunkenness, and foul language. Further evidence indicated that Ward and the lady he had introduced as his niece 'lived together as man and wife'. – Davidson to Secretary of State, 30 March 1905 (SNA B/47).

27   The certificate was signed on 7 December 1911 by Drs J.B. Addison (Chief Medical Officer), John T. Bradley (assistant medical officer, South Mahé), and Michael S. Power (assistant medical officer, Victoria). (PRO CO 530/16). The acting Governor doubted whether Lanier's imprisonment had induced Bright's disease as he claimed, and O'Brien also noted: 'Judging from the robust appearance of Mr Lanier moving about rapidly on a bicycle and the fact that he can exercise the profession of land surveyor in a rugged mountainous country such as this, ... his recovery appears to have been rapid and complete.' – Memo. by Chief Justice A.K. Young and confidential letter from O'Brien to Secretary of State, 22 January 1914 (PRO CO 530/23).

28   On 7 June 1912, an Irish Nationalist member of Parliament, Jeremiah Macveagh, asked the Secretary of State for the Colonies whether he had received complaints about the administration of the Seychelles islands. Secretary Harcourt replied that he had, but many of the complaints were trivial. However, he had ordered an inquiry into allegations respecting the conduct of one particular officer. The following month Williamson resigned from the service. No inquiry was held, and despite a protest telegram sent to London by several inhabitants, Williamson returned to Seychelles where he entered private practice. The signatories of the telegram were: Hon. Nageon, Conor, Thomasset, Merian, Stephens, H. Pare, M. Pare, Hunt, Jouanis, Decaila, Mytton, Brooks, Boullé, Chenard, Esnouf, Gardette, and Whiting. – Colonial Office minute, August 1912 (PRO CO 530/19).

29   Lanier v. Rex before Judicial Committee of the Privy Council. Leave to appeal granted, 16 December 1912 (PRO CO 530/20) and judgement delivered, 5 November 1913 (*The Times*, 6 November 1913). One result stemming from the Lanier case was the amendment in Seychelles of the law relating to the guardianship of minors, and family councils. In future the Chief Justice could not chair family councils, and stricter controls were placed on the way a guardian invested the funds of a minor.

CHAPTER FIFTEEN

This chapter is based almost wholly on the War Files at the Seychelles National Archives. C/SS/7 Vols I and II deal with the East Africa campaign; C/W/1 to C/W/5 cover the war as it affected life in Seychelles; and C/SS/8 concerns the Imperial War Graves Commission. Additional material is found in PRO CO 530/26.

1   It was not until July 1915 that the *Königsberg* was located by the British and put permanently out of action. The Germans, however, managed to salvage the cruiser's 14.1in. guns, which were subsequently used in the East African campaign.

2   Like the French commandant Quéau de Quinssy, who surrendered to a British naval squadron in 1794, O'Brien realised that Seychelles had no effective defence. 'With a picked force ... I would guarantee to land anywhere and take over the whole of Seychelles in a week,' he wrote. — O'Brien to Sir George Fiddes, 20 April 1913 (PRO CO 530/21).

3   The only Germans the Seychelles defence forces had to contend with were four seamen taken off a Norwegian sailing ship. Two were reservists, the others of service age. They were given parole, but this was revoked after one was cited by 'a respectable Seychellois' as co-respondent in a divorce suit. After four months the prisoners, under armed escort, were put aboard a BI liner for Bombay.

4   The Governor informed the Secretary of State on 8 December 1916 that normally about four to five hundred men worked on the outlying islands. Most had now been discharged because of the war, and many were unable to find work on Mahé because 'the local planters find them unsatisfactory'. He added: 'I think that the departure of these men will be an excellent thing for the country. There should now be enough work for those who remain ... Further, those who go will probably learn some much needed lessons of discipline and industry.' — quoted by A.W.T. Webb, *The Story of Seychelles* (Government Printing Office, Victoria, 1966).

5   Lieut.-General Jan Smuts was appointed to the command of the Allied forces in East Africa in February 1916. His request for labourers from Seychelles was cabled to the Governor on 29 October, a month after the capture of Dar es Salaam, capital of German East Africa. With the British and South African troops pushing ahead rapidly against the retreating Germans, problems of supply had become acute. The German commander, Col. Paul von Lettow-Vorbeck, a master of guerrilla warfare, conducted a brilliant mobile defence which lasted until the end of the war.

6   Beri-beri is caused by a lack of Vitamin B1. It is usually found in communities where highly polished rice constitutes the staple diet. Symptoms are weakness of the muscles, paralysis, oedema — swelling of the limbs — and palpitations. Death results

from cardiac failure.

7   The flogging threat was to surface again at the start of World War II, when 'malicious rumours' began circulating among volunteers for service with the Seychelles Pioneers that coloured soldiers in the British army could be flogged.

8   Dr Joseph Bartlett Addison, OBE. Trained at St Mary's Hospital, London; assistant medical officer, Seychelles, 1907; Chief Medical Officer, 1908; acting private secretary and Clerk to Executive Council, 1912; Principal Civilian Medical Officer, Hong Kong, 1924.

9   Bacillary dysentery had been introduced into Seychelles by some of those who had returned from East Africa earlier. All the affected families were isolated and their clothing, huts, and beds were burned. Few of those infected survived (SNA C/W/7 Vol. II).

10   Miss Margaret Halkett, b. 1863, Banff, Scotland. Appointed nursing sister at Seychelles' recently opened maternity home in 1911. She had previously worked at the Seamen's Hospital at Greenwich, and in Johannesburg. During the South African war she was posted to one of the 'concentration camps' set up by the British to prevent Boer families assisting their menfolk.

11   *Ankylostomiasis,* a parasitic infestation, also known as hookworm. Embryos gain access through skin, usually feet, and inhabit upper part of small intestine, where worms cause anaemia, debility, and cardiac weakness, sometimes leading to death. A medical report of 1912 had reported that hookworm was widespread in Seychelles, although successful measures had been taken to curb the disease.

12   According to Bradley, 'the pinch of the war' was felt most by the small proprietor, with about twenty acres of land. 'His daughters require to be well dressed; as they are more or less white they will not work, and as clothes, boots, hats, parasols, scents, powders, and soaps have gone up in price at least 100 per cent., he finds it hard to keep up that outward appearance of respectability on which they pride themselves.' – Bradley's annual report, 1917.

13   Fiennes apparently anticipated trouble, for he asked that the machine-gun be serviceable, with ammunition, in case it was required 'in the event of an outbreak of local disturbances'. He also sent to London, under separate cover, plans for countering any uprising.

14   Few war trophies remain. The Wilhelmstal bell is stored at the National Archives, also one of the machine-guns. Both trench mortars once stood in front of the Supreme Court building, on either side of the Queen Victoria jubilee fountain. An official of the National Archives told the author in October 1998 that the mortars were removed in the early sixties to a yard at the Union Vale prison. One is stored at La Bastille; the whereabouts of the other is unknown.

INDEX

favoured by whaleships, 122; Sultan's complaint to US, 122-3; and white women slaves, 127.

App, Auguste: friend of Allen children, 126.

Apprenticeship, 24, 37, 38; flogging and other punishments, 39, 40; end of apprenticeship, 41; work abandoned, 42; freeing of praedial apprentices, 48; new population, 70.

Arab slave ships, 19, 85, 86, 87, 90, 132; evading British cruisers, 90, 91; use of French flag, 91; condition of slaves, 112-13.

Ashanti war and deportations, 188-90.

Atwater, Derence, US consul, 106, 108, 120, 122, 126; visits Anjouan, 122; leaves Seychelles, 125.

Australia, 162, 165, 172; inaugural MM voyage, 166.

Avalasse: *See under* Cyclone.

Azores (Western Isles), 25, 31, 45.

bacca, 182-3.

Banks, Langrishe, Anglican preacher, 51.

Barallon, Arthur: loses family in avalanche, 102.

Barkly, Arthur, Chief Civil Commissioner, 138, 144, 145, 174, 184, 187; and coco de mer, 156, 157; warns that Mahé is defenceless, 160; and lighthouse on Denis island, 166; and smallpox epidemic, 166-9; leaves Seychelles, 171; biog., 221.

Barkly, Fanny, wife of above: comments on Venn's Town, 138; and on ex-Sultan Abdullah of Perak, 150; account of smallpox epidemic, 169-70.

Barkly, Sir Henry, governor of Mauritius, 92, 93; leaves Mauritius, 95.

Barrow, George, Treasurer, 142.

Baty, Sébert, PWD superintendent, 188.

Belcher, Capt. Sir Edward, RN, 42, biog., 221.

Bell, Capt. Alexander: accused of manslaughter, 79, 80.

Bénézet, Antoine, biog., 221.

beri-beri, 216, 218.

Bergne, Harold, proprietor, 188.

Best, Emma Wardlaw: and refuge for dogs, 203.

Beyts, H., protector of immigrants at Mauritus, 87; opposes sending liberated slaves to Seychelles, 88.

bigarades (wild oranges), 108.

Bird island, 17, 121, mail collected at, 126; and guano deposits, 182; and whaling ground, 204, 205; lighthouse proposal, 167-9.

Blunt, Captain Francis, Chief Civil Commissioner, 143; biog., 222.

Board of Civil Commissioners (BCC), 117, 135, 140, 143, 156, 166; criticised by Chancellor, 133; feud between members, 142; petition for greater powers, 142; and call for abolition, 144; dissolved, 173; petition to administer more islands, 176.

Board of Health, 172.

Boer War, 187, 211.

Bombay, 71, 77, 79, 92, 160, 182, 215; asylum for liberated slaves, 86.

Bonnetard, inhabitant, 110; coir factory agent, 182.

Bonnier, manager at Pointe Marianne, Diego Garcia, 128, 129.

bons, system of payment, 183, 208.

Botanical station: suggested by Griffith, 180; established in Victoria, 180; 198.

Boteler, Lieut., RN, 11, 12.

Bougainville, French navigator, 179.

Bourbon island, 2, 4, 5, 14, 15, 17, 18, 40, 45, 59; immigration from India, 58; name Réunion restored, 61.

Bouquié, D.: smallpox source victim, 167, 168.

Bowen, Sir George, governor of Mauritius, 142, 143.

Bradley, Dr John, medical officer: his opinion of Prempeh, 191; comment on Seychelles lifestyle, 198; not in favour of too much schooling, 200; 201; on inhabitants' reaction to outbreak of war, 209, 210, biog., 222.

Braley, Samuel, whaling captain, 34, 35, 36.

breadfruit tree, 155.

Bristol, Napoléon, NCO in Carrier Corps, 212.

British India Steam Navigation Company (BI), 161, 204; service compares unfavourably with MM, 164; and planters' complaints, 165; 'hotbeds of disease', 172; resumes calling, 204.

British troops, 1, 2, 5, 41, 46, 48, 53, 78; regiments: 22nd, 3; 29th, 23; 35th, 41; 82nd, 1, 12; 99th, 12, 23.

Brodie, James, Inspector of Schools, 141, 145.

Brooke, Arthur, police magistrate: suicide, 208.

Brooks, Dr James, medical officer, 101, 110; and Mrs Brooks, 120, 126; resigns, 142; brought out of retirement, 168; and smallpox epidemic, 168, 170.

Brothers of Christian Schools, 105, 139.

Brown, Robert, District Judge, 174-5, 183, 185, biog., 222.

Bruce, Sir Charles, governor of Mauritius, 195, 196, biog., 222.

Brunton, R.P, police chief, 99, 101.

Butler, immigrant, 198.

Button, Charles, conservator of forests, 154, 157.

Buxton, Thomas Fowell, abolitionist, 20.

cable: laying of submarine cable, 160; and French proposals, 161; links broken, 210.

Cable & Wireless, formerly Eastern and South African Telegraph Company, 161.

Caltaux, Hippolyte: and lease of Glorieuses, 177.

301

Campbell, Charles, magistrate, 56; inflammatory remarks and dismissal, 75; inquiry into behaviour, 76.

Campbell, Mrs, widow of Scots seaman, Praslin, 156, 157, 158.

Cape of Good Hope: place for landing liberated slaves, 85; and cable link, 160.

Cape Verde islands, 31, 45.

Capuchins: priests excite interest in Mauritius, 71; confused with Jesuits, 90.

Carnegie library, 202, 211, 220.

cemetery, 49, 70; partially obliterated by avalanche, 99; bones dug up by dogs, 109; new cemetery at Mont Fleuri, 117, 193; Carrier Corps graves, 218.

Cerf island, 134; damage by cyclone, 102; proposed site for guns, 159.

Ceylon, 77, 95-6.

Chagos archipelago, 128.

Chamberlain, Joseph, Secretary of State, 187, 188, 191, 199.

Chancellor, Rev. William, of CMS, 116, 132-42 *passim*; views on healthy living, 134; briefs Governor on industrial school, 135; and move to Capucins, 135; drawings published, 136; as Civil Chaplain, 137; criticised by Inspector of Africans, 138; returns to England, 146.

Chancellor, Mrs Katie, 132, 137, 139; character, 146.

Chastellier, Dr Evenor: and smallpox epidemic, 169.

Chauvin, Jean-François, of Exil estate, 110.

Cheyron, Félix, French consular agent, 140, 165.

Chief Civil Commissioner: *See under* Seychelles administration.

Chinese: visited by General Gordon, 156.

Church, Captain, of whaler *Diamantina*, 131.

Church Missionary Society (CMS), 114, 115, 116, 180, 184, 192, 193; statement on Venn's Town, 147.

Civil Commissioner: *See under* Seychelles: administration.

Clark, Bishop of Port-Victoria, 201, biog., 222.

Clarkes, Mr and Mrs G.: and Mico Charity school, 52.

Clément, Lorenzo, special justice, 48.

Clocktower, unveiling, 197.

cloves, 3, 57, 108, 180, 198; crop abandoned, 170.

coal: high price at Seychelles, 165.

Cockburn, Rear-Adml James: assassinated on Andaman islands, 113

Coco de mer palm and nut, 8, 43, 44, 108, 155; articles made from, 153; conservation measures, 154, 158 shape of nut fascinates General Gordon, 155; purchase of forest at Praslin, 156-8.

cocoa, 57, 180.

coconuts, 44, 57, 182, 203; thousands of trees lost in cyclone, 102, 103; widespread blight, 144, 176; exports to India, 165; growing well in Amirantes, 180; falling export earnings, 181.

coconut oil, 3, 43, 106, 180, 198; cyclone's effect on production, 103; fall in price, 144; export earnings, 176, 181.

coffee, 3, 57, 108, 180, 198; leaf disease, 170.

coir factory, 182.

Cole, Sir Lowry, governor of Mauritius, 19.

Colebrook, Maj. William, Eastern Enquiry commissioner, 8, 10, 20, biog., 223.

Collier, apostolic vicar, Mauritius, 61; Bishop of Port Louis, 67, 68, 72.

Colonial Office, 8, 75, 111, 115, 141-5 *passim*, 151, 157, 159, 173, 176, 177, 197, 202, 207, 208.

Colville, Sir Charles, governor of Mauritius, 20, 50.

Commission of Eastern Enquiry, 7, 8, 20, 31.

Commissioners of Compensation, 32, 38.

Comoro islands, 29, 86, 128; as source of slaves, 5, as source of labour, 58, 61,

Constitutional advances, 173-6; creation of Crown colony, 195.

Convent: crushed by avalanche, 100; death toll, 101; loss to Sisters, 104-5; new convent completed, 105; orphanage a drain on funds, 140; grant-in-aid reduced, 141; school praised, 143. *See also* Sisters of St Joseph de Cluny.

copra, 198, 203, 211; basis of Seychelles prosperity, 96-7; production increase, 106; export earnings, 176.

Cosgrow, Cpl Charles, Seychelles Carrier Corps, 215, 216.

cotton, 3, 17, 97.

Court House, 197.

Creole language, 112, 133, 140, 146, 199; composite language forecast, 198.

Creoles, 56, 135, 183; cruel and uncaring masters, 88; 89.

Crimea War, 92, 154.

Cross, Latham, whaling captain, 25, 32, 33.

Crozet islands, 204.

Curieuse island, 110, 157, 180; leper camp closure proposed, 76; visited by Governor Gordon, 108; and location for tortoises, 180, proposed site for Boer prisoners, 188.

Curandeau, Elie, French schooner captain: and fishing incident, 93, 94.

cyclone, 98, 99; eighty people die, 101; characteristics of cyclone 103, 104.

Dacre, Adml James, C-in-C, Cape, 60, biog., 223.

Dar es Salaam, 215.

D'Arros island, 5, 48.

Darwin, Charles, naturalist, 179, 180, 202.

Davidson, Walter, Governor, 198, 200-204; and Mrs Davidson, 203; biog., 223.

death penalty, 11, 176.

Delafontaine, Rev. F. George, Civil Chaplain, 36, 52, 53, 54, 66, 73; acquires British nationality, 70-1; leaving, 70; biog., 223.

Delapeyre, District Judge: sent back to Mauritius, 142.

Delaunay, French commandant, 15.

Deltel, Louis: seeks lease of islands from French authorities, 177.

Deltel Brothers & Co., 189.

d'Emmerez de Charmoy, Adolphe, businessman, 206.

Denis island, 17, 124, 181, 205; and lighthouse, 165, 166; repaired and rebuilt with metal tripod, 167.

Denman, Dr Robert, medical officer, 188.

d'Epinay, Adrien, Mauritius settler, 23.

Desaubins, Louis, NCO in Seychelles Carrier Corps, 212.

Des Avanchers, Léon, Capuchin priest, 62-9, 71-4, 84; arrives at Mahé, 64; claims French nationality, 65; and 'spiritual revolution', 66, leaves Mahé, 67; enthusiastic following in Mauritius, 68; appeal to Queen Victoria, 68; brief return to Mahé, 69; imprisoned in Abyssinia, 69; arrives in Seychelles from India, 71; carries out 1,300 baptisms, 72; accused of burning Bibles and marriage ceremony irregularity, 73; leaves for last time, 73; rejoins Bishop Massaïa in Ethiopia, 74; doubtful about Louis Poiret's claim to be Louis XVII, 80; biog., 224.

De Romainville, Lieut., French commandant, 99.

Desmarais, Henri, District Judge, 143.

Desprez, Bishop of St Denis, 73.

Deutsche Öst-Afrika Linie, 204.

Devereux, Lieut. William, RN, 88.

Dick, George, colonial secretary, Mauritius, 37, 57, 58.

Diego Garcia, 21, 35, 43, 122; and Seychellois workers, 128; coaling station proposed, 159.

Diego Suarez, 161, 172.

Dingwall, immigrant, 198.

dogs: howling annoys Gordon, 109; and Miss Best, 203.

Dowland, James, asst. registrar of slaves, 20, 21.

Drouin, Albert, French consul at Mauritius, 161.

Drummond, Rear-Adml Edmund Charles, 184.

Dudgeon, Major R., acting Civil Commissioner, 88.

Dumont-d'Urville, Capt. Jules Sébastien, 14, biog., 224.

Dunn, whaling captain, 32, 33.

d'Unienville, Vossary, NCO in Seychelles Carrier Corps, 212.

Dupont, Paul Rivalz, biog., 224.

Dupuy, Charles, Unofficial member, BCC, 117.

Dupuy, Eugène, magistrate, 94; acting Civil Commissioner, 102; and action taken after cyclone, 102, 103.

Dupuy, shopkeeper, 110.

Edward VII, 191, 195.

Edwards, Mrs Ada: criticisms of Administrator and District Judge, 174-5; views on Africans, 183.

East Africa, 19, 88, 89, 91, 112, 161, 216-220 *passim*; landing of liberated slaves, 86.

East India Company, 79.

Edesse, Marie, mistress of Louis Poiret, 81.

Education, 143, 144, 184; Board of Education formed, 117, 140; grants-in-aid, 140, 141-2; Inspector of Schools, 140, 141; attitude of white parents, 141; English proposed language of instruction at Government School, 145; Sweet-Escott's interest in, 199; scholarships, 199, 200; number of schools and pupils, 201; government intervention 'a mistake', 201.

Elephant dance, 109.

Elliott, clerk, 21.

Emancipation Act, 23, 37.

Empire Day, 211.

Établissement (Victoria), 2, 47.

Ethiopia (Abyssinia), 63, 69, 89.

English language: teaching at Venn's Town, 139; rejected as compulsory medium of instruction, 139; language proposed for Government School, 143-5; and promoted in schools, 199; and Creole, 200.

Estridge, Henry, Collector of Taxes: describes effect of Krakatoa volcano, 170.

Equator Hotel, 162.

Europa island, 177.

Falklands, 204.

Fallet, Dr Auguste, civil chaplain, 73.

Farquhar, Sir Robert, governor of Mauritius, 5, 18, 19, biog., 224.

Farquhar atoll (Jean de Nove), 79, 93, 176, 196; cyclone prone, 104.

Fauvel, Albert-Auguste: and history of Seychelles, 202, biog., 225.

Félicité island, 72; used as residence for Malay deportees, 148; proposed for Boer prisoners, 187-8.

Fiennes, Sir Eustace T.-W., Governor, 219, biog., 225.

fireworks, first display in Seychelles, 184.

Forbes, George, leper camp superintendent, 44, 110.

Ford, Dr, acting Civil Commissioner, 56.

Foulepoint, 18.

France: views on slave trade, 19; and Seychelles planters' petition, 23; abolition of slavery, 40, 60-1; ambitions in Indian Ocean, 59; policy on Zanzibar, 92; blocks Zanzibar designs on Comoro islands, 95; war with Prussia, 95; relies less on foreign shipping, 96; influence in Seychelles noted, 140; seizes Tamatave, 160; considered most likely enemy by Britain,

160; steamship services, 106, 161; suspected of opening British mail, 161; and Denis island lighthouse, 167, discussions with Britain on status of smaller Indian Ocean islands, 177, 178; annexes the Glorieuses, 177.

Franklyn, William, Civil Commissioner, 107, 110, 112, 116; as Chief Civil Commissioner, 117, 118, 125, 126; dies, 115; and Mrs Franklyn, 120, 126; and lighthouse, 165; biog., 225.

free labourers, or *engagés,* 91.

Freemasons, 110.

French governor's house, 108.

French language: necessary for preachers, 51; spoken by English families, 53; use in court, 75; not taught at Venn's Town, 139; use in schools, 199; and Creole, 200.

French navy, 59; voyages of discovery, 14; attack on Tamatave, 18; warships call at Seychelles, 87, 106.

French settlers, 1, 2, attend Anglican services, 51.

Frere Town, Mombasa, 115.

Fressanges, Guillaume, *juge de paix,* 33, 55, 56, 75.

Frey, General Henri: and removal of stone of possession, 162, 163; biog., 226.

Frichot, James, NCO in Seychelles Carrier Corps, 212.

Galla tribe, 63, 89.

Garden of Eden, 153, 155, 159.

Gardiner, J. Stanley, naturalist, 202.

Gardner, Capt Alan, RN, 98, 102, 104.

Gébert, proprietor of Farquhar atoll, 93, 94.

Gendron: house leased for Uganda deportees, 192.

George V, 189.

Glorieuses (Glorioso islands), 177; annexed by France, 177.

Gomm, Sir William, governor of Mauritius, 60, biog. 226.

Gordon, Sir Arthur, governor of Mauritius, 105, 112, 116, 118, 144; second visit to Seychelles, 106, 107, 110; inspects leper colony, 108, 110, 111; visits Sainte Anne, La Digue, Cousin, and Frégate islands, 108-9; views coco de mer valley, Praslin, 108; on howling dogs, 109; character, 109; watches 'elephant dance', 109; opinion on settlers and Franklyn's family, 109-10; forced to retire as governor, 116; proposes constitutional changes for Seychelles, 116-7; lists qualities for Seychelles administrators, 118; mediates in Seychelles dispute with whalers, 125; biog. 226.

Gordon, Lieut.-Colonel (later General) Charles, 144, 167, 193, 202; theory on coco de mer and Garden of Eden, 153, 155; career, 154; sends coco de mer specimens to London, 155; and sketch for Seychelles coat of arms, 156; death at Khartoum, 156; refines Garden of Eden theory in Palestine, 159; defence proposals for Seychelles rejected, 159; supports Seychelles separation from Mauritius, 160; design for Seychelles flag, 176; biog. 226.

Gordon, Miss Augusta, 155.

Gordon Square, 184, 219, 220.

Government House, 2, 50, 99, 101, 102, 126, 162, 175, 210, 219; and Admiral's Wing, 107, and celebration of Queen's Birthday, 120; and smallpox epidemic, 169; Diamond Jubilee dinner, 184; poor state of repair, 185-6; and Prempeh, 190; construction of new Government House, 202.

Government School: public support for, 145; Roman Catholic opposition, 145-6; opens, 146.

Grande Comore, 121.

Grandjean, Rev. John, Civil Chaplain, 141, 142.

Great Britain: doubts loyalty of Mauritius, 94; tension with France, 94; regards France and Russia as most likely enemies, 160.

Great Chagos Bank, 34.

Green, immigrant, 198.

Grenier, Jacques, French mariner, 13, 18.

Grey, Earl, Secretary of State: agrees to replacement for Des Avanchers, 68; advocates more self-rule for Seychelles, 117.

Griffith, Thomas Risely, Administrator, 165, 175, 176, 180; and ex-Sultan Abdullah of Perak, 150; sends coco de mer specimens to Kew, 157; purchase of coco de mer forests, 158; and opening of cable link, 161; and stone of possession, 162, 163; and measles outbreak, 171, shows the flag on Aldabra, 178; and giant tortoises, 179, 180; biog., 227.

Griffiths, George Hollier, acting Chief Civil Commissioner, 171; and petition, 174; biog., 227.

Griffiths, William Hollier, magistrate and acting Civil Commissioner, 60, 79, biog., 227.

guano, 182, 198, 203, 211.

Guérard, Paul-Louis, soap factory proprietor, 182.

Gumy, Father Justin de, 201; biog., 227.

gunboats, purchase proposed, 187.

Gurney, Russell, abolitionist, chairs inquiry into slave trade, 90.

Halkett, Miss M., hospital matron, 216.

Hamerton Treaty, 90.

Harrison, George, Government Agent, 2-55 *passim*, 78, 154; as slave-owner, 7; and Mrs Harrison, 16; quits Seychelles, 46.

Havelock, Capt. Arthur, acting Chief Civil Commissioner: inquiry into wages of child apprentices, 115; return to Mahé as Chief Civil Commissioner, 142; biog., 227.

Hazard, James, whaling captain, 122-5.

Heaton, J. Henniker, MP: supports cause of ex-Sultan Abdullah of Perak, 150, 151; biog., 228.

307

Henricksen, Harald, whaling captain, 205.
Herchenroder, Alfred, Chief Justice, 195, biog., 228.
Higginson, governor of Mauritius, 67, 68, 75-7, 110; backs Keate over Des Avanchers, 67; visit to Seychelles, 76; biog., 228.
Hoareau, Alphonse, NCO in Seychelles Carrier Corps, 212.
Hoareau, Rodolphe, Seychelles Carrier Corps volunteer, 218.
Hodoul, François, Unofficial member, BCC, 117, 145; and coco de mer, 156, 157; biog., 229.
Hodoul, Jean-François: praised for navigational skill, 15; biog., 229.
Hodoul, plantation deputy manager, Diego Garcia, 128, 129.
Holman, James, 2-12 *passim*, 27; views on slavery, 7.
Honey, Sir Montagu George de Symons, Governor, 220.
Hooker, Professor Sir Joseph: interest in coco de mer, 154, 155.
hookworm, 218.
Horne, John, botanist, biog., 229.
hospital, 24, 117, 216, 217.
Hossen, Mamode, 206.
Hudrisier, Bishop, 145-6; of Port-Victoria, 200; dies, 201; biog., 230.
Hugueteau de Chaillé, French naval officer, inquiry into Curandeau affair, 93; conversation with Ward, 94.
Humfrey, Lieut. Christopher, 29th Foot, 23.
Huteau, settler, 39.

Ignatius Galfione, Capuchin priest, 82, 83; apostolic vice-prefect, 105; apostolic vicar, 140; biog., 230.
Île de France (Mauritius), 1, 14.
Immaculate Conception, Church of, 67; first stone laid, 72; Sisters buried in church, 101; rebuilding, 105; Cathedral, 202.
Income tax: removed, 203.
India, 203; recruitment of labour by French planters, 40, 91; Seychelles tries to recruit labour, 43, 56, 57; and coco de mer nuts, 153; and BI steamship service, 164, 165; Seychelles attempts to recruit Indians from Mauritius, 182; Indian shopkeepers, 198; labour from Madras, 203.
Indian Ocean: Anglo-French rivalry, 91; uncertain status of islands, 93; French monopoly of shipping services, 96, 161; and American whaling, 119-130 *passim*.
influenza, 171,
Inhabitants: extravagant lifestyle, 198; 80 pc illiterate, 200; loyalty to Britain doubted, 200.

Jacobin deportees, 52, 81.
Jardin du Roi, 108.
Jehenne, Capt. Aimable-Constant, 15, biog., 230.

Jeremiah di Paglietta, Capuchin priest, 71; surprised to see Des Avanchers, 72; accuses Des Avanchers, 73; buried by avalanche, and rescued, 100; transferred to Chile, 101, 105; and plans for new convent, 105; biog., 230.

Jeremie, John, *procureur-général*, Mauritius, 22.

Jérémie, Father: and Seychelles Carrier Corps, 213.

Jewell, Dr N.P., Praslin medical officer, 211; and service in East Africa, 216.

Jivan Jetha, merchant, 182.

Johanna, see Anjouan.

Johnston, Sir Harry, British commissioner, Uganda, 192.

Joint stock company, 77-8.

Jouanis, Charles, auctioneer, 80.

Jouanis, Noël, Unofficial member, BCC, 146.

Jouanis family, 100, 102.

Kabarega, ex-King of Bunyoro, deportee, 191, 192; as guerrilla leader, 193; dies on way home, 193.

Keate, Robert, Civil Commissioner, 52-77 *passim*, 109; refuses entry to Des Avanchers, 65; allows Catholics use of chapel, 69; views on drinking, 70; quits Seychelles, 70; biog., 231.

Kennedy, Rear-Adml Robert, C-in-C, Cape, 163, 178.

Kew Garden, 155; coco de mer palm on show, 157.

Kilwa, 90, 212, 214, 215.

Kimberley, Earl of, Secretary of State, 117, 153; envisages Seychelles as separate colony, 145.

King's (East) African Rifles, 192, 215.

King's College secondary school, 200; closes, 201.

Kiswahili (Swahili), 89, 111.

Krakatoa volcano: effect felt in Seychelles, 170-1.

Labiche, Cupidon: first death among Carrier Corps, 214.

Lablache, police chief, 66.

labour: shortage of, 49, 56, 182, 198; and continuous employment, 182; call for more Africans, 183.

La Digue, 44, 49, 72, 102, 148, 181, 211; Gordon finds island lively, 108; absence of roads, 185.

Lagrange, Emérentienne de: and book on Louis XVII, 83.

Lamu, 86, 90.

Lanier, Louis Édouard: trial and appeal to Privy Council, 205- 8.

Laplace, Capt. Cyril, 13, 14, 15; admires Seychelles women, 16; unsure of accuracy of charts, 17; views on slavery, 17, 24; biog., 231.

Laplace, French consul, Mauritius, 92, 93, 95.

Latham, Lieut. John, 1, 2, 3, 5, 12; as slave-owner, 9; biog., 231.

Laxamanna, Malay deportee, 148, 149.
Lefèvre, settler's widow, 48.
Leganne, Georges, slave-owner, 6.
Legislative Council: *See under* Seychelles: administration.
LeMarchand, Camille, settler, 109, 112; Unofficial member, BCC, 117; critic of CMS school, 135.
LeMarchand, Lieut. France, Seychelles Carrier Corps, 212, 214, 216; pension to widow, 220; biog., 231.
Lepers, 43-4; closure of camp proposed, 76; visited by Governor Gordon, 108, 110-11; each leper with own coffin, 111; proposed removal from Curieuse island, 188.
Lepper, Dr Robert: and smallpox epidemic, 167-9; given police protection, 170.
Leprosy, medical opinion on contagion, 111.
L'Impartial newspaper, 220.
Le Petit Seychellois newspaper, 193.
Le Réveil newspaper, 185.
Le Rocher: and camp for Ashanti deportees, 190.
Lesage, Lieut. Bibye, Government Agent, 3, biog., 231.
Leveilleux, Charles, Seychelles Carrier Corps volunteer, 218.
Liberated Africans, 146; places for landing, 85, 86; employed as apprentices, 88; Seychelles and Mauritius at first deemed unsuitable, 89; useful workers, 103; report on conditions, 111; temporary halt to landings, 112; not wanting in intelligence, 112; quarantined on Longue island, 113; daily routine on HM ships, 113; Britain's duty to provide for instruction, 115; H.M. Stanley expresses concern, 114; increased powers for Inspector, 115; petitioners request more, 117; treatment, 132; numbers landed drop, 133; conversing in Swahili, 134; planters fear their advancement, 135; said to be well treated, 183.
Liberation Day, 41, 48.
Lighthouse: Governor Gordon visits site on Sainte Anne, 108; proposal for lighthouse on Bird or Denis islands, 165; erected on Denis island, 166; and on Sainte Anne, 165-6; old lighthouse re-erected on Mamelles island, 167.
Linnæan Society, 154.
Liquor laws, 32.
Lislet Geoffroy, hydrographer, 14.
Livingstone, David, 113; found by Stanley, 114.
Livingstone, Oswald, 114.
Livingstone Cottage, 114.
Logan, Ewen, acting Governor, 212-19 *passim*, biog., 232.
Loizeau, Adolphe: and racial threat 74.
Loizeau, Babette, slave-owner, 10; jailed and fined for cruelty, 11.

Loizeau, Jean, son-in-law of Louis Poiret, 81.

Long Pier: *See under* Pier.

Longue island, quarantine station, 169, 171; prepared for returning volunteers, 216.

Louis XVII: *See under* Poiret, Louis.

Louis-Philippe, King of the French, 24.

Lubin, Charles, NCO in Seychelles Carrier Corps, 212.

Luckock, Edwin, superintendent, Venn's Town, 146, 147.

MacGregor, Dr William, medical superintendent of leper colony, 111; accuses planters, 112; as Inspector of Liberated Africans, 115; biog., 232.

Mackay, George, headmaster, Victoria School, 199, 201.

McLeod, D.W., Inspector of Schools, 202.

Madagascar, 5-33 *passim*, 88, 94, 161, 162, 177, 211; French attacks on, 17, 18, 160; as source of slaves, 19, 58; and of labour, 58, 61; reopened to Europeans, 92; and mission sent by Mauritius, 92; intervention by France, 95, British gains at Merina court, 95; virtual French protectorate, 160.

Madge, Edward, Government Agent, 3, 4, 81, 84; return to Mauritius, 6; as slave-owner, 6, 7; biog., 232.

Madras, 77, 87.

Mahé, 2, 3, 15, 17, 48, 63-86 *passim*, 105, 106, 108, 111, 119, 126, 164-181 *passim*, 204, 211, 213, 217; and only natural disaster, 97; comment by H.M. Stanley, 114; Governor Gordon's first visit, 116; island 'much improved', 119; calls by American whaleships, 130; too costly to fortify, 159; and smallpox epidemic, 167-9.

Mahé Syndicate, 207.

maize, 3, 21, 42, 88.

Makarios, Archbishop of Cyprus, 147.

Malay deportees: *See under* Abdullah *and* Perak.

Mamin, settler, 48.

mangrove poles, 178.

Mantri of Larut, Malay deportee, 148, 149; allowed to reside in Sarawak, 150-1.

Marist Brothers, 145, 199.

Marseilles, 162, 166, 172, 191.

Masonic lodge, 72; at Mauritius, 96; visited by Pike, 110.

Massaïa, Bishop, 63, 68.

Mauritius, 1-56 *passim*, 73, 79, 102, 104, 106, 111, 114, 123, 143-210 *passim*, and sugar, 8, 9, 76, 182; and criminal justice, 11; planters' protest, 22, 23; recruitment of labour from India, 24, 40, 42; cost burden of Seychelles, 49; Mico charity schools, 52; population rise, 56; Anglo-French diplomatic incidents, 59-60; Capuchins excite interest, 71; 'irregularity and confusion', 75; investment in Seychelles, 77; climate believed unsuitable for

Napoleon III, 91, 95, 96.
Nageon, Étienne, schooner captain, 71.
Naz, Virgile, assistant *procureur-général*, 142.
New Oriental Bank, 176.
Newton, Rev. Ernest, Civil Chaplain, 206.
Nicolay, Sir Wm, governor of Mauritius, 32, 49, 59, biog., 233.
Nordoff, Charles, whaleman, 29.
North, Marianne, 131; visits Venn's Town, 138; biog., 233.
Nossi-Bé, 59.
Nouméa (New Caledonia), 162, 165, 166.

O'Brien, Lt.-Col Charles, Governor, 204-211 *passim*; visits Sainte Anne whaling station, 205; returns to Seychelles, 217; biog., 234.
Ohier, Pierre, resident of Glorieuses islands, 177.
Oldfield, Commander Radulphus, RN, 86, 87, 88, 91.
Oliaji, trader, 182.
Ormsby, John, asst. protector of slaves, 21, 22.
Owen, Capt. William, RN, 11, 15, 17; and protectorate at Mombasa, 85; biog., 234.

P & O steamship line, 77; withdraws service to Seychelles and Mauritius, 96.
Pallu de la Barrière: and coir factory, 182.
Palmerston, Lord, British Foreign Secretary and Prime Minister, 59, 60.
Paupers, proposed removal from Curieuse, 188.
Payet, Henri, French resident of Seychelles, 178; seeks lease of Aldabra and Cosmoledo, 178.
Pelly, Col. Lewis, consul-general at Zanzibar, 98, 99; and cyclone, 102, 104; biog., 234.
pepper, 198.
Perak (Malaya): British wage war, 149; Resident James Birch, murdered, 149; Seychelles song popular, 152.
Petit Jean, former slave, 44.
Pétrousse, Pierre Auguste, son-in-law of Louis Poiret, 81.
Phayre, Sir Arthur, governor of Mauritius: visit to Seychelles, 135; biog., 235.
Pickwood, Robert, superintendent, Venn's Town, 137, 138, 158; ordained as Anglican priest, 146.
Pier: proposed, 77; construction begins, 107.
Pierce, whaling captain, 123-5; and Mrs Pierce and son, 127.
Pierre de Possession: removal of, 162.
pigs: forbidden in Victoria, 186.
Pike, Dr M.W., Surgeon-General, 217, 218.

313

Rassool, Abdul, trader and island owner, 181, 206.

Reform Bill, 23.

Réunion, 1, 4, 61, 91, 160, 161, 162; name restored, 61; concern for defences, 95; shipping link with Suez, 96; and epidemics, 167.

Rex v. Lanier appeal, 205.

rice: imports from India, 165.

Ricketts, Dashwood, acting Civil Commissioner, 75.

Rigby, Col. C.P., consul at Zanzibar, 91; suggested Seychelles as place for landing slaves, 86; gives evidence to inquiry on slave trade, 90.

Ripon, Lord, Secretary of State, 151, 173, 175.

roads: 70, 106, 108, 117; promise of, 76; incentive to build after cyclone, 103; new pathways proposed, 143, Forêt Noire road under construction, 180; 'deplorable state' of roads, 185; engineers sent from Ceylon, 186, 187.

Robertson, Dr Patrick, leper colony medical officer, 44.

Rochon, Abbé, 18.

Rodrigues, 21, 172.

Roman Catholic Church, 52, 61, 64, 84, 133, 183, 184; in Mauritius, 52; and government attitude to priests, 67, 68; decision on Seychelles, 68; Catholics ask for protection, 69; Seychelles mission inaugurated, 71; twelve wooden churches built, 72; plans for construction of convent, 73; relations with government over education, 141-2; cathedral, 184; priests' influence on education, 201-2.

Ross, Cadet Edward, 79, 80.

Royal College, Mauritius, 196, 199.

Royal Geographical Society, 113.

Royal Navy, anti-slaving patrols, 90, 91; warships call at Port Victoria, 106.

Royston, Anglican Bishop of Mauritius, 115, 116, 139, 141; visit to Praslin with wife and daughter, 146.

rubber, 198.

Russell, Lord John, British Secretary of State, 50.

Russia: seen by Britain as most likely enemy, 160.

Ryan, Anglican Bishop of Mauritius, 73; and avalanche, 100.

Sacred Congregation for the Propagation of the Faith, 68, 69, 73, 74.

St Abbs Whaling Company, 205; liquidation, 205.

Sainte Anne island, 2, 8, 15, 16, 17, 108; plantations destroyed in cyclone, 102, and General Gordon's defence proposals, 159; and lighthouse, 165; and whaling station, 205.

Saint Brandon (Cargados Carajos), 21.

St Jorre, settler, 10.

St Louis College, 105, 139, 141; Marist Brothers take charge, 145; 199, 200, 201.

St Louis, Victoria, 99, 104, 159.

Sainte Marie island, Madagascar, 18, 93, 161.

St Paul's, Anglican church, 53, 73, 133, 184, 191; slightly damaged in cyclone, 101.

Salmon, Charles, Chief Civil Commissioner, 132, 154, 182; 'not discreet enough', 142; transferred, 142; and ex-Sultan Abdullah of Perak, 148; and opposition to payment by *bons*, 183; biog., 235.

salted fish, 181.

Savings Bank, 176.

Savoy, Province of: assumes direction of Seychelles apostolic prefecture, 105.

Savy family, 24, 108.

Savy, Amédée, police chief, 33.

Savy, Charles Dorothée, 8, 16, 31, 32, 58; biog., 235.

Savy, François, 78.

Savy, Napoléon, lawyer, 58, 78.

Schmoderer, Father Joseph, Capuchin priest: and claim regarding death of Louis Poiret, 82-4.

Schultess, Jean, hotel proprietor, 162.

Seychelles: discovery, 2; town, 2; value of exports, 3; settlers, 2, 4, 55, 57; as slave transit point, 5; and sugar growing, 9; people, 16, 31; animals, 17, 57, 63; planters leave, 24; liberation celebrated, 41; settlers try to recruit from India, 43; poverty, 54; crops, 57; arrival of Des Avanchers, 63; problem of stray dogs, 69; drunkenness, 70; improving lifestyle, 70; RC mission inaugurated, 71; racial tensions, 74-5, 78; Indian immigration ruled out, also labour from Africa, 76; landing of liberated Africans, 84, 85, 86, 88; Indian immigration considered, 87; planters eager to take liberated slaves, 87, coaling station proposed, 89; alternative to Zanzibar, 90; and French influence, 94; importance of regular shipping link, 96; opening of post office, 96; lies outside cyclonic belt, 104; recovers quickly from cyclone, 106; scorpions and spiders, 109; reference to 'Sea Shell', 123; deteriorating relations with whalers, 125; whaler *Diamantina*, of Mahé, fitted out, 131; US consul's post abolished, 131; shortage of skilled workmen, 139; as place of deportation, 147; Gordon's survey of defences, 154; opening of cable link with Zanzibar and Mauritius, 161; fear of war with France and raising of defence force suggested, 163; and smallpox epidemic, 167-9; effect of Krakatoa volcano, 170-1, measles and influenza outbreaks, 171-2; quarantine regulations, 172, Rupee as currency, 176; coat of arms, 179; Norwegians at Sainte Anne whaling station, 205; taxation, 203; Seychelles Club, 206.

Seychelles administration: powers of Civil Commissioner, 48; British criticised, 55, 175; municipal board suggested, 70; proposals for greater autonomy, 116, 117; post of Chief Civil Commissioner created, 117; judiciary, 117, 174, 175, 176; qualities needed to administer, 118; financially free of Mauritius, 140; constitutional advances proposed, 142; petition to return to total Mauritius rule, 144; Legislative Council, 158, 175, 184, 189; post of Administrator created, 173; petition on elective principles and other matters, 173-6; Executive Council, 173, 174, 199; elected representatives ruled out, 173-4; Administrator's salary, 175; Crown colony, 195, 196, 197. *See also* Board of Civil Commissioners.

Seychelles islands:
Inner islands: Anonyme 102; Cousin, 108; Frégate, 17, 102, 108; Silhouette, 42, 49, 87, 102; Mamelles island, 167; Marianne, 17, 42; Moyenne, 203; Ronde, or Round Island (Praslin), 43, 188; South-East Island, 134. *See separate entries for* Bird island, Cerf, Curieuse, Denis, Félicité, La Digue, Longue island, Mahé, Praslin, Sainte Anne.

Outer islands: African Banks, 181; Alphonse, 20, 21, group in administrative limbo, 177; Assumption, 126, 176, 177, 178; Astove, 176, 177, 178, treasure trove, 202; Bijoutier, 177; Boudeuse, 181; Coëtivy, 15, 21, 104; Cosmoledo, 94, 126, 176, 177, 178; D'Arros, 5, 181; Desnoeufs, 181; Desroches, 20, 21, 181, slave revolt, 23; Étoile, 181; Marie Louise, 48, 181; Platte, 15; Poivre, 20, 21, 81, 181; Providence, 15, 21, 176, 181; Rémire, 181; St François, 177; St Joseph, 48; St Pierre, 15, 176. *See separate entries for* Aldabra, Amirantes, Farquhar atoll.

Place names: Anse Boileau, 72, 102; Anse Consolation (Praslin), 146; Anse Marie Louise (Praslin), 146, 156, 158, 188; Anse à la Mouche, 138; Anse aux Pins, 72, 102; Anse Royale, 72, 102, 191, 210; Anse Souillac, 81; Baie Lazare, 102, 109, 185; Baie Ste Anne (Praslin), 191; Bazaar Street (Victoria), 101; Beau Vallon, 9, 102, 104; Bel Air, 99, 203; Bel Ombre, 102, 147, 210; Benezet Street (Victoria), 101; Cap Ternay, 81; Capucins, 135, 180; Cascade, 108; Fond Ferdinand (Praslin), 156, 158; Forêt Noire, 135, 180, 185; Grand' Anse (Praslin), 146; La Misère, 190; La Rosière, 52, 71; Le Rocher, 189; Mare aux Cochons, 186; Mont Fleuri, 193, 217; North-East Point, 102; Petit Paris, 102; Plaisance, 102; Pointe Capucin, 102; Pointe Conan, 192; Pointe Larue, 134; Pointe au Sel, 134, 137; Port Glaud, 81, 138; Royal Street (Victoria), 99, 101; Union Vale, 148; Vallée de Mai, 159.

Seychelles Carrier Corps: first contingent sails for East Africa, 212; death toll, 215; second contingent leaves Mahé, 215; decision to repatriate, 216; inquiry into conditions in East Africa, 217; government justifies sending volunteers, 218; graves at Mont Fleuri cemetery, 218; complaints at treatment by government, 220. *See also* World War I.

Ships: *Afrika*, 113, 114; *Alexandra,* government steam launch, 187; *Barunga,* hospital ship, 216; *Berwick Castle,* 212, 213, 214; *Brisk,* 168; *Britannia,* cable ship, 161; *Cotherstone,* 147; *Courrier des Seychelles,* 6; *Espoir,* 93; *Guildford Castle,* hospital ship, 216; *Hope,* CMS boat, 134, 146; *Humble Bee,* captured dhow, 88; *Jeune Laure,* 6; *Joséphine Loizeau,* 63, 65, 66, 69; *Julie,* 80; *Marie,* 79; *Palamcotta,* hospital ship, 216; *Radama,* 2; *Scotia,* cable ship, 161; *Tabora,* 215; *Thomas Blyth,* 31; *Trois Frères,* 66, 71; *Wave,* government cutter, 187.

British warships: *Ariel,* 87, 88; *Bacchante,* 171; *Barracouta,* 11, 12, 15; *Boadicea,* 163; *Bonaventure,* 172; *Columbine,* 112, 113; *Curlew,* 44; *Eclipse,* 184; *Forte,* 107, 110, 111; *Galatea,* 95; *Gorgon,* 88; *Daphne,* 89; *Jaseur,* 44; *Leven,* 11, 15; *London,* 159; *Lyra,* 85, 86, 87, 91; *Orestes,* 98, and working party ashore after cyclone, 102, 104; *Pearl,* 195; *President,* 60; *Redbreast,* 178; *Sulphur,* 42; *Undine,* 167; *Wasp,* 83, 87.

French warships: *Artémise,* 24; *Favorite,* 13, 14, 15, 16, 17; *Gueydon,* 195; *Prévoyante,* 15; *Surprise,* 107.

German warships: *Emden,* 210; *Königsberg,* 210, 219.

MM steamers: *Australien,* 162; *Bosphore,* 172; *Mozambique,* 95; *Natal,* 166; *Salazie,* 171; *Sydney,* 168.

P & O steamers: Nepaul, 98, 102.

American whaleships: *Amanda,* 25, 32; *Anstey Gibbs,* 33; *Annie Ann,* 123, 127, condemned at Mauritius, 124; *Arab,* 34, 35; *Charles Carroll,* 98; *Charles W. Morgan,* 204; *Cicero,* 25, 26; *Georgia,* 25, 26, 29; *Hecla,* wrecked on Bird island, 126; *Herald,* 107, 126; *Laetitia,* 131; *Merlin,* 119, 120, 121, 128, nearly wrecked on Cosmoledo, 126-7, back at New Bedford, 130; *Mermaid,* 131; *Orray Taft,* 126; *Pioneer,* 122, 123; *Sea Queen,* 130; *William Lee,* 29.

British whaleships: *Asp,* 28; *Coquette,* 27, 30; *Diamantina,* 'of and from Mahé', 131; *Greenwich,* 44; *Harpooneer,* 31, 32; *St Ebba,* 205; *Swan,* 28; *Thames,* 32, 33; *Zephyr,* 31, 32.

shipwrecks: *St Abbs,* 79, 80.
Singapore: *See under* Abdullah.
Sisters of St Joseph de Cluny, 99, 104, 202; Mother Denise and Sister St

319

Africans, 184; and public drinking fountain, 184.

Victoria School, 198-200, 220; handed over to missions, 202.

Victoria Station, London, 197.

Wade, Captain George, Civil Commissioner, 71-80 *passim*, 88, 94, 107; relations with Des Avanchers, 72, 73; and racial tension, 74; acquitted of alleged abuse of power, 78; seeks protection for Seychelles officials, 78; reluctant to accept liberated Africans, 87; dies, 84; biog., 236.

Ward, Swinburne, Civil Commissioner, 88, 107; and uncertainty over status of islands, 93; conversation with Hugueteau de Chaillé, 94; and cyclone damage, 103; and inquiry's accusing finger, 116; appointed auditor-general, Mauritius, 116; warns on destruction of coco de mer, 154; biog., 237.

Warry, Henry Morris, superintendent, Venn's Town, 138; and Mrs Warry, 138; difficulties with children, 139; lacks teacher's certificate, 141.

West Indies: and slavery, 4, 8, 23.

whales and whaling, 25-36 *passim*, 57, 204, 205; whalebone, or baleen, 26; sperm whale, 27-35 *passim*, 119, 126, 204; Moby Dick, 34; whalemen recruited in police, 45-6; brutality by captains, 124-5; deteriorating relations with Seychelles, 125; birds' eggs and turtles from islands, 127; US consul suggests whalers carry goods for sale, 130; introduction of harpoon gun, 130; whales all the year round, 204; processing at Sainte Anne, 205.

White Fathers, 192.

White Tower, 159.

Whiting, 2/Lieut. Francis, Seychelles Carrier Corps, 212, 216; biog., 237.

Wilberforce, William, 20.

Wilhelmstal bell, war trophy, 219.

Williamson, Alexander, acting Chief Justice, 206, 207; biog., 237.

Wilson, Arthur, Sub-agent and acting Government Agent: 23, 39, 41, 46, 78.

World War I: initial panic, 209; cable links broken, 210, formation of defence force, 210, funds raised in South Mahé for war, 211, unemployment rises, 211, visit by French colonial troops, 211; Carrier Corps contingent sails for East Africa, 212; Bishop refuses to allow priest to go, 213; problem of rations, and early morning tea and biscuit, 213-4; and flogging threat, 215; second contingent of Carrier Corps leaves, 215, return of sick and dying, 216, 217; Army Council orders inquiry, 217; Seychellois serve in various theatres of war, 219, war trophies, 219, War memorial, 220; Armistice Day ceremonies, 220.

Worth, Janet, wife of whaling captain, 120; created 'sensation' in Mahé, 121.

Wright, Perceval, doctor and botanist, biog., 237.

Young, Alfred, Chief Justice, biog., 237.

Young, immigrant, 198.

Members of Seychelles Executive and Legislative Councils after the swearing-in of the Govenor of the new colony, M
private secretary), W. Morel (editor of Le Réveil), L.O. Chitty (Auditor), P. Petit (member, Legislative Council), V.
Herchenroder (Chief Justice), Sweet-Escott, A.K. Young (Crown Prosecutor and Legal Adviser), E. Savy (member,